T0257624

IET SECURITY SERIES 05

Data Security in Cloud Computing

Also available:

Age Factors in Biometric Processing, M. Fairhurst (Editor)
978-1-84919-502-7
Iris and Periocular Biometrics, C. Rathgeb, C. Busch (Editors)
978-1-78561-168-1
Engineering Secure Internet of Things Systems, B. Aziz, A. Arenas, B. Crispo
978-1-78561-053-0

Forthcoming Titles:

Mobile Biometrics, G. Guo, H. Wechsler (Editors)
978-1-78561-095-0

Data Security in Cloud Computing

Edited by
Vimal Kumar, Sivadon Chaisiri and Ryan Ko

The Institution of Engineering and Technology

Published by The Institution of Engineering and Technology, London, United Kingdom

The Institution of Engineering and Technology is registered as a Charity in England & Wales (no. 211014) and Scotland (no. SC038698).

First published 2017

The Institution of Engineering and Technology
Michael Faraday House
Six Hills Way, Stevenage
Herts SG1 2AY, United Kingdom

www.theiet.org

British Library Cataloguing in Publication Data
A catalogue record for this product is available from the British Library

ISBN 978-1-78561-220-6 (hardback)
ISBN 978-1-78561-221-3 (PDF)

Typeset in India by MPS Limited

Contents

12 Data provenance in cloud 261

Alan Yu Shyang Tan, Sivadon Chaisiri, Ryan Ko Kok Leong,
Geoff Holmes, and Bill Rogers

13 Security visualization for cloud computing: an overview 277

Jeffery Garae, Ryan K. L. Ko, and Mark Apperley

Preface

It has been about a decade since the first introduction of cloud computing concepts and business models. Despite the technology maturing and cloud evolving from a 'buzzword' into an integral component utilised by almost all organisations linked to the Internet, one thing has not changed: the concerns about data security in cloud computing. Compared to traditional information technology paradigms, cloud computing is complex, multi-tiered and large scale. Cloud computing inherits the problems of the traditional paradigms, but due to the above-mentioned characteristics it also has challenges entirely of its own. Hence, it will not be unexpected that several practical problems still remain unsolved.

We would like to propose that cloud computing's security problems can only be solved if we explore these challenges from a fundamental viewpoint: the data centric viewpoint. After all, whether it is traditional Information Technology or cloud computing, everything revolves around data. The systems are in place to process data, the processes or algorithms define how the data is processed and the policies and regulations are in place to make sure data is processed in a consistent and secure manner. A data centric view of cloud security looks at everything as eventually affecting the security of data residing in the cloud. That said, another challenge exists. A researcher new to this field may also become overwhelmed by the plethora of scientific approaches proposed to handle the challenges of securing data, while maintaining a practical level of privacy. This book (audaciously) attempts to address this problem, and presents a selection of exciting research work by experts of data security in cloud computing.

A great classification for data security issues will be one, which is based on the state of data that gets affected from the issue, data-at-rest, data-in-use or data-in-transit. In practice however the boundary between the states is not always distinct. Therefore, there are many data security issues that lie at that boundary and affect two states of the data. The organization of this book is based on this classification and reflects the fuzzy boundary between the states. Chapter 1 presents an overview of data security issues in cloud computing and sets the tone for the book. Chapters 2–4 discuss data-at-rest, Chapters 4–6 discuss data-in-use, while Chapters 6–8 discuss issues in data-in-transit. Some issues, such as data leakage, Governance, Risk Management and Compliance, data provenance and security visualization, affect data in all states and cannot be categorized under this classification. These are presented towards the end in Chapters 9–13.

With our selection of interesting as well as challenging data security issues we believe this book will be of interest to readers in both industry and academia. It will be of special interest to graduate and postgraduate students in computer science providing them with the current state of the art. This field is challenging but rewarding, and it is great to witness how science has shaped data security for cloud computing. We learned a lot as editors and authors in this journey, and it is our hope that you will find this book useful as well.

Chapter 1
A data-centric view of cloud security
Vimal Kumar[1], Sivadon Chaisiri[1], and Ryan Ko[1]

Abstract

Cloud computing offers a massive pool of resources and services that cloud users can utilize for storing and processing their data. The users can flexibly control and reduce their operational expenditures, whereas resources provisioned from the clouds can be dynamically resized to meet their demand and especially budgets. The user, however, has to consider unanticipated and expensive costs from threats associated with attacks aiming for the user's data in the cloud. In this chapter, we discuss the primary causes of new attack vectors that create a multitude of data security issues in clouds. We also discuss specific data security challenges in clouds and provide a classification which can help in an easier understanding.

1.1 Introduction

Cloud computing has changed the way we view capital and operational expenses in information technology (IT) and has changed the way infrastructures are designed in the current computing age. Cloud computing has also massively removed start-up costs for new companies and has influenced how we store and process data. Organizations may choose cloud computing because of a number of key business objectives such as reduced operational costs, reduced complexity, immediate access to resources, easy scale up and down, lower barrier to innovation etc. The eventual effect of using clouds for IT needs, however, is that an organization's data leaves its premises and is offloaded to the cloud.

Across cloud computing environments, data is the fundamental asset that we need to secure. Seen from a data-centric point of view, everything else, including the cloud computing infrastructure, policies, processes and regulations, are peripherals and are used to support the storage, movement, processing, logging and handling of data. The cloud computing infrastructure which is used for the storage, movement, processing, logging and handling of data does not belong to the data owner which has

[1]Cyber Security Lab, University of Waikato, New Zealand

subscribed to the cloud services. This *separation of data owners and their data* raises new questions for data security which require novel solutions. These solutions should provide answers to user concerns such as, the trustworthiness of the cloud service providers, accountability of the cloud service provider, security of data in distributed environments and across devices, protection against insider attacks in cloud and so on. Cloud computing also introduces a *shared environment* for users and their data. The physical resources are virtualized and shared among many users. Thus, a user's application may be using the same physical hardware as many others. The opaqueness in the cloud environment means the user does not know with whom the resources are shared with. This shared environment and its opaqueness poses new challenges of its own such as the issues of data isolation, data remanence, provable data deletion, data leakage and data integrity among others. One of the characteristics of cloud computing is *globally located servers*. Cloud service providers may migrate resources from one location to another and redistribute them over multiple global data centres to achieve internal goals such as resource consolidation, better resource utilization and high network performance. This allows clouds to utilize their resources more efficiently and also provides users with faster network access and higher reliability. This geo-distribution, however, introduces security issues of its own such as the complex interplay of the data privacy laws of multiple territories, issues with the provenance, tracing and auditing of data that is distributed globally etc.

It is important to understand the threats and security issues that emerge when data is offloaded from a traditional perimeter bound IT infrastructure to a cloud or multiple clouds. In this chapter, we attempt to study the underlying causes of many of these attacks. Moreover, as these issues do not emerge in isolation, we provide a simple classification of data security issues in cloud computing on the basis of the state of data. The remainder of this chapter is organized as follows: In Section 1.2, we provide some cloud computing definitions that will be useful in understanding the chapter. In Section 1.3, we discuss three underlying causes of the new attack vectors in clouds and in Section 1.4 we discuss and classify the main data security issues in cloud computing. Finally, we conclude the chapter in Section 1.5.

1.2   Definitions and terminology

In this section, we go over the basic terminology and definitions in the cloud domain which will help in the understanding of the chapter. First, we define the main actors in a cloud computing scenario that we are going to cross in our discussion. Figure 1.1 shows the actors involved and how they interact with each other.

- Data owner is an entity which owns the data that is uploaded on the cloud. Data owner can be an organization as well as individual users.
- Cloud service provider (CSP) is the entity that provides some form of cloud computing capability.
- Cloud service partners are outside entities that help the CSP to provide cloud capabilities. The partners may or may not be CSPs themselves.

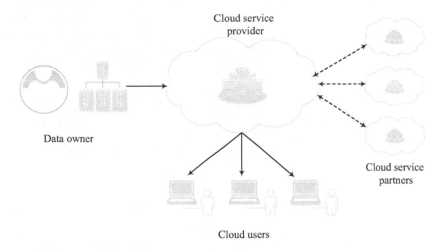

Figure 1.1   Actors in cloud computing

- Cloud users access and use data stored on the cloud capability provided by the CSP. Cloud users may or may not own the data stored on the cloud. For example, let's say **A** uploads data on the cloud and also uses this data. **A** further gives access to **B** to use the data. In this case, **A** is the data owner, whereas both **A** and **B** are cloud users.

In the rest of this chapter, we will generally distinguish data owners from cloud users; however, in places where the functions of cloud users and data owners are similar, we will use the term cloud users.

There are various views and definitions of cloud computing which define the concept with varying degree of success. One of the most popular ones is from the National Institute of Standard and Technology (NIST), which defines cloud computing as follows. *Cloud computing is a model for enabling ubiquitous, convenient, on-demand network access to a shared pool of configurable computing resources (e.g. networks, servers, storage, applications, and services) that can be rapidly provisioned and released with minimal management effort or service provider interaction* [1]. According to the NIST definition, cloud computing services can be classified based on the service model they use to create the services. There are three cloud computing service models as shown in Figure 1.2.

Infrastructure as a Service (IaaS): The services, provided in this model, allow the cloud user to interact directly with the hardware resources. The consumer is provided the capability to provision, computing power, storage and network resources. The consumer also has the responsibility of supplying software to run on the hardware resources, which can include operating systems and application software. As a result, although the user does not manage the underlying cloud resources, it has control over

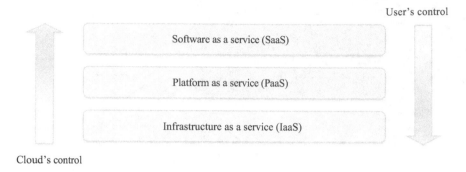

Figure 1.2   Cloud service models

operating systems security and application security while having limited control over network security [1].

Platform as a Service (PaaS): In the PaaS model, the user is provided with a development environment with tools, services and libraries. The user can create cloud services using the provided environment while bounded by the limitations of the environment. In this service model, the user has control over the applications/services which it creates but not the underlying hardware or software.

Software as a Service (SaaS): The SaaS model provides software to a cloud user that it may need. It frees the user from resource maintenance to a large extent while providing the required functionality. This model offers the least amount of control to the user. It may provide customizability of the software to fit the user's need but no control over the software, the platform or the infrastructure.

The ISO standard ISO/IEC 17728 identifies these service models as cloud capabilities and defines seven cloud service categories as follows:

1. CaaS: Communications as a Service
2. CompaaS: Compute as a Service
3. DSaaS: Data Storage as a Service
4. IaaS: Infrastructure as a Service
5. NaaS: Network as a Service
6. PaaS: Platform as a Service
7. SaaS: Software as a Service

1.3   Need for new methods

A traditional IT environment consists of various kinds of hardware, which includes computing devices such as desktop computers, laptops, mobile devices etc. These devices connect to receive and send data to a number of different servers, such as, print servers, application servers, database servers etc. All these devices and servers are located on an in-house network. In such an environment, data resides inside an organization's perimeter in various servers or user computers or simply on the company network. Data security in such an environment can be roughly divided into two parts, security of data when it goes out of the organization's perimeter and security of data within the organization's perimeter. The security concerns of traditional IT systems also apply when the operations are moved to clouds. Cloud computing, however, introduces new attack vectors thereby making security even more challenging. The three primary causes of the new attack vectors in clouds are the *disappearing perimeter*, a *new type of insider* and *contrasting business objectives*.

Disappearing perimeter: The definition of perimeter as applied to traditional IT is not useful in the case of cloud computing. The data in case of cloud computing resides on the cloud, outside of the company premises, therefore outside of the traditional *perimeter*. The cloud service provider, however, provides its own perimeter security; therefore, the data is not completely outside either. The cloud may further employ different access control and authorization mechanisms for the organization's employees and its customers, both of which access data from the cloud. This creates a huge grey area of perimeter instead of a well-defined perimeter as was the case in traditional systems. This problem is further compounded if there is a possibility of the cloud outsourcing data and applications to its clouds service partners.

A new type of insider: An insider is someone who has authorized access to a system. The insider may be fairly familiar with the system and the network architecture and therefore may also have better knowledge of the vulnerabilities and weak points of the system compared to an outsider. Traditionally, insiders are generally employees or sub-contractors who have been given access to the systems. Insider attacks have generally been a major threat to IT systems. Insiders, however, are usually traceable if proper logging and auditing mechanisms are in place. Along with the traditional insider, cloud computing introduces a new kind of insider. This insider is the employee or the sub-contractor that works for the cloud service provider or its partners. They may not work for the data owner but still have control over the data and access to it [2]. Unlike traditional insiders, the data owner has no control over such an insider.

Contrasting business objectives: Even when there are no malicious insiders, it can be hard for a data owner to place its trust in the cloud service provider. This is because both these parties have contrasting business objectives. The data owner, paying for the cloud services, wants to maximize the benefit from the cloud services and minimize expenditure while maintaining the quality of service. The service provider maintaining the resources, on the other hand, wants to maximize its return on investment by maximizing the resource utilization which may affect the quality of service. This can potentially result in misbehaviour on the part of the cloud service provider. According to [3], this misbehaviour can be one of the following types or a combination thereof. (1) Hiding failures or data corruption to maintain reputation. (2) Neglecting or deleting rarely accessed data files to save resources. (3) Attempting to gain information about the stored data. (4) Colluding with outside parties to harvest user data.

The three causes mentioned above, disappearing perimeter, new type of insider and contrasting business objectives, together lead to the perceived untrustworthiness of the cloud and play a role in rendering traditional methods of data security less effective. In the rest of this section, we discuss how three important ways of maintaining security, accountability and trustworthiness of data are affected by cloud computing.

1.3.1   Cryptography

Cryptography has been a cornerstone of data security in traditional IT and will continue to be in the cloud computing paradigm as well. Cryptography addresses two basic security constructs of data confidentiality and data integrity. Within cryptography, encryption has been an important tool along with access control to secure data on both sides of the perimeter. Encryption has been applied to data travelling on a network by way of the PKI infrastructure as well as data stored on secondary storage devices and databases. One of the main challenges in using encryption for protecting the confidentiality has been key management. As the number of authorized users grow, so do the number of keys and with the growing number of keys, key distribution and user revocation become more complex. Key management remains a challenge in cloud computing. As mentioned previously clouds, however, introduce new attack vectors and therefore new security challenges. To achieve data confidentiality, data is kept encrypted on the cloud. If, however, the encrypted data is decrypted before being processed, it will make the data vulnerable to attacks. Therefore, in the context of cloud computing, there is a need for techniques that enable operations over encrypted data. Such methods will allow confidentiality of data in the face of insider attacks and would help in increasing a user's trust in the cloud. As cloud computing has enabled new forms of data collection and sharing, it has also created new challenges in the access control of data. Previously established in-house access control methods are no longer sufficient in an environment where the perimeter has blurred beyond recognition. This has fashioned a need for functional encryption [4] and new forms of access control based on it.

Traditionally, data integrity concerns have been confined to data on the network, both inside and outside the perimeter. In cloud computing, however, the challenge of protecting the integrity of data takes a whole new form. Data owners may be concerned about unauthorized modifications, deletions and corruption of data, both malicious and accidental [3], because they have no physical control over their data. In addition, as the cloud is untrusted, there may be concerns about the validity of computations performed in the cloud. There is, therefore, a need for techniques that can validate and verify the computations performed in the cloud remotely. This becomes more challenging when the volume of data is large as is generally the case with cloud. Another important factor with data integrity in cloud is that the validation and verification should be performed at run-time when the modifications and deletions are done and the data owner be informed simultaneously. This is a challenge that owes its existence entirely to cloud computing.

While cryptography will play a huge role in solving many of the data security concerns, cryptographic techniques are generally time consuming. Therefore, any new cryptographic scheme or technique to solve these above-mentioned challenges needs to take the induced latency in account as this will affect the availability of data and services hosted in cloud.

1.3.2 Data provenance

In a traditional IT environment, logging or tracing software is used to record information about the activities of a particular component such as system usage, database operations, application execution traces, network packet traces and operating system events. Such logs can then be used in many applications such as accounting and billing, system analysis, data surveillance, IT audit, forensics and anomaly detection. In most cases, however, logs alone are not sufficient to obtain data provenance which is the derivation history of data, including necessary information about data creation, data access and data manipulation [5]. Data provenance can provide information about *who* (e.g. user) authorized *what* process (e.g. software) from *where* (e.g. a host address and an absolute directory path) to perform *which* data operation (e.g. create, read and write operations) and *when* (i.e. time of operation) involving a piece of data (e.g. a file).

In traditional systems, data provenance software such as SPADE [6], S2Logger [7], Flogger [8] and Progger [9] can be easily deployed in host and guest operating systems (i.e. physical and virtual machines). In a cloud computing environment, data owners can deploy data provenance software in self-managed virtual environments (e.g. IaaS servers and guest operating systems). In most cases, though, data owners cannot deploy such software in environments to which they have no access such as IaaS host operating systems, PaaS and SaaS, as such environments are exclusively controlled by CSPs. Hence, obtaining complete data provenance from clouds is not a straightforward task, if the CSPs do not share logs associated with their controlled environments with the data owners. This issue of tracking data provenance outside the system is a challenging research topic [10]. Data provenance in a cloud environment has to be confidential and trustworthy. In a traditional IT environment, access control, traditional data encryption and cryptographic processors (e.g. the Trusted Platform Module [11]) can be used to obtain both confidentiality and trustworthiness. In a cloud computing environment, however, the trustworthiness of cloud environments is a concern. In cloud computing, the traditional data encryption techniques as mentioned previously are not sufficient to maintain confidentiality of data provenance, and the cryptographic processors are also not commonly available. Hence, suitable encryption and trust techniques are required for securing the data provenance stored in cloud environments.

1.3.3 Privacy and security laws and regulations

Prominent public cloud service providers, such as Amazon Web Services and Microsoft Azure, typically have servers across several regions or continents, spanning across several jurisdictions [12]. Although this provides convenience, allowing the user seamless access and computation from anywhere in the world, the flow of data through the jurisdictions remains agnostic to the legal requirements for storing and processing (e.g. privacy requirements) by design [13]. Few have considered the different legal requirements across countries when they designed their data security and privacy solutions for the cloud. The subject of trans-national data privacy and assurance of the rights of data owners in regions outside their own often gives rise to larger scale problems [14,15]. One example was the 2008 disestablishment of the International Safe Harbor Privacy Principles after a Facebook user reported Facebook for their storage of his data in other regions without his knowledge, at the European Court of Justice [16]. If we look deeper into cross-boundary issues, there are two inherent sub-problems [13], which are as follows:

1.3.3.1   Gaps and misalignments

Different countries' laws are structured differently, with different definitions and coverage of citizen rights. For example, the term 'sensitive data' is defined differently across several countries, and even undefined in several countries. At the same time, the actions and consequences of breaches of principles differ from country to country.

1.3.3.2   Different expectations on technology and control

Some territories, such as the European Union, would enforce the 'right to be forgotten' but it has been widely argued that it is technically impossible to achieve its requirements. Other countries do not have a strong focus on individual rights but focus on surveillance for citizen safety. Both ends of this spectrum are valid, and a cloud service provider would need to navigate such legal minefields if they were to have successful businesses across the world.

Technologists typically struggle to know in advance or stay current with the ever-changing legal developments across all countries, and the overheads involved for staying current with these developments could be reduced if there was a global or regional alignment [13]. The European Council's General Data Protection Regulation (GDPR) [17,18], which will be launched mid-2017, is one such example. However, one can also expect even more complexities between signatories of the GDPR.

Since the beginning of public cloud proliferation, provider liabilities have hinged on service-level agreements and contracts and are mainly influenced by the local laws of the respective countries. It is commonplace to see companies encouraging users to sign biased contracts, letting go of most rights, and hosting specific data sets in countries with the most 'relaxed' laws around data privacy and sovereignty [12,15,19,20]. Conversely, most countries require sensitive data such as electronic healthcare records or banking data to remain on premise or within the country. This requirement creates a tension for the cloud service provider attempting to expand into overseas markets [15]. Can technologies which assure privacy preservation and data provenance reduce the mistrust of these cloud service providers? Also, if a cloud service provider was to liquidate, what will happen to the data? Will there be a proper process or legal safeguard for the data owners and stakeholders? In our opinion, these open challenges are not just interesting for legal professionals but also for researchers involved in the data security aspect of cloud computing.

1.4   Classification of data security issues in cloud computing

Between the time when data is generated and ultimately destroyed, it moves between its three states, data-at-rest, data-in-transit and data-in-use (as shown in Figure 1.3), residing in any one of them at any given time. This is true for data in general and

Data at rest
Data generation
Data destruction
Data in transit
Data in use

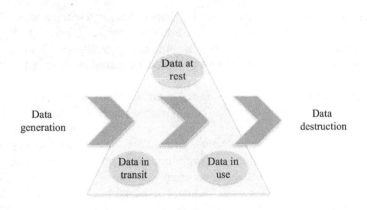

Figure 1.3 Three states of data

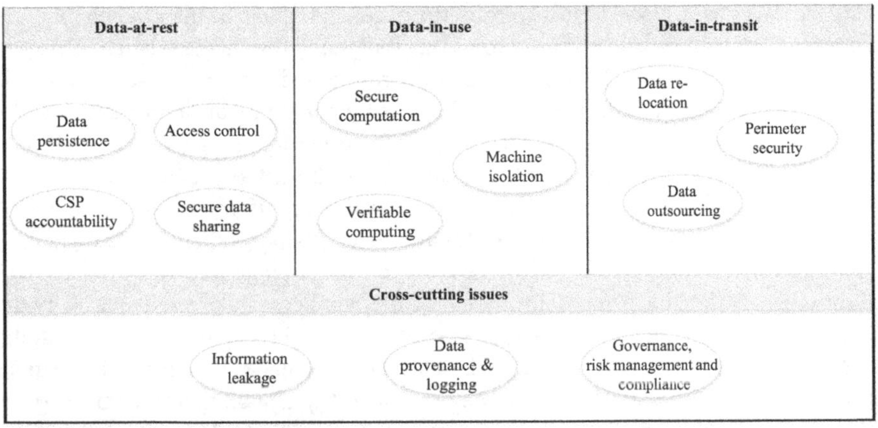

Data-at-rest
Data-in-use
Data-in-transit
Data persistence
Access control
CSP accountability
Secure data sharing
Secure computation
Machine isolation
Verifiable computing
Data re-location
Perimeter security
Data outsourcing
Cross-cutting issues
Information leakage
Data provenance & logging
Governance, risk management and compliance

Figure 1.4 Classification of data security issues

also for data in clouds. Most data security issues can be divided into three categories depending upon when the issue arises during data's lifetime. In this section, we go over each of the three states of data and the security issues that arise therein. Some security issues, however, are cross-cutting and can affect and arise during any or all of the states. We discuss these in the cross-cutting issues sub-section. Figure 1.4 shows a pictorial representation of the classification presented in this section.

1.4.1 Data at rest

Data at rest refers to data stored on secondary storage devices or persistent storage on a cloud. Persistent storage refers to specialized storage services on the cloud as well as instance storage connected to each instance. Although specialized storage services such as Amazon S3, Windows Azure and Rackspace cloud storage etc. provide data owners with highly scalable, customizable and reliable storage, instance storage can be unreliable and is wiped off when the instance terminates. In both the cases, however, data resides on the cloud, far removed from the user's machine. This loss of physical control on the data is compounded by the low trust between the data owners and CSPs as discussed in Section 1.3. This gives rise to a host of data security issues.

One of the primary challenges in cloud is, how can data owners store data securely on the untrustworthy cloud and share it with trusted users? Traditional approaches either struggle with key management (symmetric key approaches) or do not provide enough flexibility, when it comes to securing the data as well as tracking the data usage of multiple users. (Traditional PKI approaches). In [21], the authors have tried to solve this problem by using a progressive elliptic curve encryption scheme which allows data to be encrypted multiple times. A similar multi-encryption approach has been used in [22]. Reference [23] has further explored the problem of delegation of data access privileges. The challenge of secure data sharing becomes more complex when the data owner also wants to control the access of data in a fine grained manner. The users of data may have different roles, attributes and may access data in different contexts. This gives rise to the need of providing role-based, attribute-based or context-based access [24–27]. Data persistence has also emerged as an important issue in cloud computing. Cloud service providers need to be able to securely delete data once it is no more required. Failure to do so may potentially expose data to co-located users and to anyone who can lay their hands on discarded storage devices. Cryptographic solutions such as Fade [28] and FadeVersion [29] help data owners in obtaining verifiable data deletion whenever required. A related data-at-rest problem is how to verify that the data has not been modified maliciously or accidentally by the CSP. Verification of integrity of data is generally not a problem with small data but the volume and remote location of data in the cloud makes this a challenge. This remote verification also needs to be done in the untrustworthy cloud environment itself, as downloading data for performing verification is not feasible [30,31]. Another CSP accountability problem arises, when the cloud is asked to replicate data. How can the data owner make sure that the CSP genuinely has multiple copies of data, particularly when the data owner is being charged for the copies [32].

1.4.2   Data in use

Data in use, sometimes also called data in processing, is the active state of data, when it is being processed. In this state, the data may be held in primary storage of a machine such as RAM and cache memory and may also reside on registers on the CPU. To be processed by the CPU, encrypted data needs to be unencrypted and therefore stripped bare of most of the protection applied to it in the data at rest state. Thus, data in its lifetime is most vulnerable in this state.

Data stored securely in the cloud can either be processed in the cloud or on the user's machine. If the data is processed in the cloud, it needs to be decrypted and hence becomes vulnerable as mentioned above. If the data is processed on the user's machine, the user will incur the extra cost of data transfer to and from the cloud. Ideally, a user would want to perform computations on the data, in the cloud, but in a secure manner such that the data is not exposed to attackers. Solutions to this problem of secure computation in cloud are either non-cryptographic or cryptographic in nature. Non-cryptographic solutions usually entail encoding and distributing the data over multiple service providers such as in [34,34]. Multi-party computation (MPC) and fully homomorphic encryption have long been thought of as leading cryptographic candidate technologies for secure computation. MPC protocols distribute the computation of a function among multiple parties to provide secure computation of the function. FHE, on the other hand, are encryption schemes that enable operations on encrypted data. Both of these technologies, however, are inflexible and cannot be adapted to the vast range of operations that are necessary in everyday computation such as searching, index-building, programme execution etc. This has led to a variety of innovative solutions which solve the secure computation problem in a specific, application-defined domain. References [35–37] deal with the problem of secure search in the cloud, whereas [38,39] discuss privacy-preserving indexes. The work in [40] discusses secure image-processing operations over 2D images, whereas [41] describes real-time search over encrypted video data.

A problem related to secure computation is verifiable computation. In a low-trust environment, verifiable computing provides the assurance that data has been processed as expected by the user or data owner. A simple solution proposed in [42] uses two clouds, a trusted cloud for verifiable aspects of computing and an un-trusted cloud for regular computing needs. Other solutions such as the one in [43] approach this as a problem of verification of the consistency of the database. Cryptographic solutions to this problem are also discussed in [44,45]. Verifiable accounting or metering of resources used is also a challenging issue in cloud computing and one which is of interest to both cloud service providers and cloud users. Verifiable accounting can provide assurance to both the parties that the billing for the usage of resources is appropriate and in accordance to an agreed upon policy [46].

Virtualization is one of the basic technologies on which cloud computing is built. Virtualization allows the creation of multiple separate virtual machines (VM) on the same physical hardware, thus increasing resource utilization from a CSP's point of view. These VMs, however, when running concurrently, use the same physical resources such as the CPU, main memory, secondary storage and network devices. This not only can introduce non-malicious fluctuations of hardware usage efficiency but also creates a new attack vector. Attackers can try to co-locate themselves on the same physical resources as the machine they want to attack [47]. This creates a need for better isolation techniques that can allow VMs to operate in a space where they are unaffected by the co-located VMs.

1.4.3 Data in transit

Data in transit sometimes also referred to as data in motion, is the state of data, in which it is moving or is transferred from one location to another over a network. In the realm of cloud computing, data may be moving from cloud client's local storage to the CSP's cloud storage, it may be moving from the cloud storage to local storage. Data may also move between multiple clouds, and it may also move within a cloud. All these movements of data are covered under data in transit.

A CSP may move data internally between its datacentres (data relocation) to achieve internal goals such as resource consolidation, better resource utilization and high network performance as well as to provide lower latency access to its users. The service provider, however, also needs to honour any SLA agreements and local regulations; there may have been regarding the movement and location of data owner's data [16]. The data owner, on the other hand, may also need new techniques that can help it verify the movement and transit of data once uploaded to the cloud. A CSP may also delegate data to its partners or other CSPs. This may be done due to either a lack of resources with the cloud or for cost-saving measures or for efficient provisioning. The cloud partners, however, may or may not have the same level of security for the data as negotiated by the data owner with the original provider. This results in a major security challenge that we call data outsourcing, which calls for techniques that can track data as it moves in and out of the cloud.

As data travels from the data owner to the cloud and on to the cloud user, it raises another important issue in the data-in-transit category that is perimeter security. As mentioned previously, the perimeter in cloud has blurred beyond recognition and, hence, perimeter security has become an even greater challenge and requires new and innovative solutions. One such promising perimeter security technique is software-defined perimeter (SDP) [48].

1.4.4 Cross-cutting issues

So far, we have discussed data security issues that arise in the three states of data; there are, however, issues which affect data in all or more than one states of its life cycle. We discuss some of such cross-cutting issues in this sub-section.

Accidental and malicious information leakage can occur at any state of data's life cycle. Information leakage refers to the disclosure of information about data in cloud. This information can take many forms and hence can have various implications. In the seminal work in [47], the authors showed that it was not only possible to ascertain the geographic location of a VM, it was to a large extent possible to achieve co-residency with a selected VM. This attack was possible due to a VM's network information leakage. References [49,50] explore information leakage due to de-duplication in cloud storage. The authors note that when multiple data owners upload the same data to the cloud, many CSPs only keep a single copy on the cloud and simply provide access links to all data owners and users. This is called de-duplication and can be exploited to gain information about the data and its owner. Similarly, Reference [51] looks at the information leakage due to indexing in clouds.

Another cross-cutting issue in cloud computing is that of data provenance and auditing. As mentioned before, data provenance provides the derivation history of data. From a security point of view, data provenance can be used for ensuring accountability as well as in auditing and forensics. There are, however, open research areas in data provenance. For example, data provenance can be incomplete and imperfect as important records or logs of data may be partially collected or absent [10]. Without the availability of complete and perfect data provenance, provenance can result in inadmissible evidence, in any kind of auditing. Reconstruction of data provenance by utilizing existing logs [52], whereas completeness and perfection of provenance can be assured is still an on-going research problem. Overheads and scalability issues of data provenance need to be addressed too as the size of provenance data itself can grow rapidly. This has the potential to degrade performance of machines storing or collecting data provenance [53]. Maintaining security, privacy and trustworthiness of data provenance is also an open problem [54].

Finally, data governance, risk and compliance management is another key cross-cutting challenge for a data-centric view of cloud computing. The relative volatility and flow of data across and within clouds have increased the complexity for CSPS, data owners and cloud users [14]. Several researchers have attempted to automate the data governance regulation and policy compliance alignment for cloud environments hosting physical and virtual hosts, within and across countries [55]. Provenance and auditing empowers a certain level of accountability but continued research into capabilities to reduce human input reliance is required for truly automated data governance, risk management and compliance [19].

1.5 Conclusion

Data security remains one of the top concerns of data owners when moving operations to the cloud. Even after years of academic and industry research, there are still open issues that need solutions. Most of these cloud specific issues arise due to the new attack vectors. In this chapter, we have identified a disappearing perimeter, a new type of insider and contrasting business objectives of the cloud service provider and the cloud user as three primary causes of the new attack vectors. We also discussed how the new attack vectors affect cryptography, data provenance and privacy and security laws which have traditionally been used as security tools and policies for data security. We have also provided the reader with a small survey of the open issues and classified them under a simple taxonomy. We have attempted in this chapter to provide the reader with a clear understanding of the open data security issues in cloud computing and hope this will help in stimulating their interest in this exciting field of research.

References

[1]   National Institute of Standards and Technology. The NIST definition of cloud computing; 2011. ⟨http://www.nist.gov/itl/cloud/upload/cloud-def-v15.pdf⟩ [March 2017].

[2]   Chandarekaran, K. *Essential of Cloud Computing*. Boca Raton, FL, USA: CRC Press, 2014.

[3]   Yu, S., W. Lou, and K. Ren. "Data security in cloud computing", in *Handbook on Securing Cyber-Physical Critical Infrastructure* (1st ed.), chapter 15, edited

by Sajal K. Das, Krishna Kant and Nan Zhang, Morgan Kaufmann, Boston, MA, USA, 2012.

[4]   Boneh, D., A. Sahai, and B. Waters. "Functional encryption: Definitions and challenges", in *Theory of Cryptography Conference*. Berlin: Springer, 2011.

[5]   Tan, A. Y. S., R. K. L. Ko, G. Holmes, and B. Rogers. "Provenance for cloud data accountability", in R. Ko, & K.-K. R. Choo (Eds.), *The Cloud Security Ecosystem: Technical, Legal, Business and Management Issues* (pp. 171–185). Berlin, Heidelberg: Elsevier Inc., 2015.

[6]   Gehani, D. T. "SPADE: support for provenance auditing in distributed environments", in *Proceedings of the 13th International Middleware Conference*. New York: Springer-Verlag New York, Inc., 2012.

[7]   Suen, C. H., R. K. L. Ko, Y. S. Tan, P. Jagadpramana, and B. S. Lee. "S2logger: End-to-end data tracking mechanism for cloud data provenance", in *Trust, Security and Privacy in Computing and Communications (TrustCom), 2013 12th IEEE International Conference on*. Melbourne, VIC, Australia: IEEE, 2013.

[8]   Ko, R. K. L., P. Jagadpramana, and B. S. Lee. "Flogger: A file-centric logger for monitoring file access and transfers with cloud computing environments", in *Third IEEE International Workshop on Security in e-Science and e-Research* (ISSR'11), in conjunction with IEEE TrustCom'11, Changsha, China, 2011.

[9]   Ko, R. K. L., and M. A. Will. "Progger: An efficient, tamper-evident Kernel-space logger for cloud data provenance tracking", in *Cloud Computing (CLOUD), 2014 IEEE Seventh International Conference on*.Anchorage, AK, USA: IEEE, 2014.

[10]   Tan, Y. S., R. K. L. Ko, and G. Holmes. "Security and data accountability in distributed systems: a provenance survey", in *2013 IEEE 10th International Conference on High Performance Computing and Communications & 2013 IEEE International Conference on Embedded and Ubiquitous Computing (HPCC_EUC)* (pp. 1571–1578). Zhangjiajie, China: IEEE.

[11]   Taha, M. M. B., S. Chaisiri, and R. K. L. Ko. "Trusted tamper-evident data provenance", in *Trustcom/BigDataSE/ISPA, 2015 IEEE*. Vol. 1. Helsinki, Finland: IEEE, 2015.

[12]   Ko, R. K. L. "Cloud computing in plain English", *ACM Crossroads* 16.3 (2010): 5–6. ACM.

[13]   Scoon, C., and R. K. L. Ko. "The data privacy matrix project: Towards a global alignment of data privacy laws", *Trustcom/BigDataSE/I SPA, 2016 IEEE*. Tianjin, China: IEEE, 2016.

[14]   Ko, R. K., P. Jagadpramana, M. Mowbray, *et al.* (2011, July). "TrustCloud: A framework for accountability and trust in cloud computing", in *Services (SERVICES), 2011 IEEE World Congress on* (pp. 584–588). Washington, DC, USA: IEEE.

[15]   Ko, R. K. L., G. Russello, R. Nelson, *et al.* "Stratus: Towards returning data control to cloud users", in *International Conference on Algorithms and Architectures for Parallel Processing*, pp. 57–70. Cham: Springer International Publishing, 2015.

[16] Reidenberg, J. R. "Resolving conflicting international data privacy rules in cyberspace", *Stanford Law Review* 52, no. 5 (2000): 1315–1371.

[17] Mantelero, A. "The EU proposal for a general data protection regulation and the roots of the 'right to be forgotten'", *Computer Law & Security Review* 29.3 (2013): 229–235.

[18] de Hert, Paul, and Vagelis Papakonstantinou. "The new general data protection regulation: Still a sound system for the protection of individuals?", *Computer Law & Security Review* 32.2 (2016): 179–194.

[19] Ko, R. K. L. "Data accountability in cloud systems", in *Security, Privacy and Trust in Cloud Systems*, pp. 211–238. Berlin: Springer, 2014.

[20] Ko, R. K. L., S. S. G. Lee, and V. Rajan. "Understanding cloud failures", *IEEE Spectrum* (2012): 84–84. IEEE.

[21] Zhao, G., Rong, C. Rong, J. Li, F. Zhang, and Y. Tang. "Trusted data sharing over untrusted cloud storage providers." *Cloud Computing Technology and Science (CloudCom), 2010 IEEE Second International Conference on.* Indianapolis, IN, USA: IEEE, 2010.

[22] Cabaniss, R., V. Kumar, and S. Madria. "Multi-party encryption (MPE): Secure communications in delay tolerant networks", *Wireless Networks* 21.4 (2015): 1243–1258.

[23] Xue, K., and P. Hong. "A dynamic secure group sharing framework in public cloud computing", *IEEE Transactions on Cloud Computing* 2.4 (2014): 459–470.

[24] Zhou, L., V. Varadharajan, and M. Hitchens. "Enforcing role-based access control for secure data storage in the cloud", *The Computer Journal* 54, no. 10 (2011): 1675–1687.

[25] Tang, Y., P. P. C. Lee, J. C. S. Lui, and R. Perlman. "Secure overlay cloud storage with access control and assured deletion", *IEEE Transactions on Dependable and Secure Computing* 9.6 (2012): 903–916.

[26] Li, M., S. Yu, Y. Zheng, K. Ren, and W. Lou. "Scalable and secure sharing of personal health records in cloud computing using attribute-based encryption", *IEEE Transactions on Parallel and Distributed Systems* 24.1 (2013): 131–143.

[27] Zhou, Z., L. Wu, and Z. Hong. "Context-aware access control model for cloud computing", *International Journal of Grid and Distribution Computing* 6.6 (2013): 1–12.

[28] Tang, Y., P. P. Lee, J. C. Lui, and R. Perlman (2010, September). "FADE: Secure overlay cloud storage with file assured deletion", in *International Conference on Security and Privacy in Communication Systems* (pp. 380–397). Berlin, Heidelberg: Springer.

[29] Rahumed, A., H. C. Chen, Y. Tang, P. P. Lee, and J. C. Lui (2011, September). "A secure cloud backup system with assured deletion and version control", in *Parallel Processing Workshops (ICPPW), 2011 40th International Conference on* (pp. 160–167). Taipei City, Taiwan: IEEE.

[30] Erway, C., A. Kupc, U. C. Papamanthou, and R. Tamassia. "Dynamic provable data possession," in *CCS'09: Proceedings of the 16th ACM Conference on*

Computer and Communications Security (New York, NY, USA), pp. 213–222, New York, NY, USA: ACM, 2009.

[31] Wang, C., Q. Wang, K. Ren, and W. Lou. "Privacy-preserving public auditing for data storage security in cloud computing," in *InfoCom2010*, San Diego, CA, USA: IEEE, March 2010.

[32] Mukundan, R., S. Madria, and M. Linderman. "Efficient integrity verification of replicated data in cloud using homomorphic encryption." *Distributed and Parallel Databases* 32.4 (2014): 507–534.

[33] Will, M. A., R. K. L. Ko, and I. H. Witten. "Bin Encoding: A user-centric secure full-text searching scheme for the cloud", *Trustcom/BigDataSE/ISPA, 2015 IEEE*. Vol. 1. Helsinki, Finland: IEEE, 2015.

[34] Will, M. A., R. K. L. Ko, and I. H. Witten. "Privacy preserving computation by fragmenting individual bits and distributing gates", *Trustcom/BigDataSE/I SPA, 2016 IEEE*. Tianjin, China: IEEE, 2016.

[35] Wang, C., N. Cao, J. Li, K. Ren, and W. Lou. "Secure ranked keyword search over encrypted cloud data", *Distributed Computing Systems (ICDCS), 2010 IEEE 30th International Conference on*. Genova, Italy: IEEE, 2010.

[36] Cao, N., C. Wang, M. Li, K. Ren, and W. Lou. "Privacy-preserving multi-keyword ranked search over encrypted cloud data", *IEEE Transactions on Parallel and Distributed Systems* 25.1 (2014): 222–233.

[37] Ren, S. Q., and K. M. M. Aung. "PPDS: Privacy preserved data sharing scheme for cloud storage", *International Journal of Advancements in Computing Technology* 4 (2012): 493–499.

[38] Hu, H., J. Xu, C. Ren, and B. Choi. "Processing private queries over untrusted data cloud through privacy homomorphism", *Data Engineering (ICDE), 2011 IEEE 27th International Conference on*. Hannover, Germany: IEEE, 2011.

[39] Squicciarini, A., S. Sundareswaran, D. Lin. "Preventing information leakage from indexing in the cloud", *Cloud Computing (CLOUD), 2010 IEEE Third International Conference on*. Miami, FL, USA: IEEE, 2010.

[40] Mohanty, M., M. R. Asghar, G. Russello. "2DCrypt: Privacy-preserving image scaling and cropping in the cloud", *IEEE Transactions Information Forensics and Security (TIFS) 2016*.

[41] Liu, J. K., M. H. Au, W. Susilo, K. Liang, R. Lu, and B. Srinivasan. "Secure sharing and searching for real-time video data in mobile cloud", *IEEE Network* 29.2 (2015): 46–50.

[42] Bugiel, S., S. Nürnberger, A. R. Sadeghi, T. Schneider (2011, October). "Twin clouds: Secure cloud computing with low latency", in *IFIP International Conference on Communications and Multimedia Security* (pp. 32–44). Berlin: Springer.

[43] Jana, S., V. Shmatikov (2011, June). "EVE: Verifying correct execution of cloud-hosted web applications", in *HotCloud*.

[44] Rosario G., C. Gentry, B. Parno. "Non-interactive verifiable computing: outsourcing computation to untrusted workers", *Proceedings of the 30th Annual Conference on Advances in Cryptology*, August 15–19, 2010

[45] Shuo, Y., A. R. Butt, Y. Charlie Hu, S. P. Midkiff. "Trust but verify: Monitoring remotely executing programs for progress and correctness", *Proceedings of the Tenth ACM SIGPLAN Symposium on Principles and Practice of Parallel Programming*, June 15–17, 2005.

[46] Sekar, V., P. Maniatis. "Verifiable resource accounting for cloud computing services", *Proceedings of the Third ACM Workshop on Cloud Computing Security Workshop*. New York, NY, USA: ACM, 2011.

[47] Ristenpart, T., E. Tromer, H. Shacham, S. Savage (2009, November). "Hey, you, get off of my cloud: exploring information leakage in third-party compute clouds", in *Proceedings of the 16th ACM Conference on Computer and Communications Security* (pp. 199–212). Chicago, IL, USA: ACM.

[48] Software Defined Perimeter Working Group, "SDP specification 1.0", April 2014. Available: https://cloudsecurityalliance.org/download/sdp-specification-v1-0/. [retrieved Feb 21, 2017].

[49] Mulazzani, M., S. Schrittwieser, M. Leithner, M. Huber, E. R. Weippl (2011, August). "Dark clouds on the horizon: Using cloud storage as attack vector and online slack space", in *USENIX Security Symposium* (pp. 65–76).

[50] Harnik, D., B. Pinkas, A. Shulman-Peleg. "Side channels in cloud services: Deduplication in cloud storage", *IEEE Security & Privacy* 8.6 (2010): 40–47.

[51] Squicciarini, A., S. Sundareswaran, D. Lin. "Preventing information leakage from indexing in the cloud", *Cloud Computing (CLOUD), 2010 IEEE Third International Conference on*. IEEE, 2010.

[52] Magliacane, S. "Reconstructing provenance", *The Semantic Web–ISWC 2012* (2012): 399–406.

[53] Zhao, D., C. Shou, T. Malik, I. Raicu. "Distributed data provenance for large-scale data-intensive computing", *Cluster Computing (CLUSTER), 2013 IEEE International Conference on*. IEEE, 2013.

[54] Hasan, R., R. Sion, M. Winslett. "Introducing secure provenance: problems and challenges", *Proceedings of the 2007 ACM Workshop on Storage Security and Survivability*. Alexandria, VA, USA: ACM, 2007.

[55] Papanikolaou, N., S. Pearson, M. Casassa Mont, R. K. L. Ko. "A toolkit for automating compliance in cloud computing services", *International Journal of Cloud Computing 2* 3, no. 1 (2014): 45–68.

Chapter 2

Nomad: a framework for ensuring data confidentiality in mission-critical cloud-based applications

Mamadou H. Diallo[1], Michael August[1], Roger Hallman[1], Megan Kline[1], Henry Au[1], and Scott M. Slayback[1]

Abstract

Due to their low cost and simplicity of use, public cloud services are gaining popularity among both public and private sector organisations. However, there are many threats to the cloud, including data breaches, data loss, account hijacking, denial of service, and malicious insiders. One of the solutions for addressing these threats is the use of secure computing techniques such as homomorphic encryption and secure multiparty computation, which allow for processing of encrypted data stored in untrusted cloud environments without ever having the decryption key. The performance of these techniques is a limiting factor in the adoption of cloud-based applications. Both public and private sector organisations with strong requirements for data security and privacy are reluctant to push their data to the cloud. In particular, mission-critical defense applications used by governments do not tolerate any leakage of sensitive data. In this chapter, we present Nomad, a framework for developing mission-critical cloud-based applications. The framework is comprised of: (1) a homomorphic encryption-based service for processing encrypted data directly within the untrusted cloud infrastructure, and (2) a client service for encrypting and decrypting data within the trusted environment, and storing and retrieving these data to and from the cloud. In order to accelerate the expensive homomorphic encryption operations, we equipped both services with a Graphics Processing Unit (GPU)-based parallelisation mechanism. To evaluate the *Nomad* framework, we developed *CallForFire*, a Geographic Information System (GIS)-based mission-critical defense application that can be deployed in the cloud. *CallForFire* enables secure computation of enemy target locations and selection of firing assets. Due to the nature of the mission, this application requires guaranteed security. The experimental results show that the performance of homomorphic encryption can be enhanced by using a GPU-based acceleration mechanism.

[1]US Department of Defense, SPAWAR Systems Center Pacific (SSC Pacific), San Diego, CA, USA

In addition, the performance of the *CallForFire* application demonstrates the feasibility of using the *Nomad* framework to develop mission-critical cloud-based applications.

2.1   Introduction

Public cloud services are gaining popularity among both public and private sector organisations due to their low cost and ease of use. According to the U.S. National Institute of Standards and Technology, the cloud provides a pool of compute resources which can be dynamically provisioned over the Internet, and which is both scalable and measurable [1]. Public cloud service providers such as Google, Rackspace, Heroku, and Amazon Web Services provide various software services over the Internet at low cost, including services such as content management, accounting, virtualisation, and customer relationship management.

Since computers have become highly commoditised in recent years, it can make economic sense to outsource computation to clusters of distributed untrusted compute units whose ownership and locations are unknown. The cloud provides an abstraction for this compute model. Public clouds achieve cost efficiencies via economies of scale and cost sharing among many customers, and therefore provide a means for organisations to achieve high throughput computation at minimal cost without requiring significant amounts of upfront capital investment in data center infrastructure. As a result, organisations have been increasingly embracing the cloud as a platform for outsourcing the hosting of web-based services. Virtual machines form the fundamental unit of the cloud abstraction, as they can be provisioned and destroyed completely within software without labour-intensive changes to hardware configurations. This fluid computational model enables software systems to be rapidly provisioned, configured, deployed, and scaled in the cloud without the purchase of expensive dedicated hardware.

The Cloud Security Alliance [2] has identified multiple security threats to the cloud. These security threats discourage organisations, such as financial institutions, healthcare organisations, federal and state governments, and defense agencies, from using the public cloud to store their sensitive data. These threats include data breaches, data loss, account hijacking, denial of service, and malicious insiders, among others. Cloud security and privacy issues have been confirmed by different surveys [3]. For instance, virtual machine escape vulnerabilities, such as VENOM [4], enable a guest virtual machine to access and execute code on the host machine. Additionally, cross-VM side-channel attacks can take advantage of co-resident virtual machines within a cloud infrastructure. One such example of this type of attack, known as a cache attack, has been successfully demonstrated on public cloud service providers [5–11]. As security researchers continue to explore and identify threats within public cloud service offerings, more information about cloud vulnerabilities will be exposed, thereby leading to the development of exploitation tools. For example, Nimbostratus [12] is a toolset developed for fingerprinting and exploiting poorly configured Amazon Web Services deployments. Since there is no guarantee that data stored and processed in public clouds will remain confidential, organisations have a need for secure computation mechanisms to guarantee the security and privacy of such data. Fully homomorphic encryption is one such mechanism.

Starting with the first construction of fully homomorphic encryption in 2009 [13], the cryptographic research community has been actively developing new homomorphic cryptography schemes, which would enable computation on encrypted data in the cloud. A number of schemes have been developed, including lattice-based [13], and ring learning with errors (RLWEs)-based approaches [14]. As a result, significant progress has been achieved [15]. However, homomorphic encryption schemes have not matured enough to be used as the mainstream data encryption mechanism due to the fact that the homomorphic operations are computationally intensive. This computational complexity limits the practicality of current homomorphic encryption schemes.

Since secure computation techniques such as homomorphic encryption are currently impractical, public cloud service providers enable customers to perform their own encryption before storing their sensitive data in the cloud (e.g., end-to-end encrypted cloud storage provided by https://mega.nz), thereby precluding the customer from performing any computation on their data when stored in the cloud. In order to perform computations on the encrypted data stored in the cloud, it must be decrypted first, which can lead to data leakage.

To address these limitations of current cloud service providers, we propose *Nomad*, a framework for building mission-critical cloud-based applications. Nomad consists of a distributed architecture for storage and processing of encrypted data, which is deployed across trusted and untrusted cloud environments. The Nomad framework leverages cloud-based Application Programming Interfaces (APIs) to create a secure storage service hosted on virtual machines. This storage service achieves data confidentiality via a homomorphic encryption-based data storage system. To accelerate the homomorphic encryption operations within the storage system, Nomad uses a GPU-based parallelisation technique. Nomad also provides a monitoring system, which enables the system administrator to track the resource usage and state of virtual machines running in the cloud. The monitoring system informs the system administrator when the virtual machines are not meeting required performance objectives, thereby enabling the system administrator to migrate the cloud-based services to another cloud. The framework provides a means of outsourcing sensitive computations to an unsecure cloud environment, without concern for the loss of confidentiality of the data. The primary benefit of this approach is that it enables organisations and individuals to take advantage of the cost efficiencies of the cloud without having to worry about the security (i.e., data confidentiality) ramifications of using the cloud.

Within the Nomad framework, the data is encrypted and decrypted on the trusted client side. The encrypted data is homomorphically processed on the untrusted server without ever decrypting the ciphertext representation of the data. The assumption is that the untrusted environment has more computation power than the trusted environment. In our current implementation of Nomad, we use *HElib*, an open source homomorphic encryption (HE) library [16]. HElib provides low-level cryptographic operations and is computationally intensive.

We developed an end-to-end application, called *CallForFire*, to analyse the feasibility of the Nomad framework. *CallForFire* is a GIS-based defense application for target acquisition and direction of fires against acquired targets. The application includes a map for visualising observer and target locations. We performed experiments to evaluate the performance of *CallForFire*.

Contributions. The following are the main contributions of this work:

- We designed and implemented a fully homomorphic encryption-based key/value storage system. This storage system provides a means for efficient storage, retrieval, and processing of encrypted data stored in the cloud.
- We built a framework, called Nomad, around the storage system, which facilitates the development of mission-critical applications that can be deployed in the cloud. The framework simplifies the development of secure applications that are deployed in the cloud.
- We used GPU parallelisation to accelerate HElib operations on both the trusted client and the untrusted server.
- We implemented an application, called *CallForFire*, using the Nomad framework. *CallForFire* is an interactive GIS application that demonstrates the feasibility of the Nomad framework.
- We performed experiments to analyse the performance of the *CallForFire* application. For specific use cases and interactive applications such as *CallForFire*, Homomorphic Encryption is feasible, but it may still be too slow for non-interactive applications.

2.2   Nomad framework overview

The Nomad framework consists of a modular architecture, which provides flexibility when implementing systems using the framework. The framework employs a client/server design to enable rapid deployment of secure cloud-based services. The specific application services making use of the framework are decided by the application developer. By using the Nomad framework, the application developer does not have to ensure the confidentiality of the data when designing the application, since the confidentiality of the application data is guaranteed by the framework itself. The application developer needs only to configure the framework so as to match its security level to the requirements of the application. The client module is assumed to run on a trusted machine which can safely store private encryption keys. The server module is assumed to run on a semi-trusted or untrusted machine. Together, the trusted client and the untrusted server provide a platform for secure computation in untrusted environments.

The client/server architecture of the Nomad framework can be seen in Figure 2.1. The Client Management Service consists of the Client Management Engine and all of the components necessary for managing the homomorphic encryption of the plaintext application data as well as the components responsible for monitoring the health of the virtual machines. The Cloud Storage Service consists of the Cloud Management Engine and the server side homomorphic encryption and monitoring components. The Cloud Storage Service resides on virtual machines in the cloud. The specific configuration of virtual machines used depends on the application developer's implementation.

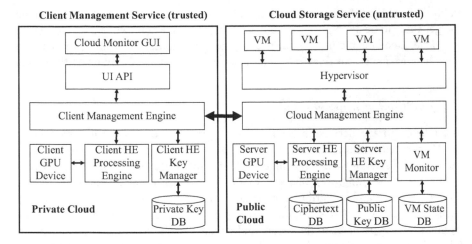

Figure 2.1   Nomad framework high-level architecture

2.2.1 Client management service

The Client Management Service is typically deployed on a trusted machine, possibly within a private cloud owned by the application developer. The components of the Client Management Service consist of the following: a Cloud Monitor Graphical User Interface (GUI), User Interface API (UI API), Client Management Engine, HE Processing Engine, HE Key Manager, Public/Private Key Database, and a GPU Device. The Client Management Engine takes commands from the UI API and translates them into tasks to be distributed to the HE Processing Engine and HE Key Manager, thereby acting as an abstraction layer between the end user and the underlying components which make up the framework. The Cloud Monitor GUI is the graphical user interface that has been implemented for developers using the framework to be able to manage and view data stored within the system, as well as to be able to view the health of the virtual machines under observation. The UI API is the programmatic interface that the application developer uses to program applications to interact with and use the framework. Due to the modular design of the framework, the application developer is free to use the UI API to create their own GUI. The HE Processing Engine performs the homomorphic encryption of the plaintext data stored in the system as well as the homomorphic decryption of the ciphertext data retrieved from the system. The GPU Device is used by the HE Processing Engine to accelerate the computations needed to homomorphically encrypt and decrypt data. The HE Key Manager is responsible for storing and retrieving the public and private keys used by the HE Processing Engine when encrypting and decrypting the trusted data. The Public/Private Key Database is the database used by the HE Key Manager for storage and retrieval of the public and private keys used for homomorphic encryption and decryption. As an example, a command to encrypt an integer value is sent via the UI API to the Client Management Engine, which then generates the public/private key pair, stores the keys in the

Public/Private Key Database, and then sends the encryption command along with the integer value to be encrypted over to the HE Processing Engine so that it can encrypt the value. Once the plaintext value is encrypted, the ciphertext result is sent back to the Client Management Engine so that it can be stored in the cloud using the Cloud Storage Service.

2.2.2 Cloud storage service

The Cloud Storage Service is deployed on a semi-trusted or untrusted machine or set of untrusted machines. It can be deployed in a public cloud on multiple virtual machines, or even on virtual machines hosted across different public cloud environments. Since the framework makes use of a web service-based client/server model, its components can be distributed geographically and still interoperate to provide a secure storage system. The Cloud Storage Service makes use of virtual machines running on a hypervisor in the cloud, and consists of the following components: a Cloud Management Engine, HE Processing Engine, HE Key Manager, VM Monitor, Ciphertext Database, Public Key Database, Virtual Machine Statistics Database, and a GPU Device. The Cloud Management Engine provides the client-facing interface to the server side of the Cloud Storage Service, and is hosted on virtual machines in the cloud. It receives commands from the Client Management Engine to store and retrieve encrypted data, and to perform operations on data stored within the system. The HE Processing Engine is the component that actually performs the homomorphic encryption operations. The ciphertext results of operations on homomorphically encrypted data are stored in the Ciphertext Database for later retrieval. The HE Key Manager manages the public keys used by the HE Processing Engine. The Public Key Database stores the public keys for access by the HE Key Manager. The public key is periodically used by the HE Processing Engine to re-encrypt the ciphertext to remove noise that accumulates over time to ensure the accuracy of the ciphertext. The VM Monitor is used for monitoring the state of virtual machines to assist the user in deciding if virtual machines need to be replicated or migrated in order to maintain system performance and ensure application availability. The VM Monitor makes use of a VM State Database to store the current and historical virtual machine state data.

2.2.3 Operational overview

When put together, the Client Management Service and the Cloud Storage Service intercommunicate to create the Nomad framework. Nomad provides a means for application developers to store encrypted application data in the cloud. This encrypted data can then be used in computations that the application performs in the cloud without ever decrypting the ciphertext. As a result, the sensitive plaintext data are never put at risk even though the systems comprising the cloud infrastructure are unknown and untrusted. This new paradigm for secure computation on untrusted systems addresses a major drawback of outsourced computation in general, and of cloud computing in particular. The Nomad framework provides the basic operations of storage, retrieval, deletion, and computation on data. Below is a description of how the system stores, retrieves, and performs computation on encrypted data. Client applications making use of the Nomad framework use the UI API to store data in the Cloud Storage Service. The Client Management Service is responsible for managing all of the keys, data, and operations for the client application. The application server is assumed to be running on virtual machines in the cloud alongside the Cloud Storage Service itself. The application data is stored as ciphertext in the cloud. All operations that the application performs on the data are performed on the ciphertext directly, as the application never has access to the underlying plaintext data. After operations have been performed on the ciphertext data in the cloud, the results are returned to the trusted client application for display and consumption by the end-user. Upon first use of the system, the user initialises the client and generates a public/private key pair. In practice, key generation would be done by a trusted third party.

Storage of encrypted data. A description of how the data is encrypted and stored in the cloud storage system follows. *Note: Assume that each user has a single public/private key pair for encryption and decryption of their data.*

1. System initialisation: In order to use the system, the user must first send a request to the *Client Management Engine* to generate a public/private key pair ($< ID_{user}, PK, SK >$). The public key and private key are denoted by PK and SK, respectively. The *Client Management Engine* sends a request to the *HE Key Manager* to generate the key pair and store it in the *Public/Private Key DB*. The *Client Management Engine* sends the User ID and Public Key ($< ID_{user}, PK >$) to the *Cloud Management Engine* for later usage. The *Cloud Management Engine* calls on the *HE Key Manager* to store the User ID and Public Key in the *Public Key DB*.

2. The user initiates a request to store their $Value_{plaintext}$ in the Cloud Storage Service.

3. The *Client Management Engine* submits a request to the *HE Processing Engine* to encrypt the plaintext value to get the ciphertext ($Enc(Value_{plaintext}, PK) = Value_{ciphertext}$).

4. The *Client Management Engine* then submits a request to the server-side *Cloud Management Engine* to store the key/value pair ($< Key_{data}, Value_{ciphertext}, ID_{user} >$). The Key_{data} can be represented by a hash function computed by the *Client Management Engine*. Note that this key (Key_{data}) is used for indexing the data within the cloud storage, not to be confused with the public key (PK) used for encryption or the private key (SK) used for decryption.

5. The *Cloud Management Engine* receives the storage request and calls on the *HE Processing Engine* to store the data ($< Key_{data}, Value_{ciphertext}, ID_{user} >$) in the *Ciphertext DB*.

Retrieval of encrypted data. The following describes how the encrypted data is retrieved from the cloud storage system and decrypted.

1. The user initiates a request to retrieve their $Value_{plaintext}$ from the Cloud Storage Service.

2. The *Client Management Engine* submits a request to the server-side *Cloud Management Engine* to retrieve the value associated with the user ID and the key which is unique to the data ($< Key_{data}, ID_{user} >$).

3. The *Cloud Management Engine* receives the retrieval request and calls on the *HE Processing Engine* to retrieve the data, $Value_{ciphertext}$, from the *Ciphertext DB*.
4. The *Ciphertext DB* responds to the query for the data associated with the tuple $< Key_{data}, ID_{user} >$ and returns the $Value_{ciphertext}$ to the *HE Processing Engine*.
5. The *HE Processing Engine* returns the encrypted data to the *Cloud Management Engine*.
6. The *Cloud Management Engine* returns the encrypted data to the *Client Management Engine*.
7. The *Client Management Engine* submits a request to the *HE Key Manager* to retrieve the Private Key, *SK*, associated with the user.
8. The HE Key Manager queries the *Public/Private Key DB* to retrieve the Private Key assigned to the user.
9. Upon receiving the Private Key from the *Public/Private Key DB*, the *HE Key Manager* returns the Private Key to the *Client Management Engine*.
10. The *Client Management Engine* sends $< Value_{ciphertext}, SK >$ to the *HE Processing Engine* along with a request to decrypt the $Value_{ciphertext}$.
11. The *HE Processing Engine* takes the $Value_{ciphertext}$ and returns the $Value_{plaintext}$ to the *Client Management Engine* ($Dec(Value_{ciphertext}, SK) = Value_{plaintext}$).
12. The *Client Management Engine* returns the $Value_{plaintext}$ to the user.

Operations on encrypted data. Following is a description of the process taken to perform an operation on the encrypted data in the cloud. Nomad supports the following binary arithmetic operations on integers in the encrypted domain: addition, subtraction, multiplication, and negation.

Note: This section assumes that the data has already been stored in the cloud storage system—refer to the Data Storage section above for details on how this is accomplished.

1. The user requests that a binary operation, *OP*, be performed on two integers (e.g., *data*1 and *data*2).
2. The *Client Management Engine* generates the request to perform the operation on the two integers and sends it to the *Cloud Management Engine* ($< ID_{user}, Key_{data1}, Key_{data2}, OP >$).
3. The *Cloud Management Engine* parses the request to identify the operation, the operands, and the user who submitted the request.
4. The *Cloud Management Engine* retrieves the two encrypted integers from the *Ciphertext Database* using their associated data IDs (Key_{data1} and Key_{data2}).
5. The *Cloud Management Engine* retrieves the public key associated with the user's ID (ID_{user}) from the *Public/Private Key Database*.
6. The *Cloud Management Engine* calls on the *HE Processing Engine* to perform the operation on the ciphertext data ($OP(PK, Data_{ciphertext1}, Data_{ciphertext2}) = Result_{ciphertext}$).
7. The *HE Processing Engine* makes use of the *GPU Device* as necessary to accelerate the operation on the two integer values.
8. The *Cloud Management Engine* then returns the $Result_{ciphertext}$ to the *Client Management Engine*.

9. The *Client Management Engine* retrieves the user's private key (*SK*) by requesting it from the *HE Key Manager*.
10. Using the private key, *SK*, the *Client Management Engine* calls on the *HE Processing Engine* to decrypt the *Result$_{ciphertext}$*
    (*Dec(Key$_{private}$, Result$_{ciphertext}$)=Result$_{plaintext}$*).
11. The *Client Management Engine* then sends the *Result$_{plaintext}$* to the user.

2.3 Homomorphic encryption background

Fully Homomorphic Encryption (FHE) is seen as the "holy grail of cryptography" [17]. The ability to outsource data processing without giving away information about the data, or which components of the data are of interest during computation, is foundational for the concepts of security and privacy in the cloud. FHE was first theorised by Rivest *et al.* [18], but there was not a successful FHE scheme until Gentry's Doctoral Thesis [13] in 2009. The success of Gentry's Doctoral work was revolutionary and there have been many advances in the field since then and a number of FHE schemes have since been developed [19,20], most notably the Brakerski, Gentry, and Vaikuntanathan (BGV) scheme [21]. The open source Homomorphic Encryption library (HElib) [16] implements this BGV scheme and is the underlying homomorphic encryption scheme used in Nomad.

2.3.1 BGV scheme

The BGV scheme for homomorphic encryption is based on the Ring Learning With Errors (RLWE) problem [22] and is built on algebraic structures, in particular rings and ideal lattices [21]. The security of RLWE schemes is based on the Shortest Vector Problem (SVP), which has been shown to be at least as hard as worst-case lattice problems. Specifically, the LWE problem and its variants are known to be secure against all currently known quantum computer attacks [23]. Moreover, RLWE cryptography schemes are generally more computationally efficient than traditional LWE schemes because of the use of ideal lattices as their foundational structure. BGV offers a choice of "leveled" FHE schemes based on either LWE or RLWE—with the RLWE scheme having better performance—where the size of the public key is linear in the depth of the circuits that the scheme can evaluate. The fundamental operation in the scheme is the *REFRESH* procedure, which switches the moduli of the lattice structure as well as the key. This process runs in almost quasilinear time when used with the RLWE version.

    RLWE [24] is formally defined as follows: For security parameter λ, let $f(x) = x^d + 1$ where $d = d(\lambda)$ is a power of 2. Let $q = q(\lambda) \geq 2 \in \mathbb{Z}$. Let $R = \mathbb{Z}[x]/(f(x))$ and let $R_q = R/qR$. Let $\chi = \chi(\lambda)$ be a distribution over R. The $RLWE_{d,q,\chi}$ problem is to distinguish the following two distributions: In the first distribution, one samples (a_i, b_i) from R_q^2. In the second distribution, one first draws $s \leftarrow R_q$ uniformly and then samples $(a_i, b_i) \in R_q^2$ by sampling $a_i \leftarrow R_q$ uniformly, $e_i \leftarrow \chi$, and setting $b_i = a_i \cdot s + e_i$. The assumption is that the $RLWE_{d,q,\chi}$ problem is infeasible. For this application, the security parameter λ is on the order of $|\lambda| = 10^2$, s is the *secret key*, e_i is generated noise, and χ is assumed to be Gaussian.

The definitions needed for the encryption scheme are as follows. Let $R = R(\lambda)$ be a ring. HElib uses $R = (\mathbb{Z})[x]/f(x)$ where $f(x) = x^d + 1$ and $d = d(\lambda)$ is a power of 2 [25]. The dimension $n = n(\lambda)$ is taken to be 1, and odd modulus $q = q(\lambda)$, a distribution $\chi = \chi(\lambda)$ over R, and an integer $N + N(\lambda)$ which is set to be larger than $(2n + 1)\log(q)$. Computations are based on the plaintext space R_2, although it is possible to use larger spaces.

The operations defined by the BGV scheme are as follows:

- **Encryption.** Given a message $m \in R_2$, let $\mathbf{m} = (m, 0, 0, \ldots, 0) \in \mathbf{R}_2^N$, where $N = \lceil(2n + 1)\rceil(\log(q))$, for an odd modulus, q. Then the output ciphertext is given as $\mathbf{c} = \mathbf{m} + \mathbf{A}^T\mathbf{r} \in \mathbf{R}_q^{n+1}$, where $\mathbf{A}$ is the matrix of public keys and $\mathbf{r}$ is a vector of noise from χ_2^N.
- **Decryption.** Given a ciphertext $\mathbf{c}$ and the secret key $\mathbf{s}$, compute $m = (\langle \mathbf{c}, \mathbf{s} \rangle \mod q) \mod 2$, where $\langle \mathbf{c}, \mathbf{s} \rangle \mod q$ is the *noise* associated with $\mathbf{s}$.
- **Arithmetic operations.** This scheme supports a number of operations including element-wise addition, subtraction, and multiplication; scalar arithmetic; and automorphic rotations that support efficient polynomial arithmetic (e.g., shift-register encoding). These operations take ciphertext as their input and produce ciphertext as their output. They produce accurate results, but the computation overhead is very high. Our aim is to reduce this computation cost to make homomorphic encryption feasible for widespread use.

2.3.2   HElib

This section describes the platform, modules, and algorithms that serve as the foundation of HElib. Figure 2.2 shows the HElib block diagram. The structure of the platform

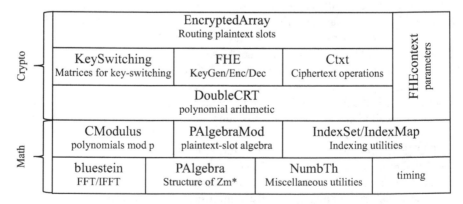

Figure 2.2   A block diagram of the Homomorphic-Encryption library. Reprinted with permission from Halevi S. An Implementation of homomorphic encryption. GitHubRepository, https://github com/shaih/HElib. 2013

is based on two major components: the underlying Math layer and the operational Cryptography layer.

The Math layer is implemented using the NTL math library [26], which consists of modules to support the creation of the mathematical structures along with definitions for operations on these structures. These modules include **PAlgebra, NumbTh, timing, bluestein, CModulus, PAlgebraMod**, and **IndexSet/IndexMap**. These are used to construct the mathematical structures needed for computation, including the structure of $\mathbb{Z}_m^*$ from **PAlgebra**, miscellaneous utilities from **NumbTh**, a way to facilitate timing within the system from **timing**, and the fast computation of arbitrary length FFTs from **bluestein**. **CModulus** enables modular arithmetic over polynomials, **PAlgebraMod** defines component-wise plaintext-slot arithmetic, and **IndexSet/IndexMap** provides indexing utilities that are needed for the complex matrix operations that are involved. The second component of the Math layer consists of a module to enable the Double-Chinese Remainder Theorem (Double-CRT) representation of polynomials. The Double-CRT representation of polynomials provides a way to efficiently perform arithmetic on large polynomials by encoding polynomials into vectors in such a way that it allows for component-wise operations. See [16] for additional details.

The second layer of the HElib platform is the Cryptography layer. The modules included in this layer are **KeySwitching**, which is used for storing the matrices needed for key-switching, and **FHE**, which consists of all of the cryptographic operations such as Key Generation, Encryption, and Decryption. The **Ctxt** module is used to perform all of the operations on the ciphertext, and the **EncryptedArray** is needed to support routing of the plaintext slots for operations. The final module that is used in HElib is **FHEContext**, which is used to keep track of all the parameters throughout the system.

HElib parameters. HElib uses the following parameters for configuration:

- k: The security parameter (default $= 80$) is analogous to the security parameter λ and is typically on the order of 10^2.
- m, p, r: provides the native plaintext space by $\mathbb{Z}[X]/(\Phi_m(X), p^r)$, where m is defined by the security parameter, k.
- d: degree of the field extension (default $= 1$). The degree of the field extension defines how polynomials will factor in the field. The default value of $d = 1$ indicates that the polynomials will split into linear (degree 1) factors.
- R: number of rounds (default $= 1$).
- c: number of columns in the key-switching matrices (default $= 2$).
- L: number of levels in the modulus chain (default is heuristically determined).
- s: minimum number of plaintext slots (default $= 0$).

2.4 GPU-based acceleration of BGV FHE

Since their introduction in the 1980s, GPUs have evolved from being used in basic display applications to more complex computations (e.g., 3D rendering). Only recently (2007) have GPUs become more widely available, as General Purpose computing on

Graphics Processing Units (GPGPUs), due to NVIDIA's Compute Unified Device Architecture (CUDA) [27]. CUDA has enabled the management of the multitude of cores that are used on GPUs.

With these advances, single GPUs are now able to function akin to a mobile high-performance computing (HPC) device. They are also easily reprogrammable, which makes them well suited for military and mobile applications. For example, a GPU on a Unmanned Aerial Vehicle (UAV) is able to process data at a near real-time rate and send time-sensitive feedback to decision makers instead of having to process later at a remote site.

We used GPU-based parallelisation as a mechanism to accelerate the processing of the algorithms in HElib. The first step in this process was to profile the HElib and Number Theory Library (NTL) code, beginning with the encoding, encryption, and arithmetic operations. Various HElib functions were profiled, including the algorithms for key generation, encryption, decryption, addition, and multiplication. The results of the HElib profiling are presented in the Implementation (Section 2.6) and Evaluation (Section 2.7) sections.

After performing the code profiling, we were able to identify portions of the code where there are combinations of algorithms which are particularly time consuming and repetitive. These algorithms are more computationally intensive than the CUDA overhead, and thus are good candidates for parallelisation on GPUs. We factored the CUDA overhead into our calculations in order to better approximate the actual speedup gained from parallelisation using the GPU. The CUDA overhead stems from the device memory allocation, host-to-device memory transfers, device-to-host memory transfers, and memory de-allocation. Table 2.5 describes the typical CUDA overhead required for GPU kernel executions. It should be noted that when executing any GPU device code, a one-time GPU initialisation cost is also incurred along with the previously mentioned CUDA overhead. This GPU initialisation time should be taken into account when porting sections of code to the GPU. Based on Amdahl's law, we identified sections of code with the most potential for parallelisation.

This approach was successfully taken to identify that parallelisation of the BluesteinInit() and BluesteinFFT() functions could be a potential source of speedup within HElib. The call sequences showed that, in general, the BluesteinFFT() function is called extensively by HElib. For example, the HElib profiling results seen in Table 2.2 show that the tasks of generating key switching matrices and performing key switching are computationally intensive, and these tasks make extensive use of the Bluestein FFT algorithm. When performing a simple workload of adding two numbers (which includes HElib initialisation, key generation, encryption, addition of two integers, and decryption), the BluesteinInit() and BluesteinFFT() functions take approximately 10% and 46% of the total execution time, respectively. These two functions were then profiled to determine portions of code which were computationally intensive and could be performed in parallel. With identified portions of code that could be calculated independently, portions of the Bluestein FFT code were ported to the NVIDIA GPU using CUDA. The performance results can be seen in the Implementation (Section 2.6) section.

2.5 Application: *CallForFire*

In order to demonstrate the utility of Nomad in a mission-critical scenario, we developed an application using the Nomad framework [24,28]. This application, called *CallForFire*, anticipates a tactical environment in the future where critical information could be communicated and processed in a cloud environment. *CallForFire* implements the "call for indirect fire" protocol used in the battlefield.

A tactic that military units use during engagements is the "call for indirect fire" to destroy enemy positions [29]. The players in the call for fire are the *Forward Observer* (*FO*), the *Fire Direction Center* (*FDC*), the *Firing Unit* (*FU*), and the *High-Value Target* (*HVT*). The *HVT* is the enemy target that needs to be destroyed. The *FDC* is the central command who has the technologies to compute and analyse fire data, and the authority to initiate a fire mission. The *FDC* receives calls for fire from the *FO*s and directs the *FU*s. The mission of the *FO* is to identify and locate *HVT*s, perform calls for fire, adjust the calls for fire, and report the outcome of the fire. Other concepts include Observer Target Line (*OTL*), which is a straight line projected from the *FO* to the *HVT*; Observer-Target Direction ($OT_{direction}$), which is the angle (azimuth) between the *FO* and the *HVT*; and Observer-Target Distance ($OT_{distance}$), which represents the distance from the observer to the target. The $OT_{distance}$ and $OT_{direction}$ are two important factors in determining the location of the *HVT*s.

*FO*s are typically sent into the field in advance to explore the area and collect intelligence. The intelligence collected is very sensitive and can directly impact the success of the mission. Any leakage of this sensitive data can jeopardise the security and safety of the defense personnel, in particular the *FO*. The data shared among the allied players must be protected to preserve its integrity, confidentiality, and availability.

The protocol is as follows: A *FO* spots a *HVT* (which could be a building, cars, etc.), collects all pertinent data about the *HVT* including $OT_{distance}$ and $OT_{direction}$, and sends it to the *FDC* to request a call for indirect fire. The *FDC* computes and analyses the firing data to determine the courses of action. If the resulting information is deemed accurate, the *FDC* initiates a fire mission to destroy the *HVT* and sends it to the *FU*. The *FU* takes action and destroys the *HVT* by firing for effect.

CallForFire uses the Military Grid Reference System (MGRS)[30] as the underlying geographical reference system. The MGRS conveniently partitions the world into 100,000-meter square grids, with each coordinate being a 5-digit integer. Each MGRS coordinate consists of three components: the grid zone designator (GZD)—a double digit integer followed by a letter, the 100,000-meter square identifier SQ_{ID}—two letters, and the numerical location (Easting and Northing) within the 100,000 meter square—both five digit integers. Given the 100,000 meter square, a reference point, and a reference bearing (direction), the numerical location of any position can be computed.

To model the computation of the *HVT* location in the MGRS, assume first that the GZD and the SQ_{ID} are known. Also assume that the (fixed) numerical location of the *FO* within the 100,000-meter square is known and the *HVT* is inside the same square. Now, let $FO_{easting}$ be the easting of the *FO*, and $FO_{northing}$ the northing of the

FO. Let also $HVT_{easting}$ be the HVT easting, $HVT_{northing}$ the HVT northing, and θ the *HVT* bearing. Then, the *HVT*'s location is calculated as follows:

$$HVT_{easting} = FO_{easting} + OT_{distance} \times \sin(\theta)$$

$$HVT_{northing} = FO_{northing} + OT_{distance} \times \cos(\theta)$$

where the easting and northing distances are measured in meters (m) and the θ is measured in angular mils (to the nearest integer) from 0 mils North.

It will be assumed that the positions of the *FO*s and *FU*s will be known to the *FDC*. Multiple *FO*s may call for fire support on the same *HVT*. When this happens, the nearest available *FU* to the *HVT* will be directed to fire on the *HVT*. The distance between the *FU* and the *HVT* is calculated as follows:

$$Distance^2_{FU-HVT} = (FU_{easting} - HVT_{easting})^2 + (FU_{northing} - HVT_{northing})^2$$

Note that the actual distance between the FU and HVT is found by taking the square root of the above equation. HElib currently does not support the square root operation, but distances can still be compared using the above formula.

2.5.1 CallForFire operational workflow

The CallForFire operational workflow describes how the call for indirect/supporting fire procedure is implemented by the CallForFire application. Nomad currently supports the following integer operations in the encrypted domain: addition, subtraction, multiplication, and negation. For this simple scenario, we assume that all locations (except the *FDC*) are inside of the same MGRS zone.

1. The *FO* detects an *HVT* in the field, estimates its distance and bearing, and enters the data into the *FO* client application.
2. The *FO* client application uses the *FDC* public key to homomorphically encrypt the *FO*'s location (easting and northing) and the *HVT*'s distance and bearing, and sends them to the *FDC*.
3. The *FDC* outsources the computation of the *HVT*'s location to the Nomad cloud service by sending the homomorphically encrypted *FO*'s location, the *HVT*'s bearing and distance, and locations of the available *FU*s over to the cloud.
4. The cloud homomorphically computes the *HVT*'s absolute location and selects the nearest *FU* to direct fire on the *HVT*.
5. The cloud sends the *HVT*'s location and *FU* selection back to the *FDC*.
6. The *FDC* decrypts the *HVT*'s location and the *FU* selection, then makes the final decision to initiate the firing operation.
7. The *FDC* encrypts the *HVT*'s location using the *FU* public key and sends the firing command to the selected *FU*.
8. The selected *FU* decrypts the *HVT*'s location and directs fire on the *HVT*.

2.6 Implementation

The Nomad framework is designed to be modular and extensible, using Thrift [31] as the underlying client/server framework. We chose Thrift, which is based on the remote procedure call (RPC) protocol, in order to abstract away the details of the communication between the client and server. The *Cloud Storage Service* uses Google's LevelDB [32] for its underlying database, but the framework can easily be adapted to use other NoSQL databases such as Apache Accumulo [33]. The current implementation of Nomad uses the Xen hypervisor [34], which is open source and used by major public cloud service providers today. The GPU-based acceleration mechanism is integrated with HElib and uses the Nvidia CUDA [27] parallel computing platform and programming model, as described in Section 2.4. For the *Client Management Service* implementation, we used the CppCMS [35] web development framework to integrate the various C++ libraries, including HElib, Thrift, LevelDB, and CUDA. Nomad's modular design allows developers to extend the framework, including using different hypervisors for virtual machine management, and choosing different key/value stores for back-end storage.

We implemented the *CallForFire* application using the Nomad framework. Open-Layers [36], an open source javascript library, is used for loading, displaying and rendering map data in the browser. Since the map data needs to be completely encrypted within the Cloud Storage Service, standard GIS databases such as Oracle Spatial and Graph or PostGIS could not be used for this purpose. Traditional GIS systems perform the computations on the server side, which means that the plaintext data must be visible to the server when using these systems, thereby precluding their use in the CallForFire application. Instead, LevelDB is used for storing the encrypted

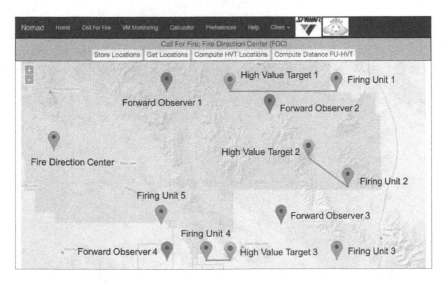

Figure 2.3   Screenshot of the CallForFire application in a web browser

GIS data. Since LevelDB provides an ordered mapping from keys to values, one of the main advantages of using LevelDB is that the keys and values are arbitrary byte arrays and are automatically compressed using the Snappy compression library [37]. The Snappy compression library has fast and reasonable compression, which is advantageous given the large size of the ciphertext. For performing operations in different geographical coordinate systems within CallForFire, we leveraged the GeographicLib [38] library.

Figure 2.3 is a screenshot of the actual *CallForFire* GUI in a web browser. It shows an example scenario with the following players: one *FDC*, four *FOs*, five *FUs*, and three *HVTs*. In this scenario, the *FDC* has computed the locations of the three *HVTs* using the information given by the *FOs*. It has also selected the nearest *FU* for each *HVT* as indicated by the lines between them on the map.

2.7   Experiments

We performed two different sets of experiments to analyse the feasibility of the overall Nomad approach. The first set of experiments focused on the optimisation of the HElib library using the GPU-based parallelisation approach. The second set of experiments analysed the feasibility of the CallForFire application. HElib uses the following main parameters: R (number of rounds), p (plaintext base), r (lifting), d (degree of the field extension), c (number of columns in the key-switching matrices), k (security parameter), L (number of levels in the modulus chain), s (minimum number of slots), and m (modulus). HElib is initialised by configuring the parameters $R, p, r, d, c, k,$ and s. The parameters L and m are automatically generated by HElib based on these other parameters.

2.7.1   *Performance of the GPU-based parallelisation*

For this set of experiments, the following HElib parameters defined in Section 2.3.2 were used for configuration: $R = 2, p = 7919, r = 1, d = 1, c = 2, k = 80, L = 3, s = 0$. Table 2.1 describes the test environment.

HElib profiling. A simple workload consisting of the encryption of two integers and their addition was used to profile HElib to identify potential subroutines for GPU

Table 2.1   Test environment

Operating system	CentOS 7
Server	Dell T630 Server
CPU	Intel Xeon CPU E5-2620 v3 2.4 GHz
Memory	16 GB Memory
GPU	NVIDIA Quadro K4000
Cores	768 CUDA Cores
Driver	CUDA Driver 7.0, Runtime 7.0
Version	CUDA Capability 3.0

parallelisation. The timing results reported are the averages (i.e., mean value) taken over 50 runs of this simple workload. Table 2.2 details the comparison between the CPU HElib and GPU HElib implementations. We used the TAU Parallel Performance System [39] to perform the code profiling. It can be seen that almost all of the HElib modules benefited from the GPU implementation. These results highlight the speedup that can be gained when these methods are ported to the GPU.

Tables 2.3 and 2.4 compare the execution time of the CPU HElib implementation to the GPU HElib implementation. It should be noted that the workload execution times reported do not include the GPU initialisation time. From these tables, it can be seen that implementing the BluesteinFFT() function using the GPU results in a speedup of $2.1\times$ compared to the CPU implementation.

Table 2.2   HElib profiling results

HElib modules	CPU HELib execution time (ms)	GPU HELib execution time (ms)
FHE context	1,278	1,136
Mod chain	412	298
Secret key	245	36
Key switching matrices	1,826	509
Encoding single value	0.108	0.114
Encrypting single value	65	65
Adding two values	1	0.465
Decrypting result	28	8
Decode result	0.116	0.0358

Table 2.3   Timing comparison of BluesteinInit( ) CPU and GPU implementation (256 threads per block)

Function call	Inclusive execution (ms)	Number of calls	Application execution (%)	Workload execution (ms)
CPU	404	8	10.1	3,970
GPU	300	8	7.7	3,836

Table 2.4   Comparison of BluesteinFFT( ) CPU and GPU implementation (256 threads per block)

Function call	Inclusive execution (ms)	Number of calls	Application execution (%)	Workload execution (ms)
CPU	1,826	268	45.7	3,970
GPU	223	268	10.2	2,119

Table 2.5   GPU overhead

	BluesteinInit()	**BluesteinFFT()**	**Average**
GPU initialisation	38.561 ms	92.713 ms	80.226 ms
CUDA memory allocation	151.01 μs	32.889 μs	32.855 μs
CUDA memory copy, host to device	NA	4.8030 μs	4.8040 μs
CUDA memory copy, device to host	6.3040 μs	6.2040 μs	6.2180 μs
CUDA free	72.231 μs	80.318 μs	72.381 μs
Over head kernel execution	230 μs/14 KB	124 μs/14 KB	116 μs/14 KB

Table 2.6   Comparison of CPU and GPU BluesteinInit/FFT implementation combinations (256 threads per block)

	CUDA overhead (ms)	**Workload execution (ms)**	**Total execution (ms)**
CPU BluesteinInit(), CPU BluesteinFFT()	0	3,970	3,970
GPU BluesteinInit(), CPU BluesteinFFT()	56	3,836	3,892
CPU BluesteinInit(), GPU BluesteinFFT()	46	2,119	2,166
GPU BluesteinInit(), GPU BluesteinFFT()	43	2,033	2,077

Table 2.5 describes the GPU overhead associated with the respective GPU implementation of BluesteinInit() and BluesteinFFT(). The GPU overhead, along with the one-time GPU initialisation, provide the minimum CPU execution time savings necessary in order to make utilising the GPU worthwhile. This cost needs to be taken into account when porting code to the GPU.

HElib GPU parallelisation. With BluesteinInit() and BluesteinFFT() ported to the GPU, combinations of the CPU and GPU implementations were profiled. Table 2.6 shows these results in detail. It should be noted that the CUDA overhead is a combination of the GPU initialisation and GPU kernel overhead as described previously. This table shows how much time savings is gained from each of the two functions when using combinations of the GPU and CPU for their implementation. For example, implementing the BluesteinFFT() function in the GPU yields significantly higher speedup than implementing the BluesteinInit() function in the GPU. This is because the BluesteinFFT() function is called many more times than the BluesteinInit() function. From this, one can infer that the time savings is proportional to the number of times each function is called.

Table 2.7   Comparison of workload execution time when varying the number of threads per block using GPU BluesteinInit/FFT implementation

	CUDA overhead (ms)	Workload execution (ms)	Total execution (ms)
32 Threads/block	47	2,051	2,099
64 Threads/block	45	2,038	2,084
128 Threads/block	47	2,043	2,090
256 Threads/block	45	2,037	2,082
512 Threads/block	44	2,040	2,084
1,024 Threads/block	45	2,038	2,084
0 Threads/block (CPU implementation)	0	3,970	3,970

Multiple threads can be assigned to process the data stored in each memory block within the GPU. This has the potential of speeding up data processing within the GPU. The number of threads per block can be customised. In Table 2.7, various numbers of threads per block were executed and profiled. The results presented in the table reveal that there is only a slight decrease in execution time when increasing the number of threads per block. This confirms NVIDIA's CUDA GPU Occupancy Calculator which details no effect of increasing the number of threads per block when utilising Compute Capability 3.0 and 64 registers per thread. Also note that the average overhead for the GPU kernel execution is 116 μs per 14 KB processed by the GPU.

2.7.2   *CallForFire performance*

We performed experiments to analyse the performance of *CallForFire* with respect to the overhead associated with Computation, Storage, and Data Transmission. We ignored the latency between browser and server. For all the experiments, the following parameters are fixed: $R = 1$, $r = 1$, $d = 1$, $c = 2$, and $s = 0$. We adjusted the parameters p and k in order to evaluate the performance tradeoffs associated with having a larger integer space and a higher security level, respectively. The parameters L and m are automatically generated by HElib based on the other parameters.

The experiments were performed using two HP Z420 desktops with 16 GB RAM and 500 GB storage, and one MacBook Pro with 2.6 GHz Intel Core i7, 16 GB RAM, and 500 GB storage. The setup is as follows: The *FO* module is run on a MacBook Pro laptop, the *FDC* module is deployed on a Z420 desktop, and the *Cloud* module is deployed on a Z420 desktop.

CallForFire computation overhead. To measure the computation overhead, we performed two sets of computations: (1) calculation of the *HVT*'s location and, (2) firing asset selection. In the *HVT* location calculation, we measured the time it took to homomorphically encrypt ten individual locations consisting of six parameters (GZD, SQ_{ID}, $FO_{easting}$, $FO_{northing}$, $OT_{distance}$, $OT_{direction}$) each, computed the numerical location (easting and northing) of the *HVT* for each *FO*, and decrypted the *HVT*

Table 2.8   *Average computation overhead in seconds with fixed p = 9576890767*
(10 digits)

Security parameter (*k*) Type	80		100		120	
	Individual	Batched	Individual	Batched	Individual	Batched
Encrypt location	702.399	63.077	782.689	71.873	831.919	77.196
Decrypt location	600.704	165.279	692.349	217.052	760.939	217.062
Compute location	212.197	21.323	221.747	27.355	237.119	23.255
Compute distance	271.294	26.386	283.755	28.794	331.041	33.288
Store location	2.474	0.249	2.799	0.284	2.811	0.282
Retrieve location	16.383	1.558	18.093	1.800	21.831	1.964

locations. We also measured the time it took to store and retrieve ten encrypted locations from the storage. In the firing asset selection, we measured the time it took to compute the distance between ten *FUs* and ten *HVTs* pairwise. We repeated both experiments 100 times and computed the averages. Table 2.8 summarises the results of these experiments and gives a comparison between the performance of *individual* and *batched* operations. When performing operations in *batched* mode, an input array with multiple elements is passed in to the storage system. The homomorphic encryption operations can then be performed on all of the elements of the array within the same operation. With *individual* operations, one data element (i.e., an integer) is placed into the input array, which is then passed to the storage system. Based on the results of these experiments, it is best to use *batch* mode when possible, which can reduce the overhead significantly.

Transmission and storage overhead. For the transmission and storage overhead, we measured the time it took for the *FO* to encrypt and transmit the location information to the *FDC*, and for the *FDC* to store the information in its database. We considered scenarios for 100 *FOs* and calculated the averages. The time it takes to transmit an encrypted location and store it in the database is about 22 times longer than when the location is not encrypted. For the storage space overhead, the average space used to store a location using FHE is 8.96 megabytes, whereas the average for a location without using FHE is 17.6 bytes. This significant storage space overhead is a limitation common to all lattice-based homomorphic encryption schemes.

2.8   Related work

Much of the early and continued support for research in FHE has come from government sources like the Defense Advanced Research Projects Agency (DARPA). Early FHE schemes were many orders of magnitude too slow for practical use, and DARPA led a multi-year effort, PROgramming Computation on EncryptEd Data (PROCEED), to improve their computational efficiency [40].

One line of research has focused on hardware-based optimisations of FHE, including the use of FPGAs to accelerate portions of the homomorphic encryption computations [41–43]. In addition to the hardware-based optimisation work that has utilised FPGAs, Worcester Polytechnic Institute showed some improvement using GPGPUs [44,45].

Another line of research has been in software-based optimisations. While BGV [21] and HElib [16] are the most widely used scheme and implementation of FHE, respectively, a number of schemes are being proposed and new implementations are coming online. FHE implementations based on the NTRU cryptographic scheme showed early progress, most notably the work by Rohloff and Cousins [46]. Ducas and Micciancio [47] released an open source implementation of FHE that reports bootstrapping times of 0.5 s for a non-packed ciphertext encrypting a single bit [48].

Some of the software-based optimisations have focused on specialised homomorphic encryption schemes for specific application domains. For instance, Rohloff *et al.* [49] propose the use of FHE for secure and efficient communication with Voice over Internet Protocol (VoIP). Pedrouzo-Ulloa *et al.* [50] developed a multivariate RLWE FHE scheme for encrypted image processing. Microsoft Research developed an implementation of the FHE-based YASHE scheme [51], *Simple Encrypted Arithmetic Library (SEAL)* [52] which will enable biological data science researchers to comply with patient privacy laws. SEAL v2.0 [53] utilises the FV [20] scheme rather than YASHE due to that scheme's improved "noise growth", allowing for smaller parameters. The YASHE and FV schemes are both RLWE-based and many researchers consider them to be promising.

2.9 Conclusion

In this chapter, we presented *Nomad*, a framework for developing secure and privacy-preserving applications in the cloud. In particular, Nomad can be used to build mission-critical cloud-based applications with ensured data confidentiality. Nomad consists of a fully homomorphic encryption-based key/value storage system that provides a means for efficient storage, retrieval, and processing of encrypted data stored in the cloud. The storage system was developed using HElib, an open source homomorphic encryption library. HElib implements the BGV homomorphic encryption scheme, which is based on the RLWE technique. We employed a GPU-based approach to parallelise some of the underlying HElib algorithms to accelerate the HElib operations. We performed experiments to analyse the performance of the GPU-based acceleration. These experiments showed a 2.1× speedup of certain HElib operations. The results of this approach are promising in that portions of HElib may be accelerated, thereby leading to more uses of homomorphic encryption in practical applications.

To analyse the feasibility of the Nomad framework, we implemented *CallForFire*, a cloud-based mission-critical defense application. *CallForFire* takes advantage of Nomad's *Cloud Storage Service* to encrypt and compute enemy target locations in the battlefield. *CallForFire* is very secure, as the data stored in the system is never decrypted within the cloud storage service, which is where all the computations take place. *CallForFire* uses very limited operations on integers and is interactive, which made it suitable for development using the Nomad framework. Despite the fact that the homomorphic operations are slow, the performance of the *CallForFire* application highlights the feasibility of such a system in a real-life scenario.

While the overall performance of HElib may still be impractical for many applications, certain interactive applications, such as *CallForFire*, can still make use of HElib in a limited context to enhance data confidentiality. Further development of secure computing techniques that protect data-in-processing, such as homomorphic encryption, will likely accelerate the adoption of cloud computing by organisations with sensitive data.

2.10   Future research challenges

Encrypted computing that ensures data security and privacy consists of two primary research areas: FHE and multi-party computation (MPC) [54]. Both FHE and MPC enable secure storage and computation. However, FHE is expensive in terms of computation with minimal communication overhead, while MPC is expensive in terms of communication with minimal computation overhead [55]. Furthermore, FHE only requires a single (possibly untrusted) server, while MPC requires each party to work from their own (trusted) server [56]. An approach for increasing the performance of HElib would be to incorporate MPC techniques into the library.

Using CUDA GPU acceleration techniques such as page-locked host memory, asynchronous memory transfers, and streams can be used to further optimise the HElib operations. Faster NVIDIA GPUs can also be used to parallelise HElib, specifically using higher compute capabilities such as the Tesla K80 with Compute Capability 3.7. HElib also can be distributed across multiple nodes to speed up the homomorphic operations.

Another approach for optimising homomorphic encryption is through hardware-based parallelisation techniques. Much of the research in hardware-based parallelisation focuses on FPGAs [42,43]. FPGAs enable the implementation of algorithms at the hardware level, which is faster than the software-based implementations. A hybrid approach that combines FPGAs and GPUs has the potential to further improve the performance of homomorphic encryption.

References

[1]   Grance T, Mell P. The NIST Definition of Cloud Computing. Recommendations of the National Institute of Standards and Technology. 2011 September.

[2]   Alliance CS. The Notorious Nine: Cloud Computing Top Threats in 2013. Top Threats Working Group. 2013.

[3]   GCN: Like it or not, cloud computing is here to stay; 2011. Available from: https://gcn.com/microsites/2011/cloud-computing-download/cloud-computing-application-development.aspx. [Online; accessed 20-Dec-2016].

[4] Venom: Virtualized Environment Neglected Operations Manipulation; 2015. Available from: http://venom.crowdstrike.com/. [Online; accessed 20-Dec-2016].

[5] Apecechea GI, Inci MS, Eisenbarth T, Sunar B. Fine grain Cross-VM Attacks on Xen and VMware are possible! IACR Cryptology ePrint Archive. 2014;2014:248.

[6] Apecechea GI, Inci MS, Eisenbarth T, Sunar B. Wait a minute! A fast, Cross-VM attack on AES. IACR Cryptology ePrint Archive. 2014;2014:435.

[7] Apecechea GI, Eisenbarth T, Sunar B. S$A: A Shared Cache Attack That Works across Cores and Defies VM Sandboxing – And Its Application to AES. In: IEEE Symposium on Security and Privacy. IEEE Computer Society; 2015. p. 591–604.

[8] Inci MS, Gulmezoglu B, Irazoqui G, Eisenbarth T, Sunar B. Seriously, get off my cloud! Cross-VM RSA Key Recovery in a Public Cloud. IACR Cryptology ePrint Archive. 2015;2015:898.

[9] D'Antoine SM. Exploiting Processor Side Channels To Enable Cross VM Malicious Code Execution. Rensselaer Polytechnic Institute; 2015.

[10] Liu F, Yarom Y, Ge Q, Heiser G, Lee RB. Last-Level Cache Side-Channel Attacks are Practical. In: IEEE Symposium on Security and Privacy. IEEE Computer Society; 2015. p. 605–622.

[11] Litchfield A, Shahzad A. Virtualization Technology: Cross-VM Cache Side Channel Attacks make it Vulnerable. CoRR. 2016;abs/1606.01356.

[12] Nimbostratus: Tools for fingerprinting and exploiting Amazon cloud infrastructures; 2015. Available from: http://andresriancho.github.io/nimbostratus/. [Online; accessed 20-Dec-2016].

[13] Gentry C. Fully Homomorphic Encryption Using Ideal Lattices. In: Proceedings of the Forty-First Annual ACM Symposium on Theory of Computing. STOC'09. New York, NY, USA: ACM; 2009. p. 169–178.

[14] Halevi S, Shoup V. Algorithms in helib. In: Advances in Cryptology–CRYPTO 2014. Berlin: Springer; 2014.

[15] Parmar PV, Padhar SB, Patel SN, Bhatt NI, Jhaveri RH. Survey of Various Homomorphic Encryption algorithms and Schemes. International Journal of Computer Applications. 2014 April;91(8). Published by Foundation of Computer Science, New York, USA.

[16] Halevi S, Shoup V. Design and Implementation of a Homomorphic-Encryption Library. 2013; IBM Research.

[17] Micciancio D. A first glimpse of cryptography's Holy Grail. Communications of the ACM. 2010;53(3):96–96.

[18] Rivest RL, Adleman L, Dertouzos ML. On data banks and privacy homomorphisms. Foundations of Secure Computation. 1978;4(11):169–180.

[19] Cousins D, Rohloff K, Peikert C, Sumorok D. SIPHER: Scalable implementation of primitives for homomorphic encryption. DTIC Document; 2015.

[20] Fan J, Vercauteren F. Somewhat Practical Fully Homomorphic Encryption. IACR Cryptology ePrint Archive. 2012;2012:144.

[21]   Brakerski Z, Gentry C, Vaikuntanathan V. Fully Homomorphic Encryption without Bootstrapping; 2011. Cryptology ePrint Archive, Report 2011/277.

[22]   Regev O. The learning with errors problem. In: 25th Annual IEEE Conference on Computational Complexity, CCC 2010; 2010.

[23]   Micciancio D, Regev O. Lattice-based cryptography. In: Post-quantum cryptography. Berlin: Springer; 2009. p. 147–191.

[24]   Diallo MH, August M, Hallman R, Kline M, Au H, Beach V. Nomad: A Framework for Developing Mission-Critical Cloud-Based Applications. In: 10th International Conference on Availability, Reliability and Security, ARES, Toulouse, France, August 24–27; 2015.

[25]   Halevi S. An implementation of homomorphic encryption. GitHubRepository, https://github com/shaih/HElib. 2013.

[26]   Shoup V. NTL: A library for doing number theory; Version 5.5.2, 2010. [Online; accessed 20-Dec-2016]. http://shoup.net/ntl/.

[27]   Nvidia. CUDA C Programming Guide; 2015. [Online; accessed 29-Jun-2014].

[28]   Diallo M, August M, Hallman R, Kline M, Au H, Beach V. CallForFire: A Mission-Critical Cloud-based Application Built Using the Nomad Framework. In: Financial Cryptography and Data Security. Berlin: Springer; 2016.

[29]   Tactics, Techniques, and Procedures for Observed Fire, Field Manual 6-30; 1991.

[30]   FM 3-25.26 Map Reading and Land Navigation; 2001.

[31]   The apache thrift software framework; 2015. Available from: https://thrift.apache.org/. [Online; accessed 20-Dec-2016].

[32]   Jeff Dean SG. Level DB: A fast and lightweight key/value database library by Google; 2015. [Online; accessed 20-Dec-2016]. https://code.google.com/p/leveldb/.

[33]   Halldrsson GJ. Apache Accumulo for Developers. Packt Publishing; 2013.

[34]   Xen Project; 2015. Available from: https://www.xenproject.org/. [Online; accessed 20-Dec-2016].

[35]   CppCMS – High Performance C++ Web Framework. Available from: http://cppcms.com/wikipp/en/page/main.

[36]   OpenLayers 3: A high-performance, feature-packed library for all your mapping needs.; 2015. Available from: http://openlayers.org/. [Online; accessed 20-Dec-2016].

[37]   snappy: A fast compressor and decompressor; 2015. Available from: http://google.github.io/snappy/. [Online; accessed 20-Dec-2016].

[38]   GeographicLib; 2015. Available from: http://geographiclib.sourceforge.net/. [Online; accessed 20-Dec-2016].

[39]   Shende S, Malony AD. The Tau Parallel Performance System. IJHPCA. 2006;20(2):287–311.

[40]   Libicki MC, Tkacheva O, Feng C, Hemenway B. Ramifications of DARPA's Programming Computation on Encrypted Data Program. RAND. 2014.

[41]   Cousins DB, Golusky J, Rohloff K, Sumorok D. An FPGA co-processor imple-
       mentation of Homomorphic Encryption. In: IEEE High Performance Extreme
       Computing Conference, HPEC 2014, Waltham, MA, USA, September 9–11,
       2014. Piscataway, NJ: IEEE; 2014. p. 1–6.

[42]   Cousins DB, Rohloff K, Peikert C, Schantz R. An update on SIPHER (scalable
       implementation of primitives for homomorphic encryption)—FPGA imple-
       mentation using Simulink. In: High Performance Extreme Computing (HPEC),
       2012 IEEE Conference on. Piscataway, NJ: IEEE; 2012. p. 1–5.

[43]   Cilardo A, Argenziano D. Securing the cloud with reconfigurable computing:
       An FPGA accelerator for homomorphic encryption. In: 2016 Design, Automa-
       tion & Test in Europe Conference & Exhibition (DATE). Piscataway, NJ: IEEE;
       2016. p. 1622–1627.

[44]   Wang W, Hu Y, Chen L, Huang X, Sunar B. Accelerating fully homomorphic
       encryption using GPU. In: IEEE Conference on High Performance Extreme
       Computing, HPEC 2012, Waltham, MA, USA, September 10–12, 2012.
       Piscataway, NJ: IEEE; 2012. p. 1–5.

[45]   Wang W, Hu Y, Chen L, Huang X, Sunar B. Exploring the feasibility of
       fully homomorphic encryption. IEEE Transactions on Computers. 2015;64(3):
       698–706.

[46]   Rohloff K, Cousins DB. A scalable implementation of fully homomor-
       phic encryption built on NTRU. In: International Conference on Financial
       Cryptography and Data Security. Berlin: Springer; 2014. p. 221–234.

[47]   Ducas L, Micciancio D. FHEW-A Fully Homomorphic Encryption Library;
       2014. Available from: https://github.com/lducas/FHEW. [Online; accessed 20-
       Dec-2016].

[48]   Ducas L, Micciancio D. FHEW: bootstrapping homomorphic encryption in less
       than a second. In: Annual International Conference on the Theory and Appli-
       cations of Cryptographic Techniques. Berlin: Springer; 2015. p. 617–640.

[49]   Rohloff K, Sumorok D, Cousins D. Scalable, Practical VoIP Teleconfer-
       encing with End-to-End Homomorphic Encryption. IEEE Transactions on
       Information Forensics and Security, Volume 12, p. 1031–1041, 2017.

[50]   Pedrouzo-Ulloa A, Troncoso-Pastoriza JR, Pérez-González F. Multivariate
       lattices for encrypted image processing. In: 2015 IEEE International Confer-
       ence on Acoustics, Speech and Signal Processing (ICASSP). Piscataway, NJ:
       IEEE; 2015. p. 1707–1711.

[51]   Bos JW, Lauter K, Loftus J, Naehrig M. Improved security for a ring-based
       fully homomorphic encryption scheme. In: IMA International Conference on
       Cryptography and Coding. Berlin: Springer; 2013. p. 45–64.

[52]   Dowlin N, Gilad-Bachrach R, Laine K, Lauter K, Naehrig M, Wernsing J.
       Manual for Using Homomorphic Encryption for Bioinformatics. Microsoft
       Research; 2015.

[53]   Laine K, Player R. Release Notes for SEAL v2.0-beta. Microsoft Research;
       2016.

[54]   Cramer R, Damgård I. Multiparty computation: an introduction. In: Contemporary Cryptology. Berlin: Springer; 2005. p. 41–87.

[55]   Choudhury A, Loftus J, Orsini E, Patra A, Smart NP. Between a Rock and a Hard Place: Interpolating between MPC and FHE. In: International Conference on the Theory and Application of Cryptology and Information Security. Berlin: Springer; 2013. p. 221–240.

[56]   Archer DW, Bogdanov D, Pinkas B, Pullonen P. Maturity and performance of programmable secure computation. IACR Cryptology ePrint Archive; 2015.

Chapter 3
Preserving privacy in pre-classification volume ray-casting of 3D images

Manoranjan Mohanty[1], Muhammad Rizwan Asghar[2], and Giovanni Russello[2]

Abstract

With the evolution of cloud computing, organizations are outsourcing the storage and rendering of volume (i.e., 3D data) to cloud servers. Data confidentiality at the third-party cloud provider, however, is one of the main challenges. Although state-of-the-art non-homomorphic encryption schemes can protect confidentiality by encrypting the volume, they do not allow rendering operations on the encrypted volumes. In this chapter, we address this challenge by proposing *3DCrypt*—a modified Paillier cryptosystem scheme for multiuser settings that allows cloud datacenters to render the encrypted volume. The rendering technique we consider in this work is the pre-classification volume ray-casting. *3DCrypt* is such that multiple users can render volumes without sharing any encryption keys. *3DCrypt*'s storage and computational overheads are approximately 66.3 MB and 27 s, respectively, when rendering is performed on a $256 \times 256 \times 256$ volume for a 256×256 image space. We have also proved that *3DCrypt* is INDistinguishable under Chosen Plaintext Attack (IND-CPA) secure.

3.1 Introduction

Cloud computing is an attractive paradigm for accessing virtually unlimited storage and computational resources. With its pay-as-you-go model, clients can access fast and reliable hardware paying only for the resources they use, without the risk of large upfront investments. Nowadays, it is very common to build applications for multimedia content hosted in infrastructures run by third-party cloud providers. To this end, cloud datacenters are also increasingly used by organizations for rendering of images [1–3]. In these cloud-based rendering schemes, the data is typically stored

---

[1]Center for Cyber Security, New York University, United Arab Emirates
[2]Department of Computer Science, The University of Auckland, New Zealand

in the cloud datacenter, and on request, the data-to-image rendering operation is performed at the cloud-end.

The data and the rendered image can contain critical information, which when disclosed raises data confidentiality and privacy issues. For example, the data can be a scanned MRI of a patient's head, whose storage and rendering were outsourced to the cloud by a hospital due to the adaption of the cloud-based medical imaging technique. If processed in plaintext, both the data and the rendered image can reveal information about the disease that the patient may be suffering from. Therefore, the data must be hidden from the third-party cloud server, which we assume is *honest-but-curious*: it honestly performs requested operation, but it can be curious to learn sensitive information. The data encryption scheme is such that rendering can be performed on the encrypted data. Although the rendered image must not disclose any information to the cloud server, an authorized user (i.e., the one holding the encryption key) must be able to discover the secret rendered image from the encrypted rendered image.

Ideally, one would like to use the fully homomorphic encryption scheme to perform any type of computations over encrypted data [4]. However, current homomorphic encryption schemes are not computationally practical. Therefore, partial homomorphic schemes have been typically used for the cloud-based encrypted processing [5]. Using the partial homomorphic Shamir's (k, n) secret sharing, Mohanty *et al.* [6] proposed the encrypted domain pre-classification volume ray-casting. Their work, however, cannot hide shape of the object from a datacenter and can disclose the color of the object when k or more datacenters collude together. Recently, Chou and Yang [7] used permutation and adjusted the color transfer function (used in rendering) such that critical information about the object can be hidden from the rendering server. Their work, however, is not secure enough.

When working on encrypted data, a lot of attention is usually paid to the actual scheme without considering key management, an aspect critical for organizations. In a typical organization, issuing the same key to all employees, who want to share data, is not feasible. In an ideal situation, each employee must have her own personal key that can be used to access data encrypted by the key of any other employee. This scenario is often referred to as the full-fledged multiuser model. When the employee leaves the organization, the employee's key must be revoked and the employee must not be able to access any data (including her own data). However, the data (including data of resigned employees) must be accessible to employees still holding valid keys.

In this chapter, we present *3DCrypt*, a cloud-based multiuser-encrypted domain pre-classification volume ray-casting framework. The proposed method is an extension of an earlier published conference paper [8]. Our method is based on the modified Paillier cryptosystem. Paillier cryptosystem is homomorphic only to addition and scalar multiplication operations, whereas the pre-classification volume ray-casting (as explained in Section 3.2.3) performs a number of operations, including additions, scalar multiplications, and multiplications. The use of Paillier cryptosystem alone therefore cannot hide shape of the object as the rendering of opacities, which renders the shape, involves multiplications. We addressed this issue using a private–public cloud model in such a way that rendering tasks can be distributed among the public and private cloud servers without disclosing both shape and color of the object to any of them.

Our contributions are summarized as follows:

- We provide a full-fledged multiuser scheme for the encrypted domain volume rendering.
- We can hide both color and shape of the object from the cloud. The color and shape are protected from the public cloud server by encrypting both the color and opacity information and by performing rendering in an encrypted domain. The color is protected from the private cloud server by performing rendering on the encrypted color information. The shape is protected from the private cloud server by hiding pixel positions of the image space.
- *3DCrypt* is such that if both the private and public cloud servers collude, they can, at most, learn shape of the object. The cloud servers can never know the secret color from gathered information. Therefore, we provide more security against collusion attacks than the state-of-the-art Shamir's secret sharing-based schemes.

Our preliminary analysis performed on a single machine shows that *3DCrypt* requires significant overhead. According to our analysis, the computation cost at the user end, however, can be affordable. Security analysis shows that *3DCrypt* is INDistinguishable under Chosen Plaintext Attack (IND-CPA) secure.

The rest of this chapter is organized as follows. Section 3.2 reviews existing approaches for encrypted domain rendering and provides an overview of pre-classification volume ray-casting. In Section 3.3, we describe our system model and threat model. In Section 3.4, we provide an overview of *3DCrypt*. Section 3.5 describes how we integrated Paillier cryptosystem to the pre-classification volume ray-casting. Section 3.6 explains construction details and Section 3.7 provides security analysis. In Section 3.8, we report results and performance analysis. Section 3.9 concludes our work.

3.2   Related work and background

In this section, we first provide a summary of existing encrypted domain volume rendering schemes and then provide an overview of 3D imaging and volume ray-casting.

3.2.1   Encrypted domain rendering

There are very few works in the direction of encrypted domain rendering using the partial homomorphic encryption. Mohanty *et al.* [6] proposed the encrypted pre-classification volume ray-casting and the encrypted post-classification volume ray-casting [9] using Shamir's (k, n) secret sharing. Their pre-classification volume ray-casting scheme, however, cannot hide shape of the rendered object from the cloud server. Furthermore, their scheme requires n datacenters and assumes that k of them must never collude. Recently, Chou and Yang [7] proposed a privacy-preserving volume ray-casting scheme that uses *block-based* permutation (which creates sub-volumes from the volume and permutes the sub-volumes) and adjustment of transfer function to hide both the volume and rendering tasks from the rendering server. Their work, however, lacks to achieve privacy due to the loss of information from the adjusted transfer table and the use of permutation.

In literature, there are alternative schemes to address privacy issues by outsourcing of volume rendering and visualization tasks to a third-party server. Koller *et al.* [10] protected the high-resolution data from an untrusted user by allowing only the user to view the low-resolution results during interactive exploration. Similarly, Dasgupta and Kosara [11] proposed to minimize the possible disclosure by combining nonsensitive information with high-sensitivity information. The major issue with such schemes is that they leak sensitive information. To minimize information loss, we consider supporting the encrypted domain rendering.

3.2.2 3D images

A 3D image has three dimensions: width, height, and depth. In contrast to 2D images (which has only width and height), a 3D image better represents the real world, which is also 3D in nature. To this end, a pixel in a 3D image is represented by four values: the R, G, B colors and the opacity.

We are increasingly using 3D images in our day-to-day life in various ways, such as in cinema (3D movies), Google map, and medical imaging (3D MRI, 3D ultrasound, etc.). Typically, a 3D image is rendered either from a stack of 2D images or from a 3D volume data. The former rendering scheme, which is known as surface rendering, produces inferior image quality than the later rendering scheme, which is known as volume rendering. In this chapter, we consider volume rendering. There are a number of ways how a 3D image can be rendered from a given volume data. Volume ray-casting is the most popular among them. We discuss volume ray-casting in the following section.

3.2.3 Volume ray-casting

Volume ray-casting is a volume rendering technique that renders an image from a volume (3D data) representing physical properties of an object in the form of a 3D grid of discrete points known as *voxels*. The image is rendered by projecting rays from each pixel of the image space to the volume as illustrated in Figure 3.1a. There are mainly two types of volume ray-casting: pre-classification volume ray-casting and post-classification volume ray-casting. The pre-classification volume ray-casting [12] incurs less computation cost than post-classification volume ray-casting. Therefore, pre-classification volume ray-casting is typically used in practice [2,13]. Pre-classification volume ray-casting, which is considered in this chapter, is executed in a pipeline of independent rendering components: *gradient* and *normal estimation, classification, shading, ray-projection, sampling, interpolation,* and *composition* as shown in Figure 3.1b. Table 3.1 summarizes operations performed by different rendering components and whether these operations can be performed in encrypted domain using Paillier cryptosystem.

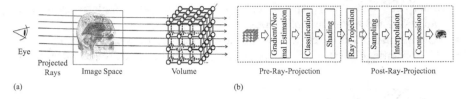

(a)   (b)

Figure 3.1   Pre-classification volume ray-casting: (a) a general overview and (b)
the rendering pipeline

Table 3.1   Rendering components of pre-classification volume ray-casting,
mathematical operations of rendering components, and their
suitability for being performed in encrypted domain using Paillier
cryptosystem

Component	Operations	Can performed in encrypted domain?
Gradient estimation	-, *k (scalar multiplication)	Yes
Normal estimation	+, *, $\sqrt{}$	No
Classification	Table lookup	No
Shading	+, *, $\int$, ...	No
Ray projection	None	Yes
Sampling	Random selection	Yes
Interpolation	+, *k	Yes
Composition	+, *	No

We call the rendering operations before and after ray-project as a *pre-ray-projection* and a *post-ray-projection*, respectively. In this work, we made the following observations about rendering components.

- The pre-ray-projection rendering operations can be preprocessed. These operations produce colors and opacities, which are used by the post-ray-projection rendering. Since the post-ray-projection rendering operations are performed dynamically (after sampling, interpolation, and classification), they do not require physical properties of the object and the exact pixel positions of the image space.
- Interpolation finds the color C_s and opacity A_s of a sample point s along a projected ray from the colors and opacities of eight neighboring voxels of the sample point. Mathematically, interpolation of color values can be defined as:

$$C_s = \sum_{v \in N(s)} C_v I_v \tag{3.1}$$

where $N(s)$ is the set of eight neighboring voxels of s, C_v is the color value, and $0 \leq I_v \leq 1$ is the interpolating factor of the voxel $v \in N(s)$. Likewise, we can interpolate opacities A_s. Therefore, for a constant I_v, this operation requires only additions and scalar multiplications.

- Composition finds the color C and opacity A along a projected ray from the colors and opacities of c sample points $\{s_1, s_2, \ldots, s_c\}$. Mathematically, composition can be defined as:

$$C = \sum_{i=1}^{c} C_{s_i} O_i \qquad (3.2)$$

and

$$A = \sum_{i=1}^{c} O_i \qquad (3.3)$$

where $O_i = A_{s_i} \prod_{j=i+1}^{c} (1 - A_{s_j})$ and A_s is the opacity of s. Therefore, for a constant O_i, this operation also requires only additions and scalar multiplications.

- After interpolation, the position and direction of a projected ray, which can disclose the coordinate of the pixel that casted it, are not required; rather, a ray must be distinguished from other rays as sample points along this ray need to be identified during the color/opacity composition.

3.3   System model

In this work, we consider a distributed cloud-based rendering system, where a cloud server stores and renders volumes on behalf of a volume data outsourcer. Figure 3.2 presents a real-world medical imaging scenario of *3DCrypt*. In our system model, we assume the following entities.

- **Volume Outsourcer:** This entity outsources the storage and rendering of volumes to a third-party cloud provider. It could be an individual or part of an organization. In the latter case, users can act as Volume Outsourcers. Typically, this entity owns the volume. The Volume Outsourcer can store new volumes on a cloud

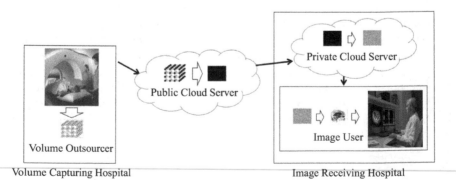

Figure 3.2   Cloud-based rendering of medical data (taken from [8])

server, delete/modify existing ones, and manage access control policies (such as read/write access rights). In our scenario, the Volume Outsourcer is part of a volume capturing hospital.

- **Public Cloud Server:** A Public Cloud Server is part of the infrastructure provided by a cloud service provider, such as Amazon S3,[1] for storing and rendering of volumes. It stores (encrypted) volumes and access policies used to regulate access to the volume and the rendered image. It performs most of the rendering on stored volumes and produces the partially rendered data.
- **Private Cloud Server:** The Private Cloud Server sits between the Public Cloud Server and the rendering requester. It can be part of the infrastructure, either provided by a private cloud service provider or maintained by an organization as a proxy server. The Private Cloud Server receives partially rendered data from the Public Cloud Server and performs remaining rendering tasks on the volume. It then sends the rendered image to the rendering requester. Note that the Private Cloud Server does not store data, and it only performs minimal rendering operations on partially rendered data received from the Public Cloud Server.
- **Image User:** This entity is authorized by the Volume Outsourcer to render a volume stored in the Public Cloud Server. In a multiuser setting, an Image User can (i) render an image (in encrypted domain) that will be accessible by Image Users (including herself) or (ii) access images rendered by other Image Users. In both cases, Image Users do not need to share any keying material.
- **Key Management Authority (KMA):** The KMA generates and revokes keys to entities involved in the system. For each user (be a Volume Outsourcer or Image User), it generates a key pair containing the user-side key and the server-side key. The server-side key is securely transmitted to the Public Cloud Server, whereas the user-side key is sent either to the user or to the Private Cloud Server depending on whether the user is a Volume Outsourcer or Image User. Whenever required (say, for example, in key lost or stolen cases), the KMA revokes the keys from the system with the support of the Public Cloud Server.

Threat Model: We assume that the KMA is a fully trusted entity under the control of the Volume Outsourcer's organization. Typically, the KMA can be directly controlled by the Volume Outsourcer. Since the KMA deals with a small amount of data, it can be easily managed and secured. We also assume that the KMA securely communicates the key sets to the Public Cloud Server and the Image User. This can be achieved by establishing a secure channel. Except for managing keys, the KMA is not involved in any operations. Therefore, it can be kept offline most of the times. This also minimizes the chances of being compromised by an external attack.

We consider an *honest-but-curious* Public Cloud Server. That is, the Public Cloud Server is trusted to honestly perform rendering operations as requested by the Image User. However, it is not trusted to guarantee data confidentiality. The adversary can be either an outsider or even an insider, such as unfaithful employees. Furthermore,

---

[1]https://aws.amazon.com/s3/

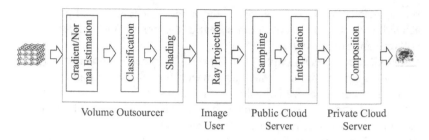

Figure 3.3   Distribution of rendering pipeline (taken from [8])

we assume that there are mechanisms to deal with data integrity and availability of the Public Cloud Server.

In *3DCrypt*, the Private Cloud Server is an *honest-and-semi-trusted* entity. The Private Cloud Server is also expected to honestly perform its part of rendering operations. The Private Cloud Server is semi-trusted in the sense that it cannot analyze more than what can perceptually be learnt from the plaintext volume. We assume that the Private Cloud Server is in conflict of interest with the Public Cloud Server. That is, both cloud servers should not collude.

3.4   Proposed approach

In this section, we present the architecture and an overview of the workflow of *3DCrypt*.

Figure 3.3 provides an overview of the pre-classification volume rendering pipeline and illustrates how we distribute the rendering pipeline among different components of *3DCrypt*. The Volume Outsourcer performs *pre-ray-projection rendering* operations: gradient/normal estimation, classification, and shading as these one-time operations can be preprocessed. The output of these operations is encrypted using Paillier cryptosystem, and the encrypted volume is sent to the Public Cloud Server. The Image User projects rays to the encrypted volume stored on the Public Cloud Server. The Public Cloud Server performs part of the *post-ray-projection rendering* operations: sampling and interpolation on encrypted colors and opacities. Then, the Public Cloud Server sends interpolated colors and opacities to the Private Cloud Server. The Public Cloud Server, however, does not share information about voxel coordinates and projected rays with the Private Cloud Server. The Private Cloud Server decrypts interpolated opacities and performs remaining post-ray-projection rendering operations: color and opacity composition using plaintext opacities and encrypted colors. Then, the Private Cloud Server sends the encrypted composite colors and plaintext composite opacities to the Image User. Finally, the Image User decrypts composite colors and creates the plaintext rendered image using plaintext colors and opacities.

Figure 3.4 illustrates the architecture of *3DCrypt*. In this system, the Volume Outsourcer is responsible for storing a volume and defining access policies for the

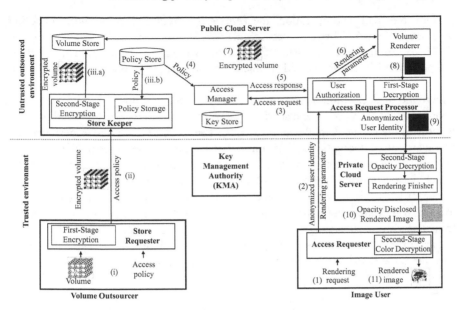

Figure 3.4   The architecture of 3DCrypt, a cloud-based secure volume storage and rendering system (taken from [8])

volume. To achieve this, the Volume Outsourcer interacts with the client module *Store Requester*. The Volume Outsourcer provides plaintext volume and access policies (Step i). The Store Requester performs the first-stage encryption on the input volume using the user-side key and then sends the encrypted volume along with associated access policies to the *Store Keeper* module of the Public Cloud Server (Step ii). On the Public Cloud Server-end, the Store Keeper performs the second stage of encryption using the server-side key corresponding to the user and stores the encrypted volume in a *Volume Store* (Step iii.a). The Store Keeper also stores access policies of the volume in the *Policy Store* (Step iii.b).

Once an Image User expects the Public Cloud Server to render a volume, his or her client module *Access Requester* receives his or her rendering request in the form of projected rays (Step 1). The module *Access Requester*, in turn, forwards the request to the *Access Request Processor* module of the Public Cloud Server (Step 2). In the request, the Access Requester sends rendering parameters (such as direction of projected rays) and user credentials (which can be anonymized) to the Access Request Processor. The Access Request Processor first performs the user authorization check to find out if the user has authorization to perform requested operations. For this purpose, the *Access Manager* is requested for checking access policies (Step 3). The Access Manager fetches access policies from the Policy Store (Step 4). Next, it matches access policies against the access request. Then, the access response is sent back to the Access Request Processor (Step 5). If the user is authorized to perform the requested operation, the *Volume Renderer* is invoked with rendering parameters (Step 6). The requested volume is retrieved from the Volume Store (Step 7). Then, most of the rendering tasks, which do not require multiplication of opacities, are performed in the encrypted manner and the partially rendered data is sent to the Access Request Processor (Step 8). The Access Request Processor performs the first round of decryption on the rendered data, hides voxel positions (e.g.permuting coordinates of the voxels), and sends the data, protected pixel positions and the user identity to the Private Cloud Server (Step 9). The Private Cloud Server performs the second round of decryption and obtains partially rendered opacities in plaintext. The plaintext opacities and encrypted colors are sent to the *Rendering Finisher* module, which performs rest of rendering tasks involving multiplication of opacities. Since the opacities are in plaintext, the multiplication of opacities with colors is reduced to a scalar multiplication. The Private Cloud Server then sends the opacity disclosed (but shape-protected as voxel positions are unknown) and color encrypted rendered image to the Access Requester (Step 10). The Access Requester decrypts the colors and shows the rendered image to the Image User (Step 11).

3.5   Solution details

3DCrypt is based on a modified Pailler cryptosystem that supports re-encryption [14–16] and is homomorphic to additions and scalar multiplications. Therefore, using this cryptosystem, we can encrypt a volume, for which rendering has been adjusted such that the post-ray-projection rendering tasks including interpolation and composition can be performed by a combination of additions and scalar multiplications. In order to provide the multiuser support, we extend the modified Paillier cryptosystem [14–16] such that each user has his or her own key to encrypt or decrypt the images. In *3DCrypt*, adding a new user or removing an existing one does not require re-encryption of existing images stored in the cloud.

The main goal of *3DCrypt* is to leverage resources of the Public Cloud Server as much as possible by storing the data volume and by performing most of the rendering tasks. To ensure confidentiality, both colors and opacities are stored in an encrypted form. Information about projected rays, however, must be available in plaintext as it is required in sampling and interpolation steps of the rendering operation. Since the Paillier cryptosystem is non-homomorphic to multiplication, composition, which multiplies opacities, cannot be computed on encrypted opacities. Thus, we employ a private cloud that can perform composition by knowing plaintext opacities. Since the knowledge of opacities and pixel positions can perceptually disclose shape of the rendered image, we consider to protect voxel positions from the Private Cloud Server. We can achieve this by permuting voxel positions to dissociate them from projected rays.

A key difficulty in integrating the Paillier cryptosystem with volume ray-casting is the incompatibility of floating point operations of ray-casting operations with the modular prime operation of the Paillier cryptosystem. One way of overcoming this issue is by converting the floating point interpolating factors and opacities to their

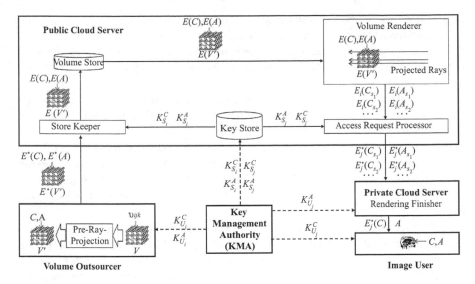

Figure 3.5   Encryption and decryption processes using 3DCrypt (taken from [8])

fixed point representatives. We can achieve this by rounding-off a float by d decimal points and multiplying 10^d with the round-off number.

Figure 3.5 provides the technical overview of *3DCrypt*'s rendering system. In *3DCrypt*, the KMA generates the color-key-set $\{K_S^C, K_U^C\}$ and the opacity-key-set $\{K_S^A, K_U^A\}$ for each user in the system (acting either as a Volume Outsourcer or as an Image User). Each key set contains a pair of keys: the user-side key and the server-side key. For each user i, the server-side keys of the color-key-set and the opacity-key-set, which are $K_{S_i}^C$ and $K_{S_i}^A$, respectively, are securely transmitted to the Public Cloud Server. The Public Cloud Server securely stores all the server-side keys in the *Key Store*, which could be accessible only to the Store Keeper and the Access Request Processor. When the user i is the Volume Outsourcer, the user-side keys of the color-key-set and the opacity-key-set, $K_{U_i}^C$ and $K_{U_i}^A$, are transmitted to the user. However, when the user i is the Image User, then the user-side key of color-key-set and opacity-key-set, $K_{U_i}^C$ and $K_{U_i}^A$, are sent to the user and the Private Cloud Server, respectively.

The workflow of our secure rendering system can be divided into three major steps: data preparation, ray-dependent rendering, and composition. We discuss each of these steps below.

3.5.1   Data preparation

This step is performed by the Volume Outsourcer prior to projection of rays. Since this step is independent of any rendering request (in the form of projected rays), this one-time step can be preprocessed. In this step, the Volume Outsourcer performs two main tasks: (i) pre-ray-projection rendering and (ii) encryption of output of the pre-ray-projection rendering using user-side keys: $K_{U_i}^C$ and $K_{U_i}^A$. As discussed in Section 3.2.3, the pre-ray-projection rendering, consisting of gradient/normal estimation, classification, and shading rendering components, maps the physical property v_{ijk} of the ijk^{th} data voxel to its corresponding color C and opacity A. After this step, an input volume V can be represented as V', where the ijk^{th} voxel of V' contains colors and opacity found by the physical property (typically represented as a floating point number) of the ijk^{th} voxel of V.

For a user i, the colors and opacities of V' are encrypted using $K_{U_i}^C$ and $K_{U_i}^A$, respectively. The encryption outputs $E_i^*(C)$ and $E_i^*(A)$ are sent to the Store Keeper as an encrypted volume $E_i^*(V')$. The Store Keeper then uses the server-side keys $K_{S_i}^C$ and $K_{S_i}^A$ to re-encrypt $E_i^*(C)$ and $E_i^*(A)$ and stores the re-encrypted volume $E(V')$ in the Volume Store.

In the encryption process, we adopt two main optimizations to decrease the storage overhead. First, we use the optimization of the modified Paillier cryptosystem. Second, we encrypt three color components—R, G, and B—in a single big number rather than encrypting them independently. We discuss both the optimizations below.

Optimization of the modified Paillier cryptosystem. The modified Paillier cryptosystem, explained in Section 3.6, is represented as: $E(C) = (e_1, e_2)$, where $e_1 = g^r$ and $e_2 = g^{rx}.(1 + Cn)$, where C is the plaintext color. Likewise, we encrypt the opacity A. Note that e_1 is independent of the plaintext color. By using a different e_1 for a different color (a typical case), we need $2k$ bits (where k is a security parameter) for storing e_1 of each color. We propose to optimize this space requirement by using one e_1 for encrypting t colors, requiring $2k$ bits for storing e_1 for all t colors. This optimization can be achieved by using the same random number r for all t colors.

Encrypting color components. As discussed in Section 3.2.3, the three color components (i.e., R, G, and B) undergo the same rendering operations. Each of them requires 8 bits in plaintext, but is represented by $2 * k$ bits (the minimum recommended value of k is 1,024) when encrypted independently. We can reduce this overhead by representing three color components as a single big number and encrypting this number in the place of encrypting the color components independently. This encrypted number will then undergo rendering in the place of rendering of color components. After decryption, we must, however, be able to recover the rendered color components from the rendered big number. One trick to create a big number from color components is by multiplying $10^{3*m*(d+f)}$ (where $d + f$ is the total rounding places during rounding operations in rendering) to m-th color component and adding all the multiplications.

3.5.2   Ray-dependent rendering

This step is performed by the Public Cloud Server after rays have been projected by the Image User. In this step, the Public Cloud Server first fetches encrypted volume $E(V')$ from the Volume Store and then performs sampling and interpolation on $E(V')$.

We use the same sampling technique as used by the conventional ray-casting. The interpolation, however, is performed on the encrypted color $E(C)$ and opacity $E(A)$. As discussed in Section 3.2.3, interpolation can be performed as additions and scalar multiplications when the interpolating factor I_{ijk} is available in plaintext. We therefore disclose I_{ijk} to the Public Cloud Server. Since the floating point I_{ijk} cannot be used with encrypted numbers, the Public Cloud Server converts I_{ijk} to an integer I'_{ijk} by first rounding-off I_{ijk} to d decimal places and then multiplying 10^d to the round-off value. *3DCrypt* is such that it allows the Public Cloud Server to run additions and scalar multiplications over encrypted numbers, as shown in (3.4) and (3.5), respectively.

$$E(C_1) * E(C_2) = E(C_1 + C_2) \tag{3.4}$$

and

$$E(C)^{I'_{ijk}} = E(I'_{ijk} * C) \tag{3.5}$$

Likewise, we can compute opacity in an encrypted manner. The interpolated color $E(C_s)$ and opacity $E(A_s)$ for each sample point s are first-stage-decrypted using the Image User j's server-side keys $K^C_{S_j}$ and $K^A_{S_j}$, respectively. The first-stage-decrypted color $E^*_j(C_s)$ and opacity $E^*_j(A_s)$ are then sent to the Private Cloud Server along with the proxy ray to which the sampling point s is associated.

3.5.3 Composition

In this step, the Private Cloud Server accumulates the colors and opacities of all the sampling points along a proxy voxel position. Since this step involves multiplication of opacities (which are non-homomorphic to Paillier Cryptosystem), the Private Cloud Server performs the second round of decryption on $E^*_j(A_s)$ using the user j's user-side key for opacity, $K^A_{U_j}$. The multiplied opacities O_s, which will be multiplied with encrypted color, however, is a floating point number. As discussed above, we can convert this float to an integer by first rounding-off the float by f places and then multiplying 10^f with the rounded-off value. Then, we can perform encrypted domain color composition using (3.4) and (3.5). Note that since the available interpolated colors are in encrypted form, the composited color $E^*_j(C)$ also remains encrypted. Furthermore, in absence of voxel positions of the image space, the composited plaintext opacity A does not reveal shape of the rendered image.

The plaintext rendered opacity A and encrypted rendered color $E^*_j(C)$ are sent to the Image User, who decrypts $E^*_j(C)$ using $K^C_{U_j}$ and views the plaintext rendered image.

3.6 Construction details

In this section, we describe the algorithms used in our proposed scheme. We instantiate two instances of the scheme: one for the color and other for the opacity.

- **Init(1^k).** The KMA runs the initialization algorithm to generate public parameters *Params* and a master secret key set *MSK*. It takes as input a security parameter

k and generates two prime numbers p and q of bit-length k. It computes $n = pq$. The secret key is $x \in [1, n^2/2]$. The g is of order: $\frac{\phi(n)}{2} = \frac{\phi(p)\phi(q)}{2} = \frac{(p-1)(q-1)}{2}$ and can be easily found by choosing a random $a \in \mathbb{Z}_{n^2}^*$ and computing $g = -a^{2n}$. It returns $Params = (n, g)$ and $MSK = x$. K_S represents the Key Store, initialised as $K_S \leftarrow \phi$.

- **KeyGen(MSK, i).** The KMA runs the key generation algorithm to generate keying material for users in the system. For each user i, this algorithm generates two key sets K_{U_i} and K_{S_i} by choosing a random x_{i1} from $[1, n^2/2]$. Then it calculates $x_{i2} = x - x_{i1}$ and transmits $K_{U_i} = x_{i1}$ and $K_{S_i} = (i, x_{i2})$ securely to user i and to the server, respectively. The server adds K_{S_i} to the Key Store as follows: $K_S \leftarrow K_S \cup K_{S_i}$.

- **ClientEnc(D, K_{U_i}).** A user i runs the data encryption algorithm to encrypt the data D using his or her key K_{U_i}. To encrypt the data $D \in \mathbb{Z}_n$, the user client chooses a random $r \in [1, n/4]$. It computes $E_i^*(D) = (\hat{e}_1, \hat{e}_2)$, where

$$\hat{e}_1 = g^r \bmod n^2 \text{ and}$$
$$\hat{e}_2 = \hat{e}_1^{x_{i1}}.(1 + Dn) \bmod n^2$$
$$= g^{rx_{i1}}.(1 + Dn) \bmod n^2$$

- **ServerReEnc($E_i^*(D), K_{S_i}$).** The server re-encrypts the user encrypted data $E_i^*(D) = (\hat{e}_1, \hat{e}_2)$. It retrieves the key K_{S_i} corresponding to the user i and computes the re-encrypted ciphertext $E(D) = (e_1, e_2)$, where

$$e_1 = \hat{e}_1 = g^r \bmod n^2 \text{ and}$$
$$e_2 = \hat{e}_1^{x_{i2}}.\hat{e}_2 = g^{rx}.(1 + Dn). \bmod n^2$$

- **ServerSum($E(D_1), E(D_2)$).** Given two encrypted values $E(D_1) = (e_{11}, e_{12})$ (where $e_{11} = g^{r_1}$ and $e_{12} = g^{r_1 x}.(1 + D_1 n)$) and $E(D_2) = (e_{21}, e_{22})$ (where $e_{21} = g^{r_2}$ and $e_{22} = g^{r_2 x}.(1 + D_2 n)$), the server calculates the encrypted sum $E(D_1 + D_2) = (e_1, e_2)$, where

$$e_1 = e_{11}.e_{21} = g^{r_1 + r_2} \bmod n^2 \text{ and}$$
$$e_2 = e_{12}.e_{22} \bmod n^2$$
$$= g^{(r_1 + r_2)x}.(1 + (D_1 + D_2)n) \bmod n^2$$

- **ServerScalMul($c, E(D)$).** Given a constant scalar factor c and an encrypted value $E(D) = (e_1, e_2)$ where $e_1 = g^r$ and $e_2 = g^{rx}.(1 + Dn)$, the server calculates the encrypted scalar multiplication $E(c.D) = (e_1^*, e_2^*)$, where

$$e_1^* = e_1^c = g^{rc} \bmod n^2 \text{ and}$$
$$e_2^* = e_2^c = g^{rcx}.(1 + cDn) \bmod n^2$$

- **ServerPreDec($E(D), K_{S_j}$).** The server runs this algorithm to partially decrypt the encrypted data for the user j. It takes as input the encrypted value $E(D) = (e_1, e_2)$, where $e_1 = g^r$ and $e_2 = g^{rx}.(1 + Dn)$. The server retrieves the key K_{S_j}

corresponding to the user j and computes the first-stage-decrypted data $E_j^*(D) = (\hat{e}_1, \hat{e}_2)$, where

$$\hat{e}_1 = e_1 = g^r \bmod n^2 \text{ and}$$

$$\hat{e}_2 = e_1^{-x_{j2}} . e_2 \bmod n^2$$

$$= g^{rx_{j1}} . (1 + Dn) \bmod n^2$$

- **UserDec($E_j^*(D)$, K_{U_j}).** The user runs this algorithm to decrypt the data. It takes as input the first-stage-decrypted data $E_j^*(D) = (\hat{e}_1, \hat{e}_2)$ where $\hat{e}_1 = g^r$ and $\hat{e}_2 = g^{rx_{j1}} . (1 + Dn))$, and his or her key K_{U_j}, and retrieves the data by computing: $D = L(\hat{e}_2 . \hat{e}_1^{-x_{j1}}) = L(1 + Dn)$, where $L(u) = \frac{u-1}{n}$ for all $u \in \{u < n^2 | u = 1 \bmod n\}$.
- **Revoke(i).** The server runs this algorithm to revoke user i access to the data. Given the user i, the server removes K_{S_i} from the Key Store as follows: $K_S \leftarrow K_S \backslash K_{S_i}$.

3.7 Security analysis

In this section, we evaluate security of the scheme used in this chapter. In general, a scheme is considered secure if no adversary can break the scheme with probability significantly greater than random guessing. The adversary's advantage in breaking the scheme should be a negligible function (defined below) of the security parameter.

Definition 3.1 (Negligible Function). *A function f is negligible if for each polynomial $p(.)$, there exists N such that for all integers $n > N$ it holds that:*

$$f(n) < \frac{1}{p(n)}$$

We consider a realistic adversary that is computationally bounded and shows that our scheme is secure against such an adversary. We model the adversary as a randomized algorithm that runs in polynomial time and show that the success probability of any such adversary is negligible. An algorithm that is randomized and runs in polynomial time is called a Probabilistic Polynomial Time (PPT) algorithm.

The scheme relies on the existence of a pseudorandom function f. Intuitively, the output a pseudorandom function cannot be distinguished by a realistic adversary from that of a truly random function. Formally, a pseudorandom function is defined as:

Definition 3.2 (Pseudorandom Function). *A function $f : \{0, 1\}^* \times \{0, 1\}^* \rightarrow \{0, 1\}^*$ is pseudorandom if for all PPT adversaries $\mathscr{A}$, there exists a negligible function negl such that:*

$$|Pr[\mathscr{A}^{f_s(\cdot)} = 1] - Pr[\mathscr{A}^{F(\cdot)} = 1]| < negl(n)$$

where $s \rightarrow \{0, 1\}^n$ is chosen uniformly randomly and F is a function chosen uniformly randomly from the set of function mapping n-bit string to n-bit string.

Our proof relies on the assumption that the Decisional Diffie-Hellman (DDH) is hard in a group $\mathbb{G}$, i.e., it is hard for an adversary to distinguish between group elements $g^{\alpha\beta}$ and g^{γ} given g^{α} and g^{β}.

Definition 3.3 (DDH Assumption). *The DDH problem is hard regarding a group g if for all PPT adversaries $\mathscr{A}$, there exists a negligible function negl such that:*

$$|Pr[\mathscr{A}(\mathbb{G}, n, g, g^{\alpha}, g^{\beta}, g^{\alpha\beta}) = 1] - $$
$$Pr[\mathscr{A}(\mathbb{G}, n, g, g^{\alpha}, g^{\beta}, g^{\gamma}) = 1]| < negl(k)$$

where $g \leftarrow \mathbb{G}$ is a group of order $\phi(n)/2$ (where $n = pq$), and $\alpha, \beta, \gamma \in \mathbb{Z}_n$ are uniformly randomly chosen.

Theorem 3.1. *If the DDH problem is hard relative to $\mathbb{G}$, then the proposed Paillier-based proxy encryption scheme (let us call it **PPE**) is IND-CPA secure against the server S, i.e., for all PPT adversaries $\mathscr{A}$ there exists a negligible function negl such that:*

$$Succ^{\mathscr{A}}_{PPE,S}(k) = Pr\left[b' = b \; \middle| \; \begin{array}{l} (Params, MSK) \leftarrow Init(1^k) \\ (K_{U_i}, K_{S_i}) \leftarrow KeyGen(MSK, i) \\ d_0, d_1 \leftarrow \mathscr{A}^{ClientEnc(\cdot, K_{U_i})}(K_{S_i}) \\ b \xleftarrow{R} \{0, 1\} \\ E_i^*(d_b) = ClientEnc(d_b, K_{U_i}) \\ b' \leftarrow \mathscr{A}^{ClientEnc(\cdot, K_{U_i})}(E_i^*(d_b), K_{S_i}) \end{array} \right] \qquad (3.6)$$
$$< \tfrac{1}{2} + negl(k)$$

Proof. Let us consider the following PPT adversary $\mathscr{A}'$ who attempts to solve the DDH problem using $\mathscr{A}$ as a subroutine. Note that for the proof technique, we take inspiration from the one presented in [17]. Recall that $\mathscr{A}'$ is given $\mathbb{G}, n, g, g_1, g_2, g_3$ as input, where $g_1 = g^{\alpha}, g_2 = g^{\beta}$ and g_3 is either $g^{\alpha\beta}$ or g^{γ} for some uniformly chosen random $\alpha, \beta, \gamma \in \mathbb{Z}_n$. $\mathscr{A}'$ does for the following:

- $\mathscr{A}'$ sends n, g to $\mathscr{A}$ as the public parameters. Next, it randomly chooses $x_{i2} \in \mathbb{Z}_n$ for the user i and computes $g^{x_{i1}} = g_1 \cdot g^{-x_{i2}}$. It then sends (i, x_{i2}) to $\mathscr{A}$ and keeps all $(i, x_{i2}, g^{x_{i1}})$.
- Whenever $\mathscr{A}$ requires oracle access to ClientEnc(.), it passes the data d to $\mathscr{A}'$. $\mathscr{A}'$ randomly chooses $r \in \mathbb{Z}_n$ and returns $(g^r, g^{rx_{i1}} \cdot (1 + dn))$.
- At some point, $\mathscr{A}$ outputs d_0 and d_1. $\mathscr{A}'$ randomly chooses a bit b and sends $(g_2, g_2^{-x_{i2}} g_3 \cdot (1 + d_b n))$ to $\mathscr{A}$.
- $\mathscr{A}$ outputs b'. If $b = b'$, $\mathscr{A}'$ outputs 1 and 0 otherwise.

We can distinguish two cases:

Case 1. If $g_3 = g^{\gamma}$, we know that g^{γ} is a random group element of $\mathbb{G}$ because γ is chosen at random. $g_2^{-x_{i2}} g_3 \cdot (1 + d_b n))$ is also a random element of $\mathbb{G}$ and gives no information about d_b. That is, the distribution of $g_2^{-x_{i2}} g_3 \cdot (1 + d_b n))$ is always uniform, regardless of the value of d_b. Further, g_2 does not leak information about d_b.

So, the adversary $\mathscr{A}$ must distinguish d_0 and d_1 without additional information. The probability that $\mathscr{A}$ can successfully output b' is exactly $\frac{1}{2}$, when b is chosen uniformly randomly. $\mathscr{A}'$ outputs 1 if and only if $\mathscr{A}$ outputs $b' = b$. Thus, we have:

$$Pr[\mathscr{A}'(\mathbb{G}, n, g, g^\alpha, g^\beta, g^\gamma) = 1] = \frac{1}{2}$$

Case 2. If $g_3 = g^{\alpha\beta}$, because

$$g_2 = g^\beta \text{ and }$$
$$g_2^{-x_{i2}} g_3.(1 + d_b n) = g^{-\beta x_{i2}} g^{\alpha\beta}.(1 + d_b n)$$
$$= g^{\beta(\alpha - x_{i2})}.(1 + d_b n)$$
$$= g^{\beta x_{i1}}.(1 + d_b n)$$

Thus, $(g_2, g_2^{-x_{i2}} g_3.(1 + d_b n))$ is a proper ciphertext encrypted under *PPE*. So, we have:

$$Pr[\mathscr{A}'(\mathbb{G}, n, g, g^\alpha, g^\beta, g^{\alpha,\beta}) = 1] = Succ_{PPE,S}^{\mathscr{A}}(k)$$

If the DDH problem is hard relative to $\mathbb{G}$, then the following holds:

$$|Pr[\mathscr{A}'(\mathbb{G}, n, g, g^\alpha, g^\beta, g^{\alpha\beta}) = 1] - Pr[\mathscr{A}'(\mathbb{G}, n, g, g^\alpha, g^\beta, g^\gamma) = 1]| < negl(k)$$
$$Pr[\mathscr{A}'(\mathbb{G}, n, g, g^\alpha, g^\beta, g^{\alpha\beta}) = 1] < \frac{1}{2} + negl(k)$$

So, we have:

$$Succ_{PPE,S}^{\mathscr{A}}(k) < \frac{1}{2} + negl(k)$$

Informally, the theorem says that without knowing the user side keys, the proxy cannot distinguish the ciphertext in a chosen plaintext attack.

3.8   Implementation and experiment

We implemented the secure ray-casting by integrating the modified Paillier cryptosystem to the volume ray-casting module of the open-source 3D visualization software VTK6.3.0. We run the implemented *3DCrypt* on a PC powered by Intel i5-4670 3.40 GHz processor and 8 GB of RAM, running Ubuntu 15.04. All the components of *3DCrypt*, i.e., the Volume Outsourcer, the Public Cloud Server, the Private Cloud Server, the Image User, and the KMA were simulated. Note that VTK is typically shipped with post-classification volume ray-casting. We modified VTK to provide pre-classification volume ray-casting. For dealing with big number cryptographic primitive operations, we integrated the MIRACL cryptographic library with VTK.

In our implementation, we chose a 1,024-bit key size. We round-off the floating point numbers used in rendering operations by machine precision to avoid round-off errors. For the modified Paillier encryption, we choose one random number r for all voxels of a volume, requiring one $e_1 = g^r$ (first cipher component) for all voxels.

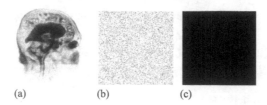

(a)   (b)   (c)

Figure 3.6   Secure rendering for the Head *image. Part figures (a)–(c) illustrate the rendered image available to the Image User, the Public Cloud Server, and the Private Cloud Server, respectively (taken from [8])*

Results. Figure 3.6 illustrates how *3DCrypt* provides perceptual security in the cloud. An image available to the Public Cloud Server is all black since the Public Cloud Server does not know the color and opacity of the pixels. The image available to the Private Cloud Server, however, contains opacity information, which can disclose shape of the image as voxel positions are disclosed to the Private Cloud Server.

Performance Analysis. In *3DCrypt*, processing by the Volume Outsourcer and the encryption by the Public Cloud Server are one-time operations, which could be performed *offline*. The overheads of these operations, however, are directly proportional to the volume size. The overhead for a volume is equal to the product of a voxel's overhead with the total number of voxels in the volume (i.e., the dimension of the volume). In our implementation, we need approximately 4,064 bits more space to store the encrypted color and the opacity of a voxel (as two encryptions of 1,024 bits key size are required for encrypting 32 bits RGBA values). Thus, we require approximately 8.6 GB of space to store a $256 \times 256 \times 256$ volume in encrypted domain (size of this volume in plaintext is approximately 67 MB). Similarly, for encrypting color and opacity of a voxel, the Volume Outsourcer requires approximately 540 ms. The Public Cloud Server requires approximately 294 ms more computation with respect to the conventional plaintext domain pre-classification volume ray-casting implemented on the same machine. Thus, the Volume Outsourcer and the Public Cloud Server require approximately 2.52 and 1.37 h, respectively, for encrypting the $256 \times 256 \times 256$ volume.

The rendering by the cloud servers and the decryption by the Image User are performed at runtime, according to the ray projected by the Image User. The overhead of performing these operations affects visualization latency, which is discussed below.

In *3DCrypt*, the overhead of transferring and performing the last round rendering operations in the Private Cloud Server is equal to the product of the number of sample points with the overhead of a sample point. The total number of sample points is equal to the sum of the sample points along all the projected rays and the number of sample points along a ray is implementation dependent. For rendering and decrypting (the first round) the color and opacity of a sample point, the Public Cloud Server requires approximately 290 ms of extra computation. For rendering and decrypting (the second round) opacity of a sample point, the Private Cloud Server requires approximately 265 ms of extra computation (with respect to the conventional plaintext domain pre-classification volume ray-casting).

In our implementation, for rendering and decrypting the $256 \times 256 \times 256$ volume data for a 256×256 image project space, the Public Cloud Server and the Private Cloud Server require approximately 16.5 and 15.2 extra minutes, respectively. Note that for this data and image space, the data overhead at the Private Cloud Server is approximately 1.75 GB.

The overhead of transferring and decrypting the color-encrypted rendered image to the Image User is equal to the product of the number of pixels in the image space (which is equal to the number of projected rays) with the overhead for a single pixel. In *3DCrypt*, the Private Cloud Server must send approximately 2,024 bits more data per pixel to the Image User. Therefore, for rendering a 256×256 image, the Image User must download 66.3 MB of more data than the conventional plaintext domain rendering. In addition, the Image User needs approximately 408 ms of computation to decrypt and recover rendered color of a pixel. Therefore, before viewing the 256×256 image, the Image User must work approximately 27 extra seconds.

3.9 Conclusions

Cloud-based volume rendering presents the data confidentiality issue that can lead to privacy loss. In this chapter, we addressed this issue by encrypting the volume using the modified Paillier cryptosystem such that a pre-classification volume ray-casting can be performed at the cloud server in the encrypted domain. Our proposal, *3DCrypt*, provides several improvements over state-of-the-art techniques. First, we are able to hide both color and shape of the rendering object from a cloud server. Second, we provide better security to collusion attack than the state-of-the-art Shamir's secret sharing-based scheme. Third, users do not need to share keys for rendering volume stored in the cloud (therefore, maintenance of per-volume keys is not required).

To make *3DCrypt* more practical, our future work can focus on decreasing performance overheads at both the cloud and the user ends. Furthermore, it would also be interesting to investigate whether we can extend *3DCrypt* for the encrypted domain post-classification volume ray-casting.

References

[1]   E. Cuervo, A. Wolman, L. P. C. *et al.*, "Kahawai: High-quality mobile gaming using GPU offload," in *Proceedings of the 13th Annual International Conference on Mobile Systems, Applications, and Services*, Florence, Italy, 2015, pp. 121–135.

[2]   KDDI Inc., "Medical real-time 3d imaging solution," Online Report, 2012, http://www.kddia.com/en/sites/default/files/file/KDDI_America_Newsletter_August_2012.pdf.

[3]   Intel Inc., "Experimental cloud-based ray tracing using intel mic architecture for highly parallel visual processing," Online Report, 2011, https://software. intel.com/sites/default/files/m/d/4/1/d/8/Cloud-based_Ray_Tracing_0211.pdf.

[4]   M. Baharon, Q. Shi, D. Llewellyn-Jones, and M. Merabti, "Secure rendering process in cloud computing," in Eleventh Annual Conference on Privacy, Security and Trust, Tarragona, Spain, 2013, pp. 82–87.

[5]   M. Mohanty, M. R. Asghar, and G. Russello, "2DCrypt: Image scaling and cropping in encrypted domains," *IEEE Transactions on Information Forensics and Security*, vol. 11, no. 11, pp. 2542–2555, 2016.

[6]   M. Mohanty, P. K. Atrey, and W. T. Ooi, "Secure cloud-based medical data visualization," in *Proceedings of the 20th ACM International Conference on Multimedia*, Nara, Japan, 2012, pp. 1105–1108.

[7]   J.-K. Chou and C.-K. Yang, "Obfuscated volume rendering," *The Visual Computer*, vol. 32, no. 12, pp. 1593–1604, Dec. 2016.

[8]   M. Mohanty, M. R. Asghar, and G. Russello, "3DCrypt: Privacy-preserving pre-classification volume ray-casting of 3D images in the cloud," in *International Conference on Security and Cryptography (SECRYPT)*, Lisbon, Portugal, 2016.

[9]   M. Mohanty, W. T. Ooi, and P. K. Atrey, "Secure cloud-based volume ray-casting," in *Proceedings of the 5th IEEE Conference on Cloud Computing Technology and Science*, Bristol, UK, 2013.

[10]   D. Koller, M. Turitzin, M. Levoy *et al.*, "Protected interactive 3D graphics via remote rendering," in *ACM SIGGRAPH*, Los Angeles, USA: ACM, 2004, pp. 695–703.

[11]   A. Dasgupta and R. Kosara, "Adaptive privacy-preserving visualization using parallel coordinates," *Visualization and Computer Graphics, IEEE Transactions on*, vol. 17, no. 12, pp. 2241–2248, 2011.

[12]   M. Levoy, "Display of surfaces from volume data," *IEEE Computer Graphics and Applications*, vol. 8, pp. 29–37, 1988.

[13]   Sinha System, "Cloud based medical image management and visualization platform," Online Report, 2012, http://www.shina-sys.com/assets/ brochures/3Di.pdf.

[14]   E. Bresson, D. Catalano, and D. Pointcheval, "A simple public-key cryptosystem with a double trapdoor decryption mechanism and its applications," in *Advances in Cryptology—ASIACRYPT 2003*, ser. Lecture Notes in Computer Science. Springer Berlin Heidelberg, 2003, vol. 2894, pp. 37–54.

[15]   G. Ateniese, K. Fu, M. Green, and S. Hohenberger, "Improved proxy re-encryption schemes with applications to secure distributed storage," *ACM Transactions on Information and System Security*, vol. 9, pp. 1–30, February 2006.

[16]   E. Ayday, J. L. Raisaro, J.-P. Hubaux, and J. Rougemont, "Protecting and evaluating genomic privacy in medical tests and personalized medicine," in *Proceedings of the 12th ACM Workshop on Privacy in the Electronic Society*, Berlin, Germany, 2013, pp. 95–106.

[17]   C. Dong, G. Russello, and N. Dulay, "Shared and searchable encrypted data for untrusted servers," *Journal of Computer Security*, vol. 19, pp. 367–397, August 2011.

Chapter 4

Multiprocessor system-on-chip for processing data in cloud computing

Arnab Kumar Biswas[1], S. K. Nandy[2], and Ranjani Narayan[3]

Abstract

Cloud computing enables cloud customers to obtain shared processing resources and data on demand. Cloud providers configure computing resources to provide different services to users and enterprises. These cloud providers satisfy the need for high-performance computing by bringing more PEs inside a chip (known as Multiprocessor System-on-Chip (MPSoC)) instead of increasing operating frequency. An MPSoC usually employs Network-on-Chip (NoC) as the scalable on-chip communication medium. An MPSoC can contain multiple Trusted Execution Environments (TEEs) and Rich Execution Environments (REEs). Security critical applications run in TEEs and normal applications run in REEs. Due to sharing of resources (for example, NoC) in cloud computing, applications running in two TEEs may need to communicate over an REE that is running applications of a malicious user (attacker). This scenario can cause unauthorized access attack if the attacker launches router attack inside the NoC. Apart from this attack, an attacker can also launch misrouting attack using router attack causing various types of ill effects. To deal with these security concerns, we discuss in detail different hardware-based security mechanisms. These mechanisms mainly employ monitoring to detect a router attack and possibly a malicious router location. The hardware-based mechanisms can provide much-needed protection to users' data in a cloud computing MPSoC platform. Apart from the threat model with practical examples, detailed hardware description of each security mechanism is given in this chapter for easy understanding of the readers.

4.1 Introduction

Cloud computing enables ubiquitous and on-demand network access to configurable computing resources. Cloud computing also enables cloud providers to provide

[1]Hardware and Embedded Systems Lab, School of Computer Science and Engineering, Nanyang Technological University, Singapore
[2]Indian Institute of Science, Bengaluru, India
[3]Morphing Machines, Bengaluru, India

services that allow collaboration, agility, scalability, and availability. An attacker can launch attacks using a vulnerability in the communication link between a user and the cloud platform, a vulnerability in the operating system (OS) or any other software elements running in the cloud or a vulnerability in the hardware cloud platform itself. In this chapter, we consider the attacks where an attacker targets the hardware cloud platform and also discuss different security mechanisms to ensure security of the information flow within a cloud platform. Cloud providers use high-performance computing resources like MPSoC that can be shared between different users simultaneously. Different processing elements (PEs) in an MPSoC are usually interconnected by a scalable medium like an NoC. An NoC mainly consists of routers and links. Routers route packets through the NoC links following a routing algorithm. For a configurable router, routing algorithm can be configured to support application requirements. The router configuration mechanism is usually not secure, enabling an attacker to launch router attack by malicious configurations. Until now, most proposed solutions in literature tried to secure the PEs (including memory) and not the communication architecture itself inside an MPSoC. If we do not protect the interconnection network similar to the PEs, the whole system can easily be made vulnerable.

Depending on how a routing path is selected inside a router, routing can be classified as deterministic (static) or adaptive [1,2]. In xpipes [3] and in Æthereal NoC [4], authors have used deterministic routing; in [5–7], authors have proposed NoC architectures using adaptive routing algorithm; and in [8–10], authors have proposed reconfigurable NoC architectures. None of these systems have considered the security vulnerability in NoC and hence router attacks are possible in these systems.

Intel introduced a 48-core Single Chip Cloud (SCC) computer in 2010 as an experimental chip for cloud computing [11] but as per our knowledge only 72-core processor TILE-Gx72 is currently available from Mellanox technologies for cloud applications [12]. Currently, Zynq UltraScale+ MPSoCs from XILINX are also available to be used in data centers for cloud applications [13]. The MPSoC consists of various intellectual property (IP) modules like block RAM and programmable logic (i.e., field programmable gate array (FPGA) for which XILINX is commonly known) and also multi-core application processing unit, real-time processing unit, and graphics processing unit (GPU) from ARM. Apart from XILINX MPSoCs, NVIDIA Tesla GPUs are used in data centers for cloud computing [14]. Regarding the programming model, MapReduce is commonly used in data centers, which allows programmers to write functional-style code which is then scheduled and parallelized automatically in a distributed system. MapReduce programming model was first proposed and implemented by Google [15], but currently it is being developed by various companies and research institutions. As a result, more capable MapReduce programming model implementations are currently available.

In literature, MapReduce is implemented in GPU chip [16], in multiprocessor chip [17], and also in a heterogeneous system with both CPU and GPU in a chip [18]. MapReduce is also implemented in a cloud platform where each computing node itself is a GPU [19,20]. In this chapter, we assume a cloud platform where each node is an MPSoC and MapReduce is used in each node and across all the nodes (i.e., the whole distributed system). We mainly consider the security aspects of such computing system. Currently, many vendors provide Security-as-a-Service

(SecaaS) to cloud customers taking many different forms. The cloud security alliance (formed by many of these vendors) provides guidelines for implementing SecaaS offerings [21]. The field of cloud security requires more research and development to ensure proper security to cloud users. Recently, Viaccess-Orca has proposed a TEE architecture called data center TEE (dcTEE) for cloud computing systems [22]. The dcTEE architecture is proposed to equip a data center with TEEs like mobile systems but taking full advantage of cloud's elasticity and scalability. We assume a similar architecture where each MPSoC contains multiple TEEs and the cloud platform (consisting of these MPSoCs) also contains distributed TEEs. We restrict our current discussion in this chapter to a single MPSoC node and consider the router attack vulnerability that can hamper the security of a chip by launching attack at the network abstraction layer itself.

An MPSoC can contain multiple secure (TEE) and nonsecure (REE) regions to provide both security and high performance. On the one hand, a secure region (TEE) ensures that sensitive data is always stored, processed, and protected with a level of trust. Non-secure regions (REEs), on the other hand, can be configured and customized to meet certain performance requirements. Specifications about TEE and REE are available in [23,24]. Figure 4.1 shows an MPSoC with two TEEs and one REE. We assume that application mapping to a set of PEs is done according to the existing literature on TEE and REE (like [22]) following the specifications in [23,24]. In case of Figure 4.1, we assume that one TEE application is mapped to the PEs (2,0), (3,0), (2,1), and (3,1) and the other TEE application is mapped to the PE (0,0). One REE application is mapped to the PEs (1,0), (0,1), and (1,1). Note that the MPSoC is used to support multi-tenant public cloud environment and different users can run their applications on the same MPSoC. Also note that all regions inside an MPSoC share the same NoC for communication. An attacker can launch unauthorized access attack using router attack in an REE if two TEEs communicate over that REE [25,26]. Apart from this unauthorized access attack, an attacker can launch misrouting attack using router attack. In this chapter, we discuss router attacks in detail that can cause various ill effects and also various hardware-based security mechanisms against the router attacks. These security mechanisms mainly employ monitoring to detect and locate a malicious router.

4.2 Current approaches to secure MPSoC cloud platforms

Various aspects of MPSoC cloud platform security are considered in literature. In [27], authors have separated the whole system into two logical domains, viz. secure and non-secure. They have provided a list of attacks that can affect an NoC-enabled MPSoC. TrustZone Technology in [28] is used to implement TEE in ARM MPSoCs with single secure region. This solution is only applicable to AMBA3 AXI/APB bus-based communication. In [29], authors have presented data protection unit in every network interface (NI) that can protect from software attacks or more specifically unauthorized access to memory locations by the PEs. The authors of [30] have proposed Quality of Security Service (QoSS) using layered NoC architecture to detect attacks based on different security rules. An authenticated encryption-based security framework in every NI for NoC-based systems is presented in [31]. The integration of ciphering techniques at the NI ensures the authenticity and confidentiality of the exchanged information between secure IP cores but the AES encryption blocks used in that solution increase the cost overhead (area and clock cycles) of the NoC. None of the above systems have considered router attacks inside NoC.

Prior works in the literature exist that consider specific hardware attacks against MPSoCs and suggest countermeasures. For example, in [32], an input buffer is proposed that can protect an MPSoC from input signal noise. The proposed input buffer can prevent glitch attack (a nondestructive hardware attack), if the glitch is applied to the input signal pin.

Recommendations to reduce the risk when adopting cloud computing are given in [33]. Like any other security area, cloud users need to adopt a risk-based approach to move to the cloud and to select correct security options. An architecture for trusted computing, called Terra, is proposed in [34]. Terra uses a trusted virtual machine (VM) monitor that partitions a tamper-resistant hardware platform into multiple, isolated VMs, providing the appearance of multiple boxes on a single, general-purpose platform. An architecture called HyperWall is proposed in [35,36] that uses hardware modules to protect guest VMs from an untrusted hypervisor. A hypervisor manages memory, processor cores, and other resources of a platform. As per our understanding, the router attack in MPSoC is presented for the first time in [25,26,37] and different hardware-based security mechanisms are also proposed to protect from router attack.

4.3   Threat model

4.3.1   *Router attack description*

An attack is any action that compromises the security of information owned by an entity/organization. Inside a router, either routing tables or hardware routing logic implementations are used to implement routing algorithm. Router attack indicates either a malicious modification of routing tables or routing logic. In this chapter, we consider only router attacks due to malicious routing tables. The nonsecure region routers are routing table-based, and hence have the flexibility to support the REE applications. The routers in the secure region of MPSoC cloud platform have routing logic implementation lacking any flexibility to get configured.

In a router, the relationship between the destination Port ID and the Routing Function can be represented as (4.1).

$$P_{ID} = F_R(S_{XY}, D_{XY}) \tag{4.1}$$

Here, P_{ID} indicates the destination Port ID, F_R indicates the routing function/algorithm, S_{XY} indicates the source address, and D_{XY} indicates the destination address. Sometimes, routing function does not depend on source address. A successful router attack results in a modified routing function F_R.

Routing table entries are configured at start/restart time or during runtime. Routing table update packets are used to configure the routers. Malicious modification of configuration information results in routing table attack. The attack can be launched by an insider who is responsible for loading the routing tables in the MPSoC cloud platform. Routing tables can be maliciously reconfigured at runtime by an application that causes generation of malicious routing table update packets. Although authentication mechanism can be implemented for the loading process, an insider attack can still break that causing single point of failure. The mechanisms presented in this chapter work at the NoC level and can also operate as a second level of protection if authentication mechanism is present for loading.

4.3.2   The malicious effects of router attack

An attacker can launch mainly two types of attacks using malicious routing tables, i.e., (i) misrouting attack and (ii) unauthorized access attack.

4.3.2.1   Effects of misrouting attack

For misrouting attack, different types of harmful effects are given below.

- **Suboptimal routing and increased delay:** Routing table attack can result in suboptimal routing which affects the real-time applications by routing the packets over unnecessarily long routes and thus affecting the quality-of-service.
- **Congestion and link overload:** The attack can lead to artificial congestion if packets are forwarded to only certain portions of the network depending on the modified routing table. Large volume of traffic through a limited capacity link can overwhelm the link making it unusable.
- **Deletion of PE:** Wrong entries in routing tables can delete a PE in an MPSoC. All packets can be diverted before reaching that particular destination PE. Similarly the PE may not be able to send any packet to any other PE, because the connected router does not route any packet from this PE anymore. This is a serious case of denial-of-service.
- **Overwhelming critical PE:** If packets are routed toward a certain critical PE at a rate that is beyond its capacity of handling, then this PE can be made unreachable to any legitimate PE. Here legitimate PE means those PEs that are not malicious and want to communicate with this critical PE.
- **Deadlock and livelock:** Improper routing tables can cause a packet to loop around and never reach its destination. It causes deadlock and livelock because no other packet can use that route.

4.3.2.2   Effects of unauthorized access attack

For unauthorized access attack, main harmful effect is given below.

- **Illegal access to data:** If the attacker can get hold of a node in nonsecure region, then he/she can route all data from secure region to that node and thus gain unauthorized access to secret information.

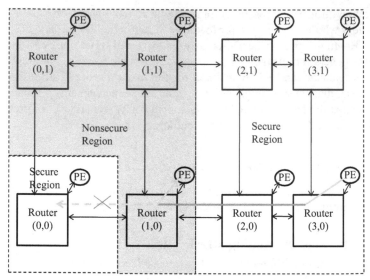

PE: Processing Element

Figure 4.1   An example of router attack in a 2 × 4 mesh NoC with two secure regions

Table 4.1   (a) Port ID assignments to different ports, (b) Normal X-coordinate and Y-coordinate routing tables at Router (1,0), and (c) Malicious X-coordinate and Y-coordinate routing tables for unauthorized access at Router (1,0)

Port name	Port ID	X table Index	Port ID	Y table Index	Port ID	X table Index	Port ID	Y table Index	Port ID
I: Eject	0								
		0	4	0	2	0	0	0	0
N: North	1								
		1	0	1	0	1	0	1	0
S: South	2								
		2	3	2	1	2	0	2	0
E: East	3								
		3	3	3	1	3	0	3	0
W: West	4								

(a)   (b)   (c)

4.3.3 Examples of router attack

A router attack example is shown in Figure 4.1. The cross on the dataflow indicates that the router (0,0) does not receive any data due to router attack at the router (1,0). Router (1,0) contains malicious routing table as given in Table 4.1(c). The port ID assignments to router ports and a normal routing table example at router (1,0) (at East input port) are also given in Table 4.1(a) and (b), respectively. Any packet coming

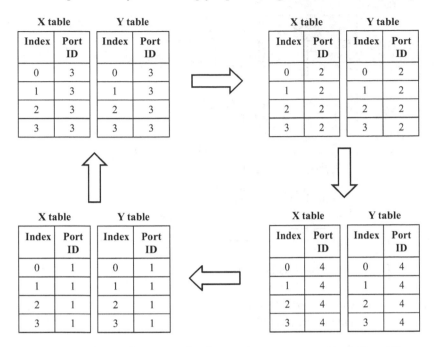

Figure 4.2   Circular path creation by four malicious routers. Each X and Y coordinate routing table represents a router at that location.

from a secure region (say PE (3,0)) and going to another secure region (say PE (0,0)) can be diverted to the eject port of this router (1,0). The packet becomes available to the nonsecure PE (1,0) and that means the attack is successful. The diversion happens irrespective of the actual destination of the packet. This is the case of unauthorized access attack. Routing logic implementation can also be maliciously changed using hardware Trojan-based attacks but that is outside the scope of this chapter.

Figure 4.2 shows an example of misrouting attack—more specifically creation of a circular path using four routers. Each X and Y table pair represents a router in that location in the figure. If all ports apart from the south port routing tables of the top right corner router of Figure 4.2 are modified, all packets entering into the router are diverted to the south port (port ID 2). There are no packets that can enter through the south input port because the bottom right corner router is diverting all packets to its West port. Hence, the circular path is created as shown in Figure 4.2.

4.4   Countermeasure for unauthorized access attack

Countermeasures for unauthorized access attack can detect, protect, and locate the router attack. The attack is detected using monitors (runtime monitor or restart monitor) located at the boundary between secure and nonsecure regions. Apart from the monitors, ejection address checker (EAC) inside every nonsecure region router can

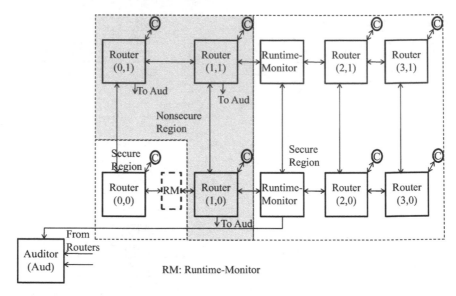

Figure 4.3   2 × 4 mesh NoC with runtime monitors in every row. The letter C inside a circle represents a PE.

detect router attack. It is assumed that every receiver returns an acknowledgment (ack) packet to the sender. Note that runtime monitor, restart monitor, and EAC are three different countermeasures introduced in this section. Also please note that the countermeasures presented in this section and the next section are transparent to normal cloud users. These are all hardware-based solutions and need to be implemented by the MPSoC provider, i.e., the cloud platform provider is responsible to utilize these security solutions in their platform.

4.4.1   Runtime monitor

Runtime monitor operates during normal operation of the MPSoC cloud platform, i.e., during runtime. The NoC fabric including runtime monitors is shown in Figure 4.3. The figure shows an MPSoC cloud platform which has two secure regions and one nonsecure region. If the secure region only accepts data and does not send out data, runtime monitor in that region is not required. For bidirectional communication, this monitor is necessary. All monitors at a secure region boundary are connected to each other like a chain. The runtime monitor block diagram is shown in Figure 4.4. Runtime monitor mainly monitors ack packet for every packet that is sent from secure to nonsecure region. Router attack in nonsecure region results in disruption of ack packet from reaching the router in secure region.

Runtime monitor has four registers, one for packet arriving from secure to nonsecure region (input register1) and another for packet going from nonsecure to secure region (input register2). The remaining two registers (input register3 and input register4) receive ack packets from the adjacent monitors. The destination checker (DC)

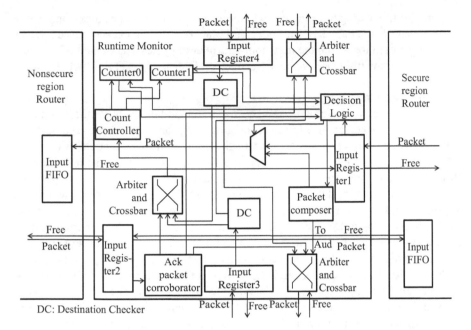

Figure 4.4 Runtime monitor block diagram with connections to secure and nonsecure region routers

module checks the ack packet's destination address. If the ack packet is destined for the current monitor, it is passed to the count controller module through the arbiter and crossbar module. Otherwise, the ack packet is sent to the next monitor through the corresponding arbiter and crossbar module. Runtime monitor has as many counters as there are routers outside this secure region in that row. In the example shown in Figure 4.3, there are two counters. The first packet arriving from the secure region destined to a particular router starts the corresponding counter. In every clock cycle, this counter is incremented by 1. It will not be reset or restarted for subsequent packets while awaiting ack packet from the destination. Source addresses of all packets traveling from secure to nonsecure region are changed in the runtime monitor with the nearest secure region router address. This ensures that all corresponding ack packets arrive at the concerned runtime monitor.

Every counter will count up to a max-count that can be expressed as:

$$\text{Max-count (in cycles)} = [T_{min} + f(\tau, I)]2N_H + T_{Pr} + T_{mon} \tag{4.2}$$

Here T_{min} is the minimum time required for a packet to leave a router after entering it. The function $f(\tau, I)$ represents a term corresponding to the network traffic condition. This function depends on traffic distribution τ and injection rate I. Max-count value is decided based on the total packet latency (packet going and ack coming) corresponding to the farthest destination. N_H is the hop count of the farthest destination. T_{Pr} and

T_{mon} are PE processing time and delay in monitor, respectively. The max-count value ensures that, in an attack free MPSoC cloud platform, an ack packet indeed reaches the runtime monitor within the max-count number of cycles. Max-count of counters does not have any influence on the performance of normal packet flow in the NoC. It only influences the malicious router detection performance, i.e., the time required to detect the location of a malicious router.

Runtime monitor has an ack packet corroborator module. It checks the destination address of ack packets received from the nonsecure region. If an ack packet is destined for the current monitor, it is passed on to the count controller module through the arbiter and crossbar module. Otherwise, the ack packet is sent to the next monitor through the corresponding arbiter and crossbar module. A counter is stopped by the count controller module if the corresponding ack packet is received within the stipulated max-count value. If not, the counter module sends a count-expired signal to the decision logic. Decision logic changes the state of the monitor from normal to "attack detected." It stops all packet movement from secure region to nonsecure region. Further, it signals the packet composer to form monitoring packets. Source address field of these packets carry the address of the nearest secure region router. As an example, in this chapter, we consider YX deterministic routing, which routes packets in the horizontal (X) direction after traversing the vertical (Y) direction. Hence, a packet traveling through the monitor has its destination in the same row as the monitor. A malicious router could be any of the routers lying in the same row as the destination router. In order to determine the exact location of the malicious router, the packet composer sends monitoring packets starting from the router closest to the monitor to the farthest router in the row (till the destination router). Payload of a monitoring packet does not contain any meaningful data. These are only used to generate ack packets in the destination PE. Counter-based technique mentioned above is used to monitor these ack packets also (generated by monitoring packets). This helps the monitor to exactly locate the malicious router. Note that all the PEs located before the malicious router are able to return ack packets. The malicious router diverts the packet and hence no ack packet arrives at the monitor and the location of that malicious router is identified. After detection of a malicious router, runtime monitor sends the router address to the auditor. This is achieved by forming a packet with the malicious router address in the payload field. The packet travels through the monitor chain and reaches the auditor at the end.

The auditor collects contents of routing table of the attacked router, so that the attack can be read off-line and analyzed. Figure 4.5 shows the block diagram of the auditor. First, it receives the malicious router address from the corresponding monitor. Then the auditor's Decision module sends an enable signal to the corresponding router. The routing table uploader module of the attacked router, after receiving this signal, uploads the routing table to the auditor.

Now there is a possibility that the attacker might send false ack packet with legitimate destination address. To mitigate this problem of source authentication in nonsecure region, router address is stored in a nonvolatile memory in the router and cannot be changed by attacker. This source address is automatically added to a packet when the packet is ejected from the PE. So, even if the attacker wants to send an ack

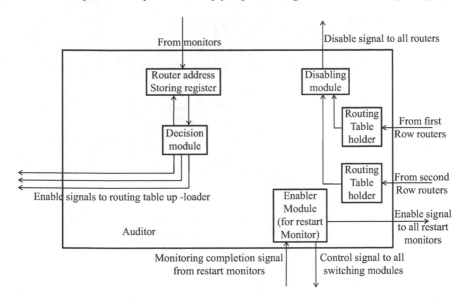

Figure 4.5   Block diagram of Auditor

packet, it will not contain a legitimate source router address. An ack packet's source address is used to reset the corresponding counter. If the ack packet does not contain legitimate source address, the corresponding counter will expire and router attack will be detected.

4.4.2   Restart monitor

Restart monitor works before starting of normal MPSoC cloud platform operation. The NoC fabric with restart monitors is shown in Figure 4.6. There is a switch in every row of the NoC at the boundary between the secure and nonsecure region. Each switch and monitor at a secure region boundary are connected to other switches and monitors, respectively, as a chain. The auditor receives data from the end of the chain and sends data to a module through the beginning of the chain. In case of enable signal (for restart monitor) and control signal (for switching module), auditor sends the signal to the first module only. That module sends the signal to the next module in the chain and in this way all modules get required signal. The block diagram of restart monitor is shown in Figure 4.7. The restart monitor is not directly connected to a secure region router as shown in Figure 4.6. After restart, auditor enables the restart monitors and disconnects the secure and nonsecure region routers using the switching module that uses simple multiplexing technique. Restart monitor does not need to detect router attacks like runtime monitor because it operates during restart time before the start of normal operations. The monitor only needs to check the existence of malicious router and its location using monitoring packets like runtime monitor. Restart monitor has only three input registers (refer Figure 4.7) instead of four unlike runtime monitor

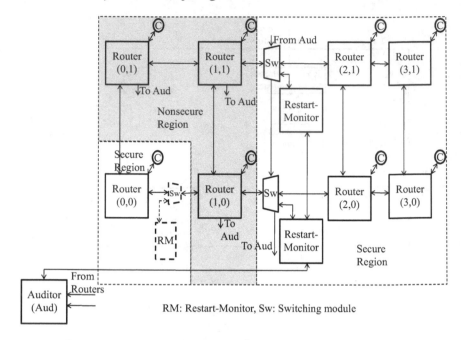

Figure 4.6   2 × 4 mesh NoC with Restart Monitors in every row

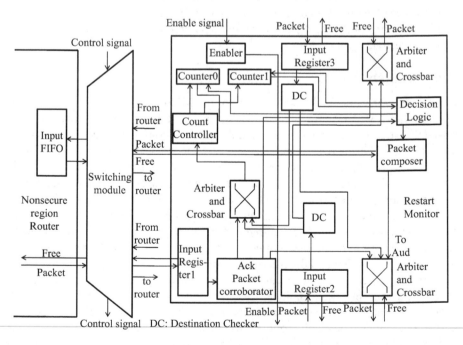

Figure 4.7   Block diagram of Restart Monitor

and requires less area. Most of the modules and their operations in restart monitor are same as runtime monitor.

After completion of monitoring all routers in the row outside this secure region, the restart monitor sends a monitoring completion signal to the auditor. Auditor then disables the monitors and sends control signal to switching modules so that the routers of secure and nonsecure region get connected for start of normal operation. Since the MPSoC cloud platform is not available for normal operation when restart monitor is monitoring the routers, there is no unauthorized access to data during this period. The only drawback of this technique is that the delay in starting normal operation of the MPSoC cloud platform is proportional to the number of routers in the NoC.

Instead of counting up to max-count as in the case of the runtime monitor, each counter in the restart monitor is set to count up to a specific value. This value is based on the topological distance of the corresponding router from the restart monitor. The count can hence be expressed as:

$$\text{Count (in cycles)} = T_{min}2N_H^i + T_{Pr} + T_{mon} \tag{4.3}$$

Here T_{min} is the minimum time required for a packet to leave a router after entering it. Count value is decided based on the total packet latency (packet going and ack coming) corresponding to a destination. N_H^i is the hop count of the i-th destination. Here $i \in \{1, \ldots, n\}$ with 1 is for the closest destination. T_{Pr} and T_{mon} are PE processing time and delay in monitor, respectively. Restart monitor can send monitoring packets one after another without waiting for ack to return—this reduces the total time required to monitor all routers. Ack packets arrive in the same order in which monitoring packets were sent. Whenever there is no ack packet from a router, the corresponding router is detected as malicious and reported to the auditor.

4.4.3 Ejection address checker

EAC is located inside every nonsecure region router and operates during normal MPSoC cloud platform operation. The block diagram of EAC is shown in Figure 4.8

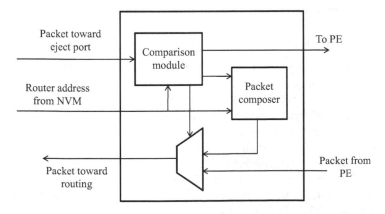

Figure 4.8   Block diagram of ejection address checker

Table 4.2   Comparison between runtime monitor, restart monitor, and EAC

	Runtime-monitor	Restart-monitor	EAC
Delay added (in clock cycles)	1	0	1
Works during	Runtime	Restart-time	Runtime
Number of routers supported	More than 1; depends on the numbers of counters	More than 1; depends on the numbers of counters	Only 1
Advantage	No initialization delay	No runtime delay; No packet loss; No reduction of throughput	No initialization delay
Disadvantage	Runtime delay; Initial loss of packets; Reduction of throughput	Initialization delay	Runtime delay; Reduction of throughput

which clearly shows that it is a hardware module which is not configurable and hence is protected from attacks similar to those directed toward routing tables. In case of unauthorized access attack, packets destined for different routers are diverted to the eject port for capturing. The EAC consists of a comparison module to compare the destination address of a packet toward the eject port with the router's address from NVM. If both addresses are same, it allows the packet to pass to the PE. If the addresses are different, comparison module signals the packet composer to form a packet to be sent to auditor. Also the state is changed to "attack detected." Packet composer takes the source address from NVM, auditor destination address, and a particular payload to indicate the attack detection. The packet is sent for routing toward the auditor. Here it is assumed that a packet can be routed to the auditor through the NoC itself.

Table 4.2 compares runtime monitor, restart monitor, and EAC.

4.4.4   Simulation and synthesis results

Bluespec System Verilog [38] is used for design and simulation of the system. NoC of Figure 4.1 is used for simulation. First, we update the routing tables with correct data for normal operation. Artificial traffic generators are used to generate traffic. Warmup period of 1,000 clock cycles, measurement period of 1,000 to 0.1 million clock cycles, and drainage period of 0.1 million to 1 million clock cycles are considered. A packet injection rate of 20%, frequency of operation of 1.11 GHz, and 32 bit packets are used in simulation. An average throughput of 222.22 million packets per second (M pkts/s) is obtained. Throughput under normal conditions are shown in Figure 4.9. In this case, the destination router (0,0) receives data correctly as shown in Figure 4.9(c) and the eject port of router (1,0) does not receive any data as shown in Figure 4.9(b). Next, we simulate attack on router (1,0) (refer Figure 4.1) by loading malicious routing table.

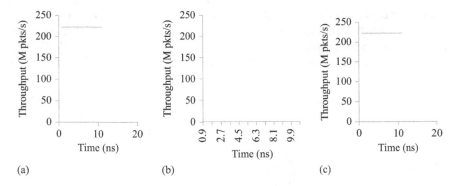

Figure 4.9   Dataflow during normal operation. (a) Secure region to nonsecure region dataflow at monitor, (b) dataflow at Router (1,0) eject port, and (c) dataflow at actual destination Router (0,0)

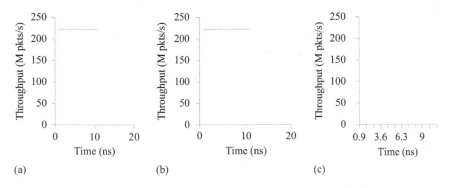

Figure 4.10   Dataflow after attack without runtime monitor in place. (a) Secure region to nonsecure region dataflow at monitor, (b) dataflow at router (1,0) eject port, and (c) dataflow at actual destination router (0,0)

It can be clearly seen from Figure 4.10 that traffic destined for router (0,0) is diverted to router (1,0) as shown in Figure 4.10(b) and (c), respectively. So, it can be seen that the attack is possible and an attacker can gain unauthorized access to all data coming from or going to a secure region of MPSoC cloud platform. Constant dataflows (i.e., horizontal lines) in Figures 4.9 and 4.10 depict absence of runtime monitors and resulting dataflow blocking. Figures 4.9(b), 4.10(c), and 4.11(c) indicate the absence of dataflow.

NoC of Figure 4.3 is used to simulate the operation of runtime monitor. This NoC is similar to Figure 4.1 except the presence of the monitors in each row. Detection of the attacked router by the runtime monitor is shown in Figure 4.11. From the start of packet transmission to the expiration of the corresponding counter, normal packet flow is continuous as shown in Figure 4.11(a). After expiration of counter, monitor detects an attack. It stops all dataflow between secure and nonsecure regions. After this time, monitor sends a simple monitoring packet to each router toward the destination from nearest to farthest to detect the location of the malicious router. So, the data rate is not zero but negligible compared to the average throughput of 222.22 M pkts/s.

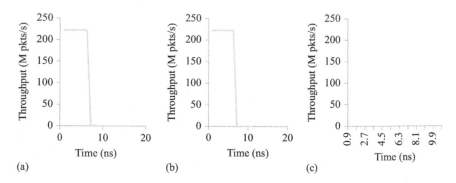

Figure 4.11   Dataflow after attack with runtime monitor in place. (a) Secure region to nonsecure region dataflow at monitor, (b) dataflow at router (1,0) eject port, and (c) dataflow at actual destination router (0,0)

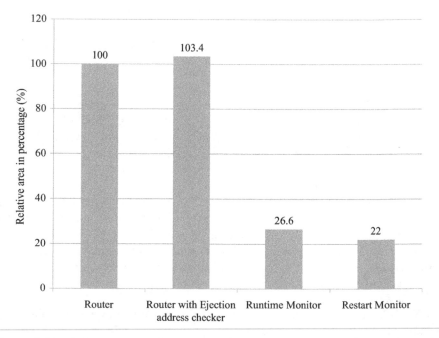

Figure 4.12   Relative areas of router including EAC, runtime monitor, and restart monitor compared to a router

Synopsys Design Compiler is used for area estimation using 65 nm Faraday technology libraries. Faraday Memaker memory compiler (65 nm technology) [39] is used for NVM area measurement. The minimum size of NVM (ROM) that can be compiled using the memory compiler is 512 bits and the area obtained is 2,305 μm^2. It becomes 18 μm^2 after scaling this to obtain 4-bit NVM area. Note that the scaled down area of a 4-bit NVM is a pessimistic estimate since the compiler generated area (for 512 bits) includes associated modules (like decoder). The router area including NVM is 8,756 μm^2. The router area including EAC is 9,056 μm^2, an increase of 3.4% compared to a normal router. The runtime monitor and the restart monitor areas are 2,329 and 1,926 μm^2, respectively. This means runtime monitor area is 26.6% and restart monitor area is 22% of a single router area. Figure 4.12 shows relative area comparisons of different solutions relative to a router area. The area overhead of different monitors are acceptable because both the monitors (runtime and restart) can monitor multiple routers.

4.5 Countermeasure for misrouting attack

Countermeasure for misrouting attack is discussed in this section. The whole MPSoC cloud platform structure is shown in Figure 4.13 including the restart monitors.

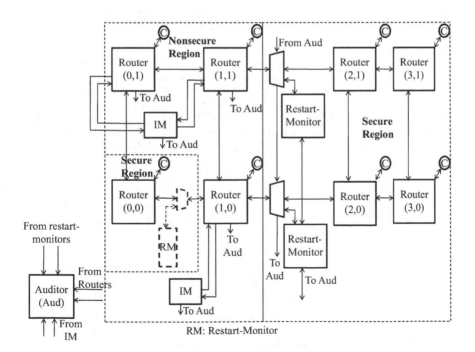

Figure 4.13   The whole MPSoC cloud platform structure including restart monitors. C in circle stands for PE.

The nonsecure region is divided into sections. Here, one section consists of a row of routers. A local monitoring module inside every nonsecure region router detects the misrouting attack. An intermediate manager (IM) coordinates these modules in a section of routers. All the IMs are managed by the auditor.

4.5.1   Local monitoring module

The block diagram of local monitoring module is shown in Figure 4.14. Input packet header checking by header checking module detects the correctness of the routed packet in deterministic XY/YX routing following routers. For XY routing, a packet is not allowed for Y-dimensional movement, unless its X-dimensional routing is complete. In addition, packets are not allowed to take X dimension if it is currently following Y dimension. Misrouting can be detected if the packet's destination address (X and Y coordinates) in its header is compared against the current router's address (X and Y coordinates). If the NoC has path diversity or is using adaptive routing, packets are not fixed to a particular path. Runtime variability in path selection reduces the effectiveness of header checking mechanism. Four 1-bit registers (malicious bit reg) indicate a malicious router detection at the corresponding input port. The correspondence between input port and 1-bit register is fixed. Whenever a malicious router is detected at an input port, the corresponding bit register is set. The decision logic checks these four 1-bit registers in every clock cycle. Whenever any bit is set, it sends a pulse to IM to set a 1-bit register in IM corresponding to this router. After detection at an input port, decision logic disables the input as well as output communication of

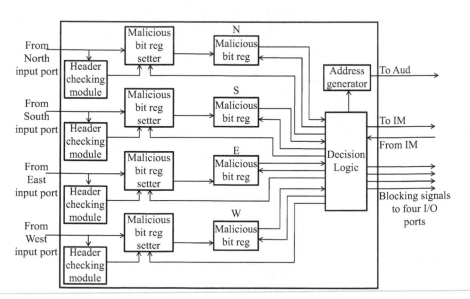

Figure 4.14   Block diagram of local monitoring module. Reg stands for register in the figure.

the concerned port. The reason is that sending data to a malicious router is waste of valuable data. The address generator module generates the malicious router address taking into consideration which input port has detected it. Malicious router is the one that has sent a wrong packet detected by header checking module. The address generator module forms a combined address message consisting of the current router address and the generated malicious router address. This message is sent to Aud whenever requested by IM. The header checking module operates in parallel with other operations at an input port like checking the routing table. So its operation does not cause any latency increment of packets. Same is true for malicious bit register setter. So it is evident that the local monitoring module in routers does not affect the MPSoC cloud platform performance.

4.5.2   Intermediate manager

The block diagram of IM is shown in Figure 4.15. IM mainly solves the scalability issue of auditor. If all the routers or more specifically all local monitoring modules are connected directly to the Aud, it becomes a bottleneck for Aud. IM handles a section (row in present case) of routers in nonsecure region and all IMs are connected to Aud. If IM manages N routers in a section, it has N 1-bit registers. Decision logic inside IM continuously checks these 1-bit registers in every clock. Whenever a bit is set by a router's local monitoring module, IM sends a pulse to Aud to set a 1-bit register corresponding to this IM. Then IM disables further setting of any malicious bit register that are not set yet inside IM. Whenever Aud requests for router address, IM takes decision based on the set malicious bit registers. It considers one router at a time among all the routers corresponding to the set bit registers. It sends a request to the selected router to send malicious router address directly to Aud. Whenever Aud sends a router address for routing table upload, IM sends this request to the corresponding router to load its routing table to Aud directly.

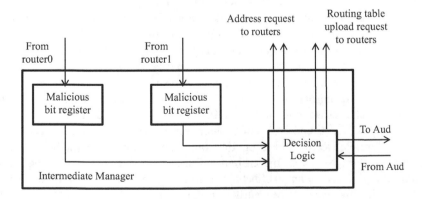

Figure 4.15   Block diagram of Intermediate Manager

4.5.3   Simulation and synthesis results

For simulation, we use the whole MPSoC cloud platform structure depicted in Figure 4.13. Our aim is to test the router's local monitoring module or more specifically the input header checking module for deterministic YX routing. We consider the router (0,1) as malicious and we send a packet into the West input port of the router (1,1) trying to go to the South output port violating the YX routing algorithm. We find that this violating packet is checked and stopped correctly in the same clock cycle in router (1,1) and the router (0,1) is correctly reported as malicious.

Synopsys Design Compiler is used for area estimation using 65-nm Faraday technology libraries. The router's area with input header checking module is 9,359 μm^2. The IM's area is 22 μm^2 and the auditor's area is 1,073 μm^2. It is to be noted that this auditor is more complex than that shown in Figure 4.5. It supports the modules (local monitoring modules and IMs) described in this section in addition to the modules shown in Figure 4.5. Detailed description of this auditor can be found in [25,37].

4.6   Summary, future research directions, and further readings

In this chapter, we have considered the attacks where an attacker targets the hardware cloud platform itself and we have also discussed different security mechanisms to ensure security of the information flow within an MPSoC cloud platform. Different PEs in an MPSoC are usually interconnected by a scalable medium like an NoC. In this chapter, we have shown a new type of security vulnerability on NoC architecture of an MPSoC cloud platform, i.e., possibility of router attack inside NoC. Until now, most of the research work was aimed at strengthening the performance, area, and power of NoC architectures. Very recently security is gaining importance in the NoC research community, but it is very important topic and must be taken into consideration at the time of system design. In future, all the cloud computing MPSoC platforms will have NoC as their on-chip communication medium. So taking NoC security into main design flow will help future cloud platform engineers to build not only a high-performance system but also a robust one which can offer fully trustworthy solution. By ensuring security of data inside each MPSoC, the cloud platform vendors can ensure security of data throughout the cloud computing system. We have discussed various monitoring-based countermeasures to deal with the router attack in an MPSoC cloud platform. We have also shown the simulation results that show that the mechanisms can successfully detect the attack and the malicious router address also. The restart monitor, the runtime monitor, the IM, and the auditor areas are 22%, 26.6%, 0.2%, and 12.2% of a router area, respectively, which is acceptable.

As a future research direction, the router attack detection methods can be improved further. Note that the current MPSoC cloud platform technology is in nanometer region and radiation effects can also change memory bits in routing tables. In future, this effect needs to be clearly distinguished from a router attack. Currently, the administrator intervention is required to rectify any malicious routing tables.

This process can be automated in future to reload correct routing tables without administrator intervention.

Interested reader can find further details of the techniques discussed in this chapter in [25,37]. We have also presented an earlier version of the work in [26].

Acknowledgments

This work was supported by the PhD scholarship from the MHRD, Government of India. We want to thank Prof Rajaraman of SERC, IISc for reviewing this chapter and suggesting some changes.

References

[1]   T. Bjerregaard and S. Mahadevan, "A survey of research and practices of network-on-chip," *ACM Computing Surveys*, vol. 38, no. 1, June 2006.

[2]   W. Dally and B. Towles, *Principles and Practices of Interconnection Networks*. USA: Morgan Kaufmann Publishers, 2004.

[3]   M. Dall'osso, G. Biccari, L. Giovannini, D. Bertozzi, and L. Benini, "Xpipes: a latency insensitive parameterized network-on-chip architecture for multiprocessor SoCs," in *Computer Design, 2003. Proceedings. 21st International Conference on*, San Jose, CA, USA, 2003, pp. 536–539.

[4]   K. Goossens, J. Dielissen, and A. Radulescu, "Æthereal network on chip: concepts, architectures, and implementations," *Design Test of Computers, IEEE*, vol. 22, no. 5, pp. 414–421, 2005.

[5]   L. Wang, H. Song, Y. Jiang, and L. Zhang, "A routing-table-based adaptive and minimal routing scheme on network-on-chip architectures," *Computers and Electrical Engineering*, vol. 35, no. 6, pp. 846–855, 2009.

[6]   T. Mak, P. Cheung, K.-P. Lam, and W. Luk, "Adaptive routing in network-on-chips using a dynamic-programming network," *Industrial Electronics, IEEE Transactions on*, vol. 58, no. 8, pp. 3701–3716, 2011.

[7]   M. Palesi, R. Holsmark, S. Kumar, and V. Catania, "Application specific routing algorithms for networks on chip," *Parallel and Distributed Systems, IEEE Transactions on*, vol. 20, no. 3, pp. 316–330, 2009.

[8]   Y. E. Krasteva, E. de la Torre, and T. Riesgo, "Reconfigurable networks on chip: DRNoC architecture," *Journal of Systems Architecture*, vol. 56, no. 7, pp. 293–302, 2010.

[9]   I. Loi, F. Angiolini, and L. Benini, "Synthesis of low-overhead configurable source routing tables for network interfaces," in *Design, Automation Test in Europe Conference Exhibition, 2009. DATE '09*, Nice, France, 2009, pp. 262–267.

[10] A. Shahabi, N. Honarmand, and Z. Navabi, "Programmable routing tables for degradable torus-based networks on chips," in *Circuits and Systems, 2007.*

ISCAS 2007. IEEE International Symposium on, New Orleans, Louisiana, USA, 2007, pp. 1065–1068.

[11]   J. Howard, S. Dighe, Y. Hoskote *et al.*, "A 48-core ia-32 message-passing processor with dvfs in 45 nm cmos," in *2010 IEEE International Solid-State Circuits Conference (ISSCC)*, San Francisco, CA, February 2010, pp. 108–109.

[12]   *TILE-Gx72 Processor Product Brief.* Mellanox Technologies, 2016. [Online]. Available: www.mellanox.com/related-docs/prod_multi_core/PB_TILE-Gx72.pdf

[13]   *Zynq UltraScale+ MPSoC Product Tables and Product Selection Guide.* Xilinx, 2016. [Online]. Available: https://www.xilinx.com/support/documentation/selection-guides/zynq-ultrascale-plus-product-selection-guide.pdf

[14]   GPU cloud computing, 2016. [Online]. Available: http://www.nvidia.com/object/gpu-cloud-computing.html

[15]   J. Dean and S. Ghemawat, "Mapreduce: Simplified data processing on large clusters," *Communications of the ACM*, vol. 51, no. 1, pp. 107–113, January 2008. [Online]. Available: http://doi.acm.org/10.1145/1327452.1327492

[16]   B. He, W. Fang, Q. Luo, N. K. Govindaraju, and T. Wang, "Mars: A mapreduce framework on graphics processors," in *Proceedings of the 17th International Conference on Parallel Architectures and Compilation Techniques*, ser. PACT '08. Toronto, Ontario, Canada: ACM, 2008, pp. 260–269. [Online]. Available: http://doi.acm.org/10.1145/1454115.1454152

[17]   C. Ranger, R. Raghuraman, A. Penmetsa, G. Bradski, and C. Kozyrakis, "Evaluating mapreduce for multi-core and multiprocessor systems," in *2007 IEEE 13th International Symposium on High Performance Computer Architecture*, Scottsdale, AZ, February 2007, pp. 13–24.

[18]   L. Chen, X. Huo, and G. Agrawal, "Accelerating mapreduce on a coupled cpu-gpu architecture," in *High Performance Computing, Networking, Storage and Analysis (SC), 2012 International Conference for*, Salt Lake City, UT, November 2012, pp. 1–11.

[19]   R. Farivar, A. Verma, E. M. Chan, and R. H. Campbell, "Mithra: Multiple data independent tasks on a heterogeneous resource architecture," in *2009 IEEE International Conference on Cluster Computing and Workshops*, New Orleans, LA, August 2009, pp. 1–10.

[20]   J. A. Stuart and J. D. Owens, "Multi-gpu mapreduce on gpu clusters," in *2011 IEEE International Parallel Distributed Processing Symposium*, Anchorage, AK, May 2011, pp. 1068–1079.

[21]   Security as a Service, 2016. [Online]. Available: https://cloudsecurityalliance.org/group/security-as-a-service/

[22]   *Trusted Execution Environments for Cloud Infrastructure: From Server Blades to Datacenters (white paper).* Viaccess-Orca and Trustonic, 2016. [Online]. Available: http://www.viaccess-orca.com/resource-center/white-papers/tee-environments-for-cloud-infrastructure.html-0

[23]   *The Trusted Execution Environment: Delivering Enhanced Security at a Lower Cost to the Mobile Market (white paper).* GlobalPlatform

Inc., February 2011. [Online]. Available: https://www.globalplatform.org/documents/whitepapers/GlobalPlatform_TEE_Whitepaper_2015.pdf

[24]   *GlobalPlatform Device Technology TEE System Architecture Version 1.0 (white paper)*. GlobalPlatform Inc., December 2011. [Online]. Available: https://www.globalplatform.org/specificationsdevice.asp

[25]   A. Biswas, S. Nandy, and R. Narayan, "Router attack toward noc-enabled mpsoc and monitoring countermeasures against such threat," *Circuits, Systems, and Signal Processing*, vol. 34, no. 10, pp. 3241–3290, 2015. [Online]. Available: http://dx.doi.org/10.1007/s00034-015-9980-0

[26]   A. Biswas, S. Nandy, and R. Narayan, "Network-on-chip router attacks and their prevention in mp-socs with multiple trusted execution environments," in *Electronics, Computing and Communication Technologies (IEEE CONECCT), 2015 IEEE International Conference on*, Bangalore, July 2015, pp. 1–6.

[27]   S. Evain and J.-P. Diguet, "From NoC security analysis to design solutions," in *Signal Processing Systems Design and Implementation, 2005. IEEE Workshop on*, Athens, Greece, 2005, pp. 166–171.

[28]   *ARM Security Technology Building a Secure System using TrustZone Technology (white paper)*. ARM Limited, April 2009. [Online]. Available: http://infocenter.arm.com/help/topic/com.arm.doc.prd29-genc-009492c/PRD29-GENC-009492C_trustzone_security_whitepaper.pdf

[29]   L. Fiorin, G. Palermo, and C. Silvano, "A security monitoring service for NoCs," in *Proceedings of the 6th IEEE/ACM/IFIP International Conference on Hardware/Software Codesign and System Synthesis*, ser. CODES+ISSS '08. ACM, Atlanta, GA, USA, 2008, pp. 197–202.

[30]   J. Sepulveda, R. Pires, G. Gogniat, W. Jiang Chau, and M. Strum, "QoSS hierarchical NoC-based architecture for MPSoC dynamic protection," *International Journal of Reconfigurable Computing*, vol. 2012, p. 10, 2012.

[31]   H. Kapoor, G. Rao, S. Arshi, and G. Trivedi, "A security framework for noc using authenticated encryption and session keys," *Circuits, Systems, and Signal Processing*, vol. 32, no. 6, pp. 2605–2622, 2013. [Online]. Available: http://dx.doi.org/10.1007/s00034-013-9568-5

[32]   A. K. Biswas, "Wide voltage input receiver with hysteresis characteristic to reduce input signal noise effect," *ETRI Journal*, vol. 35, no. 5, pp. 797–807, 2013.

[33]   *Security Guidance for Critical Areas of Focus in Cloud Computing V3.0*. Cloud Security Alliance, 2011. [Online]. Available: https://downloads.cloudsecurityalliance.org/assets/research/security-guidance/csaguide.v3.0.pdf

[34]   T. Garfinkel, B. Pfaff, J. Chow, M. Rosenblum, and D. Boneh, "Terra: A virtual machine-based platform for trusted computing," in *Proceedings of the Nineteenth ACM Symposium on Operating Systems Principles*, ser. SOSP '03. New York, NY: ACM, 2003, pp. 193–206. [Online]. Available: http://doi.acm.org/10.1145/945445.945464

[35]   J. Szefer and R. B. Lee, "Architectural support for hypervisor-secure virtualization," in *Proceedings of the Seventeenth International Conference on Architectural Support for Programming Languages and Operating Systems*,

ser. ASPLOS XVII. New York, NY: ACM, 2012, pp. 437–450. [Online]. Available: http://doi.acm.org/10.1145/2150976.2151022

[36] J. Szefer and R. B. Lee, *Hardware-Enhanced Security for Cloud Computing*. New York, NY: Springer New York, 2014, pp. 57–76. [Online]. Available: http://dx.doi.org/10.1007/978-1-4614-9278-8_3

[37] A. K. Biswas, "Securing multiprocessor systems-on-chip," PhD dissertation, Department of Electronic Systems Engineering, Indian Institute of Science, Bangalore, August 2016. [Online]. Available: http://etd.ncsi.iisc.ernet.in/handle/2005/2554

[38] Bluespec, 2013. [Online]. Available: http://www.bluespec.com

[39] Faraday Memaker, 2014. [Online]. Available: http://freelibrary.faraday-tech.com/ips/65library.html

Chapter 5

Distributing encoded data for private processing in the cloud

Mark A. Will* and Ryan K. L. Ko*

Abstract

Traditional cryptography techniques require our data to be unencrypted and to be processed correctly. This means that at some stage on a system we have no control over, our data will be processed in plain text. Solutions that allow the computation of arbitrary operations over data securely in the cloud are currently impractical. The holy grail of cryptography, fully homomorphic encryption, still requires minutes to compute a single operation. To provide a practical solution, this chapter proposes taking a different approach to the problem of securely processing data. This is achieved by each cloud service receiving an encoded part of the data, which is not enough to decode the plain-text value. The security strength is shifted from a computation problem to the sheer number possible options. Given the greater threat to data stored in the cloud is from insiders, this is the primary attack vector the presented schemes Bin Encoding and FRagmenting Individual Bits (FRIBs) aim to protect against.

5.1 Introduction

Private information in the cloud is at constant risk of attack. Recent information regarding the Yahoo hack reveals that a billion accounts were stolen [1]. Furthermore, insider attacks from cloud employees and administrators[1] are a threat, and arguably the bigger threat to customer data [3–5]. A survey by Kaspersky and B2B International revealed that 73% of companies have had internal information security incidents, and stated that the single largest cause of confidential data loss is by insiders (42%) [5]. Therefore, a current research challenge is to allow a user to control their own security, providing the ability to protect data from both insider and outsider attacks while maintaining functionality.

---

*Cyber Security Lab, University of Waikato, New Zealand
[1]An engineer at Google abused his privileged administrator rights to spy on teenagers using the GTalk service. Only after the teenagers' parents reported the administrator, Google was made aware [2].

Given how impractical solutions are currently, we have taken a different approach to the concept of processing data securely. We propose encoding and distributing data to different cloud service providers. This chapter provides a summary of two previously published works: (1) Bin Encoding [6] and (2) FRagmenting Individual Bits (FRIBs) [7]. Both schemes presented were designed to meet the following design goals.

- **No single server can reveal the full data.** To protect privacy, each server should not be able to decode any value.
- **Full cloud service.** The schemes should be easy to implement on current cloud infrastructure, for example, Amazon AWS [8] or Microsoft Azure [9], and not require any special hardware or equipment.
- **Practical performance.** Should be usable, allowing today's users of the cloud to be protected, while still getting computational functionality.
- **Accurate results.** For arbitrary secure processing, the correct result should be returned 100% of the time, where approximate string searching is best effort because of the nature of the problem.

The threat models against which we evaluate our methods are based on the following assumptions: (1) the communication channel between each distributed server and the client is secure; (2) each server encrypts user data before storing it to disk; (3) each server has no knowledge on other servers used to store data and (4) data is stored across multiple cloud service providers.

Based on these assumptions, there are two types of attacker to evaluate against: a malicious insider from the cloud service and a malicious user/outsider. Both present similar threats; however, a malicious insider has an advantage because he or she already has access to one cloud service providers system. If a malicious insider manages to bypass all internal security, for example, access policies and permissions, then they can discover parts of the distributed data. Now they become the same as any other malicious user, as they can try to break into all the other cloud service providers. This summaries into two attack vectors: breaking the data with one set of distributed data and getting all the data from each system.

5.2   Summary of distributed encoding and related work

5.2.1   *Encoding*

One of the oldest encryption techniques known is the Caesar cipher, named after Julius Caesar who used it to protect messages of high importance, such as military instructions. This is a type of substitution cipher, which maps plain-text values to their cipher-text counterparts at an shifted index in the alphabet. Decoding requires the shift number, which is the secret key. However in the case of a random one-to-one mapping as used by Mary, Queen of Scots,[2] the fixed mapping would be the secret.

---

[2] Mary's secret messages were broken via frequency analysis, which led to her execution in 1587 [10]. Hence this attack vector for string securing is covered in [6] and briefly mentioned in Section 5.5.

An everyday case where encoding has offered data privacy to people is those who can speak another language. For example, if you live in an English-speaking country and understand Mandarin Chinese, anything you type or speak will be foreign to most. Therefore, notifications on your phone's lock screen have a degree of protection if they are in another language. A substitution cipher follows this principle, where it can be thought of mapping one language to another. But where a language can be understood by many, secured data should only be understood by the intended parties.

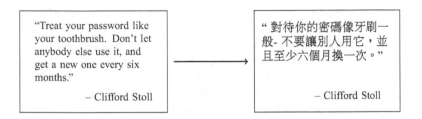

The difference between encoding and encryption is minuscule. Both transform data, but encryption keeps some part of the process a secret. Without this secret value, it should be computationally intensive to break. Therefore if only the intended parties have the secret, then the data is secured from everyone else. This traditional cryptography follows the principle defined by the Dutch cryptographer Auguste Kerckhoffs, where a cryptosystem must not depend on keeping the algorithm safe, only the secret key [11].

A lesser known principle and a widely rejected one is security through obscurity, which states that security is provided by the secrecy of the design/implementations. This should not be the only defence in place, however, can be combined with the Kerckhoffs's principle. In this chapter we keep some part of the encoding process secret, but we also distributed the data. The distribution is similar to security through obscurity, as each server should have no knowledge of others, and probably has security vulnerabilities that are not currently discovered. However if the servers are running on various hardware and software, then a single vulnerability is not enough to gain access to all servers.

An alternative to distributing data, homomorphic encryption exists in 2 flavours: partially homomorphic encryption (PHE) and fully homomorphic encryption (FHE). PHE supports a single operation over cipher text, for example, addition or multiplication, where FHE can support many operations computed over encrypted data. Cryptographic schemes supporting single homomorphic operations have been around since RSA was proposed in 1978 [12]. For some applications, only one operation is required, and in these cases PHE is an ideal solution [13–16].

Homomorphic properties have also allowed the development of secure string searching [17–23]. For large enterprises, it is sufficient to build and maintain search indexes within the corporate environment and transmit them to the cloud for use. But ordinary people who use the cloud to store personal documents would probably prefer to delegate the task of building indexes and managing search to the service provider. Current systems require the index to be downloaded, updated, and re-uploaded. Moreover, they do not support phrase or proximity searching, and at best are robust only to simple (single-character) typographical and spelling errors. Little research has been devoted to addressing these shortcomings.

Applications requiring multiple operations must therefore use FHE. FHE was only proven plausible by Gentry as late as 2009 [24], many years after PHE. Wang *et al.* [25] showed performance results of a revised FHE scheme by Gentry and Halevi [26] in 2015 for the recrypt function. Central processing unit (CPU) and graphics processing unit (GPU) implementations took 17.8 and 1.32 s, respectively, using a small dimension size of 2,048 [25]. A medium dimension size of 8,192 took 96.3 and 8.4 s for the same function [25].

Currently hardware implementations [27] of FHE schemes cannot give practical processing times, so it will be difficult to make this technology usable in the real world. Combined with the fact that quantum computing is making huge advancements [28, 29], having data protected by traditional encryption schemes (for example, Rivest et al. [12], Diffie–Hellman [30], and elliptic curves [31]) may not be as feasible in the future as it is today. Lattice-based encryption [24] could be a solution; however, it will result in even larger key sizes than current impractical FHE schemes.

5.2.2   Distribution

Cloud providers distribute their services for features like lower latency, load-balancing, and redundancy [32,33]. But rarely do they use distribution to provide better security and data protection. Currently proposed distributed processing schemes run parts of a program on different servers, so that none have a full picture on what is being processed. These, however, do not fully protect data privacy as values are in plain text while being processed on each server.

For example, one technique currently used is to distribute columns of tables in a database over many servers [34]. Then in the event of a server being compromised, only some of the data is lost. Another example is MultiParty Computation (MPC) [35], where multiple parties securely compute a function over some secret input [36–39]. Each server has its own private inputs into the function, but these often are in plain text. Other limitations of MPC include that only one server can be corrupted for correctness and the encrypted circuits can require large network transfers.

Some PHE schemes have threshold variants which allow decryption to be split across many servers [40] and have primarily been used for voting schemes [13,16,41]. This provides extra protection to the decryption key, as each server only possesses a part of it. Now if a server is compromised, no relevant data is lost. However if more servers are compromised, and additional parts of the decryption key are leaked, the easier it becomes for a malicious entity to break the key. Sections 5.3 and 5.4 follow this idea where data is distributed such that if some servers are compromised, it is still computationally difficult to get any real data. Choosing servers and cloud services to host this distributed data now becomes very important. There needs to be a range of cloud service providers to prevent insider attacks, and a range of underlying soft-wares such as operating systems to protect against a zero-day-attack compromising all servers.

To explain this idea further, distributing data is the act of splitting up some piece of information into smaller pieces. For example when complete, a puzzle is an image. But when broken up it can be hard to tell what the image should be. If we save each piece of information to a different location, then figuring out what the final image is from one piece is difficult.

If we turn off the lights, the puzzle becomes even more difficult because the image gives us no information to help solve the puzzle. This is equivalent to distributing some information which has been encoded using a known algorithm (in this case, the puzzle cutter). Without all the pieces we can't decode the information, even though we know the algorithm used.

However by not knowing the algorithm used to encode the data, we have to try each possibility to join the pieces together where only once we get the correct order will the light turn back on. But the light may turn on for false positives, because it is possible to decode something into completely the wrong thing while appearing to look correct.

This example puzzle has $20! = 2.432902008 \times 10^{18}$ combinations. Even computing a million combinations a second, it would still require thousands of years to generate all possibilities. This gives distribution of the computationally intensive property that is required for something to be considered as encryption. Therefore in this chapter, the definition of secure encoding with distribution is equivalent to encryption.

5.2.3   Custom hardware processors

The state-of-the-art secure processor, AEGIS [42], was designed to reveal only the data inside the processor. Therefore, any data leaving the processor is encrypted. This protects against a range of software and physical attacks. But AEGIS still has security vulnerabilities in the form of side-channel-attacks [43, 44]. This attack vector analyses information 'leaked' from the physical execution of a program, for example, power consumption [45] or electromagnetic radiation [46]. Other limitations of secure processors are the practicality of deployment in the cloud. By definition, the cloud should be flexible and adaptive, often viewed as abstracting services from products [47], but by creating services reliant on custom hardware, we lose the core essence of what the cloud should be. However for further security, secure processors can enhance privacy-preserving computation schemes.

5.3   String searching

5.3.1   Overview

Privacy preserving string searching is the first scheme presented to verify the idea of secure encoding with distribution. The scheme encodes documents and queries using 'Bin Encoding'. This uses a lossy encoding technique – a simple trapdoor – that maps characters individually to bins. There are several bins, and multiple characters map to the same one. Hence the original string cannot be obtained from its encoding. For example, here is a mapping with three bins A, B and C:

$$\{a, b, c, d, e, f, g, h, i\} \Rightarrow A$$
$$\{j, k, l, m, n, o, p, q, r\} \Rightarrow B$$
$$\{s, t, u, v, w, x, y, z\} \Rightarrow C$$

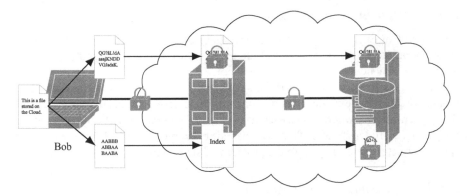

Figure 5.1   Personal user system model for Bin Encoding

(This example is for illustration; in practice, we envisage many more bins for a single index to reduce the number of false positives when searching.) Relative to this mapping, the encoded values for *hello* and *world* are *AABBB* and *CBBBA*, respectively, which can be obtained using Algorithm 1. Apart from *world*, another possibility for *CBBBA* is *slope* (among others). However, these possibilities can only be generated by someone who knows the bin mapping. Given the encoded value but not the mapping, there are countless possibilities for *CBBBA*, such as *hello* (even though the above bins map it to *AABBB*). The user's data is protected by hiding in many possible bin combinations ($>10^{20}$).

Figure 5.1 shows a typical use case. Bob is saving a file in the cloud, and would like it to be encrypted, while retaining the ability to search its contents at a later date. Before transmitting the file, his device encodes it; the computational expense is trivial. Bob separately encrypts the file using a secret key and sends both encrypted and encoded versions to the cloud service. Filenames are encrypted, while smaller documents can be padded. Note this example is not distributed, and this will be introduced in Section 5.3.6.

Algorithm 1 Bin Encoding

1: **function** BINENCODE(*string*, *binmap*)
2:      *estring* ← "
3:      **for** i ← 0 to *len*(*string*) **do**
4:          c ← *lowercase*(*string$_i$*)
5:          **if** c in *binmap* **then**
6:              *estring* ← *estring* + *binmap$_c$*
7:      **return** *estring*

5.3.2   Removing special characters

To harden Bin Encoding against language attacks, special characters such as space must be removed because they reveal too much information. For example, if spaces are visible, encoded words of length 1 will correspond with high probability to either *i* or *a* (in the English language). If the space character is encoded, its bin will occur unusually often. For example, a high-frequency letter like *T* occurs in English around 9% of the time [48], whereas space has a far greater frequency of 16%–30%, assuming an average word length of 5. This may make it easy to detect which bin contains the space character, leading again to the problem of single-letter words.

5.3.3   Approximate string searching

By encoding characters individually, approximate string searching can be supported. Using the above mapping, *hello* encodes to *AABBB*. But *hallo* also encodes to *AABBB*, so they would still match. Furthermore, if *h* and *e* were swapped, the encoded result would remain the same. Of course, this is an unrealistically simplistic example, and with more bins approximate searching will need to take into account how many bins are different, or transposed.

Modern operating systems support built-in spell checking, which perhaps reduces the importance of approximate string searching. However, this adds overhead to the client, has a limited dictionary, and users are taxed by having to confirm corrections. Thus it is advantageous for searching schemes to support approximate string matching.

5.3.4   False positives

Searching for a string over unencrypted data rarely returns false positives. However, when both query and data are encrypted, a cloud service cannot determine how accurate its results are. Lossy techniques such as Bin Encoding make it even harder to prevent false positives, for not only does the service have no knowledge of the data and query, but also it cannot be sure that two identical encoded values are actually the same. Furthermore, approximate search increases the potential for false positives if an exact match is not found. However, by looking for patterns, Bin Encoding still produces accurate results, as will be shown in Section 5.3.7.

5.3.5   Building the search index

The scheme allows the index to be built by the cloud service, rather than the client. The client need only encode the documents, which adds negligible overhead, and encrypt them. This allows multiple devices to update documents at the same time. In contrast with trapdoor searching, delegating index operations to the cloud service allows it to implement more advanced search facilities and obtain more accurate document rankings because the locations of query term hits are known.

Just how the index is built is left open, and the details are beyond the scope of this chapter. Because the cloud has no knowledge of spaces, we recommend an *n*-gram approach. For testing, we built the index using grams of the same size as the query, although in practice it is likely that fixed sized grams such as bigrams or trigrams will be used.

5.3.6 Distributed index

This section thus far describes Bin Encoding with single nondistributed index. With a single index, a larger number of bins will return more accurate results from encoded queries, because more patterns are observed. However, having many bins (>13) opens both index and queries to a wider range of attacks. In the extreme, 26 bins are simple to attack because they are a one-to-one mapping between characters and bins (assuming the alphabet is $\{A - Z\}$), enabling standard frequency and language attacks – although removing spaces made these somewhat more difficult. Therefore in practice, the index will be built using a smaller number of bins (<6) to harden it against such attacks.

Bin Encoding can be extended to store data in distributed 'environments' that are isolated from one another in such a way that if one environment is compromised by a malicious user, it will not be able to use the information or privileges gained to compromise another environment. Figure 5.2 shows a distributed index model containing four separate environments that isolate data. Three of these, B, C and D, contain indexes to the same documents built using different bin mappings. By

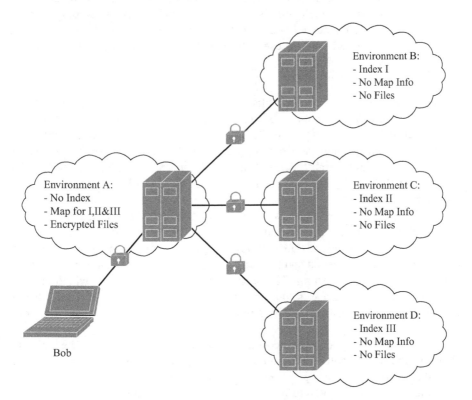

Figure 5.2   Distributed index system model for Bin Encoding

Table 5.1   Exact matching in document using distributed indexes

Search query	First result	Second result	Third result
internet	internet (100%)	interest (50%)	intended (47%)
ethics	ethics (100%)	ethica (63%)	rators (41%)
privacy	privacy (100%)	privile (31%)	rposely (31%)
hackers	archers (59%)	–	–
underwater	waterreser (41%)	underscore (34%)	undationdi (33%)
sldnfs	–	–	–

combining search results from each index, more accurate results can be returned. For example if one index gives a match on part of the document but another does not return the same match, this is likely to be a false positive.

Environment A in Figure 5.2 is responsible for distributing the query to the indexes and for combining the results to return to the user. When the user sends a query or edits a document, the number of bins for encoding can be large (e.g. 13). When Environment A receives encoded values, it uses a randomly generated mapping, different for each user, to further encode the already encoded values for each environment into a smaller number of bins. Although the user's mapping is never sent to the cloud, each index has a different mapping. Environment A also stores the encrypted files received from the user (although they could be placed elsewhere).

5.3.7   Results for searching over a document

The document we used for these results was 'Ethics and the Internet RFC1087' [49]. The distributed index setup used 13 bins to send from the client to the distribution server, before being converted into 3 indexes where each used 3 bins with different mappings. All bin mappings were randomly generated at runtime. The primary ranking used was the *n*-gram search function from the Python NGram library [50]. Results are the size of the query, so some results are segments of words or even two parts of a word because spaces are not known.

Table 5.1 contains six queries for a distributed index. The first three queries exist in the document, and this is shown by the results giving 100% matches. The remaining results (second and third) can vary depending on the bin mappings; however if the query is not misspelled and the search term is in the document, a 100% match always occurred in our testing. The bottom three queries are terms which are not in the document, and hence do not get strong matches. These results justify using distributed indices because they give similar results to a single index, but with more security.

The results for a selection of incorrect queries are given in Table 5.2. These results show that the cloud is still able to match a word/phase that the user could be meaning. Note that the query *priatcy* returns *promise* as the higher result. With a different bin mapping, *privacy* could be returned first. This is because approximate matching is more challenging for Bin Encoding, even a single wrong character in the query can

Table 5.2   Approximate matching in document using distributed indexes

Search query	First result	Second result	Third result
internat	internet (53%)	interest (50%)	interali (39%)
intranet	internet (53%)	integrit (39%)	intercon (33%)
intrenet	internet (61%)	interest (39%)	integrit (30%)
ethiks	ethics (63%)	ethica (39%)	–
ehtics	ethics (64%)	icians (42%)	ernets (41%)
priatcy	promise (42%)	privacy (38%)	product (35%)
private	privacy (46%)	privile (42%)	preadde (35%)

lead to varying results. However the important aspect is that *privacy* is returned to the user and could allow for a quick filter on the client side to move it up the list.

5.3.8   Summary

Overall the distributed index provides better security than a single index and allows for accurate results when using a small number of bins. Even if one server is compromised, the index is still protected. This is because the lossy encoding is computationally intense to reverse, similar to encryption.

5.4   Arbitrary computation

This section will extend the idea behind Bin Encoding (where encoding with distribution is comparable to encryption) from approximate string searching to arbitrary private computation like FHE. Instead of trying to build a FHE scheme which is computationally intense to break on a single machine, we started with the distributed model and tried to build a fully homomorphic scheme upon it. This shift has allowed a more practical approach to be developed which solves the same problem that existing FHE schemes target.

5.4.1   Overview

The FRIBs scheme has been designed to distribute each individual bit across many service providers, while still allowing Negative-*AND* (*NAND*) operations to be computed. We likened our proposed idea to the New Zealand terminology of 'fribs', which are small pieces of unwanted wool removed after shearing. If we say a 'bit' is the woollen fleece, then it cannot be recreated without all the fribs and wool. Distributing the bit fragments can be seen as exporting the fribs and wool to different locations, known as fragment servers. Once exported, the bit fragments can be processed securely by building functions from *NAND* gates.

The fragmentation is similar to encoding into bins, but is lossless as accurate results must be obtained. Therefore when the fribs are combined, the bit value can be

Table 5.3   Simple AND fragmentation

Value	F_0	F_1
Low	0	0
Low	1	0
Low	0	1
High	1	1

Table 5.4   Fragmentation with many states

Value	F_0	F_1
Low	0	0
Low	1	0
Low	0	1
Low	2	0
Low	0	2
Low	2	2
High	1	1
High	2	1
High	1	2

decoded. This follows the same principle of a threshold cryptosystem [40], which has N entities, but only requires t entities to decrypt a value (where $t < N$). Therefore if t entities are compromised, then the encrypted data is no longer protected.

Given a value $\{0, 1\}$ or $\{low, high\}$, the *AND* function is used to encode/fragment the bit.[3] An example is shown in Table 5.3 where a value is encoded into two fribs. A potential problem with this example is that 50% of the fribs are 0. Assuming an equal probability (50:50) between high and low bits before encoding, each servers can solve $\approx 1/3$ of the bit values (using the fact that one-half are low, and two-thirds of the fribs are 0 for low values). Depending on requirements, this could be seen as too much information leakage, even though complete values (for example, 32-bit integers or 8-bit characters) are still unknown.

One technique to reduce the number of 0 fribs is to introduce more frib states. Table 5.4 gives an example of three states for two servers, resulting in one-third of the fribs equalling 0. The fragmentation used in Table 5.4 is $F_0 \wedge F_1$, where the value 2 is *low* unless the other frib is *high*. Now each server can only solve $\approx 1/4$ of the bit values. However the easier solution is to increase the number of fribs, and only allow one frib to be 0 for an encoding, as shown in Table 5.5. This results in only $1/(N + 1)$

---

[3]Note that in this chapter we will only use the *AND* operation for fragmentation and only use two states for easier explanations and examples. Future work will demonstrate how FRIBs can be extended to support varying fragmentation algorithms, providing even more security.

Table 5.5   Fragmentation with only one server
receiving 0

Value	F_0	F_1	F_2	F_3	F_4
Low	0	1	1	1	1
Low	1	0	1	1	1
Low	1	1	0	1	1
Low	1	1	1	0	1
Low	1	1	1	1	0
High	1	1	1	1	1

fribs equalling 0, where N is the number of fribs, and a server only having knowledge of $1/(2N)$ of the bit values.

5.4.2   Distributed NAND gate

5.4.2.1   Operation

Now that the bits have been fragmented, we need to be able to compute basic operations over them such as addition and multiplication. Fragmenting values for either an addition or multiplication is trivial. For example if we have two numbers, 12 and 10, we can fragment them into $(6, 6)$ and $(8, 2)$, respectively. Adding the fragments together gives $(14, 8)$, which when joined together results in 22. Multiplication is similar, with the fragments $(3, 4)$ and $(2, 5)$, multiplication gives $(6, 20)$, outputting 120. The challenge is being able to compute both operations on the same set of data.

To compute many types of operations while only implementing a single function, a universal logic gate is used. FRIB implements a *NAND* gate, as they are preferred over *NOR* gates in electrical applications [51]. Unlike the addition or multiplication example, the result of a *NAND* function is dependent on the other fribs. Equation (5.1) compares the Exclusive-*OR* (*XOR*) and *NAND* functions, where the *NAND* function gives the wrong result. Therefore FRIBs maintain state so that when joining the fribs together, the correct result is given.

$$
\begin{array}{c|ccc|c}
  & F_0 & & F_1 & \text{Result} \\
\hline
A & 0 & \oplus & 0 & 0 \\
  & \oplus & & \oplus & \oplus \\
B & 1 & \oplus & 1 & 0 \\
\hline
  & 1 & \oplus & 1 & 0 \\
\end{array}
\qquad
\begin{array}{c|ccc|c}
  & F_0 & & F_1 & \text{Result} \\
\hline
A & 0 & \bar{\wedge} & 0 & 1 \\
  & \bar{\wedge} & & \bar{\wedge} & \bar{\wedge} \\
B & 1 & \bar{\wedge} & 1 & 0 \\
\hline
  & 1 & \bar{\wedge} & 1 & ? \\
\end{array}
\tag{5.1}
$$

5.4.2.2   Maintaining state

To keep the states of each operation we use a simple technique of concatenating each frib together to be computed/reduced later. The first operation with both fribs of 1 will be concatenated to 11. If we continued concatenating, we would lose the order of *NAND* operations, as demonstrated in (5.2) and (5.3) where the same frib values give different results.

	F_0		F_1	Result
A	11	$\wedge$	1	1
	$\overline{\wedge}$		$\overline{\wedge}$	$\overline{\wedge}$
B	11	$\wedge$	1	1
	1111	$\wedge$	11	0

	F_0		F_1	Result
A	1111	$\wedge$	11	0
	$\overline{\wedge}$		$\overline{\wedge}$	$\overline{\wedge}$
B	11	$\wedge$	1111	0
	111111	$\wedge$	111111	1

$$(5.2)$$

	F_0		F_1	Result
A	11	$\wedge$	11	0
	$\overline{\wedge}$		$\overline{\wedge}$	$\overline{\wedge}$
B	1	$\wedge$	1	1
	111	$\wedge$	111	1

	F_0		F_1	Result
A	111	$\wedge$	111	1
	$\overline{\wedge}$		$\overline{\wedge}$	$\overline{\wedge}$
B	111	$\wedge$	111	1
	111111	$\wedge$	111111	0

$$(5.3)$$

Since anything *NAND*ed with 0 results in 1, FRIBs uses 0 to maintain order. This is why the fragmentation is currently done with the *AND* function, so that if a server has a 0, it knows the bit value is *low*. Equations (5.4) and (5.5) give the same examples as in (5.2) and (5.3), but now maintains order. Equation (5.4) now gives the right frib value of 11011011 instead of 111111, which represents $11 \overline{\wedge} (11 \overline{\wedge} 11)$. But the left frib value of 110110011 has an extra 0, giving $(11 \overline{\wedge} 11) \overline{\wedge} 11$ as the order is different to the right side. The second example in (5.5) is more straightforward, as both sides are the same.

	F_0		F_1	Result
A	11	$\wedge$	1	1
	$\overline{\wedge}$		$\overline{\wedge}$	$\overline{\wedge}$
B	11	$\wedge$	1	1
	11011	$\wedge$	11	0

	F_0		F_1	Result
A	11011	$\wedge$	11	0
	$\overline{\wedge}$		$\overline{\wedge}$	$\overline{\wedge}$
B	11	$\wedge$	11011	0
	110110011	$\wedge$	11011011	1

$$(5.4)$$

	F_0		F_1	Result
A	11	$\wedge$	11	0
	$\overline{\wedge}$		$\overline{\wedge}$	$\overline{\wedge}$
B	1	$\wedge$	1	1
	1101	$\wedge$	1101	1

	F_0		F_1	Result
A	1101	$\wedge$	1101	1
	$\overline{\wedge}$		$\overline{\wedge}$	$\overline{\wedge}$
B	1101	$\wedge$	1101	1
	1101001101	$\wedge$	1101001101	0

$$(5.5)$$

5.4.2.3 Reduction

Concatenating states will affect the size of the result states, as they will get larger after each operation. Therefore at a predefined point, the states need to be reduced. Reducing the size of a frib requires information about all fribs. A separate server, known as the reduction server, is used where all N servers send their fribs to during the reduction step. Once the server has received each frib for a given value, it uses a lookup table to retrieve the reduced fribs for each server. However if each frib was sent to and returned from the reduction server in the current format, then some of the data can be decoded. The reduction servers have no knowledge of the program being run over the data, meaning any bits they can decode may still be worthless.

Since the reduction server is performing a simple lookup, we can obfuscate each frib state to a unique value. For example, each server can hash the frib with a server unique salt value, or use a random mapping. Now the reduction server cannot know the state of the fribs it has received, but protecting the reduced fribs is slightly more difficult. Instead of using a hash algorithm, we use public-key encryption on each reduced frib, such that only the single server can decrypt the frib. The lookup table is built offline and sent to the reduction server. Therefore the reduction server only receives a protected lookup table, and all the reduced fribs are already encrypted. Another security benefit given by this is that each public key for the individual servers and their reduced fragments can remain private. To further improve privacy, multiple reduction servers can be used where each one is used in a pseudo-random order.

With a maximum frib size of 32 bits, it produces $>30,000$ entries per server. Using just two servers creates a very large multi-key lookup table. Reducing the frib size to two sets of 16 bits for the lookup table gives <200 entries per server. This makes implementation more practical as the lookup table is now of a feasible size. With a maximum of <200 entries per server, each key only requires 8 bits, which can be increased by a few bits for better hashing. Splitting a frib into two 16-bit values must be done at the last operation. For example, 11011001101100011011001011 will become 110110011011 and 110110011011, allowing the same lookup table to be used to get two obfuscated values. Another lookup table can then get the encrypted values for each server using the two obfuscated values.

By using the same lookup table many times, we can increase the number of operations before the fribs need to be reduced, if the fribs have the available space to grow. Meaning that 110110011011 and 110110011011 can become four 16-bit values 110110011011, 110110011011, 110110011011 and 110110011011. Given that more servers lead to larger lookup tables, the size of the keys may need to reduce even further. Finding the balance between number of reductions and size of the fragments is important for performance.

5.4.3 Addition

The addition of two 32-bit integers can be achieved with 31 full-adders and a single half-adder. A full-adder comprised of *NAND* gates can be seen in Figure 5.3. To get the best performance for our proposed scheme, we must reduce the number of network

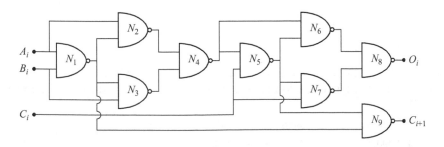

Figure 5.3 NAND gate full-adder

requests required by combining many reduction requests into a single request. First we compute all values for N_4, which for worst-case, where both A_i and B_i are 1, gives 10111001101. The frib therefore can grow up to 10 bits during this step. We can then combine all 32 fribs for N_4 into a single network payload and send them to be reduced to single bits.

How the carry bits are reduced can vary depending on implementation, however we will allow the fragments to grow as large as needed for this step. If a limitation is applied, more reduction requests will be needed. Because the first bit does not have an input carry value, N_9 input is N_1 and N_1 (equates to $!N_1$). The other carry bits involve gates N_1, N_4, N_5 and N_9, where the result from N_9 is connected to the next bits N_5 gate. Given that N_4 will be a single bit, and that the worse case value for N_1 is 11, each carry step will at most add 5 bits to the frib (11010). We only need a single 0 between each operation because we know the order is continuous. For example if the carry output for the second bit is 1101011011, we know the order of operations is $(110(10(110(11))))$.

This results in a worse-case frib size of 155 bits (16×10-bit values). We then send these carry-bit fribs to be reduced, meaning we now have single bit values for all N_4 and N_9 gates, allowing us to compute all N_8 gates with a maximum frib size of 10 bits again. This only totals three reduction requests.

5.4.4   Multiplication

Binary multiplication can be thought of as a series of *AND* operations, all added together. Equation (5.6) shows an example of multiplying 5 and 11 on an 8-bit machine. For each bit in 11, we *AND* it with each bit in 5, giving 8 values. Adding each value together gives 55.

$$
\begin{array}{r}
00000101 \\
\times\ 00001011 \\
\hline
00000101 \\
0000101 \\
000000 \\
00101 \\
0000 \\
000 \\
00 \\
+\ 0 \\
\hline
00110111
\end{array}
\tag{5.6}
$$

To make the additions more efficient, we add together the biggest and next biggest values, then the next pairing, down to the smallest and second smallest. This is shown in (5.7).

$$
\begin{array}{cccc}
00000101 & 0000 & 000000 & 00 \\
+\ 0000101 & +\ 000 & +\ 00101 & +\ 0 \\
\hline
00001111 & 0000 & 001010 & 00
\end{array}
\tag{5.7}
$$

We repeat this step in (5.8).

$$
\begin{array}{ll}
00001111 & 0000 \\
+001010 & +00 \\
\hline
00110111 & 0000
\end{array}
\qquad (5.8)
$$

And the final addition gives us the result in (5.9).

$$
\begin{array}{l}
00110111 \\
+0000 \\
\hline
00110111 \qquad \therefore\ = 00110111
\end{array}
\qquad (5.9)
$$

This gives a total of seven addition operations for this example. But by adding similar sized numbers together in parallel, we decrease the number of reduction steps required. For (5.7), each addition can combine the reduction requests into one, meaning the performance is close to that of a single addition. Therefore, the performance of this example will be slightly above three additions. For 32-bit values, there are a total of 31 additions, but it performs like ≈ 5 additions.

5.4.5 Conditional

Supporting an operation to compare two values can dramatically affect the security of a secure processing scheme. For example if a group of cipher values only encrypted the set $\{0, 1\}$, then the ability to calculate if two cipher values are equal will result in two subgroups of cipher values. Where one subgroup must contain either encrypt a 0 or 1, the other subgroup must encrypt the opposite. However because our proposed scheme has the bits fragmented across many servers, all the servers must compute over the same instruction set. This prevents a compromised server trying to compare all the fribs it has, as the other fragment servers would need to be doing the same malicious action. Therefore our scheme has the ability to support conditional operations, which can be implemented to return the result in either a secure or nonsecure manner.

5.4.5.1 Secure results

Returning results securely means the result is a fragmented bit, where <1 fragment server has knowledge of the result. This can make some programs difficult to implement as the result of the comparison is not known. Two examples are given in Algorithms 2 and 3, for an equal and greater than or equal *if* statement. For both examples, we have to increment c without knowing the result of the comparison.

5.4.5.2 Nonsecure results

Instead of returning a fragmented bit, this approach returns the whole bit by using a different lookup table than for a standard operation. This allows each server to know the result of the conditional statement, making programs easier to design and in some cases compute faster.

5.4.6 Proof-of-concept addition and multiplication

Because FRIBs relies heavily on reduction requests, the locations of the fragment and reduction servers affect performance. This is something that needs to be considered

---

Algorithm 2 If equals example

```
 1: if a = b then
 2:     c ← c + 1
 3:
 4: function IFEQUAL(a, b)
 5:     m ← a − b
 6:     inout ← 0
 7:     carry ← 0
 8:     for i ← 0 to 32 do
 9:         tmp ← m[i] + inout + carry
10:         inout ← tmp & 1
11:         carry ← tmp >> 1
12:     return !(inout | carry)
13: c ← c + (1 × ifEqual(a, b))
```

Algorithm 3 If greater than or equal example

```
 1: if a >= b then
 2:     c ← c + 1
 3:
 4: function IFGREATEREQUAL(a, b)
 5:     sign_neq ← a[31]^b[31]
 6:     c ← a − b
 7:     return (!sign_neq & !c[31]) | (sign_neq & !a[31])
 8: c ← c + (1 × ifGreaterEqual(a, b))
```

---

when choosing server locations, as the bandwidth between data centres varies. The cloud service providers used for our experiment/evaluation were Amazon Web Services, Microsoft Azure and Google Cloud Platform. All instances were running with the cheapest tier option and based in the United States.

The server configuration was a single reduction server and two fragment servers. The reduction server was in California with Amazon, a fragment server was also in California but with Microsoft and the final fragment server was in Iowa hosted by Google. We used a proof-of-concept addition algorithm with a 27-bit maximum fragment size which required 9 reductions, and averaged the time for 100 addition operations with 32-bit unsigned integers. The latency at the time of testing was 3.106 ms for Azure–Amazon, and 37.414 ms for Google–Amazon.

Our results produced an average of 346 ms for each addition operation. This is directly proportional to the largest latency time, where $37.414 \times 9 \approx 346 -$ (some small computation times). Therefore if all the fragment servers could be within 10 ms round trip from the reduction server, then addition times could be 99.274 ms.

The latency figures of Azure to Amazon could result in 37.228 ms. Allowing for a larger fragment size would also increase the performance. For example, if only five reductions are required for an addition, then we can nearly half the completion time. Currently, multiplication is reliant on addition, and in Section 5.4.4 we showed that for 32-bit integers, five addition steps are required. Therefore, we can look at the addition results to solve for the multiplication results. These performance numbers are much faster than FHE schemes described in Section 5.2.1 and show the potential of distributing encoded data.

5.5 Security analysis

Given our threat model in Section 5.1, there are two main attack vectors we need to evaluate against: decoding the data with one set of the distributed data and getting all the data from each system.

5.5.1 One set of the distributed data

Successful attacks on traditional cryptography can often decrypt all the data [52, 53], but with distributed encoding each bit fragment or bin must be tried for each possibility. For example, we have two fragment servers and the bit fragments (b_{0-7}) for a byte known to be an ASCII value in the range of 32–122. Because we only know $\approx 1/4$ of the bits, there are a number of possibilities for the value. If we know b_1 and b_3 to be zero, then we have 24 possibilities, of which 14 are letters. If we increase the number of fragment servers to four, then we might know only 1 bit. Setting only b_3 or b_1 to zero gives 48 or 46 possibilities, respectively. Once we have hundreds of ASCII fragments, forming sentences and paragraphs, the number of possibilities are massive ($14^{100} \approx 4.1 \times 10^{114}$). Therefore, privacy is preserved by the large amount of computation time to generate and test all possibilities. Note, if an attacker manages to break into more systems, then the number of possibilities will decrease as more bits are known.

Bin Encoding is different as each distributed index has a small number of bins. A malicious user knows that a character cannot exist in different bins; therefore, bin patterns can be exploited. Given an encoded query of length 5, it is reasonable to assume that it is a single word. Table 5.6 shows four possible queries, giving the number of collisions for each word encoded with three bins. The words are encoded into bins, where the mapping is the ASCII value modulo 3. We then encoded all five-letter words from the dictionary [54] using the bin mapping, and test if they match the encoded query value, giving the *Same Mapping* column in Table 5.6. The *Other Mappings* column of Table 5.6 gives the collisions when the bin mapping is not known. Note this is for a distributed index, so the same mapping collisions will be much lower when the distributed results are combined.

Having a query length of 10 as shown in Table 5.7 gives similar results to Table 5.6; however, the amount of possibilities drops quite significantly. This is because with the longer query, the probability of a letter from a word encoding to

Table 5.6   Five-letter word queries

Word	Same mapping	Other mappings	% Match in dictionary
hello	16	5,374	77.94%
world	80	5,407	79.34%
paper	20	4,963	72.05%
zoned	106	5,348	78.86%

Table 5.7   Ten-letter word queries

Word	Same mapping	Other mappings	% Match in dictionary
blacksmith	1	1,994	16.79%
underwater	2	2,861	24.10%
helloworld	0	2,629	22.13%
purringcat	0	2,156	18.15%

Table 5.8   English letter frequencies [48]

A	B	C	D	E	F	G	H	I	J	K	L	M
7.61	1.54	3.11	3.95	12.62	2.34	1.95	1.95	7.34	0.15	0.65	4.11	2.54
N	**O**	**P**	**Q**	**R**	**S**	**T**	**U**	**V**	**W**	**X**	**Y**	**Z**
7.11	7.65	2.03	0.10	6.15	6.50	9.33	2.72	0.99	1.89	0.19	1.72	0.09

different values increases. Looking at the bottom two entries in Table 5.7, *helloworld* and *purringcat*, these are actually *hello world* and *purring cat,* respectively. Therefore given an encoded string of two five-letter words, there are still words of length 10 which give a potential match.

Analysing the frequency of a bin occurring gives an estimation of the letters mapped to it. For example, given the letter frequencies in Table 5.8 [48], if a bin occurs at relatively small frequency, then it is more likely to contain letters that also have a smaller frequency. This also gives a reduction in bin combinations for an malicious user to try, because certain combinations do not fall within the estimated frequencies calculated. Figure 5.4 shows the difference between the estimated frequency obtained from counting bins in the index and the actual frequency of the letters in each bin. These results show that with enough encoded documents indexed, it is possible to predict within ±2.5% of the actual letter frequency. They also show that a smaller number of bins for the index is harder to estimate. Figure 5.5 shows the distribution of 100 million unique random bins for a 3-bin configuration, giving a total of 300 million bins, each containing 8–9 letters. The average summed frequency for a bin is around 33.3%, even though the English letter frequencies vary. Therefore when generating the bin mapping, we can check if the bin frequencies are within the majority of all possible

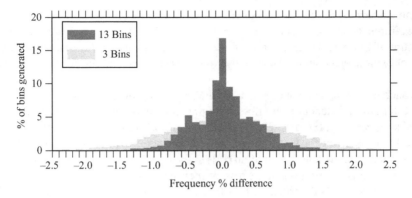

Figure 5.4   Difference in calculated and actual bin frequencies

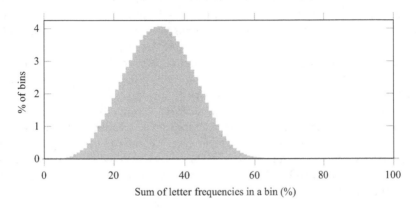

Figure 5.5   Letter frequencies in 300 million randomly generated bins

bins combinations. For example, using three bins the scheme might only accept bins with frequencies between 20% and 46%. This means that even if a malicious user knows the frequency of each bin to ±2.5%, it still gives over 20% of all possible bin combinations. Note this experiment contained only bins of even size (8–9 letters), where an implementation having a variation in the number of letters per bin would have more possible bin combinations.

Given a Bin Encoded index, it is currently possible to rebuild the encoded version of the document. However because there are no spaces, breaking the index with a dictionary attack becomes harder than breaking the individual queries. Because FRIBs does not expose character patterns, it is harder again, showing how computationally difficult distributed encoding is to break with only one set of the data.

5.5.2   Breaking into all systems

Any service implementing our schemes is ultimately responsible for the security of their own environment. Software patching, access polices, and firewall management to name a few examples. However some exploits are out of a cloud services control, for example, a zero-day vulnerability in their operating system. To reduce this risk, a mixture of Linux and Microsoft servers can be used, such that any one vulnerability cannot exploit every server. When a user/business is choosing the service providers, they should also seek information regarding security measures in place. A common approach is looking at a list of standards the service is compliant with.

International standards are now emerging for organisations using or providing cloud services, with ISO/IEC 27018:2014 (with ISO/IEC 27002 as one of its normative references) being the first International code of practice that focuses on protection of Personally Identifiable Information (PII) in the cloud. This increases the security of their service, while providing more trust to their users. The cryptography recommendations/requirements described in ISO/IEC 27018:2014 are the objectives specified in clause 10 of ISO/IEC 27002. Examples are provided for use of cryptography in the cloud, but at a minimum a cloud should implement controls for confidentiality (data encrypted when stored or transmitted) and authentication. However there is no mention of true secure processing like homomorphic encryption. To try and protect data being processed, access controls are recommended. This makes it more difficult for rogue employees or outside attackers to gain access to data in-flight. Therefore by conforming with ISO/IEC 27018:2014 will reduce the chance of a breach, and applying our scheme will enhance the security already provided.

End users also have control over their security, as the more distributed servers used, the smaller the risk of their data being compromised. Ten servers will give more security over five, but the running costs increase. Therefore evaluating against this attack vector is implementation dependent. Bin Encoding and FRIBs can protect data from rogue employees and malicious users who break into a few systems, but the cloud service providers need to try protect the data they store as well.

5.6   Little computational and network overhead

With the growth of the Internet of Things (IoTs) and mobile devices, a low powered device needs to be able to support encrypting/protecting data. For example an iPhone 5 has an A6 chip containing a 1.3 GHz dual-core processor, and an average Word document is estimated to be around 250 kBs [55]. Using Bin Encoding, even if it takes 20 clock cycles to process one character, the device would still be able to encode multiple documents per second. Also depending on the application, it is possible to do the encoding in the real time, as the document is being edited. FRIBs requires more clock cycles as it needs to choose a random fragmentation for each bit, however can still encode multiple average-sized Word documents per second. Therefore both Bin Encoding and FRIBs add little processing overhead to the client. This is because encoding requires little computation, where traditional encryption requires more complex computation by processing numbers which are larger than the processors data-path width. Sample results are given in Figure 5.6 [16] for encrypting a single vote (32-bit integer value) and generating a zero-knowledge proof.

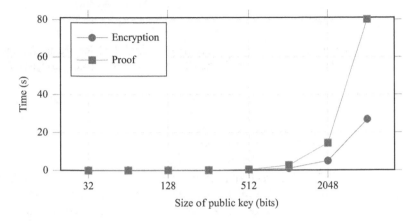

Figure 5.6   Mobile voting performance on an iPhone 5 [16].

Networking overhead is just as important because mobile data can be expensive, and the networking interface on a mobile device is one of the major consumers of power [56]. Bin Encoding can be seen as a lossy compression scheme, which will add less than half of the original file. Therefore in the worst case 50% more data needs to be transferred, but the average case will require less than 35%. The amount of data FRIBs add is directly proportional to the number of fragment servers. For example with five fragment servers, each bit gets fragmented into 5 fribs. Compression can be applied to each set of fribs, however in comparison with other homomorphic encryption schemes, a factor of 5 is good as most schemes encrypt a bit into a value within a large modulus.

5.7   Concluding remarks

With the simplicity offering superior performance and additional features, distributed encoding for secure processing offers an exciting alternative to homomorphic encryption and traditional MPC with garbled circuits. Distribution allows Bin Encoding to remove false positives in string searching without compromising security, and FRIBs the ability to protect and process data. Future work aims to further improve the strength of both schemes and provide more analysis on their security. Combining the schemes is also an option for more advanced searching and returning accurate results quickly. Bin Encoding can narrow the number of potential matches, before FRIBs performs an accurate search.

These schemes provide secure functionality in a fraction of the time compared to the holy grail of cryptography (i.e. FHE), reducing processing time from hours to seconds. By allowing for varying performance and security, users can now take control of their data in the cloud.

Acknowledgements

This research is supported by STRATUS (Security Technologies Returning Accountability, Trust and User-Centric Services in the Cloud) (https://stratus.org.nz), a science investment project funded by the New Zealand Ministry of Business, Innovation and Employment (MBIE).

References

[1]   Fox-Brewster T. Yahoo: Hackers Stole Data On Another Billion Accounts; 2016.   Online.   http://www.forbes.com/sites/thomasbrewster/2016/12/14/yahoo-admits-another-billion-user-accounts-were-leaked-in-2013 (Accessed 18/01/17).

[2]   Chen A. GCreep: Google Engineer Stalked Teens, Spied on Chats; 2010.   Online.   http://gawker.com/5637234/gcreep-google-engineer-stalked-teens-spied-on-chats (Accessed 16/01/17).

[3]   Theoharidou M, Kokolakis S, Karyda M, Kiountouzis E. The insider threat to information systems and the effectiveness of ISO17799. *Computers & Security* 2005;24(6):472–484.

[4]   Giandomenico N, de Groot J. Insider vs. Outsider Data Security Threats: What's the Greater Risk? 2017. Online. https://digitalguardian.com/blog/insider-outsider-data-security-threats (Accessed 10/03/17).

[5]   Kaspersky Lab and B2B International. Global IT Security Risks Survey; 2015.   Online.   https://media.kaspersky.com/en/business-security/it-security-risks-survey-2015.pdf (Accessed 16/6/17).

[6]   Will MA, Ko RK, Witten IH. Bin Encoding: A user-centric secure full-tet searching scheme for the cloud. In: *Trustcom/BigDataSE/ISPA, 2015 IEEE*. vol. 1. Helsinki, Finland, IEEE; 2015, pp. 563–570.

[7]   Will MA, Ko RK, Witten IH. Privacy preserving computation by fragmenting individual bits and distributing gates. In: *Trustcom/BigDataSE/ISPA, 2016 IEEE*. vol. 1. Tianjin, China, IEEE; 2016, pp. 900–908.

[8]   Amazon Web Services, Inc. Online. https://aws.amazon.com (Accessed 07/04/16).

[9]   Microsoft Azure. Online. https://azure.microsoft.com (Accessed 07/04/16).

[10]   Swain M. *Needlework of Mary Queen of Scots*. Crowood; 2013.

[11]   Kerckhoffs A. *La cryptographie militaire*. Librairie militaire de L. Baudoin; 1883.

[12]   Rivest RL, Shamir A, Adleman L. A method for obtaining digital signatures and public-key cryptosystems. *Communications of the ACM* 1978;21: 120–126.

[13]   Hirt M, Sako K. Efficient receipt-free voting based on homomorphic encryption. In: *Advances in Cryptology – EUROCRYPT 2000*. Bruges, Belgium: Springer; 2000, pp. 539–556.

[14]   Popa RA, Redfield C, Zeldovich N, Balakrishnan H. CryptDB: Protecting confidentiality with encrypted query processing. In: *Proceedings of the*

Twenty-Third ACM Symposium on Operating Systems Principles. Cascais, Portugal: ACM; 2011, pp. 85–100.

[15] Boneh D, Gentry C, Halevi S, Wang F, Wu DJ. Private database queries using somewhat homomorphic encryption. In: *Applied Cryptography and Network Security.* Banff, AB, Canada: Springer; 2013, pp. 102–118.

[16] Will MA, Nicholson B, Tiehuis M, Ko RK. Secure voting in the cloud using homomorphic encryption and mobile agents. In: *2015 International Conference on Cloud Computing Research and Innovation (ICCCRI).* Singapore: IEEE; 2015, pp. 173–184.

[17] Boneh D, Di Crescenzo G, Ostrovsky R, Persiano G. Public key encryption with keyword search. In: *Advances in Cryptology – Eurocrypt 2004.* Interlaken, Switzerland: Springer; 2004, pp. 506–522.

[18] Hwang YH, Lee PJ. Public key encryption with conjunctive keyword search and its extension to a multi-user system. In: *Pairing-Based Cryptography – Pairing 2007.* Tokya, Japan: Springer; 2007, pp. 2–22.

[19] Baek J, Safavi-Naini R, Susilo W. Public key encryption with keyword search revisited. In: *Computational Science and Its Applications – ICCSA 2008.* Perugia, Italy: Springer; 2008, pp. 1249–1259.

[20] Li J, Wang Q, Wang C, Cao N, Ren K, Lou W. Fuzzy keyword search over encrypted data in cloud computing. In: *Proceedings of the 29th Conference on Information Communications.* San Diego, CA, USA: IEEE Press; 2010, pp. 441–445.

[21] Wang C, Cao N, Li J, Ren K, Lou W. Secure ranked keyword search over encrypted cloud data. In: *Distributed Computing Systems (ICDCS), 2010 IEEE 30th International Conference on.* Genoa, Italy: IEEE; 2010, pp. 253–262.

[22] Li M, Yu S, Cao N, Lou W. Authorized private keyword search over encrypted data in cloud computing. In: *Distributed Computing Systems (ICDCS), 2011 31st International Conference on.* Minneapolis, MN, USA: IEEE; 2011, pp. 383–392.

[23] Wang J, Ma H, Tang Q et al. Efficient verifiable fuzzy keyword search over encrypted data in cloud computing. *Computer Science and Information Systems* 2013;10(2):667–684.

[24] Gentry C. Fully homomorphic encryption using ideal lattices. In: *Proc. STOC.* vol. 9; Bethesda, MD, USA; 2009, pp. 169–178.

[25] Wang W, Hu Y, Chen L, Huang X, Sunar B. Exploring the feasibility of fully homomorphic encryption. *Computers, IEEE Transactions on* 2015;64(3): 698–706.

[26] Gentry C, Halevi S. Implementing Gentry's fully-homomorphic encryption scheme. In: *Advances in Cryptology – EUROCRYPT 2011.* Tallinn, Estonia: Springer; 2011, pp. 129–148.

[27] Cao X, Moore C, O'Neill M, Hanley N, O'Sullivan E. High-speed fully homomorphic encryption over the integers. In: *Financial Cryptography and Data Security.* Christ Church, Barbados: Springer; 2014, pp. 169–180.

[28] Hirvensalo M. *Quantum Computing.* Springer; 2001.

[29]   Barz S, Kashefi E, Broadbent A, Fitzsimons JF, Zeilinger A, Walther P. Demonstration of blind quantum computing. *Science* 2012;335(6066):303–308.

[30]   Diffie W, Hellman ME. New directions in cryptography. *Information Theory, IEEE Transactions on* 1976;22(6):644–654.

[31]   Hankerson D, Menezes AJ, Vanstone S. *Guide to Elliptic Curve Cryptography.* Springer Science & Business Media; 2006.

[32]   Greenberg A, Hamilton J, Maltz DA, Patel P. The cost of a cloud: Research problems in data center networks. *ACM SIGCOMM Computer Communication Review* 2008;39(1):68–73.

[33]   Xu G, Pang J, Fu X. A load balancing model based on cloud partitioning for the public cloud. *Tsinghua Science and Technology* 2013;18(1):34–39.

[34]   Ganapathy V, Thomas D, Feder T, Garcia-Molina H, Motwani R. Distributing data for secure database services. In: *Proceedings of the 4th International Workshop on Privacy and Anonymity in the Information Society.* Uppsala, Sweden: ACM; 2011, p. 8.

[35]   Yao ACC. How to generate and exchange secrets. In: *Foundations of Computer Science, 1986., 27th Annual Symposium on.* IEEE; 1986, pp. 162–167.

[36]   Clifton C, Kantarcioglu M, Vaidya J, Lin X, Zhu MY. Tools for privacy preserving distributed data mining. *ACM Sigkdd Explorations Newsletter* 2002;4(2):28–34.

[37]   Lindell Y, Pinkas B. Secure multiparty computation for privacy-preserving data mining. *Journal of Privacy and Confidentiality* 2009;1(1):5.

[38]   Gennaro R, Gentry C, Parno B. Non-interactive verifiable computing: Outsourcing computation to untrusted workers. In: *Annual Cryptology Conference.* Santa Barbara, CA, USA: Springer; 2010, pp. 465–482.

[39]   Schoenmakers B, Veeningen M, de Vreede N. Trinocchio: Privacy-preserving outsourcing by distributed verifiable computation. In: *International Conference on Applied Cryptography and Network Security.* Guildford, UK: Springer; 2016, pp. 346–366.

[40]   Cramer R, Damgård I, Nielsen JB. Multiparty computation from threshold homomorphic encryption. In: *Advances in Cryptology—EUROCRYPT 2001: International Conference on the Theory and Application of Cryptographic Techniques Innsbruck, Austria, May 6–10, 2001 Proceedings.* Berlin, Heidelberg: Springer; 2001, pp. 280–300.

[41]   Adida B. Helios: Web-based open-audit voting. In: *USENIX Security Symposium.* vol. 17; San Jose, CA, USA; 2008, pp. 335–348.

[42]   Suh GE, O'Donnell CW, Devadas S. AEGIS: A Single-Chip Secure Processor. Information Security Technical Report. 2005;10(2):63–73.

[43]   Yang B, Wu K, Karri R. Scan based side channel attack on dedicated hardware implementations of data encryption standard. In: *International Test Conference, 2004. Proceedings. ITC 2004.* Charlotte, NC, USA: IEEE; 2004, pp. 339–344.

[44]   Köpf B, Basin D. An information-theoretic model for adaptive side-channel attacks. In: *Proceedings of the 14th ACM conference on Computer and Communications Security.* Alexandria, VA, USA: ACM; 2007, pp. 286–296.

[45]   Kocher P, Jaffe J, Jun B. Differential power analysis. In: *Advances in Cryptology – CRYPTO'99*. Santa Barbara, California, USA: Springer; 1999, pp. 388–397.

[46]   Gandolfi K, Mourtel C, Olivier F. Electromagnetic analysis: Concrete results. In: *Cryptographic Hardware and Embedded Systems – CHES 2001*. Paris, France: Springer; 2001, pp. 251–261.

[47]   Ko RK. Cloud computing in plain English. *ACM Crossroads* 2010;16(3):5–6.

[48]   Solso RL, King JF. Frequency and versatility of letters in the English language. *Behavior Research Methods & Instrumentation* 1976;8(3):283–286.

[49]   Board IA. Ethics and the Internet; 1989. Online. https://www.ietf.org/rfc/rfc1087.txt (Accessed 04/12/14).

[50]   Python NGram 3.3 Documentation. Online. https://pythonhosted.org/ngram/ (Accessed 04/02/15).

[51]   Streetman BG, Banerjee S. *Solid State Electronic Devices*, vol. 5. Prentice Hall, New Jersey; 2000. Online. http://trove.nla.gov.au/work/8960772?selectedversion=NBD22063993.

[52]   Boneh D. Twenty years of attacks on the RSA cryptosystem. *Notices of the AMS* 1999;46(2):203–213.

[53]   Zhang Y, Juels A, Reiter MK, Ristenpart T. Cross-VM side channels and their use to extract private keys. In: *Proceedings of the 2012 ACM Conference on Computer and Communications Security*. Raleigh, NC, USA: ACM; 2012, pp. 305–316.

[54]   109582 English words; 1991. Online. http://www-01.sil.org/linguistics/wordlists/english/wordlist/wordsEn.txt (Accessed 04/12/14).

[55]   FAST Search Server 2010 for SharePoint;. Online. http://technet.microsoft.com/en-us/library/gg604780.aspx (Accessed 07/01/15).

[56]   Pering T, Agarwal Y, Gupta R, Want R. Coolspots: Reducing the power consumption of wireless mobile devices with multiple radio interfaces. In: *Proceedings of the 4th International Conference on Mobile Systems, Applications and Services*. Uppsala, Sweden: ACM; 2006, pp. 220–232.

Chapter 6
Data protection and mobility management for cloud

Dat Dang[1], Doan Hoang[1], and Priyadarsi Nanda[1]

Abstract

Cloud computing has become an alternative IT infrastructure where users, infrastructure providers, and service providers all share and deploy resources for their business processes and applications. In order to deliver cloud services cost effectively, users' data is stored in a cloud where applications are able to perform requests from clients efficiently. As data is transferred to the cloud, data owners are concerned about the loss of control of their data and cloud service providers (CSPs) are concerned about their ability to protect data when it is moved about both within and out of its own environment. Many security and protection mechanisms have been proposed to protect cloud data by employing various policies, encryption techniques, and monitoring and auditing approaches. However, data is still exposed to potential disclosures and attacks if it is moved and located at another cloud where there is no equivalent security measure at visited sites.

In a realistic cloud scenario with hierarchical service chain, the handling of data in a cloud can be delegated by a CSP to a subprovider or another. However, CSPs do not often deploy the same protection schemes. Movement of user's data is an important issue in cloud, and it has to be addressed to ensure the data is protected in an integrated manner regardless of its location in the environment. The user is concerned whether its data is located in locations covered by the service level agreement, and data operations are protected from unauthorized users. When user's data is moved to data centers located at locations different from its home, it is necessary to keep track of its locations and data operations. This chapter discusses data protection and mobility management issues in cloud environment and in particular the implementation of a trust-oriented data protection framework.

Keyword

Data mobility, data protection, cloud mobility, data location

[1]University of Technology Sydney, School of Computing and Communications, Australia

6.1   Introduction

Cloud computing has been introduced as a new computing paradigm deployed in many application areas ranging from entertainment to business. It offers an effective solution for provisioning services on demand over the Internet by virtue of its capability of pooling and virtualizing computing resources dynamically. Clients can leverage cloud to store their documents online, share their information, consume, or operate their services with simple usage, fast access, and low cost on a remote server rather than physically local resources [1]. In order to deploy cloud services cost effectively, users' data is stored in a cloud where applications are able to perform requests from clients efficiently. As data is transferred to the cloud, data owners are concerned about the loss of control of their data, and cloud service providers (CSPs) are concerned about their ability to protect data effectively when it is moved about both within and out of its own environment. CSPs have provided security mechanisms to deal with data protection issues by employing various policy and encryption approaches; however, data is still exposed to potential disclosures and attacks if it is moved and located at another cloud where there is no equivalent security measure at visited sites [2]. Consequently, data mobility issues have to be addressed in any data security models for cloud.

In a realistic cloud scenario with hierarchical service chains, handling of data in a cloud can be delegated by a provider to a subprovider to another. However, CSPs do not often deploy the same protection schemes [2]. Movement of user's data is an important issue in cloud and it has to be addressed to ensure the data is protected in an integrated manner regardless of its location in the environment. When user's data is moved to data centers located at locations different from its home, it is necessary to keep track of its locations. This requirement should be taken care of by a user-provider service level agreement (SLA). The reporting service can be achieved through an agreement that enables a monitoring service from the original cloud. When a violation against the established SLA occurs, the monitoring component will be able to detect it through the corresponding CSP and trigger protection services on the original cloud, which can immediately analyze and audit the data. Moreover, data locations need to be maintained at the original cloud and encoded within the data itself, in case it loses the connection with its monitoring service. Under such circumstances, the location data can be used subsequently to trace previous locations and data operations or trigger original mobility services (MSs) if data is moved back to its original cloud. For the users, they are concerned whether their data is located in locations covered by the SLA, and data operations are protected from unauthorized users. Mechanisms should be available to report information concerning the data, such as the data location, data operation, or violation, to their owner if and when necessary.

Protecting data in the outsourced cloud requires more than just encryption [3] which merely provides data confidentiality, antitampering, and antidisclosure. The key to mitigate users' concern and promote a broader adoption of cloud computing is the establishment of a trustworthy relationship between CSPs and users. For users to trust the CSPs, users' data firstly should be protected with confidentiality maintained, and no one should be able to disclose data-sensitive information except the authorized users. Second, any actions or behaviors on the data should be enforced and recorded as the attestation to avoid false accusation to data violation. Once the breach against the SLAs subscribed between CSPs and users occurs, the attestation can be used as a proof that the CSPs violate the agreed-upon service level and, consequently, appropriate compensation may be offered to the users. Finally, the data should be able to preserve itself independently in a heterogeneous cloud environment with diverse protection frameworks.

This chapter discusses the above concerns from a novel perspective, offering a data mobility management (DMM) model with enhanced transparency and security. In this model, an active data framework that includes a location data structure and a location registration database (LRD) to deal with mobility; protocols between clouds for data movement are examined; procedures for establishing a clone supervisor at a visited cloud for monitoring purposes are investigated; and a MS to handle requests for moving the data among clouds is deployed. The data mobility model focuses on two aspects: DMM and active protection. The DMM deals with physical location changes of user's data in various cloud environments and ensures these locations be registered with the LRD and recorded within the data structure itself. The destination of a move operation is also verified to ensure that the new physical location is within the preestablished SLA. The active protection aspect deals with extending data protection when the data is moved to various locations. The active data unit [referred to as an active data cube (ADCu)] with a new location-recordable structure allows the data itself to keep record of data operations, their request parameters, and locations. Furthermore, the LRD is also used to store changes of data location and other information allowing data owners to track their data if necessary. The protocols are designed to deal with data movement from one cloud to another. The process of moving data involves a verification process and a MS at the original cloud. A clone supervisor is established at the visited cloud with the same capability as the original supervisor for monitoring operations on the data. The MS queries LRD to register the location of the data when it is first generated and update its location when it is moved to a new location. The chapter presents a comprehensive analysis of data mobility scenarios in various cloud environments. It presents the design and the implementation of the proposed DMM model as well as the evaluation of the implemented model.

The rest of the chapter is organized as follows. Section 6.2 discusses data mobility scenarios, components, and a framework for mobility in cloud. Section 6.3 reviews security mechanisms for data-in-transit. Section 6.4 presents the design, implementation, and evaluation of a trust-oriented data protection and mobility management model. The conclusion is in the Section 6.5.

6.2 Data mobility

Even with the trusted-oriented data protection framework [4], the data is still exposed to potential violations when it is moved to new cloud hosts where there are no equivalent security measures to protect it. Data mobility is still a challenge for exchanging

Table 6.1   Terms and description of components in the data mobility model

Terms	Descriptions
Original cloud	Providing cloud resources and verification procedure
Old cloud	An original cloud or a visited cloud offering cloud resources
New cloud	Creating a request to move the data with appropriate parameters
Visited cloud	A new cloud or an old cloud which stores, forwards data verification requests for permissions
Supervisor	Protecting its associated data, data locations, and the communication among clouds

information among CSPs because of the lack of models to ensure data protection and data auditing.

Clearly, mobility management is one of the most important challenges in mobile IP [5]. When a mobile is roaming away from its home network, it registers its current location to its home agent on home network. Similarly, when a data unit moves from its original cloud, similar mechanisms should be provided for the data to inform its original cloud its current locations and/or the data owner its status if necessary. The data itself, however, cannot execute these actions. For cloud data mobility, we leverage the ideas from mobile network about location register for a mobile by using a LRD located at original cloud for updating or retrieving data locations, and a recordable data structure for recording cloud host location in the data itself when there is a data request operation. Moving data to a new cloud environment, however, has to involve both the data and its supervisor (in cellular networks only the mobile phone is involved). In this model, a clone supervisor is established for monitoring the moved data and data operations. A verification procedure will process data requests at the original cloud for access permissions; however, the mobility management model may also delegate the verification and access control to the visited cloud. With the deployment of the supervisor, data protection can be achieved despite the fact that data is located at visited cloud side.

6.2.1   Components of a data mobility model

We define functions of parties involved in the mobility management model in Table 6.1:

- *Data verification:* The supervisor monitors data operations either at the original cloud or at the visited cloud. Data only accepts instructions from its supervisor. For monitoring function, the supervisor focuses mainly on detecting user's operations at the operating system level such as move, copy, and delete. When the supervisor detects such a request, it would activate the Triggerable Data File Structure (TDFS) through instructions to execute the runtime environment analysis and inspect the validity of data operations. In the proposed active data model, data operations will be verified at the shell which wraps the data in an executable status.

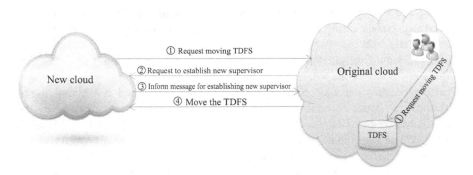

Figure 6.1   General establishing supervisor procedure

- *Data location management:* The supervisor also reports timely data locations to the original cloud as well as updating the LRD as data itself cannot send location information to original cloud, but it is able to record current location for tracing operations. It analyzes networking location in order to obtain the current network address and send back to original cloud, which is set as default source address in the report message.

6.2.2   Data mobility scenarios

It is assumed that the new cloud and the original cloud agree to establish a new supervisor at the new site. As the verification is processed at the original side, the new clone supervisor is used for dealing with data-moving cases among clouds. In this chapter, a TDFS [6] is used as data objects move among clouds. The structure is used to embed raw user's data before storing in the cloud. Details of the TDFS and the trust-oriented data protection Framework will be presented in Section 6.4. Data mobility in a cloud environment involves several cases.

In the first case, data is moved from an original cloud to a new cloud (the request may be originated from the original cloud or from the new cloud). In both scenarios, a general procedure (Figure 6.1) has to be executed between the two clouds before moving the data. The procedure is as follows:

After analyzing the request, the original cloud sends a request to the new cloud for establishing a new supervisor at the new cloud. This request is then verified by the visited cloud for the permission to install a new service. At this time, the new cloud also verifies the request to evaluate wherever it can or cannot create the service. If there is an agreement between two clouds to create the new supervisor, a confirmed message will be sent from the new cloud to the original cloud.

Following the first step, information pertaining to the supervisor and the TDFS including the type of services, the template of the supervisor, and the original location will be sent to the new cloud for creating a new instance of the supervisor.

After the supervisor is created, the TDFS will be moved to new cloud.

The new supervisor will be responsible for monitoring the TDFS at the new cloud as well as communicating with the original cloud as the new cloud does not provide the same data protection services.

If the request originated from an entity in the original cloud, the destination address of the new cloud where data is moved to has to be provided with the request. When the destination address is identified, the original cloud can communicate with the new cloud. In both scenarios, security procedures are performed by the access control component, the Cloud-based Privacy-aware Role Based Access Control (CPRBAC), and the auditing component, the Active Auditing Control (AAC) together with the associated supervisor. Having satisfied with the conditions for moving the requested data, the original cloud sends a request in order to establish the clone supervisor at the new cloud. By doing this, the link between the supervisor and its data is still kept when data is stored at another location. Details of the procedure (Figure 6.2) are as follows:

The service request from the new cloud or from within the original cloud is sent to the original cloud. This request is authorized by the access control and the auditing control components of the original cloud. If it is a valid request having correct required parameters, the supervisor is triggered to analyze data operations. As it is a "move" request, the supervisor has to communicate with mobility component for establishing a clone supervisor at the new cloud. Invalid requests against predefined policies will be triggered by the data protection unit (APDu) and captured by the auditing component. Violation triggers in the auditing may also be triggered to assist the security administrator to execute some certain security prevention operations.

The mobility component at the original cloud sends a request to the visited cloud for the permission to install a new service. The new cloud also verifies and evaluates the request to see if it can create the service. If an agreement is in place to create a new supervisor between two clouds, a confirmed message will be sent from the new cloud to the original cloud. At this step, necessary information for creating the clone supervisor will be supplied to the new cloud. Once the new supervisor is created, the mobility component invokes instructions to move the data. Hence, the new location of TDFS is also updated at LRD.

In the second case, data at an old cloud is moved to a new cloud and original cloud will process request verifications. The procedure is similar but the verification request needs to be forwarded from the old cloud to the original cloud for authorization. After analyzing the request, the original cloud sends a request to the new cloud for establishing a new supervisor at the new cloud. Once, the new service is established, the original cloud will inform the old cloud to move TDFS. Otherwise, original cloud will invoke a message for old cloud to terminate the request. Figure 6.3 depicts procedures of the second data-moving case.

In the third case, data at an old cloud is moved back to the original cloud; and in the last case, data at a cloud is moved to local storage (offline) with or without permissions. Therefore, the procedure for establishing supervisor is not performed at this stage, but the moving request has to be authorized at original cloud in order to approve for the permission.

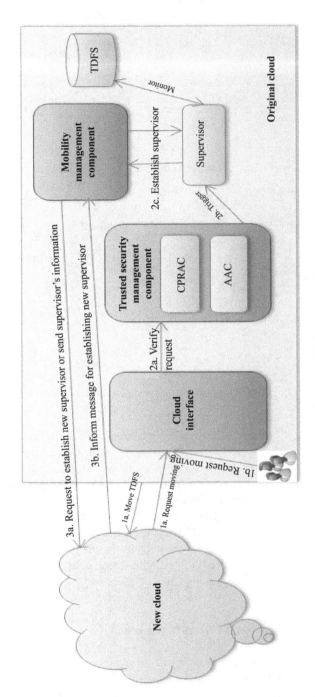

Figure 6.2   Details of establishing supervisor procedure

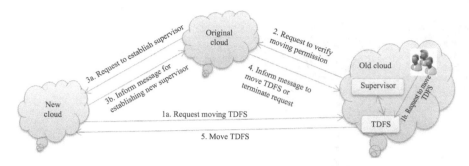

Figure 6.3   General procedure in establishing supervisor from old cloud to new cloud

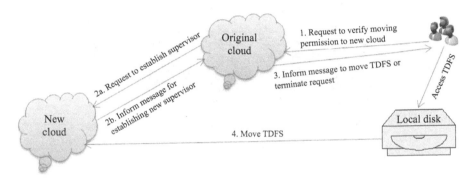

Figure 6.4   Details of processing moving request from old cloud to original cloud

For the last case, the regular verification procedure is still executed at the original to obtain the move permission. However, an exception will be raised when the original cloud detects a data move without a request or it cannot communicate with destination address provided in the request to establish supervisor. In this case, the current supervisor has to report the current TDFS location to the original cloud for updating the LRD as well as triggering the data to update this address in its core component before moving. From this point, the TDFS has to record data access locations in its location list whenever users access the data even in the offline mode. The moving operation occurs when TDFS is stored at the original cloud or at visited cloud. Figure 6.4 depicts procedures of the last moving case.

6.3   Security mechanisms for data-in-transit

Researchers have proposed various mechanisms to enhance data mobility and protect sensitive data in distributed cloud environments, which includes geographic location-based mechanisms, data-mobility-based policy and encryption mechanisms, binding user and data location, protecting cloud data using trusted third-party technologies, and data mobility based on location register database. In this section, we will present a review of these solutions for data mobility and data protection.

6.3.1 Geographic location-based mechanisms

The geographic location of data in cloud has raised user's concern about the confidentiality and privacy as the host cloud often stores user's data at some cloud storage, which may be owned by another cloud. Albeshri *et al.* [7] proposed a new approach, GeoProof as a protocol, for geographic location assurance via a proof of storage protocol and a distance-bounding protocol. It allows data owners verifying cloud locations where data is stored without relying on the word of the cloud provider. Benson *et al.* [8] introduced a theoretical framework for verifying the proofs of retrievability and on provable data possession and data geolocation. Cloud users can verify that a cloud storage provider replicates the data in diverse geolocation. Peterson *et al.* [9] introduced a new technique for sovereignty with a data possession protocol that binds network geolocation query responses with proof of data possession using a MAC-based PDP (MAC-PDP) as the interrogated server. Ries *et al.* [10] focused on verifying geographic data location in a cloud environment, detecting node movements and proving data possession for data moving among CSPs. These efforts mainly relied on the assumption of linear relationship about network latency and distance among clouds. However, in realistic network environments, this relationship is not valid. Furthermore, verifying the integrity and confidentiality of the data relies on third parties to retrieve the information from the origin of the data, and this raises an additional source of concern.

6.3.2 Data-mobility-based policy and encryption mechanisms

In policy-based approaches, cloud policies are generally translated from natural language polices which define the usage constraints of the corresponding data. For the cryptographic-based scheme, data is encrypted to ensure the confidentiality and integrity of outsourced data. Betge-Brezetz *et al.* [11] proposed a privacy control model at the virtual machines (VMs) level to protect sensitive files stored, processed, and moved in an Infrastructure as a Service cloud. The demonstration involved clouds located in different countries but run on the same platform running on Linux operating system. The model requires CSPs to build the same cloud platform and establish the same privacy control modules in order to protect the data moving among clouds. Overhead is also an issue at this VM control level. Noman and Adams [12] introduced the Data Location Assurance Solution (DLAS) for cloud computing environments by applying two cryptographic primitives: zero knowledge sets protocol and ciphertext-policy-attribute-based encryption scheme. This approach allows users to register their data at a stable cloud location (e.g. country, region) and to verify data location on request as the assurance of user's data but not focus on the solutions for moving data among clouds. Androulaki *et al.* [13] proposed a new framework focusing on location- and time-based access control to cloud-stored data. In this framework, the cloud provider stores the data reliably, whereas localization infrastructure is deployed for accessing user location. More recently, References [14–16] focused on designing a cloud information accountability framework to keep data usage transparent and traceable through embedding of enforceable access control policies and logging policies. One of the main features of their work was that the data owner can audit the copies of its data.

The cryptographic-based solutions may include encryption [17–19], verification of integrity [20–22], secure file or storage system [23,24], and dispersal storage schemes [25,26]. Policy-based mechanisms mainly focus on the provisioning of access privilege for the requests. If the adversary has sufficient hacking skills or leverages elevation of privilege to bypass the access control service, the data is still in danger. Encryption-based mechanisms impose on some constraints. For examples, the complexity of key distribution and data encryption and decryption may be introduced, especially while protecting the highly dynamic data. These approaches mainly focused on protecting data by using encryption schemes, but there were few efforts on data mobility.

6.3.3   Binding user and data location

Data-policy binding mechanism is a novel data protection scheme which encapsulates data, policy, and functional entities within its encapsulating object. The integrity of the data structure is enhanced. Any accesses on the data will enforceably activate the bundled security procedure. Chen and Hoang [27] proposed an active data binding framework in addressing data mobility and user mobility. This research concentrated on notifying data owners when their data is moved from one location to another, tracking data geographic location using Google services and integrating active data-centric framework to collect evidences of data movement. However, the lack of secured components or equivalent protection schemes at the new location results in data violation and illegal disclosure as there is no monitoring services to track the data and prevent illegal requests. Consequently, data cannot be independently survived in the heterogeneous cloud environment. Another representative research proposed in [28] introduced sticky policies which are inseparable from the associated data to enforce confidentiality protection. This technology prevents attackers from accessing data without satisfying the bundled privacy policies. Two approaches were introduced: (1) identifier-based encryption and (2) trusted platform module.

A similar data protection scheme [29] was proposed on the basis of secure data capsules. The sensitive data is cryptographically bundled with the data-use controls (DUCs) policy and provenance. They claimed that the DUCs might cover confidentiality, integrity, nonrepudiation, logging, access control, etc. However, there was no practical outcome demonstrated. References [30–32] proposed an active bundle scheme to protect disseminated sensitive data. Each bundle packages data and metadata concerning data access and dissemination policies. Through relevance a VM with each bundle, the data can be protected by enforcement of the privacy policies in the VM. Popa *et al.* [33] proposed a data traceability service for mobile computing application. A security framework for this service includes security components that ensure integrity, authenticity, confidentiality, and nonrepudiation and management components that apply the appropriate security components to users' private data.

The users can create a request to read, modify, or even transfer the data via mobile applications. When a request was raised, a message from a trace service will notify the data owner that his/her private data was accessed. This approach only considers the case that the data is accessed by the data owner, and there is no data movement among clouds. Especially, a request to send data is simply performed by creating a copy of the data. In other words, the data sent by user will not be traced by the service.

6.3.4   Protecting cloud data using trusted third-party technologies

Trusted third party technology enables establishing trustworthy service relationships. References [34–36] introduced trust computing concepts for cloud data security through trusted third-party management systems. These schemes can efficiently increase the transparency of data usage and ensure their data is not being compromised or leaked by CSPs. However, merely relying on third-party auditors (TPAs) may still disclose vulnerability once the adversary penetrates data storage service and obtains direct access privilege on data. These proposed solutions lack in protective ability on data. To cast off the constraints, data per se has to be smart to self-defend without the assistance of TPAs.

6.3.5   Data mobility based on location register database

Location register database enables subscribing and storing data locations when data is located at cloud storage. Leveraging database for data registration is a new approach to deal with changes of data location in a cloud environment. Thus, there is limited research on this scenario. Reference [12] used database for data registration and user verifications to provide DLAS at cloud. Nevertheless, data is held at the cloud to inform users that it is protected in a secure environment, and there are no data-moving operations among clouds.

However, all the above approaches have not addressed the security requirements to protect data from violation attacks when data is located at visited cloud sites. Our work, described below, is different from theirs on several aspects. First, the DMM model leverages our active data protection framework [6] in developing protocols for moving data among clouds and in establishing a new supervisor at a visited cloud for monitoring data and data operations at the new cloud as well as reporting the welfare of the data to the original cloud. Second, data is rendered active with recordable structure enabling data to store various locations when data is accessed. Third, a location register database structure is introduced to allow MSs to retrieve and inform data location. The model allows data to move among clouds of different infrastructures ranging from private cloud to public cloud while ensuring its protection regardless of the location.

6.4   A trust-oriented data protection framework

In this section, we introduce our active data mobility and protection framework [4,37].

Cloud data can be classified as *structured* or *unstructured data* in terms of management type. The term *structured data* refers to data with an identifiable structure. The most common instance of the *structured data* is the database system, where data is stored based on predefined features and properties and is also searchable by data type with access interfaces. On the other hand, *unstructured data* normally has no identifiable structure that refers to any data type. Media data, documents, and complex designated data formats like the Electronic Health Record are considered *unstructured data.*

To protect these various data types in the outsourced cloud environment, *structured data* management typically interfaces with data by using secure connection interfaces. *Unstructured data* strongly relies on third-party security mechanisms or encryption. Once third-party services are compromised, *unstructured data* would be vulnerable to violation and tampering. We concentrate on protection mechanisms for *unstructured data.*

Instead of paying attention to attacks or violations, we focus on the target data and equip it with self-describing and self-defending capability. We introduce an ADCu structure as a deployable data protection unit encapsulating sensitive data, networking, data manipulation, and security verification functions within a coherent data structure. A signed ADCu encloses dynamic information-flow tracking mechanisms that can precisely monitor the inner data and its derivatives. Any violations of policy or tampering with data would be compulsorily recorded and reported to data owners via the notification mechanisms within ADCu. This strong enforcement also triggers a log information collection procedure (which records every access to the specific data items) that will be utilized to provide transparency and accountability of data usage via disseminating the log information to data owners.

A unit of raw data is transformed into a novel data structure called a TDFS that is also referred to as an ADCu. The TDFS consists of a shell and a core as shown in Figure 6.5. The shell is equipped with active tamper-proofing codes and is executed prior to the core when the TDFS is triggered. It consists of a *shell* and a *core*. The *shell* is equipped with active tamper-proofing codes and is executed prior to the *core* when the ADCu is triggered. The ADCu is associated with a runtime environment. The *core* of the TDFS comprises an executable segment (ES), a header, and data blocks. The runnable scripts in the ES allow basic data operations, data loading, and data analysis functions. The header refers to a manifest specifying the basic information related to the data such as security header, data descriptor, and time stamp. Raw data blocks are encrypted.

At the entry point to the *shell*, the scripts invoke *verifier and identifier* to certify the validity of the request in terms of the format of request parameters and contents via request identification and verification processes. In our context, a permitted access request conforming to the configured policy is issued a certification that signifies that the access is authorized by the CPRBAC service which was proposed in our previous work [38]. Another significant component of the *shell* is the *logger* module, utilized to record significant checkpoints during transactions, data operation outcomes, and even errors when the ADCu throws exceptions. The *logger* is required to record significant intermediate information. During a single transaction, all log records marked with regular *Priority* level are stored temporarily in memory

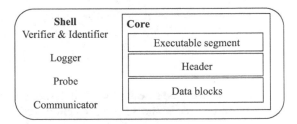

Figure 6.5   Structure of an active data cube

for performance consideration. Once the data operation finishes, the *logger* leverages the *communicator* in the *shell* to upload the log records to ADCu's external supervisor. However, a log record marked with an emergency tag will be immediately triggered by the *probe*, which then notifies the *communicator* to raise an exception. *Time Stamp* uses the Network Time Protocol to take into account the fact that cloud resources may be distributed across different time zones. Each ADCu's log information is transparent to its data owner. When the log records are stored in cloud, they are encrypted using the RSA encryption to avoid possible information leakage. Only the data owner has the corresponding key to disclose those records. In addition, sending out the log information of data usage rather than storing it inside the ADCu is activated to maintaining the light-weight feature. Increasing log information could raise the cost of storage, dissemination, or replication of the ADCu.

Each ADCu has a corresponding *supervisor* deployed in the same domain, which takes charge of monitoring external data operations (such as move and copy) that cannot be detected by the internal probe inside the ADCu, and communicating with its ADCu. If the ADCu cannot establish a proper network connection or cannot contact its supervisor, it would switch to the termination state to avoid an offline attack.

Once the verification and identification procedure succeeds, the *shell* delegates control to the data *core*. The *core* of ADCu is wrapped by an ES, a header, and data blocks. We leverage dynamic delegation approach in the ES to call back the *shell* to trigger the *core* and execute data operations. The *header* refers to a manifest specifying the basic information of supplementary data residing at the beginning of *data blocks*.

As the ADCu can only protect and manage the contents within, it cannot be triggered if adversaries attempt to execute operations such as move or delete the whole data cube. The supervisor thus is designed to monitor operational system level data manipulations that cannot be detected by the ADCu itself. An atomic data security model, called the active data protection unit (ADPu), is needed for supporting the active protection functions of the ADCu within the protection framework. The APDu is an atomic component combining two entities: a supervisor and an ADCu.

6.4.1   Mobility management model

In this section, we present the design of our DMM model. The mobility management model enhances the mobility of ADCus and its protection when deploying in cloud environment. It supports the management of data and data locations as well as ensures protection data at different clouds. The model is designed to achieve the following objectives:

- *Verification, authentication, and authorization:* requests are verified with defined policies to access the resources. The fine-grained policy structure allows users to configure and define more specific and secure protection requirements on their data. Furthermore, these requests are also audited and recorded as audit data in which evidence of data violation will be reported to data owner.
- *Mobility service:* In order to deal with the changes of data location, the MS is introduced to execute users' requests for updating, tracking data locations at LRD, and informing data owners with data operations and new locations. This addresses users' concerns when allocating their data within cloud services.
- *Location register:* When data is moved to a new cloud environment, it has to nominate its presence at the new cloud to obtain cloud services within SLAs established at its original cloud. In addition, with the introduction of the LRD, locations of data are also collected and maintained in order to serve for tracking, retrieving, and monitoring data status.
- *Data monitoring:* Data operations on the data monitored by a supervisor at original cloud or a clone supervisor at visited cloud prevent data violations against the SLAs subscribed between CSPs and users. The supervisor detects these operations and triggers its TDFS into an active state ready for executing the self-protection process.
- *Data protection:* The data is structured within an active protection structure that enables it to be monitored, triggers smart analysis, self-protection, and self-defense capability directly upon external requests. The active structure also allows the recording of data operations with itself for tracing purposes.

We focus on providing a data mobility solution for cloud data moving among clouds while ensuring data protection, auditing relevant data locations and accessed data operations. The new features of our proposed model include an active data framework with appropriate data structure and a LRD to deal with mobility; protocols between clouds for data movement; procedures for establishing a clone supervisor at the visited cloud for data protection purposes. In particular, there will be a MS agent responsible for updating and retrieving data location from the LRD. Figure 6.6 depicts the model and its four core components: (1) the data core protection component, (2) the mobility management component, (3) the trusted security management component, and (4) the cloud interface.

- **The data core protection component:** This component is designed to enable active surveillance, smart analysis, self-protection, and self-defense capabilities directly on to the data itself. The data is transformed and encapsulated in a TDFS that supports confidentiality, integrity, and intrusion tolerance [6]. To support mobility, a special encrypted element namely recordable mobility data (RMD) is designed to record user's operations when they access the data. Only the data owner who has

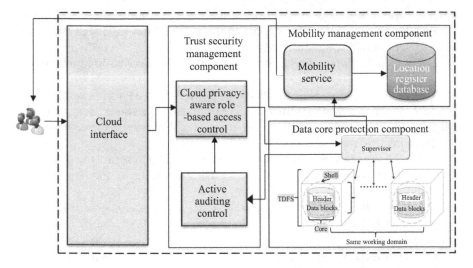

Figure 6.6 The design of data mobility management model

the decryption key can trace previous data operations. The management and coordination of cloud data for each tenant is processed by the supervisor, whose active service instance is activated when the corresponding tenant subscribes to a cloud storage service. Several supervisor service instances can be deployed to deal with a large number of requests from diverse virtual servers or machines (VMs). An atomic APDu contains an active data cube (the TDFS) and its supervisor.

• *The mobility management component:* This component includes the MS and the LRD. It aims to store and manage information about the supervisor and the TDFS at original cloud. The component centers around the location registration procedure when the TDFS is moved by maintaining connections with its responsible supervisor.

The MS is responsible for creating queries to the LRD. When the data is created, the supervisor invokes the MS to update the information about the TDFS in the LRD. In addition, the MS also supports the establishment of the new supervisor at the visited cloud.

The LRD stores the TDFS information related to data location, data operations, and data owner for data-status-monitoring purposes. The visitor location register database (VLRD) is located at the visited cloud and structured similar as LRD with some additional fields presenting for the location of visited cloud. When a TDFS is subscribed to a cloud, it needs to register and is allocated a supervisor that is responsible for the data welfare including monitoring and raising an alarm if illegal data operations are detected. Therefore, whenever a TDFS moves out of its original cloud, the supervisor will invoke a query to extract information from the database necessary for the establishment of the clone supervisor at the new cloud. Apart from the data, there are also tables holding system data, including information about servers that are allowed to connect to the system. In the design phase, we designed database tables to achieve following functions:

New data subscription: This function allows users to subscribe information about their data such as data owner and profile data.

Updating changes of location: This function supports the location update procedure when there are requests from the MS to update data locations. Despite the fact that data is stored at a visited cloud, its location is still updated if there are requests to move the data to a new cloud.

Retrieving VLRD lists: This function allows the LRD to locate the VLRD that holds the current location information of the TDFS so that the location management can be utilized.

Providing system data: This function allows the MS to access system data information about LRD and VLRD. As a result, the CSPs are able to identify cloud hosts and the location register database.

For TDFS location registration at a visited cloud, the VLRD is used for storing TDFS locations when the TDFS moves from its original cloud to a visited cloud. The VLRD is the other location register used to retrieve information about data location when data is stored at the visited cloud. Because a TDFS can be moved anywhere in clouds of different infrastructures, mobility management is very essential. When a TDFS moves about, location registration for tracking and tracing purposes is always needed. Therefore, if visited locations of TDFS are stored and managed as a distributed database system, the MS at visited cloud can query directly the VLRD rather than the home LRD.

When a request to access the data at the visited cloud is permitted, the MS will insert or update the VLRD. If the TDFS location is not stored in the VLRD, the request is forwarded to original cloud where the MS queries the LRD. When it is authorized, a new record will be added to the VLRD. When a TDFS visits a new cloud from the old cloud, the registration process in the new VLRD is as follows: (1) the MS sends a request to the new visited cloud in order to register its information in the new VLRD; (2) the new VLRD informs the MS's LRD of the TDFS's current location, the address of the new cloud; (3) the MS's LRD sends an acknowledgment including TDFS's profile; (4) the new VLRD informs the TDFS of the successful registration; and (5) the LRD sends a deregistration message to the old VLRD and the old VLRD acknowledges the deregistration.

- *The trusted security management component:* This component is for executing trusted security management. The CPRBAC service [39] is proposed to define and describe the security boundary on data operations in distributed clouds. Access resource requests that are not specified in the policy database will be rejected. The fine-grained policy structure of the CPRBAC allows users to configure and define specific and secure protection requirements on their data. Authentication and authorization are offered by the service. The AAC [38] is introduced to execute and audit users' requests in a secure and consistent manner. Users' requests must be actively audited under a distributed transaction management session. Through

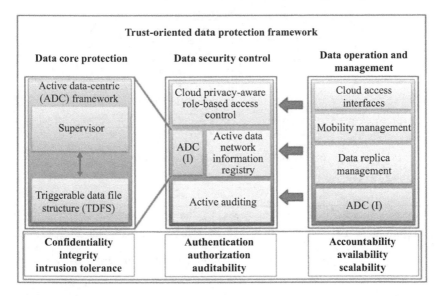

Figure 6.7   Trust-oriented data protection solution in cloud

recording audit data created as the attestations, the CSPs can report the evidences of data violations to their users. The users are more inclined to adopt the cloud solution for their businesses as they can establish more acceptable SLA with their subscribed CSPs in a firmed trustworthy relationship. The auditability can be achieved by the AAC.

- *Cloud interface:* Cloud interfaces provide data service interfaces to access active data in cloud storage systems. It forwards requests with parameters to security management component to verify access permission.

6.4.2   Trust-oriented data protection framework

In an earlier work, we proposed a trust-oriented data protection framework for data protection in cloud environments [6]. Figure 6.7 illustrates the proposed trust-oriented cloud data protection framework. The framework is structured into three blocks: the data security control block provides secure access control and data auditability functions, the data core protection block provides techniques and procedures for implementing active data protection, and the data operation and management block handles mobility and data replication management. This framework can be considered a secure data container that manipulates and verifies the data without the involvement of a third-party service. This structure presents a security and trust abstraction at a higher level than conventional data protection models that rely on the peripheral security environment and third-party protection mechanisms. Our core goal is to empower data with the capabilities of self-defense and self-protection against intrusions or violations. Data misbehavior and violation can be actively detected by the data itself,

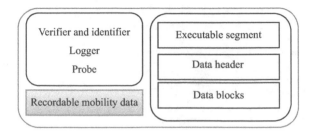

Figure 6.8   Triggerable data structure

Subject ID	Data ID	Data operation	Source address	Current address	Destination address	Time stamp

Figure 6.9   Recordable mobility data structure

reducing the risk of use by adversaries. The data core protection block employs an active security approach whereby the data is made active against any invocation, whereas the data security control block and data operation and management block support this active approach by providing data auditing and other measures including secure access control, data replication and mobility.

The management and coordination of cloud data for each tenant are processed by the supervisor, an active service instance that is activated when the corresponding tenant subscribes to cloud storage services.

In this framework, two services are proposed for data security control: the CPRBAC service and the AAC service. The CPRBAC service defines and describes the security boundary on data operations in cloud. Resource requests that are not allowed in the policy repository will be rejected. The AAC is introduced to execute and audit users' requests in a secure and consistent manner. Users' requests must be actively audited under a distributed transaction management session.

6.4.3   Implementation

6.4.3.1   Data structure design

Data is structured utilizing the active data-centric framework [6]. A special structure called recordable mobility data (RMD) is designed to record information associated with users' access request. The information includes Subject_ID, Data_ID, Operation, Time Stamp, and Cloud location. This information is transparent to its data owner. In other words, it is invisible from users' data operation. The stored information is encrypted using the RSA encryption to avoid possible information leakage. Only the data owner has the corresponding key to disclose them for tracing previous operations. The new TDFS structure is shown in Figures 6.8 and 6.9.

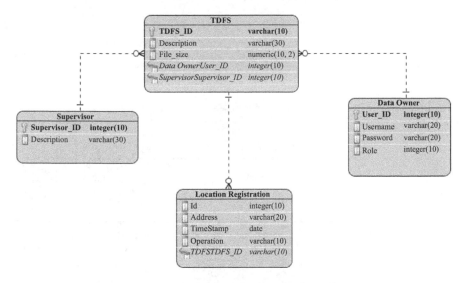

Figure 6.10   Location register database design

6.4.3.2   Location register database design

The design phase had two tasks to complete, the first was to implement the design of basic entities in the LRD's schema and the second included the design of database tables. When a TDFS registers with the LRD, information associated with the TDFS is stored in the location registration table. For implementation, we only present structure of the location registration table in the LRD. The primary keys of supervisor and data owner appears in this table for completeness. A new record, which composes of six fields including TDFS_ID, Supervisor_ID, Operation, Address, Time Stamp, and Data Owner, is inserted into the LRD as initial data location for the TDFS. Whenever a TDFS moves out of its original cloud, the supervisor will invoke the MS which will execute a query to extract information from the database necessary for the establishment of the clone supervisor at the new cloud. TDFS locations at the database are updated at the LRD to allow verifying and tracking of data (Figure 6.10).

We assume that the LRD manages n TDFSs. The set of TDFSs in the LRD is defined as $TN = \{tn_1, tn_2, ..., tn_i, ..., tn_n\}$; the set of associated supervisors is represented by $SP = \{sp_1, sp_2, ..., sp_i, ..., sp_n\}$, and the set of data operations on TDFSs at time t is represented by $OP = \{op_1, op_2, ..., op_i, ..., op_m\}$. Similarly, the set of address frequencies, the set of registered time stamps, and the set of data owners are represented by $IP = \{ip_1, ip_2, ..., ip_i, ..., ip_n\}$, $TS = \{ts_1, ts_2, ..., ts_i, ..., ts_n\}$, and $OW = \{ow_1, ow_2, ..., ow_i, ..., ow_n\}$, respectively. Let LRD table set $L = \{tn_i, sp_i, ip_i, op_i, ts_i, ow_i\}$ (Table 6.2).

Regarding the registration of TDFS's locations, a VLRD is used for storing a TDFS location when the TDFS moves from its home location in the original cloud. Because a TDFS can be moved anywhere in clouds of different infrastructures, mobility management is essential. When a TDFS moves, location registration is always

Table 6.2   LRD's data table structure

TDFS_ID	Supervisor_ID	Operation	Address	Time stamp	Data owner
tn_1	sp_1	op_1	ip_1	ts_1	ow_1
tn_2	sp_2	op_2	ip_2	ts_2	ow_2
...	...	...	...	...	...
tn_i	sp_i	op_i	ip_i	ts_i	ow_i
...	...	...	...	...	...
tn_n	sp_n	op_n	ip_n	ts_n	ow_n

Table 6.3   VLRD's data table structure

TDFS_ID	Supervisor_ID	Operation	Source address	Current address	Time stamp	Data owner
tn_1	sp_1	op_1	ip_1	cip_1	ts_1	ow_1
tn_2	sp_2	op_2	ip_2	cip_2	ts_2	ow_2
...	...	...	...	...	...	...
tn_i	sp_i	op_i	ip_i	cip_i	ts_i	ow_i
...	...	...	...	...	...	...
tn_n	sp_n	op_n	ip_n	cip_n	ts_n	ow_n

needed for tracking and tracing purposes. Therefore, if visited locations of TDFS are stored and managed as a distributed database system, the MS at visited cloud queries directly the VLRD rather than the LRD at the original cloud. A record in the VLRD composes of seven fields including TDFS_ID, Supervisor_ID, Operation, Source Address, Current Address, Time Stamp, Data Owner. VLRD's data structure inherits from LRD with an additional field as Current address. Current address A set of CIP = $\{cip_1, cip_2, ..., cip_i, ..., cip_n\}$ and VLRD table set L = $\{tn_i, sp_i, ip_i, cip_i, op_i, ts_i, ow_i\}$.

6.4.3.3   Data mobility management workflows

When a customer subscribes to a cloud service, the CSP will assign roles associated with the data for users, allowing them to access a virtual user directory and workspace. An initial set of empty active data cubes will be created according to the regular data types. After assigning roles, the supervisor will be invoked to send a request to the MS for data location registration. The request containing parameter such as UserID, DataID, Location, and Time Stamp will be processed to update to the database. Finally, the user will receive a data location registration acknowledgment message via the MS. Figure 6.11 shows the workflow for a new data location registration.

When a user needs to execute data operations such as read, insert, write, and move the data, he/she will send a request to the cloud interface including a set of parameters such as UserID, DataId, Operation and Location, and Time Stamp. In

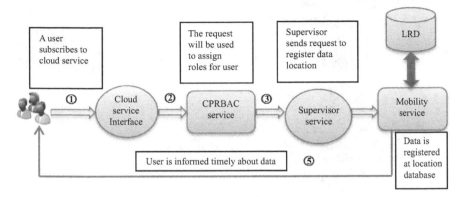

Figure 6.11   New data location registration workflow

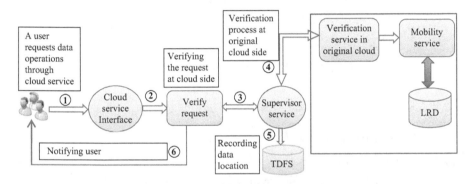

Figure 6.12   Data mobility workflow

turn, a verification process is created to perform a sequence of steps. First, it invokes the supervisor to access the data. Hence, the supervisor needs to establish the validity of the request by forwarding it to the original cloud where data location is also updated. If the request is not valid or allowed by the access policy, the supervisor will raise an alarm to notify the system administrator or related legislation organization. In fact, if desired, the data owner may be informed immediately when the original cloud detects the violation through the MS. If the request is permitted, the MS will update data location before approved verification is sent to the supervisor. From this point, data operations will be performed on the TDFS but each operation is recorded inside the TDFS for tracing purposes. Figure 6.12 presents the general procedure for data mobility workflow.

When the MS is triggered, a request is sent to LRD in order to query data location for data validation or updating new data location. Further, the MS also informs the data owner with a message concerning the accessed operations via email or mobile devices. Details of the workflow are shown in Figure 6.13.

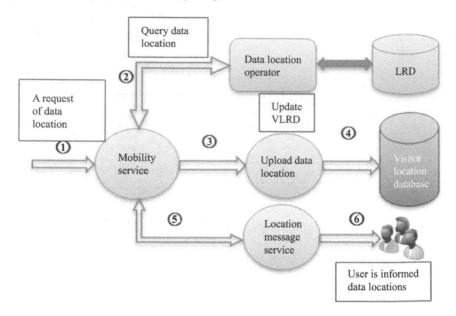

Figure 6.13   Mobility service workflow

6.4.4   Evaluation and results

6.4.4.1   Experiment setup

We performed our experiments deploying Amazon EC, Azure, and NeCTAR clouds. Our experimental environment has been set up as follows: Amazon EC2 [40] was used as the original cloud to provide cloud resources and verify requests. We created one t2.micro instance of Windows 2012 server running on Intel Xeon E5-2670 v2 2.5 GHz with 1 GB memory and another instance running MySQL to store the LRD with 5 GB storage. Packages of the model were deployed on this instance, and requests were accessed via the RMI interface. We also created an Azure cloud [41] and a NeCTAR cloud [42] as the visited clouds. We used an instance running Windows Server 2012 Datacenter with Intel Xeon E5-2660 2.2 GHz 2.19 GHz and 7 GB at Azure and another instance running Ubuntu 14.04 within 1 VCPU, 4 GB RAM at NeCTAR to send requests via the RMI interface. In order to demonstrate the working of the mobility model, a message application for notification at users' mobile phone was implemented in Java on an Android 4.4 smartphone with Quad-Core 3GB 2.7 GHz and 3GB RAM. Google cloud message (GCM) [43] was devised to send messages informing users when the data was accessed or moved at cloud side. A notification could be triggered via two sources depending on the request of data operations. If the request was to move or to copy data, the MS would inform the data owner via GCM, whereas operations such as read or write would be triggered by the probe inside the data.

The current experiments were based on following assumptions: we assumed that the runtime environment Java Virtual Machine (JVM) of the active data behaved correctly at participant clouds, and we assumed that the data would be activated when it moves to a new cloud host. We also assumed that a safe location service provider (LSP) was available on the Internet, and CSPs had the agreement to establish new supervisors. At this stage, we tested our model on cases where TDFS and regular files were moved between two clouds. Next, different clouds (with different infrastructures) involving in data-moving cases were also used to demonstrate that the model is trustworthy and behave correctly. To observe the performance of the DMM model, we first compared data operation overheads in moving regular passive data and in moving our active data. We also compared the overheads of two types of request: one came from inside the cloud and the other from outside, to evaluate the feasibility and proactivity of the system. Finally, we demonstrated security and transparency of the proposed model.

6.4.4.2 Evaluation

In our previous ADC framework, a data-moving operation was simply performed between two hosts in the private cloud environment. One host is to create a request to move the data, whereas to the other is to provide various data access scenarios to ADCu in the same cloud. In this section, we deploy various data-moving cases among clouds to address not only data mobility issues but also privacy and security. Requests will be created from both inside and outside the original cloud. Through authorization and authentication scheme based on the CPRBAC service and the LRD at the original cloud, any data-moving operations will be verified regarding user's permissions or data locations. The implementation of TDFS is based to our previous work [4] and added new fields to support data mobility.

We assume that data owners do not release sensitive information to unauthorized parties including secret keys that were used to generate signature and encrypt data and personal privacy. We assume that the LRD and CPRBAC services are trustworthy and behave correctly.

6.4.4.3 Processing data-moving case tests
Data-moving test for ADCu and normal files
We investigate a new data mobility model for ADCu by performing tests to identify the cost of moving data such as time delay on TDFS files compared to normal data. Normal files are the raw files in formats such as PDF file, XML file, or DOC file. The idea is to determine the overhead introduced by the security features and the MS performed on an ADCu of our model. We increased the file size from 300kB to 1000kB for both TDFS and normal files and compare the costs of moving operations within our model. The results are shown in Table 6.3. All results are an average of five trials. The executed time $t_{Request}$ for each request is composed of three determinants: the verification time $t_{Lookup\ service}$, the location register time $t_{Verification\ and\ mobility}$, and the data operation time $t_{Data\ operation}$

$$t_{Request} = t_{Lookup\ service} + t_{Verification\ and\ mobility} + t_{Data\ operation}$$

Processing time (ms)

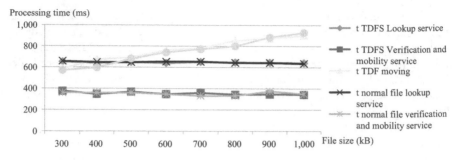

Figure 6.14   Modules processing duration

Processing time (ms)

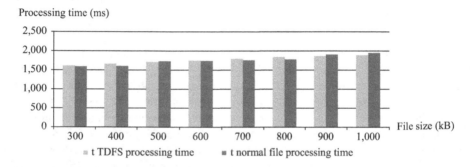

Figure 6.15   Request processing duration

1) $t_{\text{Lookup service}}$ is the time that client spent looking up server's RMI interface and sends the request.

2) $t_{\text{Verification and mobility}}$ is the security and MS latency. The CPRBAC and Location register will be processed during this period.

3) $t_{\text{Data operation}}$ is the data transfer time between the original cloud and the visited cloud.

From the results, it is clear that the processing time for a TDFS is slightly longer than that for a normal file (1765.25 ms in comparison with 1755.4 ms of the latter). The main components of the whole moving process are the lookup service time and the moving data time. The verification and MS time, the main process of the model, however, only constitutes a small amount of time (353.93 of 1765.25 ms for TDFS and 351.98 of 1755.4 ms for normal file, respectively). The comparative results are illustrated graphically in Figures 6.14 and 6.15. The *x*-axis represents the file size and the *y*-axis represents the execution time.

From our experiments, we found that the verification time and the lookup service of the model are approximately same for both TDFS and normal files. Therefore, the source of extra delay must be introduced by the transfer time. Hence, we run the same

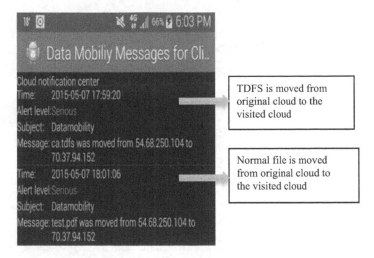

Figure 6.16   Data notification view in Samsung Galaxy Note 4

request with different data sizes. The results show that the transfer data time is indeed the significant source of latency.

This means the data protection and MS do not introduce significant overheads when the data size was increased. Overall, the amount of overheads is considered as a small price to pay for security and data protection. With our proposed model, the supervisor can trigger TDFS into an active state to self-protection; self-defense and record accessed addresses, whereas these operations on cannot perform normal files.

Figure 6.16 shows alerting messages for move requests as received by the user via the mobile phone in the move process. The message includes essential information about the moving process such as file name, moving addresses, time. It is demonstrated that the supervisor can detect data move operation and invoke the MS to send the alerting message to user's mobile device immediately when there is a request to move the data at both the original cloud and visited cloud.

Data-moving cases test among different cloud

In the following experiments, we deploy the model for different data-moving cases for ADCu described in Section 6.2. Requests were created from both inside and outside the cloud for different data-moving cases. Our primary goal is to demonstrate the efficiency, security and transparency of the proposed model. In addition, we recorded and compared the verification and MS service duration of requests from inside and outside the cloud to identify the source of latency. The results of outside requests within different data-moving cases are compared in Figures 6.17 and 6.18.

As can be seen from Figure 6.17, the verification and MS costs of the second case and the third case are substantially higher in comparison with that of the first case (the average times are 837.6 ms, 705.5 ms, and 353.9 ms, respectively) whereas there is only a small difference in the costs of the last two cases. This can be explained by the

Processing time (ms)

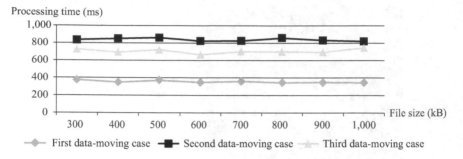

Figure 6.17   Verification and mobility service duration of different data-moving cases

Processing time (ms)

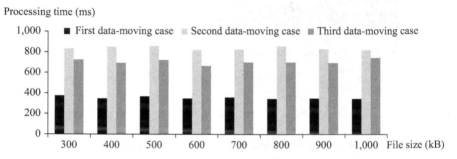

Figure 6.18   Processing duration of different data-moving cases

fact that for the last two cases, the move process requires two stages: sending requests to the old cloud and relaying these requests to the original cloud. All requests have to be forwarded to the original cloud which is responsible for verifying the requests and executing the MS even when requests are created from original cloud (the third data-moving case). We also recorded the response time of verification and MS by requests from inside cloud to compare with that of requests from another cloud. The requests from inside the cloud can be created from two sources. One is from inside the original cloud to move the data to a new cloud and the other is from a visited cloud to move the data to new cloud or back to the original cloud. As the transferring data costs are similar for both two kinds of request within moving cases on the same data. In fact, the verification and MS cost is also the same for an inside request at visited cloud for the second and third data-moving case. Thus, we only record the average response time for these two kinds of request (251.4 ms and 612.6 ms, respectively). Similarly, the average response times of the second and third data-moving case are about double that of the first data-moving case due to the relay process.

The overhead for data retrieval from a TDFS involves verification and identification, data loading, and network communication cost. To evaluate the costs of the verification and MSs, we run a number of tests. A total of 50 working threads are allocated to generate user requests in parallel. Hence, we initialized six sets of tests

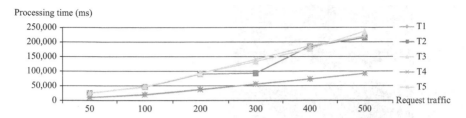

Figure 6.19   Time cost of verification and mobility services for different data-moving cases and requests

in which the number of requests ranged from 50 to 500, and each set of test runs five times circularly. Figure 6.19 illustrates the time cost of executing time cost of verification and MSs for different data-moving cases and requests. The *x*-axis represents the number of requests, and the *y*-axis represents the execution time. As we can observe, along with the increasing of the number of requests, the time cost of verification and MSs increases obviously. As we observe, the average time of inside requests for the first data-moving case (47920.1 ms) is similar to that for the outside requests (48074.55 ms). This is repeated similarly for the second data-moving case and the third data-moving case. However, the average time of requests for the second data-moving case and the third data-moving case (115285.8 ms) is approximately twice than that for the first data-moving case (47997.34 ms). It can be explained that the requests have to be forwarded back to the original cloud for executing verification and MSs. Generally, the time cost grows linearly with the increase of traffic requests. This indicates that the DMM model can efficiently avoid an exponential increase in response time when handling multiple requests. Replicas of the services to geographically separate hosts may be used to achieve load balancing and improve performance.

Figure 6.20 presented the data-moving operations for different data-moving cases. All data-moving cases will be triggered by the supervisor. The first one is triggering the MS and TDFS when data is moved from the original cloud to the visited cloud; the second one is triggering the MS and TDFS when the data at visited cloud to a new cloud; the third one is triggering the MS and TDFS when the data at visited cloud is moved back to the original cloud; and the last one is triggering the MS and TDFS when data is moved out from cloud. In all these test cases, the supervisor was able detect and trigger the MS and the TDFS when data is moved. Meanwhile, our mobile device received the alert message immediately. A message including source address and destination address actively notified the data owner when data was moved to a new cloud.

Performance analysis: Our model does not rely on complex algorithm and encryption requirement. The performance of our model in terms of the computation overhead is as follows:

Verification service: The available computation overhead on these two processes includes access request generation, policy matching, verification between access

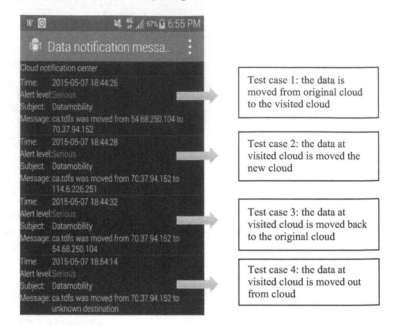

Figure 6.20　Data-moving cases notification view in Samsung Galaxy Note 4

request and targeted policy, calculating verification token, and access response generation. Among these operations, the policy matching complexity is O(N); verification complexity relies on the number of context variables required to analyze; other operations complexity are O(1).

Mobility service: The MS creates requests to query the database, which only adds negligible overhead to database as it does not incur initialization cost and database join algorithms. It only takes charge of triggering task, the other fetching data locations will be handled by the database instance.

6.4.4.4　Attack test and security analysis

In this section, we analyze possible attacks on our model. As the peripheral environment protector, the access control layer (ACL) in the entire framework resembles the firewall in a network security system that manages the incoming and outgoing network traffic to secure the internal network or computers. It blocks and defends external attacks caused by adversaries. Through authorization and authentication scheme based on the CPRBAC service, unauthorized requests would be rejected from accessing the active data stored in the cloud data storage layer. However, adversaries may leverage the elevation of privilege or illegal channel to gain the higher administration privilege (it can bypass the ACL) to directly commit an inner attack or penetrate data storage layer.

6.4.4.5 Direct access and intrusion attacks

The most direct attack is when an adversary tries to access the TDFS's content or move it to unauthorized locations. The verification process in our model operates as follows: any request to access a TDFS has to be verified at the CPRBAC for access permissions and the LRD for data's identification. Only the entity, whose request passed the verification, may continue to perform operations on the TDFS. If the TDFS's content is accessed, the shell within the TDFS will be triggered its shell protection scheme to execute verification and identification [6]. A request without any parameter is straightway regarded as an intrusion attack. Even if the adversary could input correct parameters within the request's structure, the verification process is executed to ensure the consistency of both CPRBAC and LRD. In fact, the data owner may also be informed with a notification message.

6.4.4.6 TDFS external attacks

If an attacker bypasses cloud firewall and security system and obtains a root privilege, he or she is able to execute data operations at the OS levels on the TDFS, such as copy, move, and delete the entire TDFS from cloud. These operations would not trigger the TDFS files into an active state without a supervisor's instructions, and hence, the adversary is able to expose sensitive information inside the TDFS. Data operations on TDFS are fully monitored based on the establishment of a clone supervisor in the same domain. Once the adversary performs these operations, the supervisor can detect them and then trigger the TDFS into an active state as well as notify the data owner. In the active state, the TDFS can execute self-protection process. For data owners, if their data is compromised or violated against the SLA of the subscribed cloud service, the MS can inform them through a mobile device. Furthermore, any illegal violations could be delivered to relevant governance, regulation, and compliance authorities. Figure 6.20 shows notification messages which are triggered by the supervisor.

6.5 Discussion and conclusion

6.5.1 Discussion

The last section focuses on our DMM model and the trust-oriented data protection framework. This section discusses several assumptions and measures that can be improved and extended in the future.

When an ADCu moves from its original cloud to another cloud, the responsibility to protect the data depends on the SLAs between the data owner and its original cloud provider as well as between the original cloud provider and the visited cloud provider. The mechanisms to deal with security and protection can be complex and vary depending on the agreements and assumptions. If we assume that the original cloud is mainly responsible for its registered data, then the tasks of authentication and authorization at a foreign cloud have to be done at the original cloud. This implies that the clone a supervisor established at the visited cloud has little responsibility as it will pass any requests to do with its data to the original cloud to deal with. However, if we assume that the new cloud will be mainly responsible for its visited data, the supervisor has to be generated with adequate capabilities. In this work, we assume a light-weight supervisor as it passes requests to the original cloud.

The assumptions also affect the performance of the moving process. As in our cases, requests to move data always have to be relayed back to the original cloud and, hence, the MS to processing time and the verification time can be doubled or tripled depending whether the move involves two or three clouds. If the authentication and authorization processes are delegated to the visited cloud, these processing times can be reduced.

The way the active ADCu communicates with other entities can be selectively designed. The ACDu when moved to a visited cloud may or may not be able to communicate with its owner. Even if it may, the owner may not wish to be disturbed unnecessarily, and some acceptable communications mechanisms should be developed. It is important that the ACDu must be able to protect itself and to communicate with some reliable external entity if the protection model is to be credible.

Clearly, those assumptions can be relaxed and the basic model can be extended to deal with various situations and provide more comprehensive data mobility and protection management.

6.5.2   Conclusion

This chapter discusses data protection and mobility management in cloud environments. It also presents an active framework for data protection and an extended trust-oriented framework for data mobility and protection for handling secure data mobility in a cloud environment that involves data moving within and among the original cloud and visited clouds. It also proposed a novel LRD that is capable to serve for tracing and tracking data locations. Furthermore, a new TDFS structure with recordable structure was designed to actively capture locations of requests. More importantly, a proposed establishing supervisor at visited cloud is able to deploy the equivalent data protection scheme at both cloud side to achieve an intrusion tolerant scheme. The experimental outcomes demonstrate feasibility, efficiency of the model. Further, the reliability of the system is guaranteed in terms of processing time.

References

[1]   L. Schubert and K. Jeffery, "Advances in clouds," *Report of the Cloud Computing Expert Working Group. European Commission,* 2012.

[2]   I. Foster, Z. Yong, I. Raicu, and L. Shiyong, "Cloud Computing and Grid Computing 360-Degree Compared," in *GCE'08 Grid Computing Environments Workshop,* 2008, pp. 1–10.

[3]   A. Juels and A. Oprea, "New approaches to security and availability for cloud data," *Commun. ACM,* vol. 56, pp. 64–73, 2013.

[4] L. Chen and D. B. Hoang, "Active data-centric framework for data protection in cloud environment," in *ACIS 2012: Location, location, location: Proceedings of the 23rd Australasian Conference on Information Systems*, 2012, pp. 1-11.

[5] L. Jae-Woo, "Mobility Management Using Frequently Visited Location Database," in *Multimedia and Ubiquitous Engineering, 2007. MUE'07. International Conference on*, 2007, pp. 159–163.

[6] L. Chen and D. B. Hoang, "Active data-centric framework for data protection in cloud environment," in *ACIS 2012: Location, location, location: Proceedings of the 23rd Australasian Conference on Information Systems 2012*, 2012, pp. 1–11.

[7] A. Albeshri, C. Boyd, and J. G. Nieto, "GeoProof: Proofs of Geographic Location for Cloud Computing Environment," in *32nd International Conference on Distributed Computing Systems Workshops (ICDCSW)*, 2012, pp. 506–514.

[8] K. Benson, R. Dowsley, and H. Shacham, "Do you know where your cloud files are?," presented at the Proceedings of the 3rd ACM workshop on Cloud computing security workshop, Chicago, Illinois, USA, 2011.

[9] Z. N. J. Peterson, M. Gondree, and R. Beverly, "A position paper on data sovereignty: the importance of geolocating data in the cloud," presented at the Proceedings of the 3rd USENIX conference on Hot topics in cloud computing, Portland, OR, 2011.

[10] T. Ries, V. Fusenig, C. Vilbois, and T. Engel, "Verification of Data Location in Cloud Networking," in *Fourth IEEE International Conference on Utility and Cloud Computing (UCC)*, 2011, pp. 439–444.

[11] S. Betge-Brezetz, G. B. Kamga, M. P. Dupont, and A. Guesmi, "Privacy Control in Cloud VM File Systems," in *Cloud Computing Technology and Science (CloudCom), 2013 IEEE 5th International Conference on*, 2013, pp. 276–280.

[12] A. Noman and C. Adams, "DLAS: Data Location Assurance Service for cloud computing environments," in *Tenth Annual International Conference on Privacy, Security and Trust (PST)*, 2012, pp. 225–228.

[13] E. Androulaki, C. Soriente, L. Malisa, and S. Capkun, "Enforcing Location and Time-Based Access Control on Cloud-Stored Data," in *IEEE 34th International Conference on Distributed Computing Systems (ICDCS)*, 2014, pp. 637–648.

[14] A. Squicciarini, S. Sundareswaran, and D. Lin, "Preventing Information Leakage from Indexing in the Cloud," in *Cloud Computing (CLOUD), 2010 IEEE 3rd International Conference on*, 2010, pp. 188–195.

[15] S. Sundareswaran, A. Squicciarini, D. Lin, and H. Shuo, "Promoting Distributed Accountability in the Cloud," in *IEEE International Conference on Cloud Computing (CLOUD)*, 2011, pp. 113–120.

[16] S. Sundareswaran, A. C. Squicciarini, and D. Lin, "Ensuring Distributed Accountability for Data Sharing in the Cloud," *IEEE Transactions on Dependable and Secure Computing*, vol. 9, pp. 556–568, 2012.

[17] S. Kamara and K. Lauter, "Cryptographic Cloud Storage," in *Financial Cryptography and Data Security*. vol. 6054, R. Sion, R. Curtmola, S. Dietrich,

A. Kiayias, J. Miret, K. Sako, and F. Sebé, Eds., ed: Springer Berlin Heidelberg, 2010, pp. 136–149.

[18]   N. Virvilis, S. Dritsas, and D. Gritzalis, "Secure Cloud Storage: Available Infrastructures and Architectures Review and Evaluation," in *Trust, Privacy and Security in Digital Business*. vol. 6863, S. Furnell, C. Lambrinoudakis, and G. Pernul, Eds., ed: Springer Berlin Heidelberg, 2011, pp. 74–85.

[19]   Y. Shucheng, W. Cong, R. Kui, and L. Wenjing, "Achieving Secure, Scalable, and Fine-grained Data Access Control in Cloud Computing," in *Proceedings of IEEE INFOCOM*, 2010, pp. 1–9.

[20]   A. Juels and J. Burton S. Kaliski, "Pors: proofs of retrievability for large files," presented at the Proceedings of the 14th ACM conference on Computer and communications security, Alexandria, Virginia, USA, 2007.

[21]   K. D. Bowers, A. Juels, and A. Oprea, "Proofs of retrievability: theory and implementation," presented at the Proceedings of the 2009 ACM workshop on Cloud computing security, Chicago, Illinois, USA, 2009.

[22]   H. Shacham and B. Waters, "Compact Proofs of Retrievability," presented at the Proceedings of the 14th International Conference on the Theory and Application of Cryptology and Information Security: Advances in Cryptology, Melbourne, Australia, 2008.

[23]   M. Kallahalla, E. Riedel, R. Swaminathan, Q. Wang, and K. Fu, "Plutus: Scalable Secure File Sharing on Untrusted Storage," presented at the Proceedings of the 2nd USENIX Conference on File and Storage Technologies, San Francisco, CA, 2003.

[24]   E.-J. Goh, H. Shacham, N. Modadugu, and D. Boneh, "SiRiUS: Securing Remote Untrusted Storage," *NDSS,* vol. 3, pp. 131–145, 2003.

[25]   S. Wang, D. Agrawal, and A. E. Abbadi, "A comprehensive framework for secure query processing on relational data in the cloud," presented at the Proceedings of the 8th VLDB international conference on Secure data management, Seattle, WA, 2011.

[26]   M. W. Storer, K. M. Greenan, E. L. Miller, and K. Voruganti, "POTSHARDS: secure long-term storage without encryption," presented at the 2007 USENIX Annual Technical Conference on Proceedings of the USENIX Annual Technical Conference, Santa Clara, CA, 2007.

[27]   L. Chen and D. B. Hoang, "Addressing Data and User Mobility Challenges in the Cloud," in *IEEE Sixth International Conference on Cloud Computing (CLOUD)*, 2013, pp. 549–556.

[28]   M. C. Mont, S. Pearson, and P. Bramhall, "Towards accountable management of identity and privacy: sticky policies and enforceable tracing services," in *Database and Expert Systems Applications, 2003. Proceedings. 14th International Workshop on*, 2003, pp. 377–382.

[29]   P. Maniatis, D. Akhawe, K. Fall, E. Shi, S. McCamant, and D. Song, "Do you know where your data are?: secure data capsules for deployable data protection," presented at the Proceedings of the 13th USENIX conference on Hot topics in operating systems, Napa, California, 2011.

[30] L. B. Othmane and L. Lilien, "Protecting Privacy of Sensitive Data Dissemination Using Active Bundles," in *2009 World Congress on Privacy, Security, Trust and the Management of e-Business*, 2009, pp. 202–213.

[31] R. Ranchal, B. Bhargava, L. B. Othmane, L. Lilien, K. Anya, K. Myong, and M. Linderman, "Protection of Identity Information in Cloud Computing without Trusted Third Party," in *Reliable Distributed Systems, 2010 29th IEEE Symposium on*, 2010, pp. 368–372.

[32] P. Angin, B. Bhargava, R. Ranchal, N. Singh, M. Linderman, L. B. Othmane, and L. Lilien, "An Entity-Centric Approach for Privacy and Identity Management in Cloud Computing," in *Reliable Distributed Systems, 2010 29th IEEE Symposium on*, 2010, pp. 177–183.

[33] D. Popa, K. Boudaoud, M. Borda, and M. Cremene, "Mobile cloud applications and traceability," in *RoEduNet International Conference 12th Edition Networking in Education and Research*, 2013, pp. 1–4.

[34] J. Abawajy, "Establishing Trust in Hybrid Cloud Computing Environments," in *Trust, Security and Privacy in Computing and Communications (TrustCom), 2011 IEEE 10th International Conference on*, 2011, pp. 118–125.

[35] M. Firdhous, O. Ghazali, and S. Hassan, "A trust computing mechanism for cloud computing with multilevel thresholding," in *Industrial and Information Systems (ICIIS), 2011 6th IEEE International Conference on*, 2011, pp. 457–461.

[36] W. Cong, W. Qian, R. Kui, and L. Wenjing, "Privacy-Preserving Public Auditing for Data Storage Security in Cloud Computing," in *INFOCOM, 2010 Proceedings IEEE*, 2010, pp. 1–9.

[37] T. D. Dang, D. Hoang, and P. Nanda, "Data Mobility Management Model for Active Data Cubes," in *Trustcom/BigDataSE/ISPA, 2015 IEEE*, 2015, pp. 750–757.

[38] L. Chen and D. B. Hoang, "Towards Scalable, Fine-Grained, Intrusion-Tolerant Data Protection Models for Healthcare Cloud," in *IEEE 10th International Conference on Trust, Security and Privacy in Computing and Communications (TrustCom)*, 2011, pp. 126–133.

[39] L. Chen and D. B. Hoang, "Novel Data Protection Model in Healthcare Cloud," in *High Performance Computing and Communications (HPCC), 2011 IEEE 13th International Conference on*, 2011, pp. 550–555.

[40] A. EC2. (2014). *Amazon Elastic Compute Cloud*. Available: http://aws.amazon.com/.

[41] Azure. (2014). *Microsoft Azure*. Available: https://azure.microsoft.com.

[42] N. e. C. T. a. R. (NeCTAR). Available: http://nectar.org.au/.

[43] GCM. (2014). *Google Cloud Messaging for Android*. Available: https://developer.android.com/google/gcm/index.html.

Chapter 7
Understanding software-defined perimeter

Chenkang Tang[1], Vimal Kumar[1], and Sivadon Chaisiri[1]

Abstract

In network security, a perimeter of a network of computers and other equipment is formed as a secure barrier protecting digital assets in the network from being accessed and compromised by unauthorized users. In cloud computing, building such a perimeter is challenging due to a wider and likely unknown boundary of multiple overlay networks of cloud services, resources and devices communicating with each other. To overcome this challenge, the software-defined perimeter (SDP) proposed by the Cloud Security Alliance (CSA) can be used to build a manageable secure perimeter for cloud-connected services, resources and devices. So far, SDP has proved to be a strong defense against network attacks under simulated tests and security challenges, hackathons conducted by CSA. In this chapter, we present the SDP specification and also discuss its security features and components, including zero visibility, single packet authorization, mutual transport layer security, device validation, dynamic firewalls and application binding that are behind the successful defense of SDP and a potential solution for securing data in the cloud.

7.1 Introduction

Traditionally, the security perimeter in network infrastructure has defined the boundary between the private and the public networks. Everything inside the perimeter is trusted, and everything outside the perimeter is untrusted. This perimeter deploys various security tools and technologies to protect users' data and applications from different types of attacks from the untrusted zone. Although this seems straightforward, the evolution of network, network technologies and new attack vectors have meant that protecting network infrastructure has become increasingly hard. According to SafeNet 2014 Survey [1], although 74% of IT decision-makers trust their organization's perimeter security, yet about half (44%) of them admitted that their perimeter has been breached or did not know if it had been breached. With cyber-attacks on

[1]Cyber Security Lab, University of Waikato, New Zealand

the rise, the cost of IT security is becoming an increasingly heavy burden for every organization. According to the latest Gartner report [2], the worldwide spending on information security was $75.4 billion in 2015, which will jump to $101 billion in 2018 and soar to $170 billion by 2020.

The modern network has become very sophisticated and expansive as more and more potential entry points are added into the network. With the wide use of Bring-Your-Own-Device (BYOD) and cloud computing, the traditional network perimeter is unable to protect against malicious software and unauthorized users accessing the private network and data [3]. In 2014, the Cloud Security Alliance (CSA) launched the software-defined perimeter (SDP) project, with the goal of defending against network-based attacks by reducing the perimeter surface [4]. This protocol was previously only used by US government agencies such as the Department of Defense, SDP only allows TCP connections from preauthorized users and devices based on the "need-to-know" model [5].

At the time of writing of this chapter, very little material about SDP was available. This chapter therefore attempts to provide a clear understanding of SDP and put it in the context of cloud-based perimeter security. We go over the current state of the art in perimeter security and try to explain SDP and its architecture to our readers in a lucid manner. We will use the SDP specification 1.0 [5] as our main source of information. The chapter is structured as follows: Section 7.2 introduces the idea of SDP. It also describes some similar products and software-defined systems for the cloud. Section 7.3 gives a detailed description of the SDP and how its different components work together. We describe the SDP architecture, configurations and workflow before explaining the communication that takes place between various components of SDP. In Section 7.4, we discuss why SDP is able to provide high levels of perimeter security before finally concluding it in Section 7.5.

7.2   Background and related work

Perimeter security is not a new concept as historically people have used physical barriers to prevent, or at least delay attacks on villages, castles, facilities and buildings. These barriers define the perimeter. In the early days of computing before the internet, physical access control was sufficient for perimeter security as computers were placed in secure machine rooms. Computers, however, went from being stationary and stand-alone systems, to being networked together, to being on the internet, accessible from anywhere and everywhere. When it comes to the internet, a perimeter is usually thought of as the boundary protecting intranet or enterprise LAN from attacks or intrusion as shown in the conceptual diagram in Figure 7.1.

Let us take the traditional Internet infrastructure as an example. It has a private corporate network composed of machines that provide services for outside users. Thus, external users need to build connections to the servers and send requests to the corporate network to access services, such as sending emails or querying for HTTP pages. In this scenario, a perimeter is needed to protect the corporate network and authenticate incoming users. The perimeter is not only used to block malicious traffic but also provides a method to monitor the traffic. A fixed perimeter separates

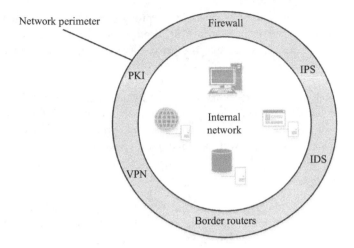

Figure 7.1   Conceptual diagram showing the perimeter enclosing an enterprise's resources

an internal network from the outside network. It may also provide a set of firewall functions that can block external access while allowing internal users to connect to outside network. Overall, a network perimeter enables users to manage their network and have better control of its security. Usually, the perimeter network is bounded by firewalls, but the firewall is not the only component in the perimeter. A series of systems may be applied to define a network perimeter, such as border routers, firewalls, intrusion detection systems, intrusion prevention systems, virtual private network (VPN), public key infrastructure (PKI). We discuss these systems below.

7.2.1   Firewalls

A firewall is a network security system which is used to monitor and control traffic in a network. The first generation of firewalls was based on packet filtering, which inspects the network addresses and port numbers to determine if the packet is allowed or blocked. The user can set up rules based on network addresses, protocols and port numbers. When packets go through the firewall, they are tested against filtering rules. If the packets do not match allowing rules, they are dropped. The second generation of firewalls was called "stateful" firewalls, which maintain the state of all packets passing through them. With such stateful information about packets, the firewalls could assess whether a new packet is the start of a new connection or a part of an existing connection [6]. The stateful firewalls can speed up the packet filtering process. When a packet has been inspected as part of an existing connection based on a state table, it will be allowed without further analysis. If the packet has not been recognized as an existing connection, it will be inspected as a new connection by firewall security rules. Application layer firewalls are the third generation of firewalls having the ability to understand certain applications and protocols as they operate and can be used to detect the misuse of certain protocols such as HTTP, FTP and DNS [7].

Proxy servers can also be used as firewalls. A proxy server acts as an intermediary for traffic between two specific networks [8]. Both sides of the network need to build connection through the proxy so that the proxy firewall can allow or block traffic based on different security rules.

Although firewalls can be used as an efficient security control for network security infrastructures, some experts feel it has become outdated as the networks have become more complicated [9]. There are many entry points and many access control roles based on different users in the modern network. Thus, modern network needs other newer techniques and methods working together to make it secure.

7.2.2   Virtual private network

VPN is a technology that creates a private network across a public network. The private network enables remote users to send and receive data with a secure connection between them and connected systems. It means VPN is an extension of the connectivity between mobile users, remote offices, customers and suppliers. Figure 7.2 shows simplified view of a VPN connection structure. Remote-access and site-to-site VPNs are two common types of VPNs. Remote-access VPN provides secure access for remote users to connect to their destination's network through a public telecommunication infrastructure. Site-to-site VPN uses gateway devices to build secure connection between two networks in two different locations.

VPN, which can form a network perimeter, has been a fairly trusted means of remote access; it, however, still has some disadvantages. The effectiveness of a perimeter created by VPN depends heavily on the security of the endpoints. These endpoints are the telecommuter's machines which are outside the network perimeter. Although one can trust the security of the perimeter, the roaming endpoints are outside of the perimeter and therefore are prone to being compromised. VPN can protect the data in transit between the endpoints from attacks; however, if an attacker

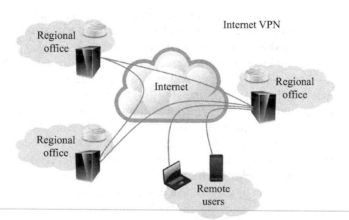

Figure 7.2   Simplified VPN connection structure

compromises an authenticated user's machine, the VPN will give the attacker an encrypted channel to connect into the network perimeter. VPN is unable to protect against such attacks which are on the rise now [10]. Furthermore, the capital costs associated with VPN gateways setup for individual servers are considerably high [4].

7.2.3   Public key infrastructure

The comprehensive setup that helps to distribute and identify public encryption keys and digital certificates and enable users to communicate with servers and other users securely is called the PKI. Sensitive information can be encrypted without PKI too, but there is no assurance of the identity of each end user and, hence, there will be no trust. A certificate authority (CA), a registration authority, a certificate database and a certificate store are the key elements of PKI. CA is regarded as a trusted third party in the PKI infrastructure. CAs verify the identity of an entity on the internet and issue a digital certificate which is bound to that entity. This certificate can then be used by the entity on the internet to prove its identity. A major weakness of PKI is that if the trusted CA is compromised, the entire PKI becomes insecure. In 2011, Dutch CA DigiNotar was broken into and the intruders managed to create more than 500 fake digital certificates. Eventually, web browser vendors had to block all the certificates issued by DigiNotar, and the company is no longer in operation [11].

7.2.4   Transport layer security

Transport layer security (TLS) protocol has evolved from secure sockets layer (SSL). Both SSL and TLS protocols provide data privacy and integrity between two communicating applications. The TLS record protocol and TLS handshake protocol are the two layers that compose TLS on the basis of the protocol specification [12]. TLS is widely used today to ensure application data exchange in a secure environment. Many applications such as web apps, file transfers, VPN connections, instant messaging and voice over IP use TLS to encrypt data over the network. According to the protocol specification in [12], the TLS record protocol provides connection security. When a connection is made, the handshake protocol is used to exchange all the information needed by client side and server side for exchanging application data. This process enables both sides to authenticate each other and to negotiate cryptographic keys and encryption algorithms. Mutual transport layer security (mTLS) is an enhanced protocol that provides mutual authentication for both the client side and the server side. With mTLS, not only the servers but the clients also need to provide a certificate for identification.

7.2.5   Other SDP-like solutions

7.2.5.1   Directory enabled networking

Directory enabled networking (DEN) is a relatively old specification proposed by Cisco and others, which binds services to clients in a network. In a DEN network, users, applications and network services are abstracted as profiles. A profile is an object that has properties and attributes describing its behavior. These profiles are integrated through a common information model that stores the necessary network information [13]. The other main component in a DEN is a set of policies. In a distributed network, a network manager needs policies to control all resources. In general, a policy defines which resources or services can be accessed by a corresponding user. With DEN, an application on the network can provide different resource access privileges to authorized users automatically. Any DEN-enabled application in the network can know the detailed information about the network from the central directory. When a user wants to access an application, the application should check the privilege of the user and provide suitable service according to the role of the user. The abstraction of a user through profiles helps DEN to provide correct access to users even when they change locations or positions within the company. Microsoft Windows NT operating system is an example of the application of DEN.

7.2.5.2   BeyondCorp

BeyondCorp is a model proposed by Google, which aims to improve the security of the traditional network architecture [14]. BeyondCorp breaks the traditional security perimeter that only allows internal users to access specific services from an internal network. Instead, in BeyondCorp, the access solely depends upon the device and the user credentials, irrespective of the location of the user [14]. The BeyondCorp system does not differentiate between local network and the internet and applies the same authentication and authorization processes for every user. This ensures that no firewalls or VPN-like systems are needed. BeyondCorp uses the concept of a managed device, wherein every device is explicitly managed by the enterprise. Only managed devices can access services. Along with managed devices with verified identities, a single sign-on system is used for all the users using those devices.

7.3   Software-defined perimeter

7.3.1   Overview of the software-defined perimeter framework

The idea of SDP security framework was proposed by CSA to keep systems secure against network attacks and protect application infrastructure [4]. As described previously, the traditional network architecture uses a fixed perimeter which consists of firewall functions to prevent external users from accessing internal resources without authentication. The traditional fixed perimeter ensures that the internal services remain secure on the basis of characteristics of blocking visibility and accessibility from outside the perimeter to the internal services [15]. However, with the development of BYOD and virtualization technology, the traditional perimeter is not enough to ensure the network to remain secure. There are too many moving devices inside the perimeter and applications and data migrating outside the perimeter for a traditional fixed perimeter to be successful. Attackers can easily access applications inside the perimeter through phishing attacks, and BYOD increases the risks as there are more devices being brought inside the perimeter [16]. Cloud computing also makes the traditional fixed perimeter seem old-fashioned and obsolete, as PaaS, SaaS and IaaS change the location of the perimeter; in fact, the location of the applications, servers and data might not even be known to provide an effective perimeter. Thus, techniques used for traditional perimeter security are not enough to protect application in today's network infrastructure due to their dependency on physical network devices.

The principles behind SDP are not entirely new. Top security organizations have previously implemented similar network architectures based on authentication and authorization before the application data exchange [4]. SDP, however, is the first approach to bring those ideas in public domain. The objective of SDP is to give application owners the ability to define and deploy perimeter functionality according to the requirements. With SDP, every server or application is initially hidden and invisible to users who want access [4]. Users need to be authenticated and provide identity in order to be authorized to access protected services. On the other hand, servers' services also need to be authenticated before users are able to access them. It means that SDP maintains the benefits of the need-to-know model and do not require a remote access gateway. In SDP, endpoint users need to authenticate and to be authorized before the real data exchange. Once both sides have been allowed to connect to each other, encrypted connections are created between requesting hosts and the application servers.

7.3.2 Software-defined perimeter architecture

In order to protect against external attacks of today and fit the distributed network topology, the network perimeter needs to be rebuilt. The solution is to shrink the perimeter directly down to the server which provides application services for users. With this solution, servers are isolated and attackers are outside the perimeter again. This method of building a perimeter creates a very strong and secure environment for servers. However, the inside users are also outside the perimeter in this circumstance. SDP attempts to solve this problem [5]. SDP is basically comprised of two components: SDP controllers and SDP hosts [5]. It separates the control channel from the data channel as shown in Figure 7.3. Control channel is used to authenticate SDP hosts. SDP hosts communicate with SDP controllers over this secure control channel. Once authenticated, the SDP hosts are then able to build connections with each other.

As shown in Figure 7.3, SDP hosts are divided into two types: initiating SDP hosts (IH) and accepting SDP hosts (AH). IHs initiate connections and thus can be thought

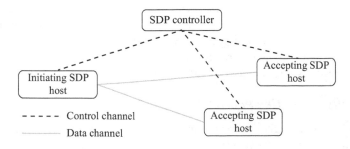

Figure 7.3   Software-defined perimeter architecture

of as clients, whereas AHs accept connections and thus are akin to servers. Before a connection can be made, an IH communicates with the SDP controller to request the list of the available AHs that it wishes to connect with. The SDP controllers may request device and user information from a database for identification and authentication before providing any information to the IH. The controller communicates with AHs periodically to update them with the authorized IHs. AHs reject all connections from all hosts except controllers and IHs which have already been authenticated by controllers. SDP can be viewed as an advanced access control system which brings a lot of benefits. SDP preauthentication mechanism enables the servers to remain invisible to unauthenticated users and systems. This characteristic isolates servers which can help to defend server exploitation. SDP's end-to-end control contributes to preventing connection hijacking. In contrast to a blanket access like in VPNs, SDP provides access for specific authorized users to get specific applications on servers. It means SDP architecture does not provide network connectivity to every port on the server. Only the authorized services or applications can be connected to, from the client side. This feature of SDP architecture makes it more secure than VPN.

7.3.3   Software-defined perimeter configurations

SDP in general can be implemented in four different configurations: (1) the client-to-gateway configuration, (2) the client-to-server configuration, (3) the server-to-server configuration and (4) the peer-to-peer configuration. In a cloud computing scenario, where a service provider uses cloud to provide services to its users, the client-to-gateway configuration appears to be more suitable. Other configurations, however, can also be used in cloud computing depending on the specific scenario. Figure 7.4 shows the client-to-gateway configuration implemented in the cloud.

In this configuration, the authenticating host acts as a gateway between the servers and the client. As shown in Figure 7.4, the servers are hidden behind the AH, which acts on behalf of the servers. There may be multiple AHs each protecting a group of servers (services) in an installation. The servers may be grouped on the basis of the kind of services they offer or load-balancing needs. This configuration helps to mitigate many attacks in which the attackers might move laterally across the servers, such as application vulnerability exploits, main in the middle attacks, pass the hash attacks [5]. For the sake of simplicity, in Figure 7.4, the AH, the servers and the controller are all shown to be in the same cloud, whereas the client is outside the cloud. SDP, however, is agnostic to the location of these components. The components shown in the figure can be located in the same cloud or each of them located in a separate cloud and the SDP configuration will still be valid. In our discussion, we will generally refer to a singular controller, AH and IH; however, in practice, there may be multiple controllers if required in a configuration along with multiple AHs and IHs.

7.3.4   Software-defined perimeter workflow

SDP workflow is entirely different from our everyday connectivity model. Figure 7.5(a) shows the steps that occur in a regular connectivity model. Clients build a TCP connection to servers before any other authentication. Then, users use credentials to

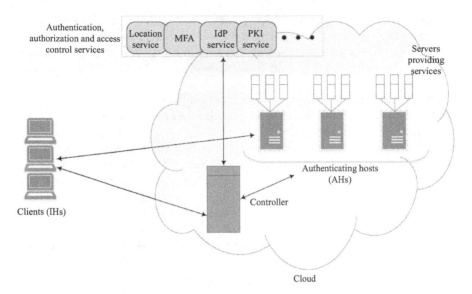

Figure 7.4   Client-to-gateway SDP configuration for cloud services

Figure 7.5   SDP workflow

log in to the server applications. In this connection model, multifactor authentication (MFA) may be applied to defend against credential theft attacks. SDP workflow rearranges the steps of normal connectivity as shown in Figure 7.5(b), it ensures preauthentication of devices and users before building connections. With SDP, MFA occurs as the first step, then users are logged in to the SDP controller [5]. Once authorized by the controller, clients get the permission to establish connections with the servers. This will be explained in the seven-step workflow below.

CSA's SDP specification 1.0 [5] describes the SDP workflow as the following seven steps:

1.   The SDP controller is brought online for SDP hosts to log in. The controller may use a variety of authentication, authorization and access control services as shown in Figure 7.4, for verification of hosts/clients that seek to be connected to services.
2.   Accepting SDP hosts are brought online. Immediately after bootup, the hosts are required to connect to the controller and send identification information

for authentication. Accepting hosts communicate with the controller but do not respond to any other unauthenticated entity. The specification does not mention how the servers are authorized by the AHs in the client-to-gateway configuration; however, this will need to be done prior to the AH connecting to the controller. When the AH communicates with the controller, it also needs to make the controller aware of the services that are behind it.

3.   An initiating host that wants to avail a service first needs to be authenticated and registered with the controller.
4.   Once the controller authenticates an IH, it selects which appropriate servers can provide the required service to the IH and which AHs do they belong to.
5.   The SDP controllers inform AHs to accept connection from the authorized IH.
6.   The SDP controllers send a list of AHs; this IH can communicate along with any other information or optional policies needed for communication.
7.   The IH starts to communicate with AHs by establishing a mutual TLS connection with each AH to perform secure communication. Note that an IH does not communicate directly with a server in the client-to-gateway configuration instead the communication is through the AH that acts as a proxy.

7.3.5   Software-defined perimeter protocol

The first and the second steps in the SDP workflow bring the SDP controller and the AHs online, this is also called onboarding. The specification by itself does not delve into the finer details of onboarding as this can vary significantly from one installation to other. This is left to the implementation and can be done either manually or through IT automation tools such as Puppet or Chef. Most cloud service providers also provide their own customized tools for easy onboarding.

7.3.5.1   Single packet authentication

One of the important building blocks of SDP is authentication. All communications, between the IH and AH, the IH and the controller and the AH and the controller need to first go through the authentication phase. The authentication in SDP is done using the single packet authentication (SPA) scheme. The SPA scheme was developed from the port knocking scheme first described in USENIX [17] in 2004. In port knocking, the firewall protecting a server is configured to drop all received packets by default. A legitimate user will send a sequence of packets to various ports of the server one by one, in accordance to a previously agreed upon sequence. Although the server drops all the packets and does not respond to the sender, a knock server keeps track of the ports which have been knocked in the sequence. If the knock sequence is legitimate, the server opens the port required by the user. This scheme has a few practical issues that are overcome by the SPA scheme, which as the name suggests uses a single packet for authentication as opposed to the multiple packets needed in port knocking.

In SPA, the communicating parties share a secret seed. The secret seed, along with a counter, is used to create a one-time password (OTP). Whenever one party wants to communicate with another party, the OTP is sent in a packet along with the counter. The receiving party tries to verify the OTP and only responds if the

IP header	TCP header	AID (32-bit)	OTP (32-bit)	Counter (64-bit)

Figure 7.6   The SPA packet

verification is successful. The SPA protocol is based on the HOTP protocol defined in RFC 4226 [18].

In SDP, an SPA packet is sent from the client to the server. Server in this case can either be the controller or the AH. The server does not need to respond to this packet. The format of the SPA packet is shown in Figure 7.6. Here, IP and TCP fields are the IP and TCP headers; AID is the agent ID or the universal identifier of the client wishing to communicate to the server. The counter is the variable input which changes in each packet and helps to protect against replay attacks and the OTP, created using the HOTP protocol. The OTP can be created by simply hashing the secret seed with the variable counter. As the seed is secret and the counter is variable, this creates a unique secret password for every packet. The SPA packet in the SDP spec 1.0 does not provide much implementation detail. The SPA implementation of fwknop [17], however, randomizes the packet by adding 16 bytes of random data to each packet. In addition, to protect the integrity of the packet, it creates an MD5 digest over the entire packet to ensure the packet is not modified before it reaches the recipient. SPA provides the following benefits to an SDP architecture:

1. It blackens the server (either AH or the controller). The server does not respond to any connection attempt from anyone unless a valid SPA packet has been received.
2. This helps in mitigating DoS attacks as the server doesn't spend any resources in processing spurious packets.
3. It helps in detecting attacks as any connection attempt that does not start with an SPA packet can immediately be classified as an attack.

7.3.5.2   Device validation

One factor in the MFA that SDP uses is device validation. In today's computing world, a large amount of computing is done by mobile devices such as laptops, mobile phones and PDAs. It is therefore important to make sure the device that one is communicating with is the correct device. Although mTLS (described in Section 7.2.4) can be used to make sure that the device requesting a connection has valid keys, it is unable to prove whether the keys belong to the communicating device and are not stolen. SDP therefore takes the additional step of validating the device with which the controller is communicating. Although mTLS proves that the device possesses the correct keys, device validation proves the authenticity of the device itself. The current SDP specification [5] does not delve into the implementation of device authentication but recommends it for additional security. Although device validation provides an additional level of security to SDP, it also creates an additional overhead of maintaining a certificate for each device. As the number of users and the number of devices per user grows, certificate management will become a challenging issue.

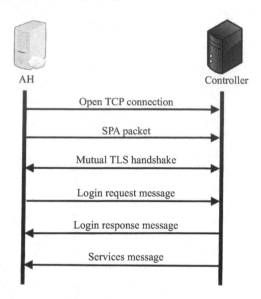

Figure 7.7   AH-controller communication

7.3.5.3   AH-controller protocol

When an AH is brought online, it first needs to communicate with the controller to login and register itself as an accepting host [5]. The sequence diagram for the AH-controller protocol is shown in Figure 7.7. This diagram only shows the message sequence in the initial login.

As all communication in SDP is done through the TCP protocol, the first step in the AH-controller communication is to open a TCP connection. Once a TCP connection has been established, the AH sends an SPA packet to get authenticated by the controller. A valid SPA packet will authenticate the AH. In SDP, every connection uses TLS and every client–server pair must use mTLS for mutual authentication. The AH, therefore, after getting authenticated initiates the mTLS handshake. Once they finish mutual TLS handshake, the AH needs to send a login request message to indicate it is ready for accepting information from the controller. The format of the packet sent by AH is shown in Figure 7.9(a). The controller then sends a response message to the AH. The response message indicates whether the login action was successful or not. If the AH login was successful, the response message should provide AH with a session ID. The format of this packet is shown in Figure 7.9(b). A valid status code along with an AH session ID indicates successful creation of a session. Next, the controller needs to tell the AH the services that are being protected. This is done by sending a service message to the AH. SDP specification [5] suggests using a JSON array to relay this information. The format of the service message is shown in Figure 7.9(d). If for example port 443 is being used to provide the Sharepoint service, the JSON specification can be something like shown in Figure 7.8 [5].

Format	Example

{"services":
[
  "port"   : \<Server port\>,
  "id"   : \<32-bit Service ID\>,
  "address" : \<Server IP\>,
  "name"   : \<Service name\>
]
}
	{"services":
	[
	  "port" : 443
	  "id" : 12345678,
	  "address" : 100.100.100.100,
	  "name" : SharePoint
	]
	}

Figure 7.8　The JSON format for AH service message

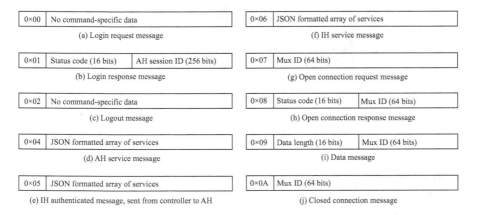

Figure 7.9　SDP communication messages

If the AH wants to logout, it needs to send a logout message to the controller to indicate that it will no longer be available for accepting any messages. The logout message is similar to the login message; however, the AH does not expect a response to the logout message. The format of the logout message is shown in Figure 7.9(c).

When a new IH has been authenticated, the controller needs to send an IH authenticated message to AH. The AH should enable this IH to access the servers on which the requested services exist. The IH authentication message format is shown in Figure 7.9(e). This would be clearer after the next subsection on IH-controller protocol.

The JSON specification is as follows:

```
{
"sid": <256-bit IH Session ID>,
"seed": <32-bit SPA seed>,
"counter": <32-bit SPA counter>
"id":<32-bit Service ID>
}
```

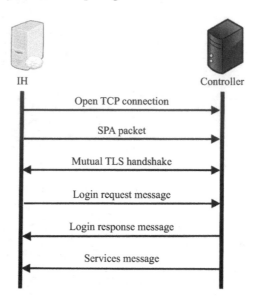

Figure 7.10   IH-controller communication

where sid is the session ID for the IH, and id is the service ID of the service the IH wants to use. Seed and counter fields will be used by the AH to validate the IH SPA packet.

7.3.5.4   IH-controller protocol

When a client, also known IH in the SDP realm, wants to request for a particular service, it first contacts the controller. As the AHs are blackened by SPA and by default drop all communication directed toward them, the only way to connect to a server is by first communicating with the controller and getting authenticated. The messages exchanged in the IH-controller communication are similar to the AH-controller communication. The sequence diagram for the IH to connect to the controller is shown in Figure 7.10.

As discussed before, all communication takes place using TCP. The IH then sends an SPA packet to the controller and gets authenticated if it has valid credentials. The IH and the controller authenticate each other using mTLS. Then, the IH sends a login request message to the controller to indicate that it wants to join the SDP, and it is available. The login request message for IH-controller communication is the same as the one used by AH and shown in Figure 7.9(a). The controller then responds to the IH with a status code indicating whether the login was successful, or not. If the login was successful the message will contain a 256 bit IH session id. The message is similar to the one sent by controller to AH in AH-controller communication and shown in Figure 7.9(b). In IH-controller communication, the message contains IH Session ID as opposed to the AH Session ID in Figure 7.9(b). If the IH wants to logout, it can

Format	Example

{"services":
 [
  "address" : \<AH IP\>,
  "id"   : \<32-bit Service ID\>,
  "name"   : \<Service name\>,
  "type"   : \<Service type\>
 ]
}
	{"services":
	 [
	  "address" : \<200.200.200.200\>,
	  "id" : \<12345678\>,
	  "name" : \<SharePoint\>,
	  "type" : \<https\>
	]
	}

Figure 7.11   The JSON format for IH service message

send a logout request message to the controller to indicating it wants to quit the SDP. There is no response from the controller for this request, and the format is as shown previously in Figure 7.9(c). When the IH has been authenticated and is logged in, the controller needs to inform the IH of the available services and the IP addresses of the servers offering those services. The controller does this by sending a service messages to the IH. The format of this message is shown in Figure 7.9(f). The JSON formatted array can hold information about multiple services. An example with one service is shown in Figure 7.11.

7.3.5.5   IH–AH protocol

Once the AH is online and knows the services, it can offer and the IH has been authenticated by the controller and has received a list of services and AHs which offer them, they are ready to perform the client–server communication. In the IH–AH protocol, the communication is always initiated by the IH. The initial message exchange during the IH–AH protocol is similar to the ones in AH-controller and IH-controller protocols. The IH opens a TCP connection and sends an SPA packet to get authenticated by the AH. Once the authentication is successful, IH and AH perform the mutual TLS handshake. This will allow both IH and AH to send and receive data securely. The IH then sends an open connection request message as shown in Figure 7.9(g) to the AH to signal its request for a service. The message consists of an 8-bit command and a 64-bit mux ID. The 64-bit mux ID is used to multiplex connections for multiple services between the same IH–AH pair. The leading 32 bits in the mux ID come from the 32-bit unique service ID of the service the IH is requesting. The trailing 32-bit identify a unique session ID for the session between the IH and the AH. The AH then responds with an open connection response message which indicates whether the connection was successful or not. The message format is shown in Figure 7.9(h). Once a connection has been established, IH and AH can begin data transmission to each other. The data transmission on either side is done with the help of the data message, whose format is shown in Figure 7.9(i). This data message will precede the actual payload, and it consists of a 16-bit field indicating the size of the payload to follow, along with the command and the Mux ID. The data message does not need a response or an acknowledgment message. If any of the IH or the AH needs to close

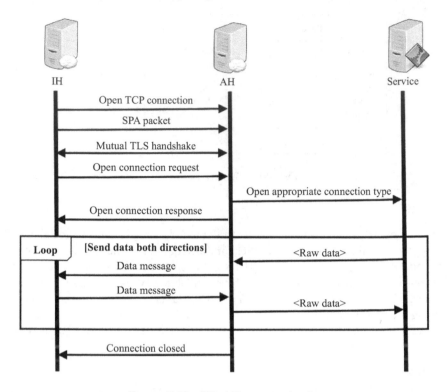

Figure 7.12   IH–AH communication

the connection a closed connection message is sent. The closed connection message is the last message of an SDP connection. The receiver of this message closes the connection without any further response. The format of the message is shown in Figure 7.9(h). The messages sent between IH and an AH that is protecting a service requested by the IH is shown in Figure 7.12.

7.4   SDP security

In this section, SDP security features and components are discussed as follows:

Zero visibility—SDP was designed to mitigate network-based attacks by dynamically employing software-based security perimeter to protect any kind of network, including clouds, demilitarized zones, data centers and even small networks [19]. So far, SDP has proved to be a good defense against network attacks under simulated tests [19,20]. In various hackathons conducted by CSA so far, no breach has been possible. Each of the four hackathons conducted by CSA has been centered around specific themes such as insider threats, DDoS attacks, credential theft and high-availability public cloud. In each of the scenarios, the attackers were provided information which mimics the information gathered by attackers in that particular scenario. However, after millions of attack attempts, the SDP architecture is yet to be breached. SDP achieves this by providing zero visibility to the outside network and utilizing multiple levels of validation and authentication before granting access to a client. In all SDP utilizes the following five layers of controls [19].

Single packet authorization (SPA)—As mentioned before, SPA blackens the server, effectively making it invisible to unauthorized devices. The first packet in SPA to the controller cryptographically verifies the authorized device. The SDP specification does not delve into the key management and distribution required for the exchange of cryptographic material, leaving the responsibility on the implementation. Successful verification of the SPA packet allows a device to further connect to an AH. If the verification fails, the connection is immediately dropped without any response to prevent clogging of network resources.

Mutual transport layer security (mTLS)—TLS is used for providing secure communication and exchange of confidential information between two entities over a network. Traditionally, TLS was only used to authenticate servers in a client–server communication; however, SDP uses mTLS, in which both the client and the server mutually authenticate each other.

Device validation (DV)—SDP performs MFA by requiring device validation. This binds the cryptographic keys to a particular device and prevents the misuse of stolen credentials. An attacker which has stolen cryptographic keys will fail the device validation step unless it also happens to have stolen the device to which the credentials belong.

Dynamic firewalls (DF)—Traditional firewalls have rules relating to the source and destination IP address and port. In SDP, the basic rule for every communication is, deny. Only devices and users, which have been authenticated, are allowed by first binding the device and the user and then dynamically inserting a rule for the binding. Thus, only authorized users and devices are able to make a connection to the protected resources.

Application binding (AppB)—In SDP, each connection is bound to a particular application. SDP creates an encrypted tunnel that binds the device, the user and the service/application the user wants to connect to. Thus, an authorized user can only interact with the application it requested. For access to other applications, the user will have to undergo a separate authentication procedure. This elimination of crosstalk prevents an authorized user to launch insider attacks by making use of vulnerabilities in applications.

7.5   Conclusion

The scenarios in the SDP hackathons mimic the real-world scenarios very closely and, therefore, it can be said with a high degree of confidence that the SDP architecture provides an easy-to-deploy and still highly secure way of protecting network infrastructure. Having said that, it must be kept in mind that SDP has not been deployed widely yet and public data about attacks on real-world deployments of SDP does not exist. There is considerable amount of excitement in the cloud and open source community, however, regarding SDP which is seen as a potential solution to the cloud perimeter security problem. At the time of writing this chapter, the first open source implementation of the client, the gateway and the controller for the client-to-gateway SDP configuration was available [21].

The security afforded by SDP, however, comes at a cost. The security cost comes in the form of connection delay introduced by SDP and reduced throughput. As explained in Section 7.3.5, before a client can establish a secure connection with a server in SDP's client-to-gateway configuration, it has to get authenticated first by the controller and then by the AH. Each of these authentications has three stages where the client first opens a TCP connection then gets authenticated using SPA and then performs a mutual TLS handshake. This has the potential to add significant a connection delay, which will be exacerbated by the network latency of the cloud itself. The other form of cost in SDP is the reduced throughput. The data message in the current version of SDP is an 88-bit message, which precedes the transmission of data. This along with mTLS's own overhead and the communication between IH and controller and the IH and AH to establish secure communication contributes in reducing the throughput of the SDP communication. The overhead and the maximum payload can give a rough idea about the throughput of SDP. The additional overhead and in turn reduced throughput caused by the SDP therefore cannot be ignored. Thus, although SDP is capable of providing unbreakable (as of yet) security, any implementation of SDP will need to consider the effects of both connection delay and reduced throughput.

The analysis and understanding of the SDP presented in this chapter are based on SDP specification version 1.0 [5] which was available at the time of writing this chapter. The SDP working group of the CSA is currently working on specification version 2.0, which will possibly be more detailed and will focus on protecting services in IoT and cloud computing.

References

[1]   SafeNet Inc, Oct. 2014, Baltimore, Available: http://www.safenet-inc.pt/news/2014/data-security-confidence-index-results/ [retrieved February 21, 2017].

[2]   S. Moore, "Gartner Says Worldwide Information Security Spending Will Grow 4.7 Percent to Reach $75.4 Billion in 2015" Gartner, 23 September 2015, Available: http://www.gartner.com/newsroom/id/3135617 [retrieved February 21, 2017].

[3]   Z. Dimitrio and L. Dimitrios, "Addressing cloud computing security issues," Future Generation Computer Systems, vol. 28, no. 3, pp. 583–592, 2012.

[4]   Software Defined Perimeter Working Group, "Software Defined Perimeter," December 2013. Available: https://downloads.cloudsecurityalliance.org/initiatives/sdp/Software_Defined_Perimeter.pdf [retrieved February 21, 2017].

[5] Software Defined Perimeter Working Group, "SDP Specification 1.0," April 2014. Available: https://cloudsecurityalliance.org/download/sdp-specification-v1-0/ [retrieved February 21, 2017].

[6] M. G. Gouda and A. X. Liu, "A model of stateful firewalls and its properties," in *2005 International Conference on Dependable Systems and Networks (DSN'05)*, 2005.

[7] A. Mohd Zafran Abdul, "Performance analysis of application layer firewall," in Wireless Technology and Applications (ISWTA), *2012 IEEE Symposium on*, 2012.

[8] O. Rolf, "Internet security: firewalls and beyond," *Communications of the ACM*, vol. 40, no. 5, pp. 92–102, May 1997.

[9] W. A. Arbaugh, "Firewalls: an outdated defense," *Computer*, vol. 36, no. 6, pp. 112–113, June 2003. doi: 10.1109/MC.2003.1204384.

[10] Mandiant, "A view from the front lines," http://www2.fireeye.com/rs/fireye/images/rpt-m-trends-2015.pdf [retrieved March 2017].

[11] N. Van der Meulen, "DigiNotar: dissecting the first Dutch digital disaster," Journal of Strategic Security, vol. 6, no. 2, p. 46, 2013.

[12] Tim Dierks, "The transport layer security (TLS) protocol version 1.2," Network Working Group, RFC 5246, 2008.

[13] Y. Xinzhong, "Directory Enabled Networks," Helsinki University of Technology, December 1998.

[14] W. Rory and B. Betsy, "BeyondCorp: a new approach to enterprise security," login, vol. 39, no. 6, pp. 5–11, 2014.

[15] J. Ari and O. Alina, "New approaches to security and availability for cloud data," *Communications of the ACM*, vol. 56, no. 2, pp. 64–73, 2013.

[16] S. Kristoffer, "Mobile device security: exploring the possibilities and limitations with Bring Your Own Device (BYOD)," (Master's Thesis), KTH, School of Electrical Engineering (EES), Communication Networks, Sweden, 2013.

[17] M. Rash, "Single packet authorization with Fwknop," December 2005, Whitepaper. http://www.cipherdyne.org/fwknop/docs/SPA.html [retrieved March 2017].

[18] D. M'Raihi, M. Bellare, F. Hoornaert, D. Naccache and O. Ranen, "Hotp: an hmac-based one-time password algorithm," Network Working Group, RFC 4226, Oct. 2004.

[19] SDP Working Group, "SDP Hackathon Whitepaper," April 2014 https://downloads.cloudsecurityalliance.org/initiatives/sdp/SDP_Hackathon_Whitepaper.pdf [retrieved March 2017].

[20] SDP Working Group, "SDP hackathon 4, Analysis and Report," March 2016 https://www.vidder.com/wp-content/uploads/2016/09/CSA-Verizon-Vidder-Hackathon4-Reliability.pdf [retrieved March 2017].

[21] Open Source Software Defined Perimeter. http://www.waverleylabs.com/open-source-sdp/ [retrieved March 2017].

Chapter 8

Security, trust, and privacy for cloud computing in Transportation Cyber-Physical Systems

Wenjia Li[1], Jonathan Voris[1], and N. Sertac Artan[2]

Abstract

Transportation Cyber-Physical Systems (TCPS) strive to achieve the seamless interoperability of a rich set of sensors embedded in vehicles, roadside units, and other infrastructure with computing platforms ranging from smartphones to cloud servers, through a variety of communication mechanisms. A successful TCPS will provide smart and scalable solutions to some of the major problems urban societies facing today including high fatalities in road crashes, time and emission costs of traffic congestion, and efficient allocation of parking spaces. However, the practicality of such a TCPS is challenged by (1) stakeholders with different and often conflicting security and privacy requirements, (2) the demands of real-time data intensive computing and communication, and (3) a high level of heterogeneity in the types of technologies deployed.

Transportation Cloud Computing, which is the integration of Cloud Computing with TCPS, is a promising solution to the challenges listed above for a scalable implementation. This chapter presents the security, trust, and privacy issues posed by integrating cloud computing with TCPS as in the first challenge above. We will survey the state of the art with respect to countermeasures which are capable of providing improved security and privacy for cloud computing in TCPS. More specifically, we will first discuss the unique challenges and the current state of the art in TCPS as well as the integration of cloud computing techniques into a TCPS application scenario. Next, we will present a comprehensive literature review on attack surface and strategies for cloud computing in TCPS. To address these attacks, we will describe various techniques to enhance security, trust, and privacy to help better safeguard cloud computing paradigms for TCPS.

[1]New York Institute of Technology (NYIT), Department of Computer Science, USA
[2]New York Institute of Technology (NYIT), Department of Electrical and Computer Engineering, USA

8.1   Introduction

There are over 1.2 billion vehicles on the roads worldwide, and the number of electric vehicles passed the 1 million mark in 2015 [1]. Transportation provides the backbone of the modern society, yet it has also been taking its toll on the environment. Moreover, traffic accidents have claimed 1.25 million lives every year since 2007, being the top cause of death among people aged 15–29 years [2]. Transportation is one of the most important application domains of Cyber-Physical Systems (CPS), which are systems in which physical components are tightly coupled with cyber components, such as networking, sensing, computing, and control.

The application of CPS in transportation sector, called transportation CPS (TCPS), will transform the way people interact with transportation systems, just as the Internet has transformed the way people interact with information. A desirable CPS must be safe, secure, and resilient to a variety of unanticipated and rapidly evolving environments and disturbances in addition to being efficient and inexpensive to maintain. Today each vehicle is equipped with 70–100 sensors [3]. For instance, one TCPS application utilizing these sensors will be vehicle prognostics, which will allow vehicle owners to assess how long the parts in their vehicles will last by the continuous monitoring and detailed reporting of the state of each part via the on-board prognostics systems [4]. This technique will allow vehicle owners to be more confident that their cars will not have any issue the next time they are behind the wheels. Moreover, drivers today can get real-time traffic information and can avoid traffic jams so that they can predict their schedule precisely. More importantly, the drivers can be alerted to an accident occurring in front of them by other vehicles or roadside units (RSUs) nearby so that they can avoid a fatal accident. The drivers can reserve parking spots ahead of time and can be directed to available parking spots as they become available in real time [5].

The effective operation of a TCPS is based on data intensive computing. By using a network of remote servers to store, manage, and process data rather than a local server or a personal computer, cloud computing has the potential to enable transportation CPS to operate in a desirable manner.

However, to reap the benefits of cloud computing, there are some challenges which must be addressed. One of the key challenges in making TCPS and Transportation Cloud Computing (TCC) ubiquitous is keeping the drivers, passengers, and pedestrians safe and secure, while preserving their privacy.

In addition, TCPS can generally be used to help enhance the safety and efficiency of the ground transportation system. One such example is the Traffic Estimation and Prediction System (TrEPS), which generally offers the predictive information that is required for proactive traffic control [6]. However, sometimes the TrEPS may receive confusing or even conflicting traffic information reported by multiple traffic sensors, some of which may have been compromised by attackers. If the trustworthiness of these traffic sensor data cannot be properly evaluated, then it is possible to result in traffic jams or even life-threatening accidents because most of the vehicles may be incorrectly redirected to the same route according to the fake traffic information. Thus, it is critical to ensure the security and trustworthiness of the TCPS.

In this chapter, first the general components of TCPS and TCC are introduced. Then, attack surfaces in TCPS are discussed in depth, followed by the current state-of-the-art security mechanisms for the TCPS. Later, both trust and privacy techniques are evaluated against the unique challenges posed in the TCPS context.

8.2 Transportation CPS

8.2.1 Vehicular and transportation networks

Following the introduction and popularity of the Mobile ad-hoc Networks (MANETs), Vehicular ad-hoc Networks (VANETs) evolved as a unique subset of the MANET, where vehicles form an ad-hoc network and communicate with other vehicles around them or to other parties, such as the roadside infrastructures. VANETs are distinguishable from other classes of MANETs by the high speeds the vehicles are traveling, the hybrid node composition, the high dynamic range of node density they exhibit, which ranges from a single vehicle communicating with the roadside infrastructure at a rural road with no nearby vehicles for miles, to vehicles in rush-hour traffic in parallel streets in a metropolitan area. Other unique VANETs attributes include their real-time requirements (e.g., emergency stop when approaching at high speed to an accident on the highway) and their access to robust battery power, computing, and networking resources.

VANETs are part of the Intelligent Transportation System (ITS). ITS is an overall architecture to systematically collect and process the data related to transportation and produced by many sources including the VANETs so that various stakeholders of transportation systems can make better, data-informed decisions. As a result, the overall transportation system can become safer and more efficient [7,8].

The Transportation (Vehicular) Clouds promises to provide the strength and flexibility of the cloud computing into the VANETs and ITS in general. In this section, we look into various networking and communication technologies developed as part of the VANETs and ITS. In Section 8.8.3, we introduce TCC.

8.2.2 Vehicle-to-everything communication

In TCPS, vehicles need to connect to various parties. The communication between vehicles and all other entities including other vehicles is generalized as vehicle-to-everything (V2X) communication. V2X can be further divided into the following subcategories depending on the parties, which the vehicles communicate:

* Vehicle-to-Vehicle (V2V) Communication
* Vehicle-to-Infrastructure (V2I) Communication
* Vehicle-to-Grid (V2G) Communication
* Vehicle-to-Pedestrian (V2P) Communication

8.2.2.1   Vehicle-to-Vehicle (V2V) Communication

In V2V, vehicles form ad-hoc networks with vehicles around them to share information such as nearby traffic conditions, and immediate dangers such as an intersection collusion warning [9].

Vehicles can also provide services to other vehicles. For instance, if two vehicles desire to communicate on the same highway but are out of radio range from each other, they can recruit the help of vehicles in between to route their traffic. Cars are parked 95% of the time [10] and parked cars can be a valuable resource to other cars (parked or in motion), and to interested third parties. In [11], the authors proposed Parked Vehicle Assistance (PVA), where they envision using parked cars as static nodes similar to RSU, however without the high cost of deploying and maintaining the necessary infrastructure for the RSU. Unlike other cars in the traffic, a parked car's location is fixed, and thus the parked cars can be used as a static backbone for the network, providing network access for both parked and moving vehicles.

For the short-range communication between vehicles and the roadside infrastructure, Dedicated Short Range Communications (DSRC) is used, which is carried over the 75 MHz band between 5.85 and 5.925 GHz [9]. The physical and medium access protocol layers on this band are collectively called as the Wireless Access in Vehicular Environment (WAVE), which is a combination of IEEE 802.11p-2010) [12] and the IEEE 1609 protocol suite [13]. Recently, Visible Light Communication (VLC) has also become a promising alternative [3].

8.2.2.2   Vehicle-to-Infrastructure (V2I) Communication

Using parked cars, other relays (such as mobile phones), or dedicated cellular/Wi-Fi connectivity built-in the vehicle [14] are promising solutions for providing Internet connectivity to vehicles. On the other hand, for remote areas with weak cellular signals, or low traffic density, dedicated roadside infrastructure, a.k.a. RSUs, can provide robust Internet connectivity, and dedicated sensors for local information. However, due to their high cost, the widespread use of these RSUs is still limited.

8.2.2.3   Vehicle-to-Grid (V2G) Communication

With the recent growing interest in electrical vehicles (EVs), the demand for electricity will definitely increase. However, as stated above, a vehicle is parked most of the time, and the EV has a sizable battery which can be charged in a fraction of the time the EV is parked. Thus, the EVs can also be considered as a large distributed energy storage over the power grid, which can be used to supply power to the grid when the demand is high.

For instance, if an EV has access to real-time power pricing when it is parked and if it knows approximately how long it will be parked, the EV can decide to buy or sell power or stay idle thus minimizes, or even eliminates, its power cost [15].

8.2.2.4   Vehicle-to-Pedestrian (V2P) Communication

According to the 2015 Global Status Report on Road Safety by the World Health Organization, 22% of the road traffic deaths in the world are pedestrian casualties [2]. Thus, research in the area of robust alert systems, which alert the pedestrians and

Table 8.1   In-vehicular communication technologies

	Max. data rate	Topology	Standards
Controller Area Network (CAN)	1 Mbps	Multi-master	ISO 11898-1 to -6
Local Interconnect Network (LIN)	20 kbps	1 Master, up to 16 slaves	ISO 17987
FlexRay	10 Mbps	Multi-drop Star Hybrid	ISO 17458-1 to -5
Media-Oriented Systems Transport (MOST)	150 Mbps	Timing master	MOST25, 50, 150

vehicles approaching to pedestrians of an imminent collision between them, is very important [16,17]. It should also be noted that some solutions such as Pedestrian Countdown Signals (PCS) are reported to actually increase the number of pedestrian–vehicle collisions [18]. Other studies reported that pedestrians may be exposed to a greater danger when crossing under time pressure [19].

8.2.3   Intra-vehicle Communication

Due to conflicting constraints in bandwidth, cost, and licensing requirements, multiple communication technologies have been proposed for intra-vehicle communication. Standards for many of these technologies have been developed, and versions and sub-modules of these standards have been ratified. Table 8.1 summarizes the commonly used intra-vehicle communication technologies and their key properties.

8.2.3.1   Controller Area Network Bus

Controller Area Network (CAN) bus is the most common communication medium for intra-vehicle communication. CAN bus is a serial bus. Communication on the CAN bus is carried via a message-based protocol, where all the messages are broadcast to all the *nodes* connected to the bus. CAN bus is a multi-master bus, which means there is no designated node that arbitrates the bus access. Instead each message carries an identifier that serves as an indicator of the priority of that particular message in the network. A critical limitation of CAN bus is its low bandwidth. Recently, the original developers of the CAN bus, Robert Bosch GmbH, developed a new communication protocol called CAN with Flexible Data Rate (CAN-FD). CAN-FD allows higher data rates [20].

8.2.3.2   Local Interconnect Network

Local Interconnect Network (LIN) bus is a low-cost serial sub-bus system for simple applications such as car seat motors, door locks, and sun roof motors, where full CAN functionality and bandwidth are not necessary [21]. LIN is a single master, multiple slave bus. A single CAN device can act as the master for multiple LIN nodes, and act as a bridge between the CAN and LIN buses. Since LIN hardware can cost much less than CAN hardware, this topology reduces the overall system cost.

8.2.3.3   Flexray

Flexray [22] was proposed for X-by-wire systems such as steer-by-wire for higher speed and fault-tolerance. FlexRay is a multi-master bus and it uses Time Division Multiple Access (TDMA) to assign fixed time slots to each node in the guaranteeing bandwidth for each device. FlexRay also has two channels for redundant communication.

8.2.3.4   Media-Oriented Systems Transport

Media-Oriented Systems Transport (MOST) [23] and similar multimedia bus systems have been proposed to satisfy the high bandwidth communication requirements of the recent in-car entertainment systems with high-quality audio and video. MOST has a single timing master and uses TDMA for its synchronous data communication where the video and audio is transmitted. It also has an asynchronous mode for sending larger size blocks, and a control channel.

8.3   Transportation cloud computing

TCC is a new and evolving paradigm to allow various transportation entities to use the traditional cloud resources made available by third parties, and also to allow the unique capabilities of these transportation entities to be utilized by third parties. In the former use, the TCPS is the consumer (customer) for the cloud service. An example of the TCPS using the cloud resources as consumers is a vehicle getting good-quality GPS location from a third-party server in the cloud [24]. In the latter use, the TCPS is the producer. For example, interested third parties can get real-time sensor data for a specific geographical area of interest from the vehicles and the RSUs in the area. This information can be indirectly related to the TCPS such as the temperature profile of the given geographical area [25]. This information can also be directly related such as the traffic conditions in the area [26]. Note that, in the last case, the TCPS is both the consumer and the producer.

Cloud offerings involving vehicular systems as consumer and/or providers are offered as services. The classification for these services in the context of TCC is given below. Note that, as TCC is an evolving technology, this list is not necessarily exhaustive.

8.3.1   Transportation cloud computing service taxonomy

The NIST cloud model identifies three service models: Software-as-a-Service (SaaS), Platform-as-a-Service (PaaS), and Infrastructure-as-a-Service (IaaS). These services in their basic form can all be considered as IaaS or be defined as part of a SaaS or PaaS, abstracting the access to the raw resources. For instance, a taxi fleet owner can collect the sensory data from their vehicles and offer real-time regional information as part of a database software offering. Services provided within the transportation cloud regardless of whether the vehicles are provider, consumer, or both can be classified into the following categories [27,28]:

8.3.1.1   Network-as-a-Service (NaaS)

Many vehicles today have Wi-Fi and cellular connectivity. Although, they may not utilize this connectivity all the time at their full capacity. Similarly, RSU can provide Internet connection to the cars that are passing by or parked as a service. The vehicles with excess bandwidth they would like to share, and the RSU's providing Internet connection can advertise these network resources. Nearby vehicles that are in need of Internet access can purchase Internet access from these providers. Furthermore, the vehicle providing Internet connectivity, and the vehicle which needs the connectivity, may be out of range of each other. In such a case, intermediate vehicles can act as relays to carry traffic between the provider vehicle and the consumer vehicle, thus providing another network service [29].

8.3.1.2   Sensing-as-a-Service (S^2aaS)

Today vehicles are equipped with many sensors such as GPS, temperature sensors, dashboard cameras. The data from these sensors can be useful for nearby users, as well as any entity who has an Interest for the information related to the geographic area a vehicle is in, regardless of where the entity is located in the world. For example, a nearby pedestrian may use his or her mobile phone GPS to get location information. However, GPS can drain the phone battery quickly. Instead, the pedestrian can collaborate with a nearby vehicle with GPS and save power [30].

When news breaks, the media and law enforcement agencies may want to have eyes on the scene rapidly, but may not have nearby camera crew that they can deploy quickly. In such a case, these agencies can tap into the dash cam of vehicles in the area to reach to visual information quickly.

8.3.1.3   Computation-as-a-Service (CaaS)

Intra-vehicle computers from manufactures such as Nexcom, Logic Supply, or Acrosser have comparable computing power to the desktop computers [3]. Yet, especially private vehicles are parked most of the time, leaving these resources idle. It is conceivable that vehicle owners may want to make the computing power in their vehicles to be made available as part of a CaaS framework.

Similarly, a vehicle may have computational needs that can be offloaded to a more traditional cloud, where the vehicle is a consumer for the CaaS. Bitam and colleagues proposed the ITS-Cloud, where conventional cloud computing resources provide the backbone of the computing services, and the vehicular computing resources (including on-board computers as well as the mobile devices in the vehicle, e.g., mobile phones provide a temporary cloud) [31,32].

8.3.1.4   Storage-as-a-Service (StaaS)

Storage can be required for keeping results of large calculations, multimedia files, as well as other resources. Unlike other services, storage requirements can be long term [33], thus their cloud model could be different than other services. Nevertheless, there are potential applications that StaaS can benefit from. One such example is given by Yu *et al.* [34], where the need of StaaS is outlined for Video Surveillance. They reported that many city buses are equipped with in-bus monitoring high-definition cameras. These cameras generate large amount of data daily, which is expensive to store on-board due to disk cost and physical space. These videos are only available to the decision makers after they are downloaded from the storage on the bus. Yu *et al.* proposed to use a roadside cloud, which assigns a virtual machine (VM) with required storage when a bus passes by a roadside coverage area for storing video files. As the bus moves from one coverage area to another (i.e., between roadside cloutlets), the VM is also migrated to the new coverage area. The video can then be requested to be transferred to a datacenter from the roadside cloutlets as needed.

8.4   TCPS attack surfaces

8.4.1   *Modern intra-vehicle data networks and the cloud*

This section concentrates on attacks which can be launched against current internal networks which control car functionality and the plausibility of doing so over the cloud. The development of intra-vehicle networks in many ways mirrors that of the early Internet, which was initially conceived as a network of friendly collaborators. Without having to worry about the presence of malicious actors or vulnerable assets, early network designers were free to focus on performance and efficiency. Since everything was intended for sharing, there was no need for attribution or access control. As the Internet scaled and commercialized, a patchwork of network security solutions eventually emerged, yet the lack of foresight lingers in the vulnerabilities of today's computer networks.

Similarly, intra-vehicle networks were designed under the assumption of a completely closed system comprised of trustworthy components with no external cloud connections. Modern cars are controlled by dozens of Electronic Control Units (ECUs) which communicate via the CAN standard [35]. Before the widespread availability of personal use wireless networks and mobile devices, gaining access to a vehicle's network was considered impractical due to their physical security. Cars are either moving at high speed or physically secured against theft.

As a result, intra-vehicular networks are designed with even fewer security considerations than the early Internet. Much like the Internet, there is no built-in access control mechanism in the CAN standard. The Internet Protocol requires source and destination addresses at a minimum, however, which provides a crude form of attribution. CAN systems, on the other hand, are strictly broadcast, making attribution all but impossible once access to the network has been gained. Since, any node in the CAN bus can broadcast messages, it is trivial for a compromised device to jam the bus by sending spoofed high-priority messages or impersonate any other device in the network. For cloud applications, where the vehicles can be used for processing or sensing data, a stealth attack can cause modifications in the calculations or in the recorded data, corrupting the data for the cloud applications. Additionally, the interconnectedness of intra-vehicle buses allows controllers of these buses to send messages to each other extending the impact of vulnerabilities in any one bus system.

Vehicles have long been viewed as valuable assets for their material worth, but until recently little attention was paid to enhancing the security of vehicles at an information level. Most early forms of protection focused on preventing physical theft or tampering, including electronic theft protection systems and mileage counter protection measures [36]. This attitude has gradually shifted as more and more computerized components have been added to cars.

The first microcontroller was added to a vehicle in 1977 when General Motors utilized one for spark plug timing in its Oldsmobile Toronado models [37]. Since then, the expansion of processors into other aspects of vehicular systems has transpired at a precipitous pace, culminating in today's incredibly complex intra-vehicular systems. Modern cars of all price levels currently require tens of millions of code and dozens of microcontrollers to function [37]. This means it is critical to provide information security as well as physical security to today's automobiles.

Just as with traditional computer systems, attacks against vehicle data networks can be classified as local or remote [38,39]. Local attacks are those that require physical access to a vehicle's network. Due to the emphasis placed on the physical security of vehicles and the fact that they are often in rapid motion, launching a direct physical attack is typically considered to be outside of the scope of vehicle threat models. However, most realistic models allow for the possibility of indirect physical access, often assumed to be made through a third party [38]. Such potential avenues of access include devices which connect to a vehicle via its On-Board Diagnostics (OBD-II) port, CD player, or media center USB input, or even an audio jack [38].

Although originally intended for trusted access by first-party devices given to specialized technicians and mechanics, the market for OBD-II tools has opened to include many third-party devices [40]. This means that the attack surface of the average vehicle must also be extended to include many third-party devices, making the coordination of security audits for all potential hardware and software involved highly impractical.

Furthermore, any vehicle or device with a network connection introduces the potential for remote system exploitation. According to a 2015 congressional report, nearly all vehicles currently on the road feature a wireless connection which could serve as a potential avenue of attack [41]. Remote attacks against vehicular systems can be further divided into the range of access provided; clearly, the further away an attack can be carried out from, the stronger the adversary. Short-range access media include Bluetooth phone and music systems, remote start and entry systems, RFID access tokens, and 802.11 network connections. Longer-range connections are typically established using cellular network connections. Note that some attacks may be hybrid forms which cross these classification boundaries. For instance, an attack launched remotely across a 4G cellular network against a device connected to a vehicle's OBD-II port would involve both indirect physical access and a long-range wireless connection.

Unfortunately, vehicle and OBD-II device manufacturers are not always forthcoming to disclose the active wireless connections on a vehicle [41]. Thus, data transmissions may occur without the vehicle owner's permission or knowledge. Even if the owners are aware of such transmissions, it may also be impossible to disable them without turning off the desirable wireless capability.

It is difficult to gauge the number of incidents in which attacks have occurred against vehicular networks in the wild due to a dearth of data in part because of manufacturers' reluctance to share such information [41]. However, such attacks are no longer theoretical in nature, having been demonstrated against actual vehicles being driven on public roadways. In 2013, Miller and Valasek demonstrated that attacks could be launched against various ECUs over a car's CAN bus with direct physical access via an OBD-II interface [42]. This included control over the speedometer, odometer, onboard navigation, steering, braking, and acceleration [42]. The authors were also able to modify the firmware of some ECUs [42], raising the possibility of advanced persistent threats which reside on an intra-vehicular network for a prolonged period of time. Threats which apply to firmware in general also apply to vehicular systems [43], with a heightened risk due to safety issues associated with transportation systems.

Initially, the automotive industry downplayed the impact of security research by emphasizing the implausibility of the direct physical access which was required. In 2015, Miller and Valasek challenged these claims when they extended their attacks by carrying them out remotely. In the specific instance tested, access was gained over a long-range cellular network to a vehicle's entertainment system, granting them the same control over critical car systems [44]. The results of this research were widespread, including a recall of over a million vehicles, lawsuits against cellular carriers, and the aforementioned congressional report on the current state of insecurity in vehicular systems [41,44].

8.4.2   Attack surfaces of future cloud-based V2X transportation networks

The previous section described how the addition of wireless communication channels to modern vehicles altered their attack surface, causing threats which were previously dismissed as impractical to be given renewed consideration. This represents only the beginning of wireless deployments in transportation systems, however. Future deployments will cause the handful of wireless channels on today's vehicles to seem quaint by comparison. Researchers are currently envisioning future transportation systems in which all vehicles and infrastructure are connected via pervasive wireless links; such environments are typically referred to as "V2X" systems [45], as described in Section 8.2.2.

This proliferation of wireless links implies a manyfold increase in the attack surface of a typical vehicle, as every new connection could potentially be utilized as an attack vector [46]. Furthermore, many aspects of V2X systems differ from typical computer networks in ways which add unique challenges. For instance, in order for RSU and other forms of infrastructure to communicate useful information they must be equipped with microcontrollers, sensors, and wireless chips. To see widespread deployment, these components will have to be as small and resource-efficient as possible. From this perspective, V2X systems are subject to many of the same constraints which "Internet-of-Things" (IoT) security solutions are subject to, including small amounts of memory and processing power, limited form factors, low-power radio standards, and limited energy availability [47,48].

Another unique requirement of V2X is their extreme flexibility with respect to speed and movement. Transportation systems are by nature dynamic and mobile, while traditional network protocols are not designed with mobility in mind; indeed, an initial design assumption of the early Internet was that nodes would not move [49,50]. The speed at which modern transportation systems are expected to move may complicate handoffs between different network cells and limit opportunities for executing protocols such as key exchange and session establishment [51]. This, combined with the aforementioned IoT device constraints, necessitates very low overhead protocols for V2X, which is a barrier to utilizing the kinds of cryptographic solutions to security found on traditional computer systems [52–54].

Further complicating the attack surface of TCPS systems which utilize remote services to process, analyze, or coordinate data is the fact that these systems open themselves to all the security issues which come with cloud services outside the context of transportation systems. These include data leakage due to improper isolation [55] or other malicious participants [56], potential loss of data availability [57], web application vulnerabilities [58], and a general lack of control over how data is handled [59].

8.5 TCPS security mechanisms

The benefits of a TCPS can only be realized if the data collected and shared by participants is authentic and trustworthy. Establishing trust in a TCPS is therefore paramount. For existing vehicular networks, this requires the difficult task of designing secure solutions while retaining compatibility with existing deployments. Fortunately, since V2X systems are currently emerging as more and more connections are established between vehicles and roadside assets, there is more room to "bake-in" security into these systems by applying the lessons learned in other domains. Many of the existing security solutions for TCPS (in particular, vehicular networks) have been primarily focusing on applying various cryptographic solutions to secure the system [60–63], and the trust management as well as privacy protection techniques have not drawn enough attention to help better secure TCPS. To address this need, in this chapter, we primarily focus on studying trust management and also privacy protection techniques to secure TCPS.

Trust is an issue for both intra-vehicle and V2X communication with any potential TCPS cloud service. However, without being able to judge the veracity of messages originating from within a vehicle or other transportation asset, it is very difficult to establish trust in the data the node relays to other parties. Most V2X trust solutions thus begin with mechanisms for enforcing trust by adding cryptographic authentication components to intra-vehicle networks. For example, the authors of [64] propose the use of symmetric key cryptography to sign messages exchanged between ECUs over the CAN bus by adding hardware security modules to each ECU. To coordinate keys between different components, an ECU acts as a key manager [64]. On the other hand, if there exists transportation infrastructure, such as RSUs, traffic sensors, and cameras, then these pre-deployed devices are generally regarded as trusted because they are connected via wired networks, which are generally better protected and thus much harder to be tampered or compromised when compared to the vehicles. Thus, in the presence of the various transportation infrastructure equipments, trust management will become a viable and indispensable solution to help better secure TCPS.

An alternative approach is to modify the CAN standard by adding new fields which can be used as indicators of intrusion [65]. In [66], the authors discuss the requirements for formally verifying trust within an intra-vehicular network, including identifying all ECUs, their connections to themselves and cloud providers, and establishing rules that govern how these entities are allowed to interact.

Under the assumption that the data collected by TCPS nodes is authenticated by one of the aforementioned techniques, the next step to creating a trustworthy system is to authenticate the messages exchanged between participant nodes. There have been several different proposals as to how to achieve this, including techniques based on asymmetric cryptography [54], group cryptography [67], and timing synchronization [68].

As mentioned in Section 8.4.2, TCPS systems that connect to the cloud will be subject to all the additional security considerations that users of cloud services face in other contexts. Fortunately, there has been a great deal of research attention provided to developing security solutions for cloud systems. These include distributed intrusion detection solutions [69,70] and encryption techniques based on identity-based cryptography [71] or homomorphic ciphers [72].

8.5.1   Trust management for TCPS

In this section, we will review various trust management schemes that have been proposed for TCPS.

8.5.1.1   Basic Principles of Trust Management

In general, the main goal of trust management is to evaluate different behaviors of other nodes and build a reputation for each node based on the observations made for behavior assessment. The reputation can then be utilized to determine trustworthiness for other nodes, make choices on which nodes to cooperate with, and even punish an untrustworthy node if necessary. The trust management system has been studied in various self-organized systems, such as ad-hoc networks [40–46], peer-to-peer systems [47–49], and wireless sensor networks [50,51]. More specifically, trust management in wireless networks can be utilized in the following three aspects: (1) node behavior assessment, (2) misbehaving node detection, and (3) proper response to node misbehaviors.

In practice, the trust management system usually relies on two types of evidences to evaluate the node behaviors. The first kind of observation is called *first-hand* observation, or in other words, direct observation [73]. First-hand observation is the observation that is directly made by a node itself, and the first-hand observation can be collected either passively or actively. If a node promiscuously observes its neighbors' actions, the local information is collected passively. In contrast, the reputation management system can also rely on some explicit evidences to assess the neighbor behaviors, such as an acknowledgment packet during the route discovery process. The other kind of observation is called *second-hand* observation or indirect observation. Second-hand observation is generally obtained by exchanging first-hand observations with other nodes in the network. The main issues of second-hand observations are related to overhead, false report and collusion [74,75].

Trust management has been proven to be an important security solution to cope with various misbehaviors in wireless networks, which act as the primary key enabling technology for TCPS. Therefore, we will start reviewing the well-known trust management schemes for wireless networks.

8.5.1.2 Trust Management for Wireless Networks

In [76], Buchegger *et al.* proposed a protocol, namely CONFIDANT (Cooperation Of Nodes, Fairness In Dynamic Ad-hoc NeTworks), to encourage the node cooperation and punish misbehaving nodes. CONFIDANT has four components in each node: a Monitor, a Reputation System, a Trust Manager, and a Path Manager. The Monitor is used to observe and identify abnormal routing behaviors. The Reputation System calculates the reputation for each node in accordance with its observed behaviors. The Trust Manager exchanges alerts with other trust managers regarding node misbehaviors. The Path Manager maintains path rankings, and properly responds to various routing messages. A possible drawback of CONFIDANT is that an attacker may intentionally spread false alerts to other nodes that a node is misbehaving while it is actually a well-behaved node. Therefore, it is important for a node in CONFIDANT to validate an alert it receives before it accepts the alert.

Michiardi *et al.* [77] presented a mechanism with the name CORE to identify selfish nodes, and then compel them to cooperate in the following routing activities. Similar to CONFIDANT, CORE uses both a surveillance system and a reputation system to observe and evaluate node behaviors. Nevertheless, while CONFIDANT allows nodes exchange both positive and negative observations of their neighbors, only positive observations are exchanged amongst the nodes in CORE. In this way, malicious nodes cannot spread fake charges to frame the well-behaved nodes, and consequently avoid denial of service attacks toward the well-behaved nodes. The reputation system maintains reputations for each node, and the reputations are adjusted upon receiving of new evidences. Since selfish nodes reject to cooperate in some cases, their reputations are lower than other nodes. To encourage node cooperation and punish selfishness, if a node with low reputation sends a routing request, then the request will be ignored and the bad reputation node cannot use the network.

Patwardhan *et al.* [78] studied an approach in which the reputation of a node is determined by data validation. In this approach, a few nodes, which are named as Anchor nodes here, are assumed to be pre-authenticated, and thus the data they provide are regarded as trustworthy. Data can be validated by either agreement among peers or direct communication with an anchor node. Malicious node can be identified if the data they present is invalidated by the validation algorithm.

Li *et al.* [79] proposed a novel trust management scheme for MANETs, in which the trust of a mobile node is evaluated from multiple perspectives rather than merely one single trust scalar. More specifically, the proposed scheme evaluates trustworthiness from three perspectives: collaboration trust, behavioral trust, and reference trust. Different types of observations are used to independently derive values for these three trust dimensions. This research work was extended in [80], in which declarative policies are used to better evaluate the trust of a mobile nodes under different environmental factors.

In [81], the authors proposed a cluster-based hierarchical trust management scheme for wireless sensor networks to effectively deal with selfish or malicious nodes, in which the authors consider both trust attributes derived from communication and from social networks to evaluate the overall trust of a sensor node. To demonstrate the utility of the proposed hierarchical trust management protocol, the authors apply it to trust-based geographic routing and trust-based intrusion detection. For each application, the authors identify the best trust composition and formation to maximize application performance.

He *et al.* [82] proposed ReTrust, an attack-resistant and lightweight trust management approach for medical sensor networks. In this approach, the authors delegate the trust calculation and management functionality to master nodes (MNs) so that there will be no additional computational overhead for resource-constrained sensor nodes (SNs), which is a critical factor for medical sensor networks. Moreover, the authors also discuss the possibility to use the ReTrust approach to detect and fight against two types of malicious attacks in medical sensor networks, namely on-off attacks and bad mouth attacks.

Chen *et al.* [83] studied a dynamic trust management protocol for secure routing optimization in delay tolerant networks (DTNs) in the presence of well-behaved, selfish and malicious nodes, in which the concept of dynamic trust is highlighted in order to determine and apply the best operational settings at runtime in response to dynamically changing network conditions to minimize trust bias and to maximize the routing application performance. Furthermore, the trust-based routing protocol can effectively trade off message overhead and message delay for a significant gain in delivery ratio.

In [84], Wei *et al.* presented a unified trust management scheme that enhances the security in MANETs that uses recent advances in uncertain reasoning that originated from the artificial intelligence community. In the proposed trust management scheme, the trust model has two components: trust from direct observation and trust from indirect observation. With direct observation from an observer node, the trust value is derived using Bayesian inference, which is a type of uncertain reasoning when the full probability model can be defined. On the other hand, with indirect observation, which is also called secondhand information that is obtained from neighbor nodes of the observer node, the trust value is derived using the Dempster–Shafer theory (DST), which is another type of uncertain reasoning when the proposition of interest can be derived by an indirect method.

Ren *et al.* [85] proposed a novel trust management scheme for unattended wireless sensor networks (UWSNs), which are characterized by long periods of disconnected operation and fixed or irregular intervals between sink visits. The absence of an online trusted third party implies that existing WSN trust management schemes are not applicable to UWSNs. To address this limitation, the authors studied a trust management scheme for UWSNs to provide efficient and robust trust data storage and trust generation. For trust data storage, the authors employed a geographic hash table to identify storage nodes and to significantly decrease storage cost. In addition, the authors used subjective logic-based consensus techniques to mitigate trust fluctuations caused by environmental factors. Finally, the authors exploited a set of trust similarity functions to detect trust outliers and to sustain trust pollution attacks.

In [86], an energy efficient collaborative spectrum sensing (EE-CSS) protocol, based on trust management, is proposed. The protocol achieves energy efficiency by reducing the total number of sensing reports exchanged between the honest secondary users (HSUs) and the secondary user base station (SUBS) in a traditional collaborative spectrum sensing (T-CSS) protocol.

8.5.1.3   Trust Management for Transportation CPS

Recently, there have been some emerging research efforts which primarily focus on trust establishment and management for vehicular networks which serve as the key enabling technology for TCPS.

In general, vehicular networks have their own unique features in addition to the features which are common to the generalized wireless networks. For instance, the traveling velocity for nodes in vehicular networks is generally much higher than those in generalized wireless networks, which makes it even more challenging for those vehicular nodes to successfully exchange information (such as which nodes are trustworthy or untrustworthy according to their prior interactions and observations) before they move out of the wireless communication range between each other [60]. Moreover, the outcome of successful security attacks in vehicular networks is generally severe or even life-threatening. For example, one compromised vehicle may transmit false hazard warnings to all neighboring vehicles, which can cause a chaotic situation such as traffic or even an accident if the false warnings are not properly handled. Alternatively, a compromised vehicle can forge messages to masquerade as an emergency vehicle so that it can mislead other vehicles to slow down and yield [87].

To address these unique challenges in vehicular networks, various trust management schemes have been studied in the recent years. In [88], the authors attempt to address the presence of both malicious and selfish nodes in vehicular networks via the trust management approach. More specifically, a distributed trust model named DTM^2 was proposed based on the Spence's Job Market model which was originated from economics. In this model, a sender node transmits a special *signal* with the message that it wants to send. This signal indicates that the message is authentic for the potential receivers. The sender node will have to pay a cost to utilize the signal, which is determined on both the value of the signal and its own behavior. In other words, the more uncooperative or malicious the behavior of the sender node, the more costly the signal will be. By this means, the proposed model discourages the sender nodes from behaving in a malicious fashion. Similarly, cooperation of the sender nodes will be rewarded proportionally to the signal's value. This research idea was extended in [89].

Liao *et al.* proposed a trust-based approach to decide the likelihood of the accuracy of V2V incident reports considering the trustworthiness of the report originator and those vehicles who have forwarded it [90]. In particular, the approach leverages the existing V2I communication facilities to collect vehicle behavior information in a crowdsourcing fashion so as to build a more comprehensive view of vehicle trustworthiness.

The authors in [91] identified that the problem of information cascading and oversampling, which are generally common in social networks, also adversely impacts trust management schemes in VANETs. Moreover, the authors also demonstrated that simple voting approach for decision making can lead to oversampling and yield incorrect results in VANETs. To address this issue, the authors proposed a new voting scheme, in which each vehicle has different voting weight according to its distance from the event. In other words, the vehicle which is more closer to the event possesses a higher weight.

In a recent study conducted by Li *et al.* [92], an attack-resistant trust management scheme (ART) was proposed for VANETs, in which the trustworthiness in vehicular networks is separately evaluated in multiple dimensions: data trust is evaluated based on the data sensed and collected from multiple vehicles; node trust is assessed in two aspects, i.e., functional trust and recommendation trust, which indicate how likely a node can fulfill its functionality and how trustworthy the recommendations from a node for other nodes will be, respectively.

8.5.2 Privacy for TCPS

In addition to safety, security, and trust, privacy is a foremost concern in the design of TCPS. Drivers have long been accustomed to a modicum of privacy while in their vehicles. Much as intra-vehicular networks lacked security mechanisms due to the assumed difficulty of accessing the network medium, as described in Section 8.2.3, vehicular privacy considerations were taken for granted due to the inherent difficulty of attacking a moving vehicle. However, with the rich variety of sensors available to emerging vehicular CPS, steps must be taken to protect the privacy of vehicle occupants. Although riders of public transportation have reduced expectations of privacy due to the shared nature of these services, providing privacy safeguards in these contexts becomes even more critical due to the additional stakeholders involved.

A variety of sensors, both in and outside of vehicles, may compromise user privacy [93]. TCPS threaten the privacy of transportation networks in two main ways. First, sensors within a vehicle can be used to eavesdrop on or monitor the vehicle's occupants. For example, small cameras and microphones included in vehicles with communication features can be used to capture audio and video of the vehicle's occupants. Second, sensors may record information regarding the activity of a driver which he or she would prefer not to disclose [94]. Geolocation is the most obvious form this may take, although other sensor data, such as accelerometers and gyroscopes, can also reveal data about a vehicle's location [95]. Connected vehicles can also be tracked by their connections to cell towers or wireless access points as they travel through an environment, providing even better location granularity than GPS coordinates [96].

Different privacy preservation techniques have been developed which provide varying degrees of privacy guarantees under differing contexts. Various techniques involving pseudonym rotations based on vehicle time and location have been proposed [97]. In [98], threshold authentication is used to preserve the privacy of V2X messages while still allowing for the possibility of verifying message trustworthiness.

Users of a TCPS may also be tracked based on other devices which they carry, such as cell phones, laptops, or payment tokens. Transportation payment tokens are increasingly equipped with short-range wireless capabilities, frequently based on Radio Frequency Identification (RFID) technology [99]. To protect against information leakage by payment tokens, techniques from the field of RFID security can be applied which utilize contextual sensing to determine when it is safe or unsafe to transmit data [100–102].

Although it may at first seem that privacy and the public nature of mass transportation are at odds with one another, cryptographic techniques can be used to provide riders with privacy assurances. In one such proposed approach, e-cash techniques are combined with re-authentication to create session tickets which can be used to pay for transportation services without revealing the identity of the passenger [103].

Once collected, transportation cloud services must also take privacy considerations into account during processing by the backend. Common techniques for providing privacy assurances include aggregating and masking data [104]; however, it can be difficult to verify the efficacy of such mechanisms on a third-party system.

8.6 Conclusion

In recent years, we have witnessed a rapid growth to the number of smart and interconnected devices that have been deployed to the transportation systems, such as on-board sensors equipped in each vehicle, traffic monitoring sensors installed in RSU, and smart phones carried by pedestrians. All these devices sense the surrounding traffic and other transportation-related information, some of which will be further processed using the integrated computational capabilities, and each device will closely interact and exchange information with other devices via the communication links. All these smart devices together with the transportation infrastructure compose the TCPS, which has the potential to revolutionize the traditional transportation system.

However, it has also been noted that TCPS is vulnerable to various security threats. Therefore, it is essential to better secure TCPS. In this chapter, we first summarize the basic idea of TCPS and how cloud computing plays a role in it. The attack surface of TCPS is then described in details. We then provide a comprehensive overview regarding the current state-of-the-art security mechanisms for TCPS. More specifically, we focus on both trust and privacy techniques which aim at addressing the unique challenges posed in the TCPS context.

As for the future research directions, we envision that the following research challenges should be better addressed regarding the security, trust, and privacy issues in TCPS.

1.   What type of trust should be evaluated in the context of TCPS. Traditionally, we are primarily interested in knowing about the trustworthiness of a node or device. However, given that the data (such as real-time traffic information) are also sensitive or even life-dependent in TCPS, we may also need to keep track of how trustworthy the data are in TCPS. In addition, it is worthwhile to point out that there may also be some correlations between the data trustworthiness and device trustworthiness. For example, it is generally the case that the data should be more trustworthy if it comes from a trustworthy node.

2.   How to share data across different administrative domains in TCPS which should still maintain the security and privacy. It is well understood that TCPS can involve nodes from various administrative domains, such as vehicle manufacturers, highway administration, and travelers. As they belong to different organizations, they generally have different levels of security and privacy concerns or requirements. Therefore, it would be impractical to specify one single sharing strategy that can satisfy all these needs. On the other hand, it may be better to use declarative policies that can properly and accurately capture the security and privacy requirements that each of them has.

References

[1]   Z. Shahan, "1 million electric cars will be on the road in September," https://cleantechnica.com/2015/08/08/1-million-electric-cars-will-be-on-the-road-in-september/, accessed: 16-09-2016.

[2]   "Global status report on road safety," World Health Organization, 2015.

[3]   S. Abdelhamid, H. S. Hassanein, and G. Takahara, "Vehicle as a resource (VaaR)," *IEEE Network*, vol. 29, no. 1, pp. 12–17, January 2015.

[4]   B. Fleming, "Advances in automotive electronics," *IEEE Vehicular Technology Magazine*, pp. 4–13, December 2015.

[5]   W. He, G. Yan, and L. D. Xu, "Developing Vehicular Data Cloud Services in the IoT environment," *IEEE Transactions on Industrial Informatics*, vol. 10, no. 2, pp. 1587–1595, May 2014.

[6]   Y. Lin and H. Song, "Dynachina: Real-time traffic estimation and prediction," *IEEE Pervasive Computing*, vol. 4, p. 65, 2006.

[7]   G. Karagiannis, O. Altintas, E. Ekici *et al.*, "Vehicular networking: A survey and tutorial on requirements, architectures, challenges, standards and solutions," *IEEE Communications Surveys & Tutorials*, vol. 13, no. 4, pp. 584–616, Fourth Quarter 2011.

[8]   J. Zhang, F. Y. Wang, K. Wang, W. H. Lin, X. Xu, and C. Chen, "Data-driven intelligent transportation systems: A survey," *IEEE Transactions on Intelligent Transportation Systems*, vol. 12, no. 4, pp. 1624–1639, December 2011.

[9]   H. Abid, L. T. T. Phuong, J. Wang, S. Lee, and S. Qaisar, "V-Cloud: Vehicular Cyber-physical Systems and Cloud Computing," in *Proceedings of the 4th International Symposium on Applied Sciences in Biomedical and Communication Technologies*, ser. ISABEL '11. Barcelona, Spain: ACM, 2011, pp. 165:1–165:5.

[10] D. Z. Morris, "Today's cars are parked 95% of the time," *Fortune Magazine*, March 2016.

[11] N. Liu, M. Liu, W. Lou, G. Chen, and J. Cao, "PVA in VANETs: Stopped cars are not silent," in 2011 Proceedings IEEE INFOCOM, Shanghai, China, 2011, pp. 431–435.

[12] "IEEE 802.11p, Amendment 6: Wireless Access in Vehicular Environments," July 2010.

[13] "IEEE 1609—Family of Standards for Wireless Access in Vehicular Environments (WAVE)," September 2009.

[14] G. Araniti, C. Campolo, M. Condoluci, A. Iera, and A. Molinaro, "Lte for vehicular networking: A survey," *IEEE Communications Magazine*, vol. 51, no. 5, pp. 148–157, May 2013.

[15] G. K. Venayagamoorthy, P. Mitra, K. Corzine, and C. Huston, "Real-time modeling of distributed plug-in vehicles for v2g transactions," in *2009 IEEE Energy Conversion Congress and Exposition*, San Jose, CA, USA, September 2009, pp. 3937–3941.

[16] E. Coelingh, A. Eidehall, and M. Bengtsson, "Collision warning with full auto brake and pedestrian detection—A practical example of automatic emergency braking," in *Intelligent Transportation Systems (ITSC), 2010 13th International IEEE Conference on*, Funchal, Madeira Island, Portugal, September 2010, pp. 155–160.

[17] A. Angelova, A. Krizhevsky, and V. Vanhoucke, "Pedestrian detection with a large-field-of-view deep network," in *Proceedings of ICRA 2015*, Seattle, WA, USA, 2015.

[18] S. A. Richmond, A. R. Willan, L. Rothman *et al.*, "The impact of pedestrian countdown signals on pedestrian–motor vehicle collisions: A reanalysis of data from a quasi-experimental study," *Injury Prevention*, 2014;20:155–158.

[19] B. A. Morrongiello, M. Corbett, J. Switzer, and T. Hall, "Using a virtual environment to study pedestrian behaviors: How does time pressure affect children's and adults' street crossing behaviors?" *Journal of Pediatric Psychology*, 2015;40(7):697–703.

[20] S. Woo, H. J. Jo, I. S. Kim, and D. H. Lee, "A practical security architecture for in-vehicle can-fd," *IEEE Transactions on Intelligent Transportation Systems*, vol. 17, no. 8, pp. 2248–2261, August 2016.

[21] ST Microcontroller Division Applications, "LIN (Local Interconnect Network) Solutions," *Application note AN1278*.

[22]   "FlexRay Communications System Protocol Specification Version 3.0.1."

[23]   MOST Cooperation, "Multimedia and Control Networking Technology (MOST) Specification Rev. 3.0 E2," July 2010.

[24]   J. Liu, B. Priyantha, T. Hart, H. S. Ramos, A. A. F. Loureiro, and Q. Wang, "Energy efficient GPS sensing with cloud offloading," in *Proceedings of the 10th ACM Conference on Embedded Network Sensor Systems*, ser. SenSys'12. Toronto, Canada: ACM, 2012, pp. 85–98.

[25]   D. Hasenfratz, O. Saukh, C. Walser *et al.*, "Deriving high-resolution urban air pollution maps using mobile sensor nodes," *Pervasive and Mobile Computing*, vol. 16, Part B, pp. 268–285, 2015, selected Papers from the *Twelfth Annual IEEE International Conference on Pervasive Computing and Communications (PerCom 2014)*, Budapest, Hungary.

[26]   J. Aslam, S. Lim, X. Pan, and D. Rus, "City-scale traffic estimation from a roving sensor network," in *Proceedings of the 10th ACM Conference on Embedded Network Sensor Systems*, ser. SenSys '12. Toronto, Canada: ACM, 2012, pp. 141–154.

[27]   M. Whaiduzzaman, M. Sookhak, A. Gani, and R. Buyya, "A survey on vehicular cloud computing," *Journal of Network and Computer Applications*, vol. 40, pp. 325–344, 2014.

[28]   L. Gu, D. Zeng, and S. Guo, "Vehicular cloud computing: A survey," in *2013 IEEE Globecom Workshops (GC Wkshps)*, Atlanta, GA, USA, December 2013, pp. 403–407.

[29]   S. Olariu, I. Khalil, and M. Abuelela, "Taking vanet to the clouds," *International Journal of Pervasive Computing and Communications*, vol. 7, no. 1, pp. 7–21, 2011.

[30]   X. Sheng, J. Tang, X. Xiao, and G. Xue, "Sensing as a service: Challenges, solutions and future directions," *IEEE Sensors Journal*, vol. 13, no. 10, pp. 3733–3741, October 2013.

[31]   S. Bitam and A. Mellouk, "ITS-cloud: Cloud computing for intelligent transportation system," in *Global Communications Conference (GLOBECOM), 2012 IEEE*, Anaheim, CA, USA, December 2012, pp. 2054–2059.

[32]   S. Bitam, A. Mellouk, and S. Zeadally, "VANET-cloud: A generic cloud computing model for vehicular Ad Hoc networks," *IEEE Wireless Communications*, vol. 22, no. 1, pp. 96–102, February 2015.

[33]   S. Arif, S. Olariu, J. Wang, G. Yan, W. Yang, and I. Khalil, "Datacenter at the airport: Reasoning about time-dependent parking lot occupancy," *IEEE Transactions on Parallel and Distributed Systems*, vol. 23, no. 11, pp. 2067–2080, November 2012.

[34]   R. Yu, Y. Zhang, S. Gjessing, W. Xia, and K. Yang, "Toward cloud-based vehicular networks with efficient resource management," *IEEE Network*, vol. 27, no. 5, pp. 48–55, September 2013.

[35]   I. ISO, "Road vehicles—Interchange of digital information—Controller area network (can) for high speed communication (first edition)," 1898.

[36]   A. Weimerskirch, "Do vehicles need data security?" SAE Technical Paper, Technical Report, 2011.

[37] R. N. Charette, "This car runs on code," *IEEE Spectrum*, vol. 46, no. 3, p. 3, 2009.

[38] S. Checkoway, D. McCoy, B. Kantor *et al.*, "Comprehensive experimental analyses of automotive attack surfaces," in *USENIX Security Symposium*. San Francisco, CA, USA, 2011.

[39] I. Studnia, V. Nicomette, E. Alata, Y. Deswarte, M. Kaâniche, and Y. Laarouchi, "Survey on security threats and protection mechanisms in embedded automotive networks," in *Dependable Systems and Networks Workshop (DSN-W), 2013 43rd Annual IEEE/IFIP Conference on*. Budapest, Hungary: IEEE, 2013, pp. 1–12.

[40] "Connected car devices," http://postscapes.com/connected-car-devices/, accessed: 10-08-2015.

[41] E. Markey, "Tracking & hacking: Security & privacy gaps put American drivers at risk," *US Senate*, 2015.

[42] C. Miller and C. Valasek, "Adventures in automotive networks and control units," *DEF CON*, Las Vegas, NV, USA, vol. 21, pp. 260–264, 2013.

[43] A. Cui, M. Costello, and S. J. Stolfo, "When firmware modifications attack: A case study of embedded exploitation." in *NDSS*, San Diego, CA, USA, 2013.

[44] C. Miller and C. Valasek, "Remote exploitation of an unaltered passenger vehicle," *Black Hat USA*, Las Vegas, NV, USA, 2015.

[45] N. Lu, N. Cheng, N. Zhang, X. Shen, and J. W. Mark, "Connected vehicles: Solutions and challenges," *IEEE Internet of Things Journal*, vol. 1, no. 4, pp. 289–299, 2014.

[46] T. Bécsi, S. Aradi, and P. Gáspár, "Security issues and vulnerabilities in connected car systems," in *Models and Technologies for Intelligent Transportation Systems (MT-ITS), 2015 International Conference on*. Budapest, Hungary: IEEE, 2015, pp. 477–482.

[47] T. Heer, O. Garcia-Morchon, R. Hummen, S. L. Keoh, S. S. Kumar, and K. Wehrle, "Security challenges in the ip-based internet of things," *Wireless Personal Communications*, vol. 61, no. 3, pp. 527–542, 2011.

[48] S. Raza, H. Shafagh, K. Hewage, R. Hummen, and T. Voigt, "Lithe: Lightweight secure coap for the internet of things," *IEEE Sensors Journal*, vol. 13, no. 10, pp. 3711–3720, 2013.

[49] D. Le, X. Fu, D. Hogrefe *et al.*, "A review of mobility support paradigms for the Internet," *IEEE Communications Surveys and Tutorials*, vol. 8, no. 1–4, pp. 38–51, 2006.

[50] W. M. Eddy, "At what layer does mobility belong?" *IEEE Communications Magazine*, vol. 42, no. 10, pp. 155–159, 2004.

[51] A. M. Vegni, R. Cusani, and T. Inzerilli, *Seamless Connectivity Techniques in Vehicular Ad-hoc Networks*. INTECH Open Access Publisher, 2011.

[52] J. J. Blum, A. Eskandarian, and L. J. Hoffman, "Challenges of intervehicle ad hoc networks," *IEEE Transactions on Intelligent Transportation Systems*, vol. 5, no. 4, pp. 347–351, 2004.

[53]   T. L. Willke, P. Tientrakool, and N. F. Maxemchuk, "A survey of inter-vehicle communication protocols and their applications," *IEEE Communications Surveys & Tutorials*, vol. 11, no. 2, pp. 3–20, 2009.

[54]   F. Kargl, P. Papadimitratos, L. Buttyan *et al.*, "Secure vehicular communication systems: Implementation, performance, and research challenges," *IEEE Communications Magazine*, vol. 46, no. 11, pp. 110–118, 2008.

[55]   A. Tripathi and A. Mishra, "Cloud computing security considerations," in *Signal Processing, Communications and Computing (ICSPCC), 2011 IEEE International Conference on*. Xi'an, Shaanxi, China: IEEE, 2011, pp. 1–5.

[56]   Y. Chen, V. Paxson, and R. H. Katz, "What's new about cloud computing security," *University of California, Berkeley Report No. UCB/EECS-2010-5 January*, vol. 20, no. 2010, pp. 2010–2015, 2010.

[57]   A. Juels and A. Oprea, "New approaches to security and availability for cloud data," *Communications of the ACM*, vol. 56, no. 2, pp. 64–73, 2013.

[58]   S. Subashini and V. Kavitha, "A survey on security issues in service delivery models of cloud computing," *Journal of Network and Computer Applications*, vol. 34, no. 1, pp. 1–11, 2011.

[59]   D. Zissis and D. Lekkas, "Addressing cloud computing security issues," *Future Generation Computer Systems*, vol. 28, no. 3, pp. 583–592, 2012.

[60]   M. Raya and J.-P. Hubaux, "Securing vehicular ad hoc networks," *Journal of Computer Security*, vol. 15, no. 1, pp. 39–68, 2007.

[61]   X. Lin, R. Lu, C. Zhang, H. Zhu, P.-H. Ho, and X. Shen, "Security in vehicular ad hoc networks," *IEEE Communications Magazine*, vol. 46, no. 4, pp. 88–95, 2008.

[62]   M. N. Mejri, J. Ben-Othman, and M. Hamdi, "Survey on vanet security challenges and possible cryptographic solutions," *Vehicular Communications*, vol. 1, no. 2, pp. 53–66, 2014.

[63]   J. Shao, X. Lin, R. Lu, and C. Zuo, "A threshold anonymous authentication protocol for vanets," *IEEE Transactions on Vehicular Technology*, vol. 65, no. 3, pp. 1711–1720, 2016.

[64]   H. Schweppe, Y. Roudier, B. Weyl, L. Apvrille, and D. Scheuermann, "Car2x communication: securing the last meter-a cost-effective approach for ensuring trust in car2x applications using in-vehicle symmetric cryptography," in *Vehicular Technology Conference (VTC Fall), 2011 IEEE*. San Francisco, CA, USA: IEEE, 2011, pp. 1–5.

[65]   P. Carsten, T. R. Andel, M. Yampolskiy, J. T. McDonald, and S. Russ, "A system to recognize intruders in controller area network (can)," in *Proceedings of the 3rd International Symposium for ICS & SCADA Cyber Security Research*. Ingolstadt, Germany: British Computer Society, 2015, pp. 111–114.

[66]   G. Ellison, J. Lacy, D. Maher, Y. Nagao, A. Poonegar, and T. Shamoon, "The car as an Internet-enabled device, or how to make trusted networked cars," in *Electric Vehicle Conference (IEVC)*, Greenville, SC, USA, 2012, pp. 1–8.

[67]   J. Guo, J. P. Baugh, and S. Wang, "A group signature based secure and privacy-preserving vehicular communication framework," *Mobile Networking for Vehicular Environments*, vol. 2007, pp. 103–108, 2007.

[68] Y.-C. Hu and K. P. Laberteaux, "Strong vanet security on a budget," in *Proceedings of Workshop on Embedded Security in Cars (ESCAR)*, Berlin, Germany, vol. 6, 2006, pp. 1–9.

[69] S. Roschke, F. Cheng, and C. Meinel, "Intrusion detection in the cloud," in *Dependable, Autonomic and Secure Computing, 2009. DASC'09. Eighth IEEE International Conference on*. Chengdu, China: IEEE, 2009, pp. 729–734.

[70] S. Whalen, N. Boggs, and S. J. Stolfo, "Model aggregation for distributed content anomaly detection," in *Proceedings of the 2014 Workshop on Artificial Intelligent and Security Workshop*. Scottsdale, AZ, USA: ACM, 2014, pp. 61–71.

[71] G. Wang, Q. Liu, and J. Wu, "Hierarchical attribute-based encryption for fine-grained access control in cloud storage services," in *Proceedings of the 17th ACM Conference on Computer and Communications Security*. Chicago, IL, USA: ACM, 2010, pp. 735–737.

[72] A. López-Alt, E. Tromer, and V. Vaikuntanathan, "On-the-fly multiparty computation on the cloud via multikey fully homomorphic encryption," in *Proceedings of the Forty-Fourth Annual ACM Symposium on Theory of Computing*. New York, NY, USA: ACM, 2012, pp. 1219–1234.

[73] S. Buchegger and J.-Y. L. Boudec, "A robust reputation system for mobile ad-hoc networks," in *Proceedings of P2PEcon*, Berkeley, CA, USA, 2003.

[74] Q. He, D. Wu, and P. Khosla, "Sori: A secure and objective reputation-based incentive scheme for ad-hoc networks," in *Proceedings of 2004 IEEE Wireless Communications and Networking Conference, WCNC'04*, Atlanta, GA, USA, vol. 2, March 2004, pp. 825–830.

[75] S. Buchegger and J.-Y. L. Boudec, "The effect of rumor spreading in reputation systems for mobile ad-hoc networks," in *Proceedings of WiOpt 2003: Modeling and Optimization in Mobile, Ad Hoc and Wireless Networks*, Sophia-Antipolis, France, 2003.

[76] S. Buchegger and J.-Y. Le Boudec, "Performance analysis of the confidant protocol," in *MobiHoc '02: Proceedings of the 3rd ACM International Symposium on Mobile ad hoc Networking & Computing*. New York, NY, USA: ACM, 2002, pp. 226–236.

[77] P. Michiardi and R. Molva, "Core: A collaborative reputation mechanism to enforce node cooperation in mobile ad hoc networks," in *Proceedings of the IFIP TC6/TC11 Sixth Joint Working Conference on Communications and Multimedia Security*. Deventer, The Netherlands: Kluwer, B.V., 2002, pp. 107–121.

[78] A. Patwardhan, A. Joshi, T. Finin, and Y. Yesha, "A data intensive reputation management scheme for vehicular ad hoc networks," in *Proceedings of the Third Annual International Conference on Mobile and Ubiquitous Systems— Workshops, Mobiquitous'06*, San Jose, California, USA, July 2006, pp. 1–8.

[79] W. Li, A. Joshi, and T. Finin, "Coping with node misbehaviors in ad hoc networks: A multi-dimensional trust management approach," in *2010*

Eleventh International Conference on Mobile Data Management, Kansas City, MO, USA, May 2010, pp. 85–94.

[80]   W. Li, A. Joshi, and T. Finin, "Cast: Context-aware security and trust framework for mobile ad-hoc networks using policies," *Distributed and Parallel Databases*, vol. 31, no. 2, pp. 353–376, 2013.

[81]   F. Bao, I. R. Chen, M. Chang, and J. H. Cho, "Hierarchical trust management for wireless sensor networks and its applications to trust-based routing and intrusion detection," *IEEE Transactions on Network and Service Management*, vol. 9, no. 2, pp. 169–183, June 2012.

[82]   D. He, C. Chen, S. Chan, J. Bu, and A. V. Vasilakos, "Retrust: Attack-resistant and lightweight trust management for medical sensor networks," *IEEE Transactions on Information Technology in Biomedicine*, vol. 16, no. 4, pp. 623–632, July 2012.

[83]   I. R. Chen, F. Bao, M. Chang, and J. H. Cho, "Dynamic trust management for delay tolerant networks and its application to secure routing," *IEEE Transactions on Parallel and Distributed Systems*, vol. 25, no. 5, pp. 1200–1210, May 2014.

[84]   Z. Wei, H. Tang, F. R. Yu, M. Wang, and P. Mason, "Security enhancements for mobile ad hoc networks with trust management using uncertain reasoning," *IEEE Transactions on Vehicular Technology*, vol. 63, no. 9, pp. 4647–4658, November 2014.

[85]   Y. Ren, V. I. Zadorozhny, V. A. Oleshchuk, and F. Y. Li, "A novel approach to trust management in unattended wireless sensor networks," *IEEE Transactions on Mobile Computing*, vol. 13, no. 7, pp. 1409–1423, July 2014.

[86]   S. A. Mousavifar and C. Leung, "Energy efficient collaborative spectrum sensing based on trust management in cognitive radio networks," *IEEE Transactions on Wireless Communications*, vol. 14, no. 4, pp. 1927–1939, April 2015.

[87]   P. Papadimitratos, L. Buttyan, T. Holczer *et al.*, "Secure vehicular communication systems: Design and architecture," *IEEE Communications Magazine*, vol. 46, no. 11, pp. 100–109, November 2008.

[88]   N. Haddadou and A. Rachedi, "Dtm2: Adapting job market signaling for distributed trust management in vehicular ad hoc networks," in *2013 IEEE International Conference on Communications (ICC)*, Budapest, Hungary, June 2013, pp. 1827–1832.

[89]   N. Haddadou, A. Rachedi, and Y. Ghamri-Doudane, "A job market signaling scheme for incentive and trust management in vehicular ad hoc networks," *IEEE Transactions on Vehicular Technology*, vol. 64, no. 8, pp. 3657–3674, August 2015.

[90]   C. Liao, J. Chang, I. Lee, and K. K. Venkatasubramanian, "A trust model for vehicular network-based incident reports," in *Wireless Vehicular Communications (WiVeC), 2013 IEEE 5th International Symposium on*, Dresden, Germany, June 2013, pp. 1–5.

[91]   Z. Huang, S. Ruj, M. A. Cavenaghi, M. Stojmenovic, and A. Nayak, "A social network approach to trust management in vanets," *Peer-to-Peer Networking and Applications*, vol. 7, no. 3, pp. 229–242, 2014. [Online]. Available: http://dx.doi.org/10.1007/s12083-012-0136-8

[92]   W. Li and H. Song, "Art: An attack-resistant trust management scheme for securing vehicular ad hoc networks," *IEEE Transactions on Intelligent Transportation Systems*, vol. 17, no. 4, pp. 960–969, April 2016.

[93]   M. Zimmer, "Surveillance, privacy and the ethics of vehicle safety communication technologies," *Ethics and Information Technology*, vol. 7, no. 4, pp. 201–210, 2005.

[94]   C. Woodyard and J. O'Donnell, "Your car may be invading your privacy," http://www.usatoday.com/story/money/cars/2013/03/24/car-spying-edr-data-privacy/1991751/, accessed: 05-08-2015.

[95]   C. Karatas, L. Liu, H. Li *et al.*, "Leveraging wearables for steering and driver tracking," in *International Conference on Computer Communications*. San Francisco, CA, USA, IEEE, 2016.

[96]   I. A. Junglas and R. T. Watson, "Location-based services," *Communications of the ACM*, vol. 51, no. 3, pp. 65–69, 2008.

[97]   D. Eckhoff, R. German, C. Sommer *et al.*, "Slotswap: Strong and affordable location privacy in intelligent transportation systems," *IEEE Communications Magazine*, vol. 49, no. 11, pp. 126–133, 2011.

[98]   Q. Wu, J. Domingo-Ferrer, and U. González-Nicolás, "Balanced trustworthiness, safety, and privacy in vehicle-to-vehicle communications," *IEEE Transactions on Vehicular Technology*, vol. 59, no. 2, pp. 559–573, 2010.

[99]   J. Gifford, "Rfid applications in transportation operations," in *Research Opportunities in Radio Frequency Identification (RFID) Transportation Applications Conference*, Washington DC, USA, 2006.

[100]   T. Halevi, S. Lin, D. Ma *et al.*, "Sensing-enabled defenses to rfid unauthorized reading and relay attacks without changing the usage model," in *Pervasive Computing and Communications (PerCom), 2012 IEEE International Conference on*. Lugano, Switzerland: IEEE, 2012, pp. 227–234.

[101]   T. Halevi, H. Li, D. Ma, N. Saxena, J. Voris, and T. Xiang, "Context-aware defenses to rfid unauthorized reading and relay attacks," *IEEE Transactions on Emerging Topics in Computing*, vol. 1, no. 2, pp. 307–318, 2013.

[102]   N. Saxena and J. Voris, "Still and silent: Motion detection for enhanced rfid security and privacy without changing the usage model," in *International Workshop on Radio Frequency Identification: Security and Privacy Issues*. Istanbul, Turkey: Springer, 2010, pp. 2–21.

[103]   T. S. Heydt-Benjamin, H.-J. Chae, B. Defend, and K. Fu, "Privacy for public transportation," in *International Workshop on Privacy Enhancing Technologies*. Cambridge, UK: Springer, 2006, pp. 1–19.

[104]   R. N. Fries, M. R. Gahrooei, M. Chowdhury, and A. J. Conway, "Meeting privacy challenges while advancing intelligent transportation systems," *Transportation Research Part C: Emerging Technologies*, vol. 25, pp. 34–45, 2012.

Chapter 9
Review of data leakage attack techniques in cloud systems
Zirak Allaf[1] and Mo Adda[1]

Abstract

Manipulating and delivering data in heterogeneous environments such as those underlying cloud systems is a critical task because of confidentiality issues. Cloud technology remains vulnerable to data leakage attacks due to its applications in gathering information about multiple independent entities (e.g. end users and VMs) and sharing cloud resources. Furthermore, the number of threats are increased when the cloud users are using cloud computing services compared to PC users, due to loss of control, privacy and outsourced data storage. Consequently, hackers exploit security vulnerabilities to launch attacks to take advantage of sensitive data such as secret keys.

When data is manipulated and shared between different parties in cloud systems, it will be vulnerable to threats in cloud systems. This chapter explores data vulnerability throughout its life cycle to categorise existing data leakage attack techniques in terms of where they can be implemented and what can be stolen in this untrusted environment, and also classifies data leakage attack techniques according to the type of data, such as files and secret keys. Furthermore, this study explores core technologies upon which cloud computing is built, such as the web, virtualisation and cryptography, and their vulnerabilities prone to such attacks. We also propose existing data leakage detection and protection techniques to mitigate and alleviate such attacks.

9.1 Introduction

Cloud computing is a new model of client server paradigm that uses Internet services to enable a number of technologies offering better solutions to end users without a required knowledge for any of these technologies and services. The richness of various models in cloud computing makes it a ubiquitous computational environment, wherein cloud users can access cloud services anywhere, at any time through the Internet. Moreover, boosting hardware resources on demand and improving flexibility

---

[1]School of Computing, University of Portsmouth, UK

to respond quickly to requirements without IT management efforts. However, this leads to the introduction of threats to the shared resources in cloud systems.

Cloud computing offers hardware and software services to its cloud consumers to organise and maintain availability to continue to meet their needs. However, the usefulness and various access techniques of cloud models cannot be a suitable solution to guarantee the maintenance of data integration and protection, especially when the data is manipulated and outsourced in an undisclosed location by a third party (cloud providers) outside the owner's control. Thus, security is the major requirement in cloud infrastructure, and data in particular is a critical asset that is vulnerable to data leakage attacks.

This chapter studies major known hardware and software vulnerabilities which lead to data leakage attacks and their countermeasures. In this chapter, we discuss the critical characteristics of how attackers exploit the hardware and software characteristics of on-board resources in their attack and introduce a comparison, mainly concerning data leakage attack techniques, especially targeting credential data (e.g. cryptographic keys). This chapter is structured as follows: in Section 9.2, we describe data state, and Section 9.3 demonstrates the core technologies that are utilised in the cloud and their vulnerabilities prone to such attack. In Sections 9.4 and 9.5, we classify recent data leakage attack techniques, mitigation, and countermeasures, followed by the conclusion.

9.2   Data state and vulnerabilities

While data is obviously an important asset to organisations, it is necessary to clarify what it exactly constitutes in a computational environment to grasp the concept of data leakage attack in terms of the type, size or state of data being compromised. Shabtai *et al.* [37] classified the state of data in its process life cycle into three states: Data-At-Rest (DAR), Data-In-Motion (DIM) and Data-In-Use (DIU) in computer systems. These categorisations reflect the states of data from the time it is created/stored, processed through computational resources, such as CPU components and main memory and transmitted over cloud systems. It is represented differently while reposing in hardware resources such as files, memory contents and network packets. In recent years, data leakage attacks have been achieved on all data states [9,36,41,56] as is shown in Table 9.1. In the following subsections, we will explain data states and possible threats to each state and will focus on data leakage attack while the data state is DIU.

9.2.1   Data-At-Rest

In this state, data is stored in storage devices. In computer systems, the internal hard disk of a computer is a permanent storage for data; DAR is a representation of data when it is stored in such devices. In cloud computing, there is a concern about the location transparency of data due to the complexity of the cloud infrastructure being hidden from cloud consumers; cloud consumers do not know where their data is or has been stored. This disruption causes hesitancy among organisations considering involvement in cloud systems, worrying about who deals with sensitive data. Moreover, consumers are also worried about malicious insiders who co-locate on the same storage. Ristenpart *et al.* [36] proposed a hard disk-based convert channel attack against arbitrary VMs on Amazon EC2. They successfully identified cloud storage co-residency and transmitted data between the VMs when they were accessing the same storage devices.

Another concern about large files, due to limited space in main memory, is that the OS loads a portion of the file in contiguous pages in main memory, and the rest remains on the storage device of the system (it is coordinated with the same physical addresses that it – the file – originated from). Bernstein [6] exploited this feature to construct a covert channel attack to identify which parts of the file have already been loaded and those still on the disk by time variation. Accessing those parts of the file that have been accessed recently takes shorter time than those that have not been touched.

9.2.2 Data-In-Motion

DIM describes the transfer of data over networks, which is delivered from a source to a destination. Data will be at risk in this media due to eavesdropping attack, which is able to inspect packets. Cryptographic technology have been used to protect the data such as Secure Shell (SSH). However, such protection techniques are still vulnerable to information leakage attack. Song *et al.* [40] showed a possible leakage attack against network packages; particularly, when they are currying credential information and moving through SSH. The authors developed a Hidden Markov Model (HMM) and key sequence prediction algorithm to guess correct pressed keys, which forms the password, by victim.

In cloud systems, Software-as-a-Service (SaaS) enables web technology to deliver applications as a service to end users. The data in this state represent request/response between client and server while they communicate. The data needs to be protected by encrypting it from eavesdropping attack. However, this does not stop attackers from malicious intentions, they can still analyse pocket size and timing to leak sensitive information [9].

9.2.3 Data-In-Use

In a DIU state, data is loaded into computational resources (mainly CPU components such as registers, caches and main memory). Generally, to load data from storage devices to CPU registers, it must pass through several hierarchical buffers, including main memory and CPU caches (L1, L2 and L3) prior to reaching the registers, where it is primed for operations such as read and write. According to the applications, data might have different alignment and organisations while loading into main memory regarding the data types, such as array, list, linked list, class and structure. In a multitasking environment, physical resources are shared between processes in different layers, such as OS (page sharing) and application (shared libraries), the data frequently being used by those resources; therefore, the OS alternates the processes in using those resources in the case that a region of memory is shared between processes, such as buffer lookup table in AES [6]. Recent work has shown vulnerabilities of DIU in multitasking systems in both layers' OS (page sharing) [12,42], the achieved memory deduplication attack and Application (shared library).

9.3   Core technology vulnerabilities in cloud computing

Cloud computing has emerged from existing technologies, mainly such as the web, cryptography and virtualisation to offer best solutions to companies, organisations and enterprises. These technologies can cover a wide range and variety of application domains, such as education, health sector, social networks, governments, on-line shopping. However, when two or more technologies contribute in handling data in the cloud, this will introduce vulnerabilities that attackers can exploit to achieve malicious intent to steal data. We list the common technologies in the cloud that have been compromised for data leakage attacks.

9.3.1   Web technology

In the SaaS model, web technology is enabled to deliver application as a service to web clients. Web technology is a client/server paradigm to provide communications through networks. Today, most desktop applications have been transferred to web application due to the ease and low cost of installation, user-friendly interface, no client update required, an independent platform and undergoing continuous technological enhancement. However, end users only need to install a web browser application to communicate with the server. This communication is carried out through networks, which might reveal sensitive information such as application states and state-transits. This information needs to be protected against network sniffers by utilising encryption techniques. However, this does not stop attackers from stealing information. Chen *et al.* [9] showed that leaking sensitive information is still viable.

9.3.2   Virtualisation technology

Virtualisation technology (VT) abstracts hardware resources (CPU, RAM, IO and network) to create multiple virtual machines (VMs) with hardware virtualisation features, each of which is represented independently in the system. Moreover, each VM runs on top of an additional layer called hypervisor. Key responsibilities of the layer are monitoring and managing shared resources between VMs through sandboxing technique. This to amplify a small number of hardware resources to serve a large number of VMs. The sharing memory technique is widely used in software industries to improve memory efficiency, such as Kernel Same Page (KSP) in KVM. However, it has a significant impact on the system security, particularly data leakage attacks. Through this, opportunities for building hidden communication channels will arise. This provides malicious VMs ability to take advantage of exploiting hardware vulnerabilities, which leads to information leakage, wherein data exchange will be performed through unauthorised processes. This technology incorporates security threats, particularly susceptibility to data leakage attacks. In this subsection, we focus on the features that are prone to such attacks, such as resource sharing, and more details are provided in the subsequent sections.

9.3.3   Cryptography

Cryptography can be considered as a set of algorithms which primarily relies on mathematical theories with computational supports to be practised in computer systems. It is widely used in various domains as a data protection solution from malicious parties who intend to steal interesting information. It can be used by OS or application layers and for different purposes, such as email services, health records, banking.

It can be an OS level solution to protect data by storing encrypted data on physical storage devices. In modern OS settings, during OS installation, one of the optional steps is asking to encrypt user files before storing them on the internal storage device during the use of the OS. In cloud systems, this is good for cloud consumers because they are worried about storage location transparency. Moreover, it can be used at application level on top of OS level. Particularly in web applications, software industries integrate cryptographic algorithms with page contents to encrypt any data that exchanges between client/server for any request/response. This is to protect data from eavesdropping [9]. This can be useful in the cloud when Platform-as-a-Service (PaaS) becomes mainstream to deliver enterprise applications through web technology to web users.

Although cryptography has widely been used in computer and cloud systems, it is still vulnerable to information leakage attacks. In this chapter, we focus on side/covert channel attacks, in computer and cloud systems, such attacks attempt to gain sensitive information, such as secret keys against cryptographic algorithms. The attacks take advantage of software implementation and hardware architecture vulnerabilities or a combination of both, rather than attacking underlying implementation of the algorithms or brute force attacks. For instance, brute force attacks rely on guesswork, wherein the attackers attempt a list of keys or passwords to find the right one.

9.4   Side and covert channel attack classification

Information leakage channel-based attack is an action of exploiting hardware and software vulnerabilities to provide unauthorised communications between two processes, in either a virtualised or non-virtualised environment, which are sharing the same physical resources.

Studies in recent years have shown that information leakage channel-based attacks are prevalently targeting cryptosystems by exploiting improper utilisation of physical resources in a shared environment and poor software implementation. The key role in motivating attackers to target cryptosystems is their essential usage in a client/server and cloud environment to protect data (as mentioned in Section 9.3.3) while it is moving through untrusted communication channels and is processing in an untrusted computational environment. Because these environments rely heavily on co-residency and sharing features, this affords opportunity to the attackers to have a good chance of being a neighbour of its victim with a virtual isolation, which is vulnerable to computational analysis.

9.4.1 Targeted data types

Recent studies showed that side and covert channel attacks have targeted different types of data. The following shows the most attractive data by attackers.

9.4.1.1 Cryptographic keys

Keys are sets of letters or symbols to form a string that can be combined with plain text through cryptographic algorithms to produce cipher text and vice versa. It is the core source of cryptographic operations' encryption and decryption. The size of cryptographic keys varies: 64, 128, 256 bits, etc. In case of choosing short keys, Brute Force attacks can be conducted, because in a modern CPU with a large number of cores, it might be possible to find the right key by checking the maximum possible keys in reasonable time. However, long keys, even with modern CPUs, will take a very long time (e.g. to crack a 128-bit AES key takes 150 trillion years [34]).

There are different types of keys and their utilisation depends on the nature of the algorithms. In AES, the algorithm uses a secret key for encryption and decryption, However, in the RSA algorithm, two keys, private and public keys, are required, one for encryption and one for decryption. When an encryption algorithm starts combining a key with plain text to generate cipher text, it meets a sequential number of mathematical operations (e.g. division, multiplication and mode). The attackers take advantage of these operations, because they can clearly degrade CPU performance during cryptographic operations.

9.4.1.2 Files

Ubiquitous features in the cloud (such as shared storage method and synchronisation services) cause cloud users to habitually store their documents remotely on untrusted storage out of end users' control, such as Dropbox, Google Drive and SkyDrive, particularly sharing similar data methods [10]. Such shared characteristics can be found in web-based applications and will be delivered through PaaS. Authors have addressed the weakness of the implementation of the web applications, which leads to data leakage attack. References [35,36,53,55] used a file on a shared storage between spy and victim processes to build a covert channel attack.

9.4.2 Source of leakage

There are a number of characteristics offered by cloud technologies to offer high-quality services, such as resource pooling, multi-tenancy and rapid elasticity [29]. However, they are vulnerable to information leakage attacks, particularly resource sharing features, which are fundamental for cloud computing to gain sufficient performance to lease sufficient number of cloud tenants. Consequently, studies have shown that this feature is prevalently exploited by attackers for their malicious intentions.

Stealing sensitive data is possible at all data states (DAR, DIP and DIT) (see Table 9.1) as they all have special consideration and techniques to achieve the attacks. Data in multitasking/users' systems can be processed by different resources, such as CPU caches, memory, storage and network media. Each media has its own characteristics on which the attackers rely during experiments. So, it is crucial to focus on the common features that have already been exploited by previous studies.

9.4.2.1 CPU architecture

Past studies showed that CPU is the most targeted resources by attackers. It is the main physical resource in computational models due to interconnection with on-board resources such as main memory and IO devices through buses. Modern CPUs have multiple cores to offer more efficient performance and facilitate to accommodate a sufficient number of programs concurrently. Each core represents a logical isolated processor inside the CPU die. The CPU has different cache levels.

In computer systems, the size and speed of memories are ordered from small and high to large and slow (e.g. registers, L1, L2, L3 and main memory). The basic function of CPU caches is to buffer data requested from the main memory, due to the trade-off performance between fast-to-slow and small-to-large memories supply the CPU when it is operating on the requested data. Each core can have its own L1 and L2 caches, or only L1 privately, while L2 is shared between two or more cores, depending on the CPU architecture design, and cores from L3 and above are shared for all CPU cores. Ge *et al.* [11] demonstrated modern microprocessors' architecture and their compromising to information leakage attacks in fine-grained details.

CPU cache is the main source of information that attackers relay on to perform side and covert channel attacks. By reviewing such attacks since last 15 years, it can be noticed that the attackers utilised one of the cache levels as primary communication channel between two processes (attack and victim) that provides the state of the victim process unintentionally. Earlier attacks targeted L1 and L2 cache as communication channels between attack and victim processes, which reside on the same core. However, core migration makes noise to the measurement when operating system alternates assigning processes to a core [60]. Researchers then continued to explore faster and higher bitrate attacks against L1 in cross-core settings. Until 2014, unified cache L3 has gained most of the attention due to higher resolution with less time required to recover sensitive information [56].

9.4.2.2 Timing

Most of the published side and covert channel attacks relied on timing to achieve the attacks. The attackers are interested in hardware activities at granularity level such as number of cycles to access a single cache line in L1 cache. They utilise timing to measure cache accesses, using own data, to synchronise with victim's data on the same cache in shared hardware settings. Modern processors such as Intel, which has offered a hardware support, is a special counter register, for timing with a high resolution for every operation. At the same time, Intel offers Read Time Stamp Counter (RDTSC) instruction to read value of the counter register.[1] The attackers use RDTSC instruction to measure cache accesses, using own data, to synchronise with victim's data on the same cache. The utilisation of RDTSC has been proposed in attack implementation code by different techniques such as prime+prob [28,35] and flush+reload [56].

9.4.2.3   CPU power consumption

Attackers monitor CPU power consumption activities over time to deduce mathematical operations, such as multiplication and division which use more CPU components than add and subtraction operations. This information will be beneficial for attackers who are targeting cryptographic algorithms to extract secret keys. This is because when a computer is running cryptographic algorithms, CPU executes a series of multiplications and divisions which causes the CPU to consume more power. The attacker then analyses the variation of the power consumption to deduce some or all of the secret key bits. This chapter will not be focusing on that feature [5,50].

9.4.2.4   Page sharing

Memory page sharing is a notable technique which is the predominant method used in memory management systems to reclaim memory. This technique is widely utilised in OSs and hypervisors, such as KVM KSP [4] and ESX Transparent Page Sharing (TPS) [45]. In this technique, the OS or hypervisor scans memory pages to find identical pages (same contents), in every specific period of time, to maintain only one copy of the pages and remove identical ones [32,47]. In virtualisation, when a hypervisor runs multiple VMs of the same OS, it can reclaim a sufficient memory. Alto *et al.* [46] statistically showed that more than 40% of memory can be saved when 10 VMs are running.

For instance, let's assume that a file with 10 pages are shared by two VMs (VM1 and VM2); when VM1 makes modifications on two pages, a copy-on-write mechanism will take place by OS, which creates two private copies of the pages and refers them to the VM1. VM2 no longer has access to the VM1's private copies. So, each VM has two private and eight shared pages. VM1 can observe a variation in writing time between shared and private pages. Writing on shared pages is longer than private pages. As the result, previous studies have shown how this feature has been exploited by covert channel attackers in computer [49] and cloud systems [7,42,53].

9.4.2.5   Shared library

Shared libraries are code that is compiled in a way that other programs can link with it during run-time. As a shared library is loaded into memory, the same memory locations are shared with multiple programs which are linked with it. This saves memory space; instead of having multiple copies for each program, only one copy will be utilised. Another advantage is that it is easy to maintain; any modification on the library does not affect the linked programs, and all the programs have the most recent version of the library once it is loaded.

---

[1] RDTSC is an assembly instruction, and it can be used in C and C++ in-line assembly. For more detail on how to use RDTSC in modern Intel CPUs, see [33].

However, shared libraries are another factor to provide shared variables between independent processes. This has a negative impact on data protection. The most visible vulnerability against shared libraries in past and recent studies is the usage of OpenSSL implementation of AES [6,60], which provides a dynamic shared library libcrypto, so as to be linked with multiple programs in UNIX-based OSs. AES utilises a lookup or S-Box table, which is an array of values that will be used during the encryption rounds. When a victim uses this table during encryption, an attacker can observe recently accessed elements from the lookup table by the victim.

9.4.3 Types of channel attacks

In recent years, side and covert channel attacks have been practised as two common types of information leakage attacks; they target hierarchical memory accesses by analysing time variations of the accesses. These two types of attacks are similar in achievements, except a covert channel attack is broader than a side channel attack technique, which can be deployed in various layers, such as network [20,38], OS [21], I/O [36,39] and application [12]. On the other hand, side channel attack is used specifically against cryptosystems to retrieve cryptographic keys by utilising CPU components.

9.4.3.1 Covert-channel attacks

This notion dates back to late 1969 and the pioneering work of Lampson [26]. He described the possibility of creating intended communication channels between two processes to exchange information. The insider process (has privilege) transmits information (state of the process) indirectly through other means, such as hardware contention, to spy process (has no privilege) on shared resources. This can occur in different layers with different bitrate transmission, such as OS [55], CPU cache [36], virtual memory (pages) [22], network packets [52]. This attack bypasses system security such as firewall and Intrusion Detection System (IDS) because it is hidden to access control mechanisms. Covert channel attack limitations are having low bit-rate and being expensive to set up.

In 2005, [35] examined covert channel attack in both L1 and L2 cache with bitrate 200 and 100 kps, respectively, in native system. Based on the experiment, he emphasised that L2 covert channel attack is more practical than L1, because L1 is noisier than L2 due to process core migrations. A year later, Wang and Lee [49] introduced an approach to build a covert channel SMT/FU whereby the attacker addressed OS vulnerability, shared pool of Functional Unit FU, to interfere with the victim's process.

In 2009, when cloud computing came to the stage, Ristenpart *et al.* [36] introduced the first practical high-level covert channel attack against CPU component L2 cache with a very low bitrate, 0.2 bps. Then, in 2011, Xu *et al.* [55] deepened the study to improve the bitrate to 3 bps by exploiting memory bus. Then, in 2015, Maurice *et al.* [28] showed the barrier of limiting bitrate between two processes in a covert channel attack in addressing uncertainty due to more frequent core migration. They utilised inclusive cache L3 to overcome this issue and their result surprisingly showed higher than previous attacks, namely 751 bps with the same attack settings.

9.4.3.2   Side-channel attacks

Side channel attack is mounted against cryptosystems to extract secret keys by the means of sources that provide interesting information rather than Brute Force attacks or attacks against mathematical implementation of the algorithms, wherein attackers rely on deducing the secret keys used by the victim. The popular algorithms paid attention to by researchers in the past decade are RSA [1,56], AES [31] , DES [2]. Attackers monitor shared resources to collect fine-grain information to identify the targeted data usage by victims. The attacker does not need privilege to yield the information, and the resources sharing will be enough to meet the attack's requirements. Side channel attack is classified into three classes: time-driven, trace-driven and access-driven [17,60].

In last 15 years, a large number of side channel attacks, those which rely on CPU caches (L1, L2 and L3 or LLC) to extract cryptographic keys, have been extensively studied and successfully practised on native and cloud systems. They have analysed the time access variations by tracing CPU cache utilisation.

The first practical attack against cryptographic algorithm DES was in 2003, and was proposed by Tsunoo et al. [44]. They retrieved about 90% of the secret key by taking approximately 10^{23} samples.

In 2005, AES algorithm became a target of researchers. It was first practised by Bernstein [6] in which the attacker remotely analysed the overall execution time of the algorithm. In addition, he published the full implementation of the attack. This attack was extended and refined in 2007 by Neve et al. [30]. They addressed the limitation in Bernstein's attack, as a result of which they were able to retrieve the entire key bits with fewer samples.

Further, Gullasch et al. [17] developed a cache channel attack to recover the full key bits in AES in native settings. The attacker recorded cache activities for approximately 2.8 s about 100 encryption calls. They were first attacked compressed lookup table. Moreover, in the improvement of Bernstein's side channel attack in 2013 by Aly and ElGayyar [3], the authors reproduced the attack on modern CPUs with the latest version of AES.

With the popularity of the cloud computing phenomenon, the use of cryptography increasingly rose due to its heterogeneousness. From that point onwards, researchers have been focusing on addressing the weaknesses of logical isolation between cloud entities on the same physical machine. Ristenpart et al. [36] were the first in practically addressing internal hardware vulnerabilities in Amazon EC2 cloud systems. Their proposed attacks were in high level and low resolution. In 2012, Zhang et al. [60] dramatically improved the resolution of the attack by utilising L1. However, in 2014, Yarom and Falkner [56] introduced a surprisingly high-resolution side channel attack utilising L3 with unrelated processes (each assigned on a different core). Since then, LLC has become the most targeted hardware that attackers rely on to extract secret keys [13,22].

9.4.4 Techniques

Time+Evict (TE) [31,43]: In this technique, it is assumed that a shared library is linked to both attacker and victim program concurrently such as lookup table in AES. They both have access to the lookup table. The attacker monitors cache line(s) that are synchronised with the array.[2] The attacker first finds the average time taken for one encryption, then triggers the encryption function and evicts cache lines, that have already touched the array. After the eviction, the attacker triggers a series of encryption and measures them. If any encryption call takes longer than the average time, it indicates that the evicted cache line(s) has(ve) been accessed recently by the victim.

Prime+Probe (PP) [28,60]: In this technique, an attacker process monitors victim process by filling the CPU cache (unified cache such as L3 or LLC between them) with its data. This is to check which attacker's cache lines have been evicted by the victim's data. To do that, the attacker process utilises a busy loop that sleeps for a specific time with each iteration to wake the attacker process up and measure variation of access time to its cache lines. Longer time indicates the cache line is evicted by the victim and needs to be loaded from a higher memory level. This technique can be applied in all memory levels.

Flush+Reload (FR) [17,56]: This technique is the inverse of prime+probe. Both the attacker and the victim should have access to the same data concurrently; this is a feature of shared library as is referred to in Section 9.4.2.5. The attacker targets a range of addresses in a shared library, which is loaded in to the main memory, and flushes one or more cache line(s) which is referenced in the address range. The attacker needs to be sure that the cache lines(s) have been removed from the cache hierarchy (L1, L2, and L3). After the flush, the attacker waits until the victim accesses some data in the address range. When the victim attempts to access the flushed cache line(s), he must access them in main memory, due to the flush performed by the attacker. Finally, the attacker scans and encodes the time accesses; shorter time indicates the cache line(s) have been recently accessed by the victim.

Flush+Flush (FF) [13,14]: This attack technique is composed of two flushes. This attack defers from flush+reload technique by avoiding reload stage, which causes the cache to be free of misses. Thus detections, which rely on cache misses, of such attack will be difficult. In this technique, the attacker relies on time variation of series flush in instruction rather than monitoring cache line accesses.

9.4.5 A generic attack model

As mentioned earlier, several attack techniques have been widely used in leaking sensitive data in cloud systems. They are similar in achieving these techniques with exception of having different system settings and CPU architecture for their utilisation.

As mentioned earlier, covert and side channel attacks provide an ability to attackers by transferring the underlying hardware activities, such as measuring time variation of memory accesses to high level. This is the core mechanism of such attacks, which allows the attackers to infer victim propriety through a resource sharing feature.

---

[2]The lookup table is represented as an array when it is loaded into main memory.

In the following, we describe a generic attack model in cloud systems and general steps to achieve such attacks. In addition, we historically show the previous attacks, over the last 15 years, against various shared resources.

In the earlier sections, the vulnerabilities of cloud components which might lead to the occurrence of data leakage attacks were demonstrated. The achievement of data leakage attacks depends on the attacker's attitudes to what they are stealing (e.g. secret keys). The aforementioned showed the importance of cryptographic algorithms in real systems to protect data in various application domains by encrypting data with secret keys. This has motivated attackers to deploy sophisticated attack techniques to gain the secret keys. The scope of this attack model will be targeting secret keys. A data leakage attack will be achieved in a two-step placement and running the attack.

After identifying the data type by an attacker, the attacker needs to place its malicious processes on the same physical machine as the victim is co-allocated, due to the nature of the attack, which is co-resident. Placing a new instance of VM in a lab is cheaper compared to real systems such as EC2 [36,55]. This is because cloud providers, in real systems, attempt to hide the complexity of cloud infrastructure and data storage to prevent cloud cartography. Thus, the attacker needs further action to take place to find its victim. To overcome this problem, Ristenpart *et al.* [36] successfully established a covert channel attack in a real cloud system, Amazon EC2, by discovered EC2 mapping (internal and external network address spaces corresponding to an entity creation) by utilising network probing technique. This was useful for the early stage for the attacker to find the internal map of EC2 to place the attack process with the victim so as to be in the same zone in EC2. This affords a chance of being co-allocated on the same physical server in the same zone.

The next step is observation. In this stage, the attacker utilises the attack techniques, such as prime+prob and flush+reload, as mentioned previously in Section 9.4.5. The attacker starts monitoring victim's activities against shared hardware. In recent years, these attacks have been studied very well across various on-board resources such as CPU caches (L1 [60], L2 [48] and L3 or LLC [56]) and memory pages [59]. Table 9.1 depicts relevant attacks against physical resources.

Stealing secret keys from cryptographic algorithms depends on the nature of the algorithms. For instance, AES algorithm [6,8] encrypts plain text using lookup table. This array holds a list of values that will be used during the encryption rounds. This table is the most critical component in the algorithm and has been targeted by attackers. AES attackers are interested in cache line accesses and cache contentions to find out recent use of cache lines, which hold the candidate elements in the lookup table by the victim.

However, the RSA algorithm [56], instead of having S-Box, depends on the mathematical operations square and multiply. Thus, the attackers are interested in tracing the execution of the victim's program rather than memory accesses.

In attacks against L1 cache. Zhang *et al.* [60] constructed a side channel attack utilising L1 instruction cache to extract AES secret keys from a co-resident victim VM with attacker VM; both were running libgcrypt shared library. The authors addressed source of noise (hardware and software) against the attack VM and were able to reduce

Table 9.1   Side and covert channel attack classifications

Data leakage attack techniques in cloud systems							
Data stat	Type	Technique	Application	Resource	Data type	System	Pubs
DAR	CC	PP	–	L1	File	IaaS	2009 [36]
	CC	PP	–	L1	File	IaaS	2011 [55]
DIP	SC	–	DES	L1	Key	Native	2003 [44]
	CC	PP	RSA	L1, L2	key	native	2005 [35]
	SC	PP	AES	L1	Key	native	2005 [6]
	CC	SMT/FU	program	L2	file	native	2006 [49]
	SC	SMT/cache	AES	L2	key	native	2006 [49]
	SC	–	RSA	I-cache	Key	native	2007 [1]
	SC	ET, PP	AES	Page	–	native	2008 [31], 2010 [43]
	SC	PP	–	I-cache	–	native	2010 [2]
	CC	PP	browser	Pages	file	PaaS	2010 [9]
	SC	ET, PP	AES	L3	key	native	2011 [17]
	CC	PP	–	L2	file	cloud	2011 [55]
	CC	PP	browsers	pages	file	IaaS	2011 [42]
	CC	PP	browsers	pages	file	IaaS	2011 [42]
	SC	PP	AES	L2	key	native	2011 [17]
	SC	FR	AES	L3	key	native	2014 [23]
	CC	PP	browsers	pages	file	PaaS	2014 [61]
	CC	FF	RSA	L3	Key	IaaS	2014 [56]
	SC	FR	AES	L3	Key	IaaS	2015 [22]
	CC	FF	browser	L3	file	IaaS	2015 [13,14]
	SC	FR	AES	L3	key	native	2015 [19]
	SC	PP	AES	L2	key	IaaS	2015 [57]
	SC	FR	AES	LL3	key	native	2015 [15]
	SC	PP, FR	AES	LL3	key	native	2016 [24]
	SC	PP, FR	AES	LL3	key	native, IaaS	2016 [18]
DIT	CC	Timing	database	–	Dataset	IaaS	2012 [41]
	CC	–	database	–	Dataset	IaaS	2012 [41]

the noise during the observation stage by using a combination of SVM and HMM to deduce key-bits with low false negative.

In attacks against L2 cache, Ristenpart *et al.* [36] introduced a cross-VM covert channel attack against CPU L2 cache. The authors targeted large-sized files to convey messages between two VMs. The aim was to identify VMs' co-residency on the shared storage devices. The authors were interested in hard disk contention patterns by recording access time variations to certain portions of the files between the VMs. Subsequently, Xu *et al.* [55] carried out the previous attack and improved the resolution of the previous covert channel model with a higher bandwidth and lower error rate.

Following this, attackers improved leakage attack by utilising different resources, such as L3, with less time to recover entire keys. In previous studies, sharing cores between attack and victim VMs was one of the requirement settings of the attacks. Before 2014, the most targeted cache levels were L1 and L2 and the attack and the victim process needed to be paired on the same core with the attacker process. Zhang *et al.*'s [60] attack model utilised IPI interrupt to force the victim process to migrate from a different core and allocate it with the attacker process. However, Yarom and Falkner [56] introduced a new direction of side channel attacks by utilising L3 cache and taking advantage of the inclusiveness feature. They proposed a flush + reload technique to extract the components of the private key, approximately 97.7% bits of the key, from the GnuPG implementation of RSA. Here, the attacker and victim process resided on different cores, in shared page settings. They successfully constructed an LLC-based channel between two unrelated processes in a virtualised environment.

As mentioned earlier, the deduplication feature is a key function in virtualisation, so that the host is able to reclaim a large amount of memory against identical contents. The results of the previous studies showed that this feature has been exploited in cloud systems. Suzaki *et al.* [42] proposed a matching technique to identify running applications (sshd and apache2 on linux OS and Firefox and IE6 on Windows XP) and discover that a targeted file is downloaded in a browser on the victim's VM. Bosman *et al.* [7] proposed a side channel JavaScript-based attack against Windows Edge Browser to retrieve HTTP hashed password. This weakness encouraged CPU industries to disable this feature. However, this has not stopped attackers from leaking information against hardware resources. Irazoqui *et al.* [22] took up the challenge that, even with the disabling deduplication feature, leaking information is still feasible. The authors utilised huge sized pages, in which the attacker can gain full physical addresses from virtual addresses. When in cache addressing, the same physical addresses are utilised for cache addressing.

In shared page settings, [56] successfully constructed LLC-based channel between two unrelated processes in virtualised environment. As mentioned earlier, deduplication feature is a key function in virtualisation so that the host OS is able to reclaim a large amount of memory against identical contents. This feature is exploited by [42,53,55]. This weakness encouraged CPU industries to disable this feature. However, this does not stop attackers from leaking information from hardware level. Irazoqui *et al.* [22] took the challenge that even with disabling deduplication feature, leaking information is still feasible.

9.5   Mitigation countermeasures

In the past decade, variety of side and covert channel attack techniques and their analysis on hardware usage at granularity level have been studied to gain unauthorised information. It is crucial for cloud users and cloud providers to understand the aspects involved in performing such attacks to address them.

Past studies showed that side and covert channel attacks in computer and cloud systems can be successfully achieved through running programs on top of the operating system using shared hardware resources. Reflecting on that, protection and countermeasures of such attacks have mainly been addressed from previous studies into four protection aspects, OS-based, application-based, hardware-based and analysis- or profile-based detection. We will expand the discussion by exploring existing protection techniques and mechanisms against such attacks. They can be categorised as follows.

9.5.1   OS level

Previous studies proved that the OS failed to hide the granularity of underlying hardware activities in multitasking systems. Moreover, it failed in maintaining the shared libraries used by higher-level applications on top of it. Thus, researchers have offered various solutions to customise existing OSs to mitigate such attacks.

Recent intensive studies have shown various exploitations to achieve such attacks. This has led to drastic changes by CPU designers and software industries to mitigate and put barriers in front of attackers to prevent such malicious intentions. In previous works, attacks against memory deduplication in virtualised systems led software industries to make changes in the system settings by disabling such features by default in their systems, such as Amazon EC2 [22,28]. Zhou *et al.* [62] proposed CACHEBAR, which is a kernel space solution, to provide a concrete protection of shared pages between cross-VMs in PaaS.

Irazoqui *et al.* [22] proposed S$A against LLC cache in large page settings to retrieve AES secret keys. Because an attacker, in large size page addressing, can reveal enough physical addresses to produce cache addresses, the authors, based on the attack limitation, showed solutions to their attack by disabling large size pages and supporting private cache slices per each VMs, which prevents cache interferences between VMs. As such, an attacker will not be successful in deducing which cache slices have been used by the victim.

9.5.2   Application level

The weaknesses in implementation of cryptographic algorithms might lead to side channel attacks [6]. Cryptographic software, like OpenSSL, provides shared libraries to several multiple programs concurrently to save memory and updating issues. However, this leads to potential threats to the software, as we showed massive attacks on the cryptographic software. In Section 9.4.2.5, the mechanism of shared libraries is shown, and this has a negative impact on using lookup table from being leaked by attackers. Solutions have been proposed, but failed in practice. [6] showed a constant-time solution against side channel attack, but it is impractical to implement a constant-time high-speed AES algorithm.

9.5.3   Hardware level

Extensive studies in the past decade have addressed many of the hardware vulnerabilities that give rise to the attacks. The most targeted hardware resources are CPU caches. This has led CPU industries to make physical changes in microprocessors to mitigate the attacks. Based on the investigation studies has done by Percival [35] in information leakage attacks against L1 cache, he recommended CPU industries to disable sharing caches between core and threads to avoid cache line evictions.

Modern CPUs support hardware configurations to enable/disable hardware settings, such as multi-threading. Multi-threading supports cache synchronisation between threads of the same core, which has the basic characteristic of some previous side channel attacks, in which case, disabling multi-threading stops the attack [25]. The authors proposed SEALTHMEM as an alternative technique to mitigate such attacks.

As the Orange Book selected the AES algorithm as a proper solution to protect data, AES has been paid attention by researcher and CPU designers. In 2008, Intel [16] announced a new set of instructions, AES-NI. The CPU executes them on a dedicated hardware for AES operations to speed up performance and security issues [54]. However, this solution has not been adopted by some of the platforms and software libraries, such as OpenSSL. Thus, the gap is still available for such side channel attackers.

Cloud providers intend to change the infrastructure of cloud systems. After presenting a series of channel-based attacks, [36,51,55] revealed the viability of building a communication channel between them to separate VMs in Amazon EC2, by revealing mapping of internal hardware resources. Amazon enhanced service delivery to cloud consumers by providing dedicated instances. The service emphasises on concrete isolation between tenants' VMs. The physical resources assigned to the VMs of one tenant are not shared with the VMs of other tenants.

Since 2014, [22,28,56] targeted inclusive feature on Intel microprocessors to bridge between unrelated processes to exchange data. On the other hand, [21] failed to set up the attack on AMD processors due to the difference in inclusive behaviour between the processes. Sometimes it is hard to make physical change in microprocessors, because it influences CPU performance.

Most of the recent attacks targeted hardware vulnerabilities, such as L1, L2 and LLC caches, while they achieve their attacks. However, there are hardware- and software-proposed solutions to detect and prevent such attacks. Liu *et al.* [27] proposed hardware and OS level protection models on LLC. They utilised performance optimisation characteristics to protect LLC, which is shared for all cores of a CPU. Then, they used the recent Intel cache technology, Cache Allocation Technology (CAT), to protect LLC against side channel attack at OS level. Finally, they introduced a combination of hardware and software support, CATalyst, which isolates LLC slices and bounds each slice to one core. Thus, cross-cores cannot interfere with each other.

9.5.4 Analysis or profile-based detection

Detecting side/cover channel attacks against microprocessor components is undetected and due to the attacks activities are hidden to access control mechanisms of the system. This is because the attackers do not use legitimated accesses or modification on the targeted resources, instead they exploit vulnerabilities prone to hardware design and software implementation. Consequently, recent studies showed that the best practice to countermeasure side/covert channel attacks is to use computer performance analysis, because the nurture of this attack degrades performance of the system.

Zhang *et al.* [58] designed a protection model (CloudRadar) to detect cross-VMs side channel attacks in public cloud services PaaS against LLC without any hardware and software configuration settings. Their model is based on the combination of signature-based and anomaly-based detection techniques that relay on the use of hardware performance counters.

9.6 Conclusion

This chapter has reviewed previous studies on data leakage attack techniques (side and covert channels) and highlighted the essential resources and their characteristics that have been used in such attacks. Furthermore, it introduced the technical requirements to achieve such an attack. This chapter has demonstrated the importance of data and its usage by different technologies in cloud environment while it is moved through insecure communication channels and manipulated in untrusted computational environments. It has also categorised data leakage attack techniques according to the architectural layers in which the attack can be achieved and the resources have been used to perform such attacks, highlighting what type of data is targeted by this attack.

References

[1] Onur Aciiçmez. Yet another microarchitectural attack: Exploiting i-cache. In *Proceedings of the 2007 ACM Workshop on Computer Security Architecture*, CSAW '07, pages 11–18. New York, NY, USA: ACM, 2007.

[2] Onur Aciiçmez, Billy Bob Brumley, and Philipp Grabher. New results on instruction cache attacks. In *International Workshop on Cryptographic Hardware and Embedded Systems*, pages 110–124. Springer, 2010.

[3] Hassan Aly and Mohammed ElGayyar. Attacking AES using Bernstein's attack on modern processors. In *Progress in Cryptology – AFRICACRYPT 2013*, pages 127–139. Springer, 2013.

[4] Andrea Arcangeli, Izik Eidus, and Chris Wright. Increasing memory density by using ksm. In *Proceedings of the Linux Symposium*, pages 19–28. Citeseer, 2009.

[5] Utsav Banerjee, Lisa Ho, and Skanda Koppula. Power-based side-channel attack for AES key extraction on the atmega328 microcontroller, 2015.

[6] Daniel J Bernstein. Cache-timing attacks on AES, 2005.

[7] Erik Bosman, Kaveh Razavi, Herbert Bos, and Cristiano Giuffrida. Dedup est machina: Memory deduplication as an advanced exploitation vector, 2016.

[8] Samira Briongos, Pedro Malagón, José L Risco-Martín, and José M Moya. Modeling side-channel cache attacks on AES. In *Proceedings of the Summer Computer Simulation Conference*, page 37. Society for Computer Simulation International, 2016.

[9]   Shuo Chen, Rui Wang, XiaoFeng Wang, and Kehuan Zhang. Side-channel leaks in web applications: A reality today, a challenge tomorrow. In *2010 IEEE Symposium on Security and Privacy*, pages 191–206. IEEE, 2010.

[10]   Cheng-Kang Chu, Wen-Tao Zhu, Jin Han, Joseph K Liu, Xu Jia, and Zhou Jianying. Security concerns in popular cloud storage services. *IEEE Pervasive Computing*, 12(4):50–57, 2013.

[11]   Qian Ge, Yuval Yarom, David Cock, and Gernot Heiser. A survey of microarchitectural timing attacks and countermeasures on contemporary hardware. *Journal of Cryptographic Engineering*, pages 1–27, 2016.

[12]   Daniel Gruss, David Bidner, and Stefan Mangard. Practical memory deduplication attacks in sandboxed javascript. In *European Symposium on Research in Computer Security*, pages 108–122. Springer, 2015.

[13]   Daniel Gruss, Clémentine Maurice, and Klaus Wagner. Flush+ flush: A stealthier last-level cache attack. *arXiv preprint arXiv:1511.04594*, 2015.

[14]   Daniel Gruss, Clémentine Maurice, Klaus Wagner, and Stefan Mangard. Flush+ flush: A fast and stealthy cache attack. *arXiv preprint arXiv:1511.04594*, 2015.

[15]   Daniel Gruss, Raphael Spreitzer, and Stefan Mangard. Cache template attacks: Automating attacks on inclusive last-level caches. In *24th USENIX Security Symposium (USENIX Security 15)*, pages 897–912, 2015.

[16]   Shay Gueron. Advanced encryption standard (AES) instructions set. *Intel*, http://softwarecommunity. intel. com/articles/eng/3788.htm, accessed 25, Aug 2008.

[17]   David Gullasch, Endre Bangerter, and Stephan Krenn. Cache games-bringing access-based cache attacks on AES to practice. In *2011 IEEE Symposium on Security and Privacy*, pages 490–505. IEEE, 2011.

[18]   Berk Gulmezoglu, Mehmet Inci, Gorka Irazoki, Thomas Eisenbarth, and Berk Sunar. Cross-vm cache attacks on AES, 2016.

[19]   Berk Gülmezoğlu, Mehmet Sinan Inci, Gorka Irazoqui, Thomas Eisenbarth, and Berk Sunar. A faster and more realistic flush+ reload attack on AES. In *International Workshop on Constructive Side-Channel Analysis and Secure Design*, pages 111–126. Springer, 2015.

[20]   Hermine Hovhannisyan, Kejie Lu, and Jianping Wang. A novel high-speed ip-timing covert channel: Design and evaluation. In *2015 IEEE International Conference on Communications (ICC)*, pages 7198–7203. IEEE, 2015.

[21]   Ralf Hund, Carsten Willems, and Thorsten Holz. Practical timing side channel attacks against kernel space aslr. In *Security and Privacy (SP), 2013 IEEE Symposium on*, pages 191–205. IEEE, 2013.

[22]   Gorka Irazoqui, Thomas Eisenbarth, and Berk Sunar. S$a: A shared cache attack that works across cores and defies vm sandboxing and its application to AES. In *2015 IEEE Symposium on Security and Privacy*, pages 591–604. IEEE, 2015.

[23]   Gorka Irazoqui, Mehmet Sinan Inci, Thomas Eisenbarth, and Berk Sunar. Wait a minute! A fast, cross-vm attack on AES. In *International Workshop on Recent Advances in Intrusion Detection*, pages 299–319. Springer, 2014.

[24]   Mehmet Kayaalp, Nael Abu-Ghazaleh, Dmitry Ponomarev, and Aamer Jaleel. A high-resolution side-channel attack on last-level cache. In *Proceedings of the 53rd Annual Design Automation Conference*, page 72. ACM, 2016.

[25]   Taesoo Kim, Marcus Peinado, and Gloria Mainar-Ruiz. Stealthmem: System-level protection against cache-based side channel attacks in the cloud. In *Presented as Part of the 21st USENIX Security Symposium (USENIX Security 12)*, pages 189–204, 2012.

[26]   Butler W Lampson. Dynamic protection structures. In *Proceedings of the November 18–20, 1969, Fall Joint Computer Conference*, pages 27–38. ACM, 1969.

[27]   Fangfei Liu, Qian Ge, Yuval Yarom *et al.* Catalyst: Defeating last-level cache side channel attacks in cloud computing. In *2016 IEEE International Symposium on High Performance Computer Architecture (HPCA)*, pages 406–418. IEEE, 2016.

[28]   Clémentine Maurice, Christoph Neumann, Olivier Heen, and Aurélien Francillon. C5: cross-cores cache covert channel. In *International Conference on Detection of Intrusions and Malware, and Vulnerability Assessment*, pages 46–64. Springer, 2015.

[29]   Peter Mell and Tim Grance. The nist definition of cloud computing, 2011.

[30]   Michael Neve, Jean-Pierre Seifert, and Zhenghong Wang. A refined look at Bernstein's AES side-channel analysis. In *Proceedings of the 2006 ACM Symposium on Information, Computer and Communications Security*, pages 369–369. ACM, 2006.

[31]   Dag Arne Osvik, Adi Shamir, and Eran Tromer. Cache attacks and countermeasures: The case of AES. In *Topics in Cryptology – CT-RSA 2006*, pages 1–20. Springer, 2006.

[32]   Ying-Shiuan Pan, Jui-Hao Chiang, Han-Lin Li, Po-Jui Tsao, Ming-Fen Lin, and Tzi-cker Chiueh. Hypervisor support for efficient memory de-duplication. In *Parallel and Distributed Systems (ICPADS), 2011 IEEE 17th International Conference on*, pages 33–39. IEEE, 2011.

[33]   Gabriele Paoloni. How to benchmark code execution times on intel ia-32 and ia-64 instruction set architectures. Intel Corporation, September, 123, 2010.

[34]   N Penchalaiah and Ravala Seshadri. Effective comparison and evaluation of des and rijndael algorithm (AES). *International Journal of Computer Science and Engineering*, 2(05):1641–1645, 2010.

[35]   Colin Percival. Cache missing for fun and profit, 2005.

[36]   Thomas Ristenpart, Eran Tromer, Hovav Shacham, and Stefan Savage. Hey, you, get off of my cloud: Exploring information leakage in third-party compute clouds. In *Proceedings of the 16th ACM conference on Computer and communications security*, pages 199–212. ACM, 2009.

[37]   Asaf Shabtai, Yuval Elovici, and Lior Rokach. *A Survey of Data Leakage Detection and Prevention Solutions*. Springer Science & Business Media, 2012.

[38]   Gaurav Shah and Matt Blaze. Covert channels through external interference. In *Proceedings of the 3rd USENIX Conference on Offensive Technologies (WOOT'09)*, pages 1–7, 2009.

[39]   Gaurav Shah, Andres Molina, Matt Blaze *et al.* Keyboards and covert channels. In *Usenix security*, volume 6, pages 59–75, 2006.

[40]   Dawn Xiaodong Song, David Wagner, and Xuqing Tian. Timing analysis of keystrokes and timing attacks on ssh. In *Proceedings of the 10th Conference on USENIX Security Symposium*, volume 10, SSYM'01, Berkeley, CA, USA:USENIX Association, 2001.

[41]   Salvatore J Stolfo, Malek Ben Salem, and Angelos D Keromytis. Fog computing: Mitigating insider data theft attacks in the cloud. In *Security and Privacy Workshops (SPW), 2012 IEEE Symposium on*, pages 125–128. IEEE, 2012.

[42]   Kuniyasu Suzaki, Kengo Iijima, Toshiki Yagi, and Cyrille Artho. Memory deduplication as a threat to the guest os. In *Proceedings of the Fourth European Workshop on System Security*, page 1. ACM, 2011.

[43]   Eran Tromer, Dag Arne Osvik, and Adi Shamir. Efficient cache attacks on AES, and countermeasures. *Journal of Cryptology*, 23(1):37–71, 2010.

[44]   Yukiyasu Tsunoo, Teruo Saito, Tomoyasu Suzaki, Maki Shigeri, and Hiroshi Miyauchi. Cryptanalysis of des implemented on computers with cache. In *International Workshop on Cryptographic Hardware and Embedded Systems*, pages 62–76. Springer, 2003.

[45]   Marcel van den Berg. Paper: Vmware esx memory resource management: Transparent page sharing, 2013.

[46]   INC VMWARE. Understanding memory resource management in vmware esx server. Palo Alto, California, USA, 2009.

[47]   Carl A Waldspurger. Memory resource management in vmware esx server. *ACM SIGOPS Operating Systems Review*, 36(SI):181–194, 2002.

[48]   Cong Wang, Qian Wang, Kui Ren, Ning Cao, and Wenjing Lou. Toward secure and dependable storage services in cloud computing. *Services Computing, IEEE Transactions on*, 5(2):220–232, 2012.

[49]   Zhenghong Wang and Ruby B Lee. Covert and side channels due to processor architecture. In *ACSAC*, volume 6, pages 473–482, 2006.

[50]   Jun Wu, Yong-Bin Kim, and Minsu Choi. Low-power side-channel attack-resistant asynchronous s-box design for AES cryptosystems. In *Proceedings of the 20th Symposium on Great Lakes Symposium on VLSI*, pages 459–464. ACM, 2010.

[51]   Zhenyu Wu, Zhang Xu, and Haining Wang. Whispers in the hyper-space: High-speed covert channel attacks in the cloud. In *Presented as Part of the 21st USENIX Security Symposium (USENIX Security 12)*, pages 159–173, 2012.

[52]   Zhenyu Wu, Zhang Xu, and Haining Wang. Whispers in the hyper-space: high-bandwidth and reliable covert channel attacks inside the cloud. *IEEE/ACM Transactions on Networking (TON)*, 23(2):603–614, 2015.

[53] Jidong Xiao, Zhang Xu, Hai Huang, and Haining Wang. A covert channel construction in a virtualized environment. In *Proceedings of the 2012 ACM Conference on Computer and Communications Security*, pages 1040–1042. ACM, 2012.

[54] Leslie Xu. Securing the enterprise with intel AES-NI. Intel Corporation, 2010.

[55] Yunjing Xu, Michael Bailey, Farnam Jahanian, Kaustubh Joshi, Matti Hiltunen, and Richard Schlichting. An exploration of l2 cache covert channels in virtualized environments. In *Proceedings of the Third ACM Workshop on Cloud Computing Security Workshop*, pages 29–40. ACM, 2011.

[56] Yuval Yarom and Katrina Falkner. Flush+ reload: A high resolution, low noise, l3 cache side-channel attack. In *23rd USENIX Security Symposium (USENIX Security 14)*, pages 719–732, 2014.

[57] Younis A Younis, Kashif Kifayat, Qi Shi, and Bob Askwith. A new prime and probe cache side-channel attack for cloud computing. In *Computer and Information Technology; Ubiquitous Computing and Communications; Dependable, Autonomic and Secure Computing; Pervasive Intelligence and Computing (CIT/IUCC/DASC/PICOM), 2015 IEEE International Conference on*, pages 1718–1724. IEEE, 2015.

[58] Tianwei Zhang, Yinqian Zhang, and Ruby B Lee. Cloudradar: A real-time side-channel attack detection system in clouds. In *International Symposium on Research in Attacks, Intrusions, and Defenses*, pages 118–140. Springer, 2016.

[59] Yinqian Zhang, Ari Juels, Alina Oprea, and Michael K Reiter. Homealone: Co-residency detection in the cloud via side-channel analysis. In *2011 IEEE Symposium on Security and Privacy*, pages 313–328. IEEE, 2011.

[60] Yinqian Zhang, Ari Juels, Michael K Reiter, and Thomas Ristenpart. Cross-vm side channels and their use to extract private keys. In *Proceedings of the 2012 ACM Conference on Computer and Communications Security*, pages 305–316. ACM, 2012.

[61] Yinqian Zhang, Ari Juels, Michael K Reiter, and Thomas Ristenpart. Cross-tenant side-channel attacks in paas clouds. In *Proceedings of the 2014 ACM SIGSAC Conference on Computer and Communications Security*, pages 990–1003. ACM, 2014.

[62] Ziqiao Zhou, Michael K Reiter, and Yinqian Zhang. A software approach to defeating side channels in last-level caches. *arXiv preprint arXiv:1603.05615*, 2016.

Chapter 10

Cloud computing and personal data processing: sorting-out legal requirements

Ioulia Konstantinou[1] and Irene Kamara[1]

Abstract

Cloud computing facilitates and accelerates the collection and processing of (personal) data and the development of new services and applications. When data collection involves personal data, specific risks and challenges for privacy and data protection of the individuals arise. The interference with privacy and data protection necessitates the implementation of appropriate safeguards. Therefore, new impacts and risks need to be analysed and assessed. In the cloud computing context, privacy and data protection should not be inferior to the level of protection required in any other data processing context. Looking at the European legal framework, the EU has thorough legislation for the protection of personal data. The new General Data Protection Regulation introduces detailed provisions establishing obligations and new instruments, such as certification. In addition, the EU data protection legislation has what is often called an *extra-territorial effect*, which entails that under conditions is applicable to natural or legal persons not established in the EU jurisdiction. The extra-territorial effect of the EU data protection legislation makes the EU legislation relevant for service providers who are not established in the EU but are processing personal data of EU citizens. This chapter aims to provide an overview of the legal requirements applicable to cloud-based applications and data processing, drawing examples primarily from the EU legal framework. This overview can serve as an

[1]Vrije Universiteit Brussel, Research Group on Law, Science, Technology and Society (LSTS), Belgium.

This research is partially based on research conducted for the Research Project SeCloud and the report Konstantinou I., *et al.* 'Overview of applicable legal framework and general legal requirements: Deliverable 3.1 for the SeCloud project' SeCloud project, 2016.

'Security-driven engineering of Cloud-based Applications' ('SeCloud') project is a 3-year project running from 2015 to 2018, funded by Innoviris, the Brussels Institute for Research and Innovation. It aims at addressing security risks of cloud-based applications in a holistic and proactive approach, built upon different aspects of the security problems: not only technical, but also organisational and societal ones. See more information on http://www.securit-brussels.be/project/secloud/

The project is comprised of four perspectives: architecture, infrastructure, programming and process. The 'process' perspective of SeCloud aims at assisting overcoming legal barriers when developing cloud-based applications.

index of key obligations and responsibilities for cloud service providers and cloud clients, but also for further research purposes (i.e. comparative analysis with other legal frameworks).

Keywords

cloud computing, personal data, General Data Protection Regulation, responsibilities, legal requirements, data transfers

10.1 Introduction: the emergence of cloud and the significance of a secure cloud

Cloud computing enables ubiquitous, convenient, on-demand network access to a shared pool of configurable computing resources [1]. In 2016, the European Commission stated that:

> The Cloud makes it possible to move, share and re-use data seamlessly across global markets and borders, and among institutions and research disciplines [2].

ENISA, the European Union Agency for Network and Information Security, highlighted scalability, elasticity, high performance, resilience and security together with cost-efficiency as benefits of cloud computing for public authorities [3]. The possibilities of opening-up with cloud computing enable numerous applications such as in mobile health, Internet of Things and online commerce, but at the same time pose significant risks to the protection of personal data of the individuals, the data of which are stored in the cloud. Data security risks include loss of governance, isolation failure, insecure or incomplete data deletion [4]. In addition, the exercise of the individuals' rights to access, modify or erase personal data concerning them is more challenging to be exercised in the cloud context. In the cloud model [1], users' data are transferred to cloud-based applications and are stored either by these applications or by third parties (cloud services), along with data of other users. Cloud applications and the entities related to the applications, often collecting and processing personal data, have responsibilities and legal obligations to protect and process such data in compliance with the law.

The EU has thorough legislation for the protection of personal data. The new General Data Protection Regulation (GDPR) [5], which was recently finalised, introduces detailed provisions for the protection of personal data. In addition, EU data protection legislation has what is often called an *extra-territorial effect*: under conditions, which are explained in the next section; it is also applicable outside of the EU 'territory' (jurisdiction). Therefore, the EU legislation is *relevant* not only to organisations established in the EU, but also to organisations established outside the EU.

The chapter is structured as follows: first, there is a discussion on the 'extra-territorial effect' of the EU data protection law. This section intends to demonstrate the relevance of the EU data protection law to non-EU cloud actors.[2] In addition, the EU data protection law, being stringent and detailed, serves as a good example for analysing the legal obligations of 'cloud players'. Next, the EU data protection legal framework is briefly presented. The fourth section introduces the legal concepts of data controller and data processor. As the legislation uses different terms than cloud provider, cloud client, etc., this section is significant because it helps identify which cloud actor has which legal obligations. The obligations and roles of controller and processor might vary in different contexts, when for instance a cloud service provider (CSP) has access to the data stored in the cloud, whereas in other cases, the CSP does not have access rights to the data. The fifth section is divided into two parts: the first part focuses on the compliance of cloud players with general personal data principles. The second part delves into the specific technical and organisational measures. The sixth section of the chapter analyses the regulation of data flows. It provides a detailed overview of the international data transfers issue: when the EU data protection law allows data transfers outside of its jurisdiction and under which conditions. Finally, Section 10.7 summarises and concludes the chapter.

10.2   Cloud computing and the extra-territorial effect of EU data protection law

Cloud computing entails data transfers from one data centre to another. From a legal point of view, the location of the data centre, but also the cloud client and the CSP, are in principle crucial to determine the applicable law. In general, data flows raise several questions as to the governing law, applicable to the data processing operations. Within the EU, there is a new personal data protection legal framework, the GDPR, which will be directly[3] applicable to all EU Member States from 2018 onwards.

Even beyond the CSPs established in the EU Member States, the GDPR is relevant to cloud clients and CSP that might not be established in the EU. As De Hert and Czerniawski explain, the GDPR introduces new factors, beyond 'territory', to assess whether an EU Member State has jurisdiction over a data protection case [6]. Article 3 of the GDPR introduces new criteria for deciding GDPR applicability: 'offering goods or services to' or 'monitoring the behaviour of' data subjects in the EU by a controller or processor not established in the EU [7]. The wording *in the Union*

---

[2]Cloud actors in the context of this article are the cloud service provider and the cloud client.

[3]It is important to explain the difference between an EU Directive and an EU Regulation. An EU Directive is a legislative act that sets out a goal that all EU Member States must achieve. However, it is up to the individual Member State to devise their own laws on how to reach these goals. Therefore, it requires implementation by the Member States, as it is only a framework law. An EU Regulation, on the other hand, is a binding legislative act, directly applicable in its entirety across the EU. No national implementation is required. As it is immediately applicable and enforceable by law in all Member States, it offers higher levels of law harmonisation across the EU. http://europa.eu/eu-law/decision-making/legal-acts/index_en.htm and http://ec.europa.eu/legislation/index_en.htm.

implies physical presence of the individual whose personal data are processed (data subject) in the EU, but not necessarily residence.

Article 3 GDPR provides:

1. *This Regulation applies to the processing of personal data in the context of the activities of an establishment of a controller or a processor in the Union, regardless of whether the processing takes place in the Union or not.*
2. *This Regulation applies to the processing of personal data of data subjects who are in the Union by a controller or processor not established in the Union, where the processing activities are related to:*
   (a) the offering of goods or services, irrespective of whether a payment of the data subject is required, to such data subjects in the Union; or (b) the monitoring of their behaviour as far as their behaviour takes place within the Union.
3. *This Regulation applies to the processing of personal data by a controller not established in the Union, but in a place where Member State law applies by virtue of public international law.*

Basically, the GDPR applies to (1) EU companies that process personal data, regardless of whether the processing takes place in the EU or not and (2) non-EU companies which process personal data of data subjects who are in the EU, and these processing activities are related to (i) the *offering of goods or services* to EU data subjects or (ii) *monitoring individuals' behaviours* that occur within the EU.

To provide an example: when a US-established cloud provider offers targeted services to individuals in the EU, *irrespectively of whether the individuals' are citizens of an EU Member State or US citizens residing in France,* the legal relationship of the US cloud provider with the US citizen is governed by the EU GDPR regarding the data processing activities concerning those individuals'. This is because the EU legislation does not depend on its protection on whether the individual is an EU citizen, but the protection is offered to any individual, given that the other conditions of Article 3 GDPR are met.

This extra-territorial effect of the EU data protection legislation (GDPR) has been discussed and criticised [8], among others as facilitating legal uncertainty for a CSP. A CSP might be subject to different legislations and thus be caught in a network of different and sometimes conflicting legal rules [6]. Despite the discussion revolving around the effect and the criticism, cloud computing actors as analysed below need to be aware of the broadened applicability of the EU data protection framework. If their processing activities fall in the scope of the GDPR, they shall comply with their legal obligations.

10.3   The EU legal framework on data protection

In this section, we provide a brief overview of the EU data protection legal framework, with some comments on the applicability of the Directive 95/46/EC and the new GDPR.

10.3.1 The Data Protection Directive 95/46/EC

From 1995 until 2018, the protection of personal data in the EU is regulated with the Data Protection Directive 95/46/EC. Personal data processing operations resulting from the use of cloud computing services and falling within the territorial scope criteria of EU data protection law need to respect the EU data protection provisions of Directive 95/46/EC as transposed in the national law of the EU Member States [9]. Processing operations fall within the scope of EU Data Protection Directive when personal data is processed in an automated way, and the data processing takes place in the context of the activities of an establishment of a controller located in the EU or by a controller located outside the EU that makes use of equipment located in the EU [10]. When processing in a cloud computing environment involves the processing of personal data about the provision of publicly available electronic communications services in public communications networks (telecom operators), the processing also needs to comply with the specific legal instrument of the EU data protection law, the e-Privacy Directive 2002/58/EC [11].[4]

10.3.2 The new General Data Protection Regulation

Following the technological emergence and the proliferation of online services, the EU regulator initiated in 2012 a reform process of the Data Protection Directive. The first draft for a GDPR aimed at providing a single set of rules within the EU for the processing of personal data by private companies and the public sector.[5]

After 3 years of negotiations, the European Parliament and the Council of the European Union reached an informal agreement on the final draft of the EU GDPR in 2015. On 14 April 2016, the EU GDPR 679/2016 was adopted at EU level. The GDPR is now officially EU law and will directly apply in all EU Member States, replacing EU and national data protection legislation. Although the GDPR was adopted on 24 May 2016, it will enter into force from 25 May 2018, giving the organisations subject to its scope a 2-year period to adapt their processing activities to the new legal framework.[6] The new rules on the one hand build upon the general principles set forth in Directive 95/46/EC and on the other hand aim at updating them in accordance with the needs of the digital environment, simplifying administrative burdens and reinforcing the rights of individuals, the accountability of controllers and processors of personal data and the powers of supervisory national authorities [10]. The GDPR introduces some new

[4]Directive 2002/58/EC applies to providers of electronic communication services made available to the public and requires them to ensure compliance with obligations relating to the secrecy of communications and personal data protection, as well as rights and obligations regarding electronic communications networks and services. In cases where cloud computing providers act as providers of a publicly available electronic communication service, they will be subject to this regulation. The Directive is currently under legislative reform.

[5]Directive 95/46/EC needed to be implemented at a national level, requiring transposition into national law by the national legislature of each member state. The General Data Protection Regulation is directly applicable in all Member States. It applies automatically in each Member State and does not require any national implementation by the Member States.

[6]Article 99 GDPR.

obligations for data controllers, such as 'privacy by design' and 'privacy by default', accountability, data protection impact assessments (DPIAs), personal data breach notifications, as well as the right to be forgotten and the right to data portability. The technologically neutral approach of EU data protection rules in Directive 95/46/EC is maintained. The GDPR embraces the technological developments but does not focus on any specific technologies. Therefore, it also applies to cloud computing services [12].

10.4   Data controller, data processor and cloud computing actors: assigning roles and responsibilities

The EU data protection legislation uses two key terms to signify the persons responsible to comply with the legal obligations: *data controller* and *data processor*. Article 4(7) GDPR defines a *controller* as 'the natural or legal person, public authority, agency or any other body that alone or jointly with others determines the purposes and means of the processing of personal data'. Article 4(8) GDPR defines a data processor as the 'natural or legal person, public authority, agency or any other body that alone or jointly with others, processes personal data on behalf of the controller'.

   One of the most important and challenging aspects of the data protection legal framework in the cloud computing context is the applicability of the notions of 'controller' and 'processor'. The allocation of these roles is the crucial factor that decides the responsibility for compliance with data protection rules. Cloud computing involves a range of various and different actors. To establish the specific obligations, duties and responsibilities of each actor according to the data protection legal framework, it is, first, necessary to define, refine and assess the role of each of these actors involved. Article 29 Working Party (WP29), an advisory body comprised of EU national data Protection authorities,[7] in its Opinion 1/2010 on the concepts of 'controller' and 'processor' has stressed out that:

   the first and foremost role of the concept of controller is to determine who shall be responsible for compliance with data protection rules, and how data subjects[8] can exercise the rights in practice. In other words: to allocate responsibility [13].

Therefore, two general key criteria can be extracted from the WP29 opinion on how to determine who the controller is and who the processor in each case: allocation of responsibility and responsibility for compliance.

---

[7]Under the GDPR, Article 29 Working Party will be replaced by the European Data Protection Board (EDPB).
[8]The data subject is the person whose personal data are collected, held or processed. (https://secure.edps.europa.eu/EDPSWEB/edps/site/mySite/pid/74#data_subject.)

10.4.1 Cloud client and cloud service provider

Personal data processing is defined in Article 4(2) GDPR as 'any operation or set of operations which is performed on personal data or on sets of personal data, whether or not by automated means'. Such operations include collection, recording, organisation, structuring, storage, adaptation or alteration, retrieval, consultation, use, disclosure by transmission, dissemination or otherwise making available, alignment or combination, restriction, erasure or destruction of personal data.

The cloud client usually determines the ultimate purpose of the processing and decides on the outsourcing of this processing and the delegation of all or part of the processing activities to an external organisation. The cloud client therefore acts in principle as a data controller [10,14,15]. The cloud client, acting as data controller, is responsible for complying with data protection legislation. The cloud client may assign the CSP the selection of the methods and the technical or organisational measures to be used to achieve the purposes of the controller [16]. The CSP is the entity that provides the various forms of cloud computing services. When the cloud provider supplies the means and the platform, acting on behalf of the cloud client (data controller), the CSP is usually considered a data processor. The suggested way to ensure compliance by the data processor is to strictly apply the requirements of Article 32 GDPR on the security of processing and Article 28 GDPR on the responsibilities of processors [10,13,16].

However, the precise role of the CSP should be examined *on a case-by-case basis*. It may occur that in some cases, the CSP processes personal data, when for instance the CSP has access to the stored data. In such cases, it is important to determine whether the cloud provider is merely acting as a 'data processor' *on behalf of* the data controller, whether it is a data controller (for instance, processes the data for its own purposes) or a *joint controller* together with the cloud client [15].[9]

The European Data Protection Supervisor (EDPS) further adds that:

> the cloud client/data controller may not be the only entity that can solely determine the 'purposes and means of the processing'. More and more often, the determination of the essential elements of the means, which is a prerogative of the data controller, is not in the hands of the cloud client. In this respect, the cloud provider, who happens to have the technical background, typically designs, operates and maintains the cloud computing IT infrastructure (be it simply the basic hardware and software services as in IaaS,

[9]Per ICO (Information Commissioner's Office, the UK Data Protection Authority) identifying the data controller in a private cloud should be quite straightforward because the cloud customer will exercise control over the purpose for which the personal data will be processed within the cloud service. If a cloud provider simply maintains any underlying infrastructure, then it is likely to be a data processor. In a community cloud, more than one data controller is likely to access the cloud service. They could act independently of each other or could work together. If one of the data controllers also acts as a cloud provider, it will also assume the role of a data processor in respect of the other data controllers that use the infrastructure. When using a public cloud, a cloud client may find it difficult to exercise control over the operation of a large cloud provider. However, when an organisation contracts for cloud computing services based on the cloud provider's standard terms and conditions, this organisation is still responsible for determining the purposes and the means of the personal data processing. (pp. 7–9).

or the platform as in PaaS, or the overall service, including the application
software, as in SaaS) [10].

Furthermore, it is often the CSP the one who develops standard contracts or Service Level Agreements (SLAs) to be offered to the cloud client based on its technical infrastructure and business type. The cloud client has, therefore, no or very little leeway to modify the technical or contractual means of the service [10].

Data processors need to consider the deployment model/service model of the cloud in question (public, private, community or hybrid/IaaS, SaaS or PaaS) and the type of service contracted by the client. Processors are responsible for adopting security measures in line with those in EU legislation as applied in the controller's and the processor's jurisdictions. Processors must also support and assist the controller in complying with (exercised) data subjects' rights [16]. The GDPR, in that respect, introduces a broader perspective compared to the Directive 95/46/EC provisions with regard to the role of the processors in personal data processing, who, under the Directive 95/46/EC, are only indirectly liable. Under the new regime, certain EU data protection law requirements, for instance on accountability, data security and data breach notifications, will apply for the first time directly to data processors. Apart from these requirements, Article 82 GDPR specifically holds processors directly liable (par.1) and establishes the conditions under which individuals may claim damages from them (par.2): in cases where a processor has not complied with GDPR obligations addressed specifically to processors or in cases it has acted contrary to or outside of the lawful instructions of the data controller [17]. Article 28(3) GDPR provides for detailed rules on the terms of the contract which appoints processors.

10.4.2   Sub-contractors

Cloud computing services may involve many contracted parties who act as data processors. Data processors may also sub-contract services to additional sub-processors. In that case, the data processor has an obligation to provide the cloud client with any relevant information regarding the service sub-contracted, e.g. its type, the characteristics of current or potential sub-contractors and guarantees that these entities act/will act in compliance with the GDPR. To ensure the allocation of clear responsibilities for data processing activities, all the relevant obligations must also apply to the sub-processors through contracts between the cloud provider and sub-contractor, describing the provisions, terms and requirements of the contract between the cloud client and the cloud provider [14]. These conditions are also mentioned in Article 28(4) GDPR, which stresses that in case of sub-contracting for specific processing activities, the same data protection obligations as set out in the contract or another legal act between the controller and the processor shall be imposed on the sub-processor. These obligations should provide sufficient guarantees, specifically around data security. In case of sub-processor's non-compliance with the imposed obligations, the initial processor remains fully liable to the controller for the performance of these obligations.

The data processor may sub-contract its activities on the basis of the agreement of the data controller (or else 'consent' if a natural person). This consent must be given at the beginning of the service and must be accompanied with an obligation on behalf of the data processor to inform the data controller on any intended changes concerning the addition or replacement of sub-contractors. The controller reserves the right to object to such changes or terminate the contract at any time [14]. This opinion is enshrined in Article 28(2) GDPR, which basically introduces sub-contracting only upon controller's consent [17].

Article 29 Working Party proposes that there should be guarantees for *direct liability* of the processor towards the controller for any breaches caused by the sub-processor(s). Another proposal is the creation of a third-party beneficiary right in favour of the controller in the contracts signed between the processor and sub-processor(s) or the signature of these contracts on behalf of the data controller, rendering him a party to the contract [14]. Even though, the Article 29 Working Party opinions are not mandatory, cloud actors should consider the 'soft law'[10] interpretation of the legislation by the EU regulators, in this case the data protection authorities.

The following table summarises the terminology and basic roles described above:

Table 10.1   Basic roles of cloud actors from an EU data protection perspective

Cloud actor	Activity	Role from data protection perspective	Definition	
Cloud client	Determines the purpose of the processing and decides on the delegation of all or part of the processing activities to an external organisation	***Data controller or joint controller***	A data controller, 'alone or jointly with others, determines the purposes and means of the processing of personal data'. Art. 4(7) GDPR	
Cloud service provider	Provides the various types of cloud computing services	*When the cloud provider supplies the means and the platform, acting on behalf of the cloud client (data controller), the cloud provider is a **data processor**. Also possible joint controller*	A data processor, 'processes personal data on behalf of the controller'. Art. 4(8) GDPR	AQ1
Sub-contractors	If the cloud client (data controller) consents, the cloud providers (data processors) may also sub-contract services to additional sub-processors (sub-contractors)	*From a data protection perspective, the sub-contractors are **data processors***	–	

---

[10]'Soft law' could be defined as rules that are neither legally binding nor completely lacking legal significance. These rules, which are not directly enforceable, include guidelines, policy declarations, codes of conduct, etc. 'Soft law' is often contrasted with 'hard law', which refers to traditional, directly enforceable, law.

10.5   Duties and responsibilities of the cloud computing actors

This section discusses the key legal requirements for the cloud client and the CSP that emanate from the GDPR. The requirements are divided into two categories: (1) compliance with the general data processing principles and (2) implementation of technical and organisational measures.

10.5.1   Compliance with the general personal data processing principles

Personal data processing in the context of cloud computing is deemed lawful if it is performed in compliance with the basic principles of EU data protection law along with the other applicable obligations. These basic principles include: lawfulness, transparency towards the data subject, purpose specification and limitation, accuracy, storage limitation, integrity and confidentiality and accountability.

10.5.1.1   Transparency

The principle of transparency is crucial for fair and legitimate processing of personal data in cloud computing. In accordance with Articles 5(1)(a) and 12 GDPR, the cloud client, when acting as data controller, is obliged to provide the data subject, whose personal data or data related to the data subject are collected, with the controller's identity and the purpose of the processing. Further relevant information shall also be provided, such as the recipients or categories of recipients of the data, which can also include processors and sub-processors, to the extent that such further information is necessary to guarantee fair processing towards the data subject [18]. Transparency in the above sense is also enshrined in Recitals 39 and 58 GDPR.

Transparency must also be guaranteed in the relationship between cloud client, CSP and sub-contractors. The cloud client can assess the lawfulness of the processing of personal data in the cloud only if the CSP keeps the cloud client up-to-date about incidents that might occur, access requests and other issues.

Another aspect of transparency in the cloud computing context is the necessary information the cloud client, when acting as data controller, must obtain, regarding all the sub-contractors involved in the respective cloud service and the locations of all data centres in which personal data may be processed. This is crucial, because only under this condition, an assessment can be made on whether personal data may be transferred to a third country outside of the European Economic Area which does not ensure an adequate level of protection within the meaning of the GDPR [14].

10.5.1.2   Purpose specification and limitation

The principle of purpose specification and limitation, as defined in Article 5(1)(b) GDPR, requires that personal data must be collected for specified, explicit and legitimate purposes and not be further processed in a way incompatible with those purposes. The cloud client, when acting as data controller, therefore, is competent to determine the purpose(s) of the processing prior to the collection of personal data from the data subject and inform the data subject accordingly. The cloud client is not allowed to process personal data for other purposes, incompatible or conflicting with the original purposes. Furthermore, the CSP, when acting as a data processor, is not allowed use personal data for its own purposes [15,18,19]. If he does, then the CSP is a data controller, and subsequently, all the relevant obligations for data controller apply to this CSP.

Moreover, further processing, inconsistent with the original purpose(s), is also prohibited for the cloud provider or one of its sub-contractors. In a typical cloud computing scenario, a larger number of sub-contractors may be involved; therefore, the risk of further personal data processing for incompatible purposes may be quite high. In order to mitigate the risk of further processing, the contract between CSP and cloud client should entail technical and organisational measures and provide guarantees for the logging and auditing of relevant processing operations on personal data that are performed by the cloud provider or the sub-contractors, either automatically or manually (e.g. by employees).

10.5.1.3   Storage limitation

Article 5(1)(e) GDPR requires personal data to be kept in a form which permits the identification of data subjects for no longer than necessary for the purposes for which the data were collected. Personal data that are not necessary any more must be erased or anonymised. If the data cannot be erased due to legal retention rules (e.g. tax regulations), access to this personal data should be prohibited and blocked. The responsibility to ensure that personal data are erased as soon as they are not necessary lies with the cloud client, when acting as data controller. Erasure of data is a crucial issue not only throughout the duration of a cloud computing contract but also upon its termination. It is also relevant in case of substitution or withdrawal of a sub-contractor [20]. In addition to cloud client's responsibility, per Article 28(3)(g) GDPR, cloud providers must also delete or return all the personal data processed within the cloud to the controller at the end of the data processing services [17].

The principle of storage limitation is applicable to personal data irrespective of whether they are stored on hard drives or other storage media. As personal data may be kept at the same time on different servers at different locations, each dataset must be deleted irreversibly (i.e. previous versions, temporary files and even file fragments) [14,19].

Secure erasure of personal data practically means that either the storage media is destroyed or demagnetised or the personal data stored is deleted through overwriting, which requires special software tools [14]. The cloud client should make sure that the cloud provider ensures secure erasure in the above sense and that the contract between the provider and the client provides for the erasure of personal data. The same applies for contracts between CSPs and sub-contractors [20].

10.5.1.4   Responsibility and accountability in the cloud

The principle of accountability is explicitly introduced in the GDPR. According to Articles 5(2), 24 and 28 GDPR, data controllers and processors must be able to ensure *and demonstrate* compliance with the GDPR requirements. Responsibility and accountability are also expressed by the introduction of specific obligations such as data protection by design and by default, data security breach notifications and Data Protection Impact Assessments. Apart from the general improvement of the data subject's protection in relation to the Data Protection Directive, these enhanced responsibilities of the data controller are also considered a major improvement for the protection of personal data in the cloud computing environment [21].

However, the EDPS[11] observes that some of the new obligations may be difficult to comply with if the data controller is considered to be the cloud client. As mentioned earlier, in many cases, the cloud client may be considered the data controller, due the capacity of the cloud client to determine the means and the purposes of processing. However, in practice, it is not always easy to match the concepts of the controller one-to-one with the concept of the cloud client. The EDPS identifies mainly the following of the data controller obligations, as being difficult to be carried out by the cloud client: that is the implementation of policies to ensure that personal data processing is compliant with the GDPR, data security requirements, DPIA, data protection by design, data breach notifications. This is mainly because in practice such measures are usually implemented by the CSP. The cloud client, especially in business-to-consumer relationships, has little or no control over issues such as the security policies of the CSP. It is therefore paradoxical to assign responsibility to the cloud client for such issues [10].

The processor, on the basis of Article 28 GDPR, is required to co-operate with the controller in order to fulfil the latter's obligation to respond to data subjects' rights and assist the data controller in ensuring compliance with the security requirements, data breach notifications, DPIA and prior consultation. However, the ultimate responsibility lies on the controller [10].

10.5.2   *Technical and organisational measures of data protection and data security*

The cloud clients, when acting as data controllers, are obliged[12] to choose cloud providers (processors) that guarantee the implementation of adequate technical and organisational security measures governing the personal data processing and can demonstrate accountability and compliance with these measures. These technical and organisational measures should target to protect confidentiality, integrity and availability of data, by preventing inter alia unauthorised access, modification, erasure or removal [19]. In addition, attention should be drawn to the complementary data protection goals of transparency, isolation, intervenability, accountability and portability [14]. Article 32 GDPR highlights the implementation of technical and organisational measures on behalf of the controller and the processor to achieve a high level of security in personal data processing. Article 32 GDPR attributes several criteria the

---

[11]The European Data Protection Supervisor (EDPS) is an independent supervisory authority established in accordance with Regulation 45/2001, on the basis of article 286 of the EC Treaty. The EDPS' mission is to ensure that the fundamental rights and freedoms of individuals – in particular their privacy – are respected when the EU institutions and bodies process personal data.
[12]Article 28(1) GDPR.

controller and the processor need to consider when selecting technical and organisational measures. Such criteria include the state of the art, the scope, context and purposes of processing, but also the costs of implementation.

Under the GDPR, both the controller and the processor are obliged to assess the risks identified through the processing and the nature of the data processed and designate their measures accordingly. Regarding technical and organisational measures in cloud computing, the EDPS highlights that all parties involved, controllers and processors, should perform risk assessments for the processing under their control, due to the complexity of cloud computing. Comprehensive risk assessment and security management in a cloud environment requires co-operation and co-ordination between the different parties involved, as the overall level of security is determined by the weakest link. In a cloud environment used by multiple clients, security failures of one client could affect the security of other clients, unless the service has provided robust and secure measures to separate services and data between clients and make mutual interference impossible [12]. Informing cloud users on the risk assessment and security measures of the cloud provider and better understand their effectiveness and limitations would enable cloud users, accordingly, to also take necessary measures, as the EDPS further observes [10].

Compliance with security obligations may be achieved for data controllers when they have extensive and accurate information allowing them to make the assessment that the CSP fully complies with its security obligations as processor or controller. The introduction of data breach notification in the GDPR (Articles 33 and 34) imposes the obligation on data controllers to inform data protection authorities and, when the breach is likely to result in high risk to the rights and freedoms of individuals, data subjects about personal data breaches. CSPs, therefore, would have to report any personal data breaches that occur in their services, either directly (to the supervisory authorities and the individuals), in case they act as controllers, or indirectly (to the cloud client who is the data controller) if they act only as processors [12].

10.5.2.1 Availability

Providing availability means ensuring timely and reliable access to personal data. Availability risks include infrastructure problems, such as, among others, accidental or malicious loss of network connectivity and accidental hardware failures (either on the network or the storage/processing systems) [14]. It is the responsibility of the data controllers, check whether the data processor has adopted reasonable measures to cope with the risk of interferences, such as backup internet network links, redundant storage and effective data backup mechanisms [14].

10.5.2.2 Integrity

Data integrity relates to the maintenance and the guarantee of the authenticity, accuracy and consistency of data over their entire life cycle. Data integrity can be compromised during processing, storage or transmission of the data. In these cases, the integrity of the data may be maintained, when the data are not maliciously or accidentally altered. The notion of integrity can be extended to IT systems, requires that the processing of personal data on these systems remains unmodified [14]. Personal data modifications can be detected by cryptographic authentication mechanisms such as message authentication codes, signatures or cryptographic hash functions (which do not require secret keys, unlike message authentication codes and signatures). Interference with the integrity of IT systems in the cloud can be prevented or detected by means of intrusion detection/prevention systems (IPS/IDS) [14].

10.5.2.3   Confidentiality

The cloud client, when acting as a data controller, must guarantee that the personal data under its responsibility can only be accessed by authorised persons. In a cloud environment, encryption may significantly contribute to the confidentiality of personal data, if applied correctly [15]. Encrypting personal data does not mean that the individual is no more identifiable. As the technical data fragmentation processes that may be used in the framework of the provision of cloud computing services, such as encryption, do not render data irreversibly anonymous, data protection obligations still apply [20]. Encryption of personal data may be used in all cases when 'in transit' and when available to data 'at rest' [15]. This should be particularly the case for data controllers who intend to transfer sensitive data to the cloud or who are subject to specific legal obligations of professional secrecy. In some cases, (e.g. an IaaS storage service) a cloud client may not rely on an encryption solution offered by the CSP but may choose to encrypt personal data prior to sending them to the cloud. Encrypting data at rest requires attention to cryptographic key management as data security then ultimately depends on the confidentiality of the encryption keys [19].

Communications between CSP and cloud client as well as between data centres should also be encrypted. Remote administration of the cloud platform should only take place via a secure communication channel. If a cloud client plans to not only store but also to further process personal data in the cloud, he must bear in mind that encryption cannot be maintained during processing of the data [19]. When encryption is chosen as a technical measure to secure data, security of the *encryption key* is crucial, through a robust key management arrangement. It is also important to note that the loss of an encryption key could render the data useless. This could amount to the accidental destruction of personal data and therefore a breach of the security and confidentiality principle [15]. Further technical measures aiming at ensuring confidentiality include authorisation mechanisms and strong authentication (e.g. two-factor authentication). Contractual clauses may also impose confidentiality obligations on employees of cloud clients, CSPs and sub-contractors [14].

10.5.2.4   Isolation

Isolation is linked to the purpose limitation principle. Even though not a legal term, it can be generally said that in technical terms, isolation of the data serves the data protection principle of purpose limitation. In cloud infrastructures, resources such as storage, memory and networks are shared among many users. This creates new risks for data and renders the possibility of disclosure and further processing for illegitimate purposes quite high. Isolation as a protective goal, therefore, is meant to address this issue and ensure that data are not used beyond their initial original purpose and maintain confidentiality and integrity [14].

Isolation may be achieved first by adequate governance and regular review of the rights and roles for accessing personal data. The implementation of roles with excessive privileges should be avoided (e.g. no user or administrator should be authorised to access the entire cloud). More generally, administrators and users must only be able to access the information that is necessary for their legitimate purposes (least privilege principle) [14].

10.5.2.5 Intervenability

The data subjects have the rights of access, rectification, erasure, restriction and objection to the data processing [22]. The cloud client must verify that the cloud provider does not impose technical and organisational obstacles to the exercise of those rights, even in cases when data are further processed by sub-contractors. The contract between the client and the CSP should demand that the cloud provider is obliged to support the client in facilitating exercise of data subjects' rights and to ensure that the same is safeguarded for its relation to any sub-contractor [14].

10.5.2.6 Portability

The use of standard data formats and service interfaces by the cloud providers is very important, as it facilitates inter-operability and portability between different cloud providers. Therefore, if a cloud client decides to move to another cloud provider, any lack of inter-operability may result in the impossibility or at least difficulties to transfer the client's (personal) data to the new cloud provider ('vendor lock-in'). The same problem also appears for services that the client developed on a platform offered by the original cloud provider (PaaS). The cloud client should check whether and how the provider guarantees the portability of data and services prior to ordering a cloud service. Preferably, the provider should make use of standardised or open data formats and interfaces. Agreement on contractual clauses stipulating assured formats, preservation of logical relations and any costs accruing from the migration to another cloud provider could be considered guarantees [14].

Data portability is defined in Article 20 and Recital 68 GDPR as an instrument to further strengthen the control of the data subject over its own data: the data subject should be allowed to receive personal data concerning the data subject which it provided to a controller in a structured, commonly used, machine-readable and inter-operable format, and to transmit it to another controller. To implement this right, it is important that, once the data have been transferred, no trace is left in the original system. In technical terms, it should be possible to verify the secure erasure of data [10,12].

10.5.2.7 IT accountability

In terms of data protection, IT accountability has a broad scope: it refers to the ability of the parties involved in personal data processing to provide evidence that they took appropriate measures to ensure compliance with the data protection principles [14].

IT accountability is particularly important to examine personal data breaches, based on the degree of responsibility of each cloud actor.

Furthermore, cloud providers should provide documentary evidence of appropriate and effective measures that ensure the application of the data protection principles outlined in the previous sections. Procedures to ensure the identification of all data processing operations, to respond to access requests, the allocation of resources including the designation of data protection officers who are responsible for the organisation of data protection compliance, or independent certification procedures are examples of such measures. In addition, data controllers should ensure that they are prepared to demonstrate the setting up of the necessary measures to the competent supervisory authority upon request [12].

10.5.3   Data protection impact assessments in cloud computing

Article 35 GDPR introduces an obligation for the data controller or the processor acting on the controller's behalf to carry out DPIAs in the event that the relevant processing operations present significant risks to the rights and freedoms of the data subjects.[13] As the use of cloud computing services for personal data processing could sometimes involve specific data protection risks, DPIAs constitute a useful instrument for the identification of these risks and the determination of appropriate mitigation measures. The EDPS highlights the importance of carrying out DPIAs on the use of cloud computing services by the public sector, especially when the processing may involve sensitive data (such as health data, data revealing political opinions, etc.) [10,23].

10.5.4   Audits and certifications

Another crucial aspect that directly affects the accountability principle and the application of its requirements in the cloud computing context is the interaction of various parties along the end-to-end value chain to deliver the service to the end customer. It is of utmost importance that these multiple actors trust each other to act responsibly and in co-ordination and take appropriate measures to ensure that data processing operations are carried out in compliance with data protection rules [10,24].

In this respect, internal and trusted third-party audits and subsequent certifications are valuable in attesting verifying responsibility and accountability when multiple actors are involved. Such audits should themselves be based on appropriate certification schemes. The GDPR establishes data protection certification mechanisms in Articles 42 and 43, which include third-party audit with strong involvement of the data protection authorities [25].

Articles 24 and 25 GDPR frame the responsibility of the data controller and specify the data protection by design and by default measures to be taken. Among others, the GDPR requires that the controller implements mechanisms to ensure that the effectiveness of those data protection measures can be verified. This can be done

---

[13]The list of the processing operations where data protection impact assessments should be mandatory is non-exhaustive.

by independent internal or external auditors. Article 28, accordingly, specifies the data protection measures that the processors must take. Besides these provisions, cloud-computing-specific codes of conduct drawn up by the industry and approved by the relevant data protection authorities could also be a useful tool to improve compliance and trust among the various actors. The codes of conduct model are present both in Directive 95/46/EC and the GDPR (Articles 27 and 40, respectively, Recitals 77 and 98 GDPR are also relevant) [10].

10.6 Data flows and appropriate safeguards

Data flows are an important part of the cloud computing model. From a legal perspective, the transfer of data from one cloud server to another could mean application of different legislation, per the governing law. The governing (applicable law) depends as discussed in Section 10.2, on the location, but also other conditions, such as the target of the offered cloud service [26]. Cloud computing services rely on the continuous flows of data of cloud clients across CSPs' infrastructure. Data are being transferred from the cloud clients to cloud providers' servers and data centres located in various parts of the world. The cloud client is therefore rarely able to know in real time where the data are located or stored or transferred [10].

The EU data protection legislation, both the Directive 95/46/EC and the new GDPR, include safeguards and provisions that enable such transfers. A cloud client or CSP acting as data controller need to both preserve the necessary safeguards for the protection of personal data in the framework of the general accountability principle, but also make use of the means established in the legislation for legitimate data transfers. Due to the challenges with continuous relocation of data, applying the data transfers requirements of EU data protection legislation in the cloud computing environment is challenging and has limitations [27].

The GDPR adopts similar data transfer rules to the existing Directive 95/46/EC regime. At the same time, there are some important novelties that lead to key implications. Article 44 GDPR requires that not only controllers but also *processors* implement appropriate safeguards for international data transfers [10]. This constitutes a significant step for the cloud computing environment, which imposes significant obligations also to CSPs acting as data processors [10,12].

10.6.1 Adequacy decisions[14]

The application of data transfer rules is usually based on an assessment of whether there is an adequate level of protection in the countries where the data are going to be transferred.[15] This assessment is made by the European Commission and followed

---

[14]Under the current legal framework, the Commission has adopted several adequacy decisions with respect to Andorra, Argentina, Australia, Canada, Switzerland, Faeroe Islands, Guernsey, State of Israel, Isle of Man, Jersey, US PNR and the US Safe Harbor. Such decisions will remain in force until amended, replaced or repealed by a Commission Decision (article 45(9) GDPR).
[15]Article 46 GDPR.

by an adequacy decision. However, as stated above, cloud computing services most frequently do not have any stable location of the data and personal data may not remain permanently in each location. Furthermore, some service providers may refuse to inform where the cloud servers are located [10]. Adequacy decisions, including the EU-US Data Privacy Shield [28], have limited geographical scope and may have uncertain results if challenged in court [29]. However, they usually require less effort from the part of data controller, in comparison to the other ways to transfer data outside the EU, while preserving a high level of data protection, guaranteed by the EU data protection law.

10.6.2 Alternative ways for data transfers by means of 'appropriate safeguards'

Article 46 of the GDPR provides a restrictive list of conditions under which personal data may be transferred by a data controller or processor to a third country outside the EU or an international organisation in the absence of an *adequacy decision, without the authorisation of the supervisory authority*. Necessary requirement for all the alternative grounds for transfers is the availability of enforceable data subject rights and of effective legal remedies for the data subjects. According to Article 29 Working Party, though, such alternative ways should not be the grounds for recurrent, massive or structural transfers, but rather be relied upon 'exceptionally' [30].[16] In practice, in the absence of an adequacy decision, the alternative ways for transfers are the only way to ensure that a CSP continues to provide its services in compliance with the EU data protection law.

Taking a closer look at the alternative grounds for data transfers, in this section, we outline the grounds of Article 46 GDRP, which is relevant to cloud computing data flows. *Standard data protection clauses* (Article 46(2)(c)(d)) are either adopted by the European Commission or adopted by the national data protection authorities and approved by the European Commission for governing international data transfers between two controllers or one controller and a processor. They are, therefore, based on a bilateral approach. When the cloud provider is processor, model clauses 2010/87/EC is an instrument that can be used between the processor and the controller as a basis for the cloud computing environment to offer adequate safeguards in the context of international transfers [27].

The EDPS has commented that Article 46 GDPR facilitates the use of several types of contractual clauses, either standard or ad hoc. This flexibility might be particularly useful for CSPs, as they have the option to enter whichever category they wish, tailored to their specific needs. However, whichever are the clauses chosen by

---

[16]More specifically, *these exemptions, which are tightly drawn, for the most part concern cases where the risks to the data subject are relatively small or where other interests (public interests or those of the data subject himself) override the data subject's right to privacy. As exemptions from a general principle, they must be interpreted restrictively. Furthermore Member States may provide in domestic law for the exemptions not to apply in particular cases. This might be the case, for example, where it is necessary to protect particularly vulnerable groups of individuals, such as workers or patients.* [10].

the CSPs, they should all contain minimum guarantees on essential aspects. These guarantees might include the requirement to enter into written agreement with sub-processors, by which they commit to the same data protection obligations, prior information/notices of the cloud customer on the use of sub-processors, audit clause, third-party beneficiary rights, rules on liability and damages, supervision, etc. [10]. In addition to the standard contractual clauses (SCCs), cloud providers could offer customers provisions that build on their pragmatic experiences as long as they do not contradict, directly or indirectly, the SCCs approved by the Commission or prejudice fundamental rights or freedoms of the data subjects [31]. Nevertheless, the companies may not amend or change the SCCs without implying that the clauses will no longer be 'standard' [31].

Another ground is *binding corporate rules* (BCRs). BCRs are personal data protection policies adhered to by the controller or processor established in an EU Member State. These policies facilitate transfers of personal data to a controller or processor in one or more third countries within a group of undertakings or a group of enterprises engaged in a joint economic activity (Article 4(20) GDPR). Thus, BCRs refer to data transfers within the same company, for instance the CSP establishments in several countries or companies with a joint economic activity. Article 29 Working Party has developed (based on the Directive 95/46/EC) BCRs for processors which will allow the transfer within the group for the benefit of the controllers without requiring the signature of contracts between processor and sub-processors per client [32]. Such BCRs for processors would enable the provider's client to entrust their personal data to the processor while being assured that the data transferred within the provider's business scope would receive an adequate level of protection [14]. The GDPR includes (Article 47 GDPR) detailed minimum content requirements for the BCRs to be a valid ground for data transfers, such as: the legally binding nature, complaint procedures, personnel training, tasks of the data protection officer and others.

Another ground for data transfers likely to be widely used in the case of cloud computing is the *soft law* grounds, i.e. approved codes of conduct and approved data protection certifications. Adherence to approved codes of conduct and certifications based on the conditions of the GDPR may bring several benefits to data controllers and processors in terms of accountability, administrative fines imposed by the data protection authorities (Article 83 GDPR) and data transfers. The process of conforming to such soft law instruments might entail intensive third-party audits (for instance from accredited certification bodies indicated in Article 43 GDPR) and follow-up activities to maintain the certification and the seal. The cloud clients and service providers, however, might consider choosing this option, as it is more flexible than standard data protection clauses and BCRs. Transfers by means of codes of conduct or certification mechanisms need to be accompanied with binding and enforceable commitments on behalf of the controller or processor in the third country, that they shall apply the appropriate safeguards, including those concerning data subject rights.

Data transfers in the absence of an adequacy decision can also be based on contractual clauses between controller or processor and the controller, processor or recipient of the personal data in the third country or organisation, after authorisation of the competent supervisory authority (Article 46 (3) GDPR). This ground can also be relevant for cloud actors.

10.7   Conclusions

The use of cloud computing models facilitates and accelerates the creation and processing of big data collections and the production of new services and applications. When these big data collections contain personal data, specific risks and challenges for privacy and data protection arise, and appropriate safeguards are imperative to be implemented.

Privacy and data protection in the context of cloud computing must not, in any case, be inferior to the level of protection required in any other data processing context. The cloud computing model can only be developed and applied legally if the data protection standards are not lowered compared to those applicable in conventional data processing operations.

The extra-territorial effect of the new EU GDPR induces not only broader legal rules but also new challenges. Not only EU, but also non-EU cloud computing service providers are highly affected and need to be aware of the updated EU data protection framework to process personal data in compliance with their legal obligations. Cloud providers, not established in the EU, that offer targeted services to individuals in the EU, irrespectively of whether these individuals are citizens of an EU Member State, are governed by the GDPR regarding the data processing activities concerning those individuals.

The cloud client-cloud provider relationship is often a data controller–processor relationship. Exceptionally, the cloud provider may act as a controller and, therefore, have full responsibility for compliance with all the legal obligations deriving from EU data protection law, or a joint controller together with the cloud client. The cloud client, when acting as a data controller, is also responsible for selecting a CSP that guarantees compliance with EU data protection legislation. The GDPR renders both data controllers and data processors directly liable for certain EU data protection law requirements, such as accountability, data security and data breach notifications.

As far as contracts between CSPs and cloud clients are concerned, sub-processors may only be delegated if the controller consents to such activity. Furthermore, CSPs' contracts with sub-contractors should stipulate the provisions of the original contract with the cloud client.

The GDPR requirements in the context of cloud computing may be divided into two broad categories: (1) compliance with the fundamental data processing principles and (2) technical and organisational measures implementation.

Transparency entails the detailed provision of information on behalf of the cloud providers to the cloud clients about all data protection relevant aspects of their services and, accordingly, the relevant notifications to the data subjects by the cloud clients. The purpose specification principle guarantees that the cloud client does not process personal data for further purposes, other than the original(s), by the cloud provider or any sub-contractors. Furthermore, once personal data are no longer necessary for the specific purposes they were collected and processed, the cloud client must ensure that they are erased from wherever they are stored. Finally, the cloud client and the CSP must be able to ensure and demonstrate accountability through the adoption and implementation of appropriate data protection policies and technical and organisational measures that their processing activities comply with the requirements of the EU Data Protection Law.

Regarding technical and organisational measures, such measures should be guaranteed and included in the contract between the cloud client and the cloud provider and be reflected in the provider and sub-contractors' relationship. Technical measures must ensure availability, integrity and confidentiality of the data. Isolation is a protective goal, which is meant to address the risk that data is used beyond its initial original purpose and to maintain confidentiality and integrity.

Moreover, the data subjects have the rights to access, rectification, erasure, blocking and objection. The exercise of the data subject rights should be assisted by the cloud service provider. Interoperability and data portability are facilitated using standard data formats and service interfaces by the cloud providers.

In case of cross-border transfers, the EU data protection legislation, both the Directive 95/46/EC and the new GDPR, includes safeguards and provisions that enable such transfers. A cloud client or cloud provider acting as data controller needs to preserve the necessary safeguards for the protection of personal data in the framework of the general accountability principle, but also make use of the means established in the legislation for legitimate data transfers. The GDPR requires that not only controllers but also processors implement appropriate safeguards for international data transfers. In the absence of an adequacy decision, transfers of data to non-adequate third countries require specific safeguards via the use of special arrangements (e.g. the EU-US Privacy Shield), Standard Contractual Clauses or Binding Corporate Rules.

References

[1]   Mell P., Grance T. 'The NIST definition of cloud computing'. *Communications of the ACM*. 2010;53(6):50.

[2]   European Commission. *European Cloud Initiative – Building a Competitive Data and Knowledge Economy in Europe*. Communication from the Commission to the European Parliament, the Council, the European Economic and Social Committee and the Committee of the Regions, COM (2016) 178 final, 2016. Available from: https://ec.europa.eu/digital-single-market / en / news/ communication-european-cloud-initiative-building-competitive-data-and-knowledge-economy-europe.

[3]   ENISA. *Security Resilience in Governmental Clouds*. 2011. Available from: https://www.enisa.europa.eu/publications/security-and-resilience-in-governmental-clouds.

[4]   ENISA. *Cloud Computing: Benefits, Risks and Recommendations for Information Security*. 2009. Available from: http://www.enisa.europa.eu/act/rm/files/deliverables/cloud-computing-risk-assessment/at_download/fullReport.

[5]   European Parliament and Council of the European Union. Regulation 2016/679 of the European Parliament and of the Council of 27 April 2016 on the protection of natural persons with regard to the processing of personal data and on the free movement of such data, and repealing Directive 95/46/EC (General Data Protection Regulation), L 119/14.5.2016.

[6]   De Hert, P., Czerniawski M. 'Expanding the European data protection scope beyond territory: Article 3 of the General Data Protection Regulation in its wider context'. *International Data Privacy Law.* 2016; 6(3):230–243. doi:10.1093/idpl/ipw008.

[7]   Hon W.K., Hörnle J., Millard C. 'Data protection jurisdiction and cloud computing – When are cloud users and providers subject to EU data protection law. The cloud of unknowing'. *International Review of Law, Computers & Technology.* 2012; 26(2–3):129–164, p. 33. Available from: http://www.tandfonline.com/doi/abs/10.1080/13600869.2012.698843.

[8]   Svantesson D.J.B. 'Extraterritoriality and targeting in EU data privacy law: The weak spot undermining the regulation'. *International Data privacy Law.* 2015;5:230–33.

[9]   European Parliament and Council. Directive 95/46/EC of the European Parliament and of the Council of 24 October 1995 on the protection of individuals with regard to the processing of personal data and on the free movement of such data (Data Protection Directive). OJ L 281, 23.11.1995.

[10]   European Data Protection Supervisor. 'Opinion of 16 November 2012 on the Commission's Communication on "Unleashing the potential of Cloud Computing in Europe"'. 2012. Available from: https://secure.edps.europa.eu/EDPSWEB/webdav/shared/Documents/Consultation/Opinions/2012/12-11-16_Cloud_Computing_EN.pdf, p. 14.

[11]   European Parliament and the Council. Directive 2002/58/EC of the European Parliament and of the Council of 12 July 2002 concerning the processing of personal data and the protection of privacy in the electronic communications sector (Directive on privacy and electronic communications), OJ L 201, 31.07.2002 p. 37, as amended by European Parliament and the Council, Directive 2009/136/EC of the European Parliament and of the Council of 25 November 2009, OJ L 337, 18.12.2009.

[12]   Hon W.K., Kosta E., Millard C., Stefanatou D. 'Cloud accountability: The likely impact of the proposed EU data protection regulation'. *Queen Mary School of Law Legal Studies Research Paper.* 2014(172). Available from: http://papers.ssrn.com/sol3/Papers.cfm?abstract_id=2405971.

[13]   Article 29 Data Protection Working Party. 'Opinion 1/2010 on the concepts of "controller" and "processor" WP 169'. 2010. Available from: http://ec.europa.eu/justice/data-protection/article-29/documentation/opinion-recommendation/files/2010/wp169_en.pdf.

[14]   Article 29 Data Protection Working Party. 'Opinion 05/2012 on Cloud Computing' WP 196, 2012. Available from: http://ec.europa.eu/justice/data-protection/article-29/documentation/opinion-recommendation/files/2012/wp196_en.pdf.

[15] Information Commissioner's Office. 'Guidance on the use of Cloud Computing', 2012. Available from: https://ico.org.uk/media/for-organisations/documents/1540/cloud_computing_guidance_for_organisations.pdf.

[16] Hon W.K., Millard C., Walden I. 'Who is responsible for "personal data" in cloud computing? – The cloud of unknowing, Part 2'. *International Data Privacy Law.* 2012; 2(1):3–18. Available from: http://idpl.oxfordjournals.org/content/2/1/3.short.

[17] Webber M. 'The GDPR impact on the cloud service provider as a processor' *Privacy and Data Protection (PDP Journals).* 2016;16(4):11–14.

[18] Kamarinou D., Millard C., Hon W.K. 'Privacy in the clouds: An empirical study of the terms of service and privacy policies of 20 cloud service providers'. *Queen Mary School of Law Legal Studies Research Paper* 209, 2015. Available from: http://papers.ssrn.com/sol3/Papers.cfm?abstract_id=2646447.

[19] International Working Group on Data Protection in Telecommunications. 'Working paper on cloud computing – Privacy and data protection issues – "Sopot Memorandum"'. 2012. Available from: https://datenschutz-berlin.de/content/europa-international/international-working-group-on-data-protection-in-telecommunications-iwgdpt/working-papers-and-common-positions-adopted-by-the-working-group.

[20] Hon WK., Millard C., Walden I. 'The problem of "personal data" in cloud computing: What information is regulated? – The cloud of unknowing'. *International Data Privacy Law.* 2011;1(4):211–228. Available from: http://idpl.oxfordjournals.org/content/1/4/211.short.

[21] Article 29 Data Protection Working Party. 'Opinion 08/2012 providing further input on the data protection reform discussions'. WP 199, 2012. Available from: http://ec.europa.eu/justice/dataprotection/article-29/documentation/opinion-recommendation/files/2012/wp199_en.pdf.

[22] Articles 15-22 GDPR.

[23] European Data Protection Supervisor. 'Opinion of 7 March 2012 on the data protection reform package'. 2012. Available from: https://secure.edps.europa.eu/EDPSWEB/webdav/site/mySite/shared/Documents/Consultation/Opinions/2012/12-03-07_EDPS_Reform_package_EN.pdf.

[24] Article 29 Data Protection Working Party. 'Opinion 3/2010 on the principle of accountability'. WP 173, 2010. Available from: http://ec.europa.eu/justice/policies/privacy/docs/wpdocs/2010/wp173_en.pdf.

[25] Kamara I., De Hert P. 'Data protection certification in the EU. Possibilities, actors and building blocks in a reformed landscape; data protection certification in the EU general data protection regulation', in Rodrigues R. and Papakonstantinou V. (eds.) *Privacy and Data Protection Seals*, TMC Asser Press, 2017 (forthcoming).

[26] Konstantinou I., Quinn P., De Hert P. 'Overview of applicable legal framework and general legal requirements: Deliverable 3.1 for the SeCloud project'. SeCloud project, 2016.

[27] Hon W.K., Millard C., Walden I. 'Data export in cloud computing – How can personal data be transferred outside the EEA. The cloud of

unknowing, Part 4'. 2012. Available from: http://papers.ssrn.com/sol3/papers.cfm?abstract_id=2034286.

[28]   European Commission. Available from: http://ec.europa.eu/justice/data-protection/international-transfers/eu-us-privacy-shield/index_en.htm.

[29]   Judgment of the Court (Grand Chamber) of 6 October 2015 (request for a preliminary ruling from the High Court (Ireland)) – Maximillian Schrems v Data Protection Commissioner, Case C-362/14.

[30]   Article 29 Data Protection Working Party. 'Working document 12/1998: Transfers of personal data to third countries: Applying Articles 25 and 26 of the EU data protection directive'.1998. Available from: http://ec.europa.eu/justice/policies/privac1y/docs/wpdocs/1998/wp12_en.pdf.

[31]   European Commission. 'Can companies include the standard contractual clauses in a wider contract and add specific clauses?' Published by the EC on http://ec.europa.eu/justice/policies/privacy/docs/international_transfers_faq/international_transfers_faq.pdf.

[32]   Article 29 Data Protection Working Party. 'Working document 02/2012 setting up a table with the elements and principles to be found in Processor Binding Corporate Rules'. 2012. Available from: http://ec.europa.eu/justice/data-protection/article-29/documentation/opinion-recommendation/files/2012/wp195_en.pdf.

Chapter 11

The Waikato Data Privacy Matrix

Craig Scoon[1] and Ryan K. L. Ko[1]

Abstract

Data privacy is an expected right of most citizens around the world, but there are many legislative challenges within the boundary-less cloud computing and World Wide Web environments.

The Waikato Data Privacy Matrix outlines our global project for alignment of data privacy laws, by focusing on Asia Pacific data privacy laws and its relationships with the European Union and the United States. Some alignment already exists for the European Union and United States, there is a lack of research on Asia Pacific alignment within its region and across other regions. The Waikato Data Privacy Matrix also suggests potential solutions to address some of the issues that may occur when a breach of data privacy occurs, in order to ensure an individual has their data privacy protected across the boundaries within the Web.

11.1 Introduction

Privacy of an individual is a widely discussed issue in the legal arena, but with the introduction of cloud services, privacy concerns have also made their way into the computing realm [1]. Laws made by governments can sometimes be confusing to an everyday citizen. In recent years, legislation has been enacted to protect the privacy of an individual or society, but this has come under fire [2]. These discussions have been fuelled by the large amount of media coverage and publicity about leaks of personal data, and breaches of data privacy, including the case of the 2013 National Security Agency (NSA) leaks [3]. A result of this publicity has meant an increased awareness in data privacy limitations and rights, which highlighted a need for clarification around trans-national legislation and an effective way of aligning them with other countries so an everyday user (e.g. consumer and small businesses) can understand any privacy concerns that may relate to them or their data processed or stored by third parties.

[1]Cyber Security Lab, University of Waikato, New Zealand

The emergence of the Internet of Things (IoT) [4] and the adoption of cloud services [5] presents important research foci towards ensuring users and vendors can put trust in these technologies and services by knowing the requirements of different countries' legislation. The amount of data and personal information stored or transferred to servers across trans-national jurisdictions, in which devices reside, creates a need for a better understanding of global data privacy legislation that may create repercussions for their business or privacy.

There are many legislative challenges within boundary-less cloud computing and World Wide Web environments. Despite its importance, the legal side of the security ecosystem seems to be in a constant effort to catch-up. There are recent issues showing a lack of alignment that caused some confusion. An example of this is the "right to be forgotten" case in 2014 that involved a Spanish man and Google Spain. He requested the removal of a link to an article about an auction of his foreclosed home, for a debt that he had subsequently paid. However, misalignment of data privacy laws caused further complications to the case.

The Waikato Data Privacy Matrix (WDPM) provides an easy way to cross reference different trans-national legislation that align with a set of predefined domain areas. Assisting a user to see what laws are governing their data wherever in the world that data may be located. The WDPM can also be utilised by governments, and in particular the legislature, to see gaps which may appear in their own legislation and allow them to propose changes to improve or align with the rest of the countries.

11.2 Background

11.2.1 Justification

Many users of cloud services do not have a legal background or legal understanding. Cloud services have been incorporated into everyday life, and the geographical boundaries which once contained a legal jurisdiction are now being blurred. Legislation is an important function in society, set down by the legislature, to govern what are acceptable behaviours, and punishments if these behaviours are not followed.

Cloud users and vendors need to know what legislation will impact on them and their data wherever it is in the world.

The Department of the Prime Minister and Cabinet (DPMC) in New Zealand released the updated Cyber Security strategy, on 10 December 2015, replacing the 2011 version. The strategy outlines the government's response to addressing the threat of cybercrime to New Zealanders. Connect Smart conducted a survey in 2014 on cyber security practises; 83% of those surveyed said they had experienced a data breach in some way (22% saying they had email accounts compromised). The scary side to that statistic is 61% of those did nothing to change their behaviour [6]. The new version has four principles:

- partnerships are essential
- economic growth is enabled
- national security is upheld
- human rights are protected online

Cyber resilience involves detection, protection and recovery from cyber incidents, and looking to create action plans for disaster recovery from cyber incidents.

Cyber capability refers to educating the public and providing them with the necessary tools they may need. It focuses on individuals, businesses, government departments and organisations to build better cyber security capabilities and awareness. The success of this goal will allow all levels of New Zealanders to have the knowledge and tools available to protect themselves against a cyber threat. This principle should also have the potential to increase the skills in the cyber security industry, allowing businesses and organisations to have the technical staff to support the rest of their information technology (IT) team.

Addressing cybercrime looks at prevention of cybercrime, but also has an extra component, in the "National Plan to Address Cybercrime", which identifies cybercrime issues and challenges and ways they can be addressed. Most of this is from awareness so the public can help themselves.

International co-operation is the last goal which is vital to mitigating risk within cybercrime. This looks at building international partnerships within the Asia Pacific (APAC) region.

New Zealand is not the only country to release a new cyber security strategy [7]. Australia released their 4-year strategy in April 2016 which outlines five themes:

- a national cyber partnership
- strong cyber defences
- global responsibility and influence
- growth and innovation
- a cyber smart nation

The Australian and New Zealand strategies have similar goals in mind – ultimately educating citizens, and providing tools and international co-operation.

Thousands of new businesses are started every year, some of these will not even get off the ground and out of the ones that do, around 10% will fail within the first year and around 70% will fail within 5 years [8]. One of the biggest points of failure comes down to the business revenue. Even a company which is semi established that needs to break out into an overseas market to get more customers, may not have enough revenue to hire a legal team or even a single professional, to give them all of the legal advice to successfully launch their business in an overseas jurisdiction. Legal bills can be very expensive. Although legislation is freely available in most countries around the world it may not be easy to navigate.

11.2.2   Cloud computing

Cloud computing started in 1999 when Salesforce became one of the first major companies to move into the cloud business. Salesforce started the concept of providing enterprise-level applications to any user providing they had Internet access [9].

Amazon Web Services were launched in 2002 offering a suite of cloud-based services for customers, including storage and computation. In 2006 Amazon introduced its Elastic Compute Cloud (EC2) to the public [10]. A survey conducted by Synergy Research Group in 2016 found that Amazon controlled 31% of the cloud market share for the first quarter in 2016 [11]. This is the same as the result for this survey when conducted for 2015 fourth quarter, with Microsoft, IBM and Google coming in under Amazon [12].

In January 2016, RightScale – an organisation deploying and managing applications in the cloud – conducted its annual State of the Cloud Survey of the latest cloud computing trends which focuses on cloud users and cloud buyers. There were 1,060 IT professionals who participated in the survey, and of these participants 95% were using cloud services [13]. To utilise cloud computing, it is essential to have multiple data centres located in different parts of the country or the world, to ensure lower latency for the customers using the cloud service. Google has many data servers scattered across the globe, but it is unclear the precise number of data centres that Google operates [14]. Although this is good for users who have their data stored in these places, it makes it difficult to know what laws apply to their data. Even if a user has data stored in the United States (US) their data may be subjected to different state laws depending on which part of the country it is stored in. What makes matters more unclear is when a user has their data stored in multiple data centres in different parts of the world. Internet addresses are not physical addresses, which allows them to be easily spoofed, making it harder to locate where the data came from or showing the data is residing in an entirely different country. There is a clear need for policy makers to collaborate on these laws so there is a global alignment which does not produce any surprises for users of these services.

11.2.3 NSA leaks

In 2013, Edward Snowden – a former employee of defence contractor in Booz Allen Hamilton at the NSA – released classified information relating to numerous global surveillance programs, many of which were run by the NSA and the Five Eyes Alliance. Snowden met with two reporters from the British daily newspaper – *The Guardian*, where he revealed top secret classified information relating to the clandestine surveillance program known as PRISM, and other information about covert spying operations carried out by the US government on its citizens. It was originally thought that Snowden downloaded 1.5 million documents but only shared around 200,000 [15] with the two original journalists from *The Guardian*. However this has not been confirmed.

The leaked documents revealed how the Foreign Intelligence Surveillance Court (FISC) had ordered Verizon – an American telecommunications company – to hand over millions of customers' telephone records [16]. This was not so the NSA could pry into the content of these calls, but it did allow the NSA's computers to look through the millions of phone records for patterns or unusual types of behaviour [17]. This practice had been going on for approximately 7 years, on a 3 monthly renewal system.

The documents also revealed top-secret procedures that showed steps the NSA must take to target and collect data from "non-US citizens" and how it must minimise data collected on its own US citizens. There were also documents relating to a program codenamed "EvilOlive" [18] which collected and stored large amounts of Internet metadata from US citizens, including sender, recipient, and time stamp of email correspondences from Internet users [19].

Since the leaks, the Information Technology and Innovation Foundation (ITIF), an industry-funded think tank that focuses on the intersection of technological innovation and public policy, estimated the leaks could cost cloud computing companies up to $35 billion in lost revenue [3].

The fallout from this exposure forced countries that were using data centres in the US to open data centres in their own countries or look for other places to store data. Russia received this news and passed a new law which required all tech companies inside Russian borders to only use servers located within Russia. This is one way of not having to worry about a global alignment, but it is an extremely high cost for the companies to use backyard data centres [3]. It also forced users of cloud services to look into where their data was going to be stored or if it would be moved from the US centres to another part of the world where the laws were unknown to them.

11.2.4   PRISM

The PRISM program was launched in 2007 after the enactment of the Foreign Intelligence Surveillance Act (FISA). PRISM was carried out by the NSA to collect stored Internet communications and use data mining techniques to look for patterns of terrorist or other potential criminal activity within the communications. There were at least nine major US Internet companies participating in this program which included Microsoft in 2007, Yahoo in 2008, Google, Facebook and Paltalk in 2009, YouTube in 2010, AOL and Skype in 2011 and Apple in 2012 [20]. The basic idea behind the program was for the NSA to have the ability to request data on specific persons of interest. Permission is given by the FISC, a special federal court setup by the FISA. There are still questions about the operation of the FISC and if its actions are in breach of the US constitution.

11.2.5   Trans-national agreements

To protect data privacy within the European Union (EU), the data protection directive was enacted in 1995. This directive only applied to a participating EU member country which meant that data could not be transferred outside of the EU. The EU–US Umbrella Agreement is a framework to enable co-operation between law enforcement efforts between the EU and US which covers all categories of personal data exchanged between the two countries. This agreement is purely for the purpose of prevention, detection, investigation and prosecution of criminal offences, including terrorism [21].

11.2.6   Safe harbor to privacy shield

The Safe Harbor Agreement was launched in 2000 after the European Commission and the Department of Commerce of the United States agreed it had adequate protection for transferring data from the EU to the US. Thirteen years later, the Safe Harbor Agreement began to come under fire in the wake of the Snowden leaks, and by

October 2015 the Court of Justice of the European Union (CJEU) had declared the Safe Harbor invalid, after the case of Max Schrems.

After the invalidation, a draft of the new EU–US Privacy Shield [22] emerged. The draft Privacy Shield was announced in February 2016, and is an adaption of the Safe Harbor Agreement. In a press release in February 2016 the European Commission stated that the new Privacy Shield would "provide stronger obligations on companies in the European Union (EU) to protect the personal data of Europeans and stronger monitoring and enforcement by the US Department of Commerce and Federal Trade Commission, including through increased co-operation with European Data Protection Authorities" [23]. Three new elements were included in the new Privacy Shield framework:

- strong obligations on companies handling Europeans' personal data, and robust enforcement
- clear safeguards and transparency obligations on US government access
- effective protection of EU citizens' rights with several redress possibilities

The Privacy Shield was signed off on 8 July 2016 by the European Commission and the Department of Commerce of the United States. The new and approved version of the Privacy Shield contains numerous clarifications for the privacy principles.

The Privacy Shield was open to companies from 1 August 2016, so by August 2017 the questions around how legitimate this Privacy Shield will be, should be answered. All going well, it should be able to restore and start to rebuild trust with the citizens around the use, protection, and stewardship of data [24].

The new and approved version of the Privacy Shield contains numerous clarifications for the privacy principles.

The first relates to data integrity and purpose limitation, which clarifies the purpose of data usage and that it is reliable for its intended use; meaning it must be up to date and complete.

The choice principle allows the data subject to opt-out if their data will be disclosed to a third party or used for a different purpose, and clarifies the use for direct marketing.

The principle on accountability for onwards transfers clarifies the obligation to all parties involved, of the processing of data being transferred to ensure the same level of protection despite the location of that party.

The access principle is probably the most important principle in the Privacy Shield. It allows a data subject to query an organisation if they are processing any personal data related to them, which the organisation needs to respond to, in a reasonable time. Although, the problem here is what constitutes reasonable. This is a subjective interpretation of the word so this may cause some problems in the future. It also allows for the data subject to correct, amend, or delete personal data that is inaccurate or has been processed in violation of the principles. This aligns with the EU directives and regulations.

The principle on Recourse, Enforcement and Liability clarifies how complaints are handled, and sets out eight levels of redress that must be handled in a specific order, which would be used for EU citizens if their complaint is not resolved to their satisfaction [25].

Since the Privacy Shield was built upon parts of the Safe Harbour Agreement, companies still need to self-certify. It has the extra principle components, meaning citizens from the EU are protected better than before, and there is more transparency in this agreement.

11.2.7   General data protection regulation

Currently in the EU there are numerous directives in place which aim to protect personal data. The EU Data Protection Directive [26], which is the main document within the EU for data protection, regulates how data can be processed within the EU. In addition there are two other directives which compliment the Data Protection Directive. The first of these is the 2009 E-Privacy Directive which replaced the former 2002 E-Privacy directive [27], and the second one is the Data Retention Directive [28].

The General Data Protection Regulation (GDPR)[1] is a new regulation from the EU that will come into force from 25 May 2018, replacing the existing EU Data Protection Directive. The GDPR will help to strengthen and unify data protection for individuals who reside within the EU.

The GDPR will introduce or further define the following areas [29]:

- Increased Territorial Scope
- Tougher Sanctions
- Consent
- Breach Notification
- Right to Access
- Right to be Forgotten
- Data Portability
- Privacy by Design
- Data Protection Officers

Once in force, the GDPR will be legally binding on all member states of the EU. This will also extend the scope to *all* organisations who may operate within the EU or process data of EU citizens whether they are headquartered there or not [30,31].

There has been much discussion around the effects the GDPR will have on the data privacy landscape. The general consensus is that the GDPR will have a positive effect. The new principles in the GDPR aim to give back the control to citizens over their data. The GDPR will set the new standard for data privacy.

---

[1] Regulation on the protection of natural persons with regard to the processing of personal data and on the free movement of such data, and repealing Directive 95/46/EC.

11.3   Legal cases

Privacy concerns are an ongoing issue that may only get more complicated as the technological landscape evolves. In recent years there have been some important landmark legal cases which reaffirm the need for a project of the calibre of the WDPM.

11.3.1   Schrems v. Data Protection Commissioner

The Schrems[2] case is probably the biggest and most important privacy case in recent history, resulting in the invalidation of the Safe Harbor Agreement.

Maximillian Schrems, an Austrian law student and privacy activist, was studying abroad at Santa Clara University, completing his PhD, where he wrote a term paper on Facebook's lack of awareness of European privacy law [32]. During his research, Mr Schrems sent a request to Facebook for their records on him and received a CD with over 1,200 pages of data. This sparked the start of his journey down the road that would eventually lead him to the CJEU.

Mr Schrems then filed 23 complaints, against Facebook, to the Irish Data Protection Commissioner. These complaints related to the level of protection which was provided for data in the US. Most of Mr Schrems data for Facebook was transferred from one of Facebook's subsidiary companies in Ireland through to servers in the US, where his data was then processed. This was permitted through the Safe Harbor Agreement.

The complaints made by Mr Schrems further added concerns to the lack of protection for data offered in the US previously highlighted by the release of the documents in 2013 by Edward Snowden around the spying of the NSA [33].

11.3.2   Google Spain v. AEPD and Mario Costeja González

This Google case[3] was another important privacy case which resulted in the new EU "Right to be Forgotten" ruling [34].

In 1998, a Spanish citizen – Mario González – had two short articles published about him by a Spanish newspaper – *La Vanguardia*. The newspaper reported Mr González's home was to be auctioned to pay off his social security debts. Subsequently, these two articles were published on the Internet. Twelve years later in 2010, Mr González made a complaint to the national data protection agency in Spain against the newspaper, as well as Google Spain and Google Inc. He alleged that when any Internet user typed his name into a Google search engine, they would see the two articles published in 1998. Mr González had since rectified these issues and moved on with his life, making these articles now irrelevant; yet, the articles were still available, which he argued were prejudicial to his present and future living.

---

[2]Case C-362/14 Schrems v. Data Protection Commissioner [2015] ICLR.
[3]Google Spain SL, Google Inc. v. Agencia Española de Protección de Datos (es), Mario Costeja González [2014] C-131/12.

Mr Gonzålez requested all personal information relating to him be either removed from the newspaper or the pages in question amended [35]. He then requested Google Spain and Google Inc. to remove or conceal his personal data, so it would not appear in the search results nor in the links to the newspaper [36].

The Spanish Court referred this case to the CJEU where it ruled in favour of Mr Gonzålez, and he won the right for Google Spain and Google Inc. to remove the links from online circulation; however, the articles are still online but are harder to find now with the links gone.

11.3.3   Apple v. FBI

To give some background on why this case is important to the data privacy debate – in early December 2015 a husband and wife walked into the building of the Inland Regional Centre in San Bernardino, California, to carry out a terrorist attack. They shot and killed 14 people and seriously injured a further 22 people. The two attackers were then shot by police [37]. The police seized the iPhone 5C of one of the shooters.

Once the FBI had the iPhone, they had ten attempts to guess the password before the data on the phone would be erased. The FBI filed a motion to compel Apple to help them access the contents of the phone by bypassing the security. The Judge ordered Apple to provide "reasonable technical assistance". For Apple to allow this type of access, they would have to write a completely new version of their iPhone Operating System (iOS). The new version would essentially allow a backdoor into the iPhone by bypassing the security features built in to the current iOS, allowing the FBI to use a brute force attack to crack the pass code to the phone [38].

Although Apple said it was possible for them to build the backdoor into their system, they said it was too dangerous and once it was created anyone could use it to gain access to an iPhone. Apple said they regularly receive requests from law enforcement agencies asking for their help to unlock phones, but have not done this, keeping their customers' privacy their priority.

The FBI managed to unlock the phone, through the use of a third party, a week before the trial was set to be heard. The FBI has never confirmed how they accessed the phone or which third party helped them [39].

The publicity which came out of this case was enormous. In recent years, the US Government has attempted to get Apple and other technology companies to build a form of backdoor into their products, so law enforcement agencies have the ability to bypass the security measures where a phone is involved in an investigation. Apple changed their software in 2014 to ensure their phones could not be unlocked or decrypted [40]. This was a reassuring step for Apple customers, showing that their privacy, and privacy of their data, was important to the company.

> *"While we believe the FBI's intentions are good, it would be wrong for the government to force us to build a backdoor into our products. And ultimately, we fear that this demand would undermine the very freedoms and liberty our government is meant to protect."*
> Tim Cook, *Chief Executive Officer of Apple*

11.3.4   The right to be forgotten concept

The "right to be forgotten" is a concept where an individual within the EU has the ability to request search engines remove links to pages that detail certain information about a person which may be inadequate, irrelevant or no longer relevant. This issue, relating to a person's right to privacy, which came out of the Google Spain case, not only affects Google search engine but any search engine which holds a "presence" in the EU, including both Yahoo and Bing [41].

Currently the "right to be forgotten" only applies to individuals (does not cover companies), living within a member country of the European Union which includes all nationalities residing within the EU. The "right to be forgotten" has been limited by the CJEU. An individual may refer to any person, including celebrities or other people who live in the public eye, although they would still come under the right to be forgotten, this may not guarantee they can be forgotten. The CJEU has specified that search engines must consider the public's right to information as it is of more importance when dealing with someone in the public eye. Although they may want something removed, they may not be able to have that, due to their position in society.

There may be exceptions to this which could include scams that are the kind of public interest items Google has said will be excluded from "right to be forgotten". Professional malpractice, criminal convictions, or public conduct of government officials would also fall under this exception [42].

The Court has made it clear that journalistic work must not be touched; it is to be protected [42].

For someone to be forgotten, a form is filled out and submitted to Google. If successful, the link to the page would be removed but this only applies to search engines within the EU. If Alice lives in Sweden and was to have something removed, Bob would not be able to see it on Google.fr (France) and Google.ge (Germany), but if it was to be looked up on Google.co.nz it would still be visible [41].

Although the form can help to get the correct information to Google, there are some issues. If someone has two variations of their name, for instance "Matt Smith" and "Matthew Smith", the form will only allow for one of these to be removed. This means two forms would need to be filled out [43].

In 2012, European Union Agency for Network and Information Security (ENISA) published a paper outlining the pros and cons of the new Bill that was being looked at which would later become the "right to be forgotten". It also laid out the technical aspects of how it could be enforced [44].

11.4   Related work in legal alignment

11.4.1   DLA Piper

The DLA Piper Data Protection Laws of the World Handbook [45] was launched in 2012. The handbook allows a user to choose two of the 89 countries and compare data privacy legislation. This website is helpful to a user to give them some idea of relevant legislation in the countries specified; however, it will mostly give the main piece of legislation relating to data privacy. The handbook then summarises the selected topic, for example, if the user clicks on "Authority" it will give an overview of who the authority is. In New Zealand's case it just gives contact details for the Office of the Privacy Commissioner.

11.4.2   Forrester Global Heat Map

The Forrester Global Heat Map [46] gives a user minimal access without registering for the site. Once registered, a user can buy the report for US$499 [47]. Not all of the countries are represented for free and the user does not get any usable information. Of the seven countries that can be clicked on – Russia, Taiwan, China, Singapore, Thailand, the UK and the US – only the UK and the US give information which is not helpful to the user.

11.4.3   International Data Protection Legislation Matrix

The International Data Protection Legislation Matrix [48] was developed by the US Department of Commerce and has not been updated since 2005. It is a table of 51 Areas which includes 50 countries and the EU (it does not include the US). It lists the relevant legislation, and a hyperlink to that legislation. The document then tells the user the status of the legislation and some key details about the legislation.

11.4.4   Baker & McKenzie's Global Privacy Handbook

This handbook [49] is written and updated by Baker & McKenzie, a global law firm with offices in 47 countries [50]. The user can utilise their tool to select and compare a single country or multiple countries, out of the available 56 countries. The user can then select a single topic or multiple topics to view and compare. The application will then give the user a summary of the legislation. It does not mention which legislation is used or is applicable in the country.

11.5   Proposed solution

A possible solution is the WDPM, which is a Rosetta Stone like matrix which helps to align data privacy laws throughout Asia Pacific, the EU and the US. It does this by having a set of seven predefined domains which include a control specification. (The Rosetta Stone [51] was a stone uncovered in 1799 with writing inscribed on it in two languages – Egyptian and Greek, these are done in three scripts – hieroglyphic, demotic and Greek.) The first domain is "Legislative Framework" which includes six "control specifications". Next to each control specification it lists the name of the documents relevant to that specification. The document name in the first domain gives the user the full name of the document and a link they can click which will take them to that document.

The WDPM directs a user to a specific section, article, schedule or part in the applicable legislation. This reduces the user hunting through government or other websites to find the relevant legislation they need and then directs them to the specific part of that legislation where they can see what the law states. The WDPM allows a user to see if there are any similar laws to do with that control within some of the countries located in the Asia Pacific, the EU or the US.

One example of the WDPM is the control specification from the pre-collection process domain. It directs the user to many different documents that relate to whether consent is required from the individual involved in the collection. In New Zealand there are three documents identified. The Privacy Act 1993 – which is the legislation, section 6 which in the Act, is titled "Information Privacy Principles" and then to principle 3. The use of the WDPM allows users to quickly and painlessly find and identify the relevant information relating to consent. When a user looks at the country in question they are also able see Australia, China and the UK which helps the user to see immediately that there is some law around consent in these countries.

The contributions from a variety of privacy experts have helped shape the WDPM, as well as the advise of over 20 experts from academia and industry. This has helped to provide some peer review of the information and directions within the WDPM.

The WDPM only focuses on general data privacy legislation at a federal level, meaning only legislation which covered the country as a whole was looked at. Due to the scope of the project only general data privacy was researched, this did not include legislation relating to health and finance. There were only 12 countries included in the WDPM as a start; the next step would be to add multiple other countries to create a more global and comprehensive alignment tool. The delivery for the WDPM is also an important step as the current form of the WDPM is a large Excel spreadsheet, but a web application will need to be introduced to make the user experience even better.

To ensure the WDPM is a truly global tool, a wider range of countries will also need to be added.

11.5.1   Data privacy matrix road map

The WDPM started off as a project which looked at aligning data privacy laws within the Asia Pacific region. Out of the APAC countries there were five countries chosen – New Zealand, Australia, China, Malaysia and Singapore, because these countries all participate in providing major cloud services. It was a logical choice to look at the alignment of these countries first. The next step is to align the UK and the US. For the EU countries there have been six countries chosen – United Kingdom, Sweden, France, Poland, Estonia and Germany. These countries have been chosen as they are among the most influential EU countries [52]. Estonia has been chosen as it is a leader in cybersecurity and e-government. It was decided at the beginning that WDPM would be at a high level of legislation covering federal legislation. State and local laws have been left out at this point, but may be introduced at a later time. It also does not look at tortious or civil laws as these are not as black and white as the federal legislations.

11.6 Concluding remarks

Data privacy is an increasingly important topic being widely discussed. With the advancement of Cloud services and technologies, and the upcoming implementation of the GDPR, it does not seem like these discussions will slow down. The WDPM is a tool to allow users to compare data privacy laws across the globe; so even though the GDPR will be the one document within the EU, it will still need to align with the rest of the non-EU countries to see how their data privacy legislation aligns.

11.6.1 Vision

To help to complete the future work and promote the WDPM and data privacy, the Data Privacy Foundation Inc. has been setup. The foundation has the following vision:

> **(a)** To assist in achieving global alignment of data privacy laws by identifying gaps and shortfalls in country and regional laws and legal systems, thereby ensuring full legal protection of data.
> **(b)** To establish the premier, knowledge based, definitive global authority on data privacy.
> **(c)** To provide knowledge, tools, training, consultancy and events to assure data privacy across the globe.
> **(d)** To establish, build, and sustain data privacy knowledge databases by harnessing collaborative, open source, scalable contributions and technologies.
> **(e)** To facilitate delivery of data privacy at a level not achievable or limited by any one organisation or country.

The foundation will help to create a comprehensive and robust global alignment tool for all types of data privacy legislation. There is a lot of work to be done to include these extra additions but this is a crucial development to create a truly global tool, and the benefit of having the foundation will help to extend the reach of this research.

By having access to federal and state legislation combined with case law, users and governments have a tool which gives them extensive information and direction to data privacy legislation around the globe.

References

[1] Vic (J.R.) Winkler, "Cloud Computing: Privacy, confidentiality and the cloud," June 2013 (Last Accessed on 24 October 2016). [Online]. Available: https://technet.microsoft.com/en-us/library/dn235775.aspx

[2] I. Georgieva, "The Right to Privacy under Fire – Foreign Surveillance under the NSA and the GCHQ and Its Compatibility with Art. 17 ICCPR and Art.

8 ECHR," *Utrecht J. Int'l & Eur. L.*, vol. 31, p. 104, February 27, 2015 (Last Accessed on 24 October 2016). [Online]. Available: www.utrechtjournal. org/articles/10.5334/ujiel.cr/

[3] N. Arce, "Effect of NSA Spying on US Tech Industry: $35 Billion? No. Way More," June 10, 2015 (Last Accessed on 22 July 2016). [Online]. Available: http://www.techtimes.com/articles/59316/20150610/effect-of-nsa-spying-on-us-tech-industry-35-billion-no-way-more.htm

[4] K. L. Lueth, "Why the Internet of Things Is Called Internet of Things: Definition, History, Disambiguation," December 19, 2014 (Last Accessed on 24 October 2016). [Online]. Available: https://iot-analytics.com/internet-of-things-definition/

[5] L. Columbus, "Roundup of Cloud Computing Forecasts And Market Estimates, 2016," March 13, 2016 (Last Accessed on 24 October 2016). [Online]. Available: http://www.forbes.com/sites/louiscolumbus/2016/03/13/roundup-of-cloud-computing-forecasts-and-market-estimates-2016/#5557f3c574b0

[6] Department of the Prime Minister and Cabinet (New Zealand), "National Plan to Address Cybercrime," December 10, 2015 (Last Accessed on 24 August 2016). [Online]. Available: http://www.dpmc.govt.nz/sites/all/files/publications/nz-cyber-security-cybercrime-plan-december-2015.pdf

[7] Department of the Prime Minister and Cabinet (Australia), "Australia's Cyber Security Strategy," April 21, 2016 (Last Accessed on 24 August 2016). [Online]. Available: https://cybersecuritystrategy.dpmc. gov.au/assets/img/PMC-Cyber-Strategy.pdf

[8] S. Nicholas, "Surviving and Thriving with Your New Business," September 22, 2015 (Last Accessed on 24 August 2016). [Online]. Available: http://www. stuff.co.nz/business/better-business/72295224/Surviving-and-thriving-with-your-new-business

[9] "The History of Cloud Computing" (Last Accessed on 27 August 2016). [Online]. Available: http://www.eci.com/cloudforum/cloud-computing-history.html

[10] A. Mohamed, "A History of Cloud Computing" (Last Accessed on 27 August 2016). [Online]. Available: http://www.computerweekly.com/feature/A-history-of-cloud-computing

[11] Business Cloud News, "AWS, Google, Microsoft and IBM Pull Away from Pack in Race for Cloud Market Share," April 29, 2016 (Last Accessed on 27 August 2016). [Online]. Available: http://www.businesscloudnews.com/2016/04/29/aws-google-microsoft-and-ibm-pull-away-from-pack-in-race-for-cloud-market-share/

[12] J. Tsidulko, "Keeping Up with the Cloud: Top 5 Market-Share Leaders," February 11, 2016 (Last Accessed on 27 August 2016). [Online]. Available: http://www.crn.com/slide-shows/cloud/300079669/keeping-up-with-the-cloud-top-5-market-share-leaders.htm/pgno/0/6

[13] K. Weins, "Cloud Computing Trends: 2016 State of the Cloud Survey," February 9, 2016 (Last Accessed on 6 April 2016). [Online]. Available: http://www.rightscale.com/blog/cloud-industry-insights/cloud-computing-trends-2016-state-cloud-survey

[14] "Google Data Centres," February 9, 2016, (Last Accessed on 7 April 2016). [Online]. Available: https://www.google.com/about/datacenters/inside/locations/index.html

[15] M. B. Kelly, "The US Now Thinks Snowden 'Probably Downloaded' 1.5 Million Documents That Haven't Been Found," June 6, 2014, (Last Accessed on 22 July 2016). [Online]. Available: http://www.businessinsider.com.au/clapper-says-snowden-took-less-than-they-though-2014-6

[16] "Verizon – about us" (Last Accessed on 12 July 2016). [Online]. Available: http://www.verizon.com/about/our-company/history-timeline

[17] "Court Order to Spy on Verizon Users Is a 3-Month Renewal of Ongoing Practice: Feinstein," June 6, 2013 (Last Accessed on 22 July 2016). [Online]. Available: http://nypost.com/2013/06/06/court-order-to-spy-on-verizon-users-is-a-3-month-renewal-of-ongoing-practice-feinstein/

[18] P. Szoldra, "SNOWDEN: Here's Everything We've Learned In One Year of Unprecedented Top-Secret Leaks," June 7, 2014 (Last Accessed on 22 July 2016). [Online]. Available: http://www.businessinsider.com.au/snowden-leaks-timeline-2014-6?r=US&IR=T

[19] J. Schellhase, "After Two Years of Edward Snowden Revelations, What Have We Learned About NSA Spying?" May 6, 2015 (Last Accessed on 22 July 2016). [Online]. Available: http://all-that-is-interesting.com/snowden-revelations/3

[20] T. Sottek and J. Kopstein, "Everything You Need to Know About PRISM," July 17, 2013 (Last Accessed on 3 April 2016). [Online]. Available: http://www.theverge.com/2013/7/17/4517480/nsa-spying-prism-surveillance-cheat-sheet

[21] "Questions and Answers on the EU–US Data Protection Umbrella Agreement," September 8, 2015 (Last Accessed on 3 April 2016). [Online]. Available: http://europa.eu/rapid/press-release_MEMO-15-5612_en.htm

[22] G. Maldoff, "We Read Privacy Shield So You Don't Have To," March 7, 2016 (Last Accessed on 4 April 2016). [Online]. Available: https://iapp.org/news/a/we-read-privacy-shield-so-you-dont-have-to

[23] EU Commission, "EU Commission and United States Agree on New Framework for Transatlantic Data Flows: EU–US Privacy Shield," February 2, 2016 (Last Accessed on 24 August 2016). [Online]. Available: http://europa.eu/rapid/press-release_IP-16-216_en.htm

[24] S. Colclasure, "The EU Privacy Shield One Week In: A Privacy Exec's Perspective," August 10, 2016 (Last Accessed on 24 August 2016). [Online]. Available: http://venturebeat.com/2016/08/10/the-eu-privacy-shield-one-week-in-a-privacy-execs-perspective/

[25] F. Gilbert and M.-J. Van Der Heijden, *EU–U.S. Privacy Shield 2.0 Signed, Sealed and Delivered.* Bloomberg BNA – Privacy and Security Law Report, July 7, 2016, iSSN 1538-3423 (Last Accessed on 24 August 2016). [Online]. Available: https://www.bna.com/euus-privacy-shield-n57982076797/

[26] "EU Data Protection Directive," 1995 (Last Accessed on 6 April 2016). [Online]. Available: http://eur-lex.europa.eu/legal-content/EN/TXT/PDF/?uri=CELEX:31995L0046&from=en

[27] Council of European Union, "Directive 2009/136/EC," 2009 (Last Accessed on 3 August 2016). [Online]. Available: http://eur-lex.europa.eu/legal-content/EN/TXT/HTML/?uri=CELEX:32009L0136&from=EN

[28] Council of European Union, "Directive 2006/24/EC," 2006 (Last Accessed on 3 August 2016). [Online]. Available: http://eur-lex.europa.eu/LexUriServ/LexUriServ.do?uri=OJ:L:2006:105:0054:0063:EN:PDF

[29] EUGDPR.org, "GDPR Key Changes," (Last Accessed on 13 December 2016). [Online]. Available: http://www.eugdpr.org/key-changes.html

[30] A. Macrae, "GDPR – The Good, the Bad and the Ugly," February 23, 2016 (Last Accessed on 12 January 2017). [Online]. Available: https://www.tripwire.com/state-of-security/security-awareness/gdpr-the-good-the-bad-and-the-ugly/

[31] A. Olshanskaya, "Why the GDPR Is Good for Business," December 15, 2016 (Last Accessed on 12 January 2017). [Online]. Available: https://iapp.org/news/a/why-the-gdpr-is-good-for-businesses/

[32] S. M. Lisa Mays, "The Schrems Decision: How the End of Safe Harbor Affects Your FCPA Compliance Plan," November 12, 2015 (Last Accessed on 27 August 2016). [Online]. Available: http://www.globaltradelawblog.com/2015/11/12/the-schrems-decision-how-the-end-of-safe-harbor-affects-your-fcpa-compliance-plan/

[33] "The Court of Justice Declares that the Commission's US Safe Harbour Decision Is Invalid," October 6, 2015 (Last Accessed on 4 April 2016). [Online]. Available: http://curia.europa.eu/jcms/upload/docs/application/pdf/2015-10/cp150117en.pdf

[34] "Google Spain v. AEPD and Mario Costeja González (C-131/12)," 2014 (Last Accessed on 6 April 2016). [Online]. Available: http://curia.europa.eu/juris/document/document_print.jsf?doclang=EN&docid=152065

[35] "Factsheet on the 'Right to Be Forgotten' Ruling" (Last Accessed on 7 April 2016). [Online]. Available: http://ec.europa.eu/justice/data-protection/files/factsheets/factsheet_data_protection_en.pdf

[36] L. Laudati, "Summaries of EU Court Decisions Relating to Data Protection 2000–2015," January 28, 2016 (Last Accessed on 27 August 2016). [Online]. Available: https://ec.europa.eu/anti-fraud/sites/antifraud/files/caselaw_2001_2015_en.pdf

[37] E. Ortiz, "San Bernardino Shooting: Timeline of How the Rampage Unfolded," December 3, 2015 (Last Accessed on 27 August 2016). [Online]. Available: http://www.nbcnews.com/storyline/san-bernardino-shooting/san-bernardino-shooting-timeline-how-rampage-unfolded-n473501

[38] T. Cook, "Answers to Your Questions about Apple and Security," February 16, 2016 (Last Accessed on 29 August 2016). [Online]. Available: https://www.apple.com/customer-letter/answers/

[39] A. Kharpal, "Apple vs FBI: All You Need to Know," March 29, 2016 (Last Accessed on 29 August 2016). [Online]. Available: http://www.cnbc.com/2016/03/29/apple-vs-fbi-all-you-need-to-know.html

[40] K. Zetter, "Apple's FBI Battle Is Complicated. Here's What's Really Going On," February 18, 2016 (Last Accessed on 29 August 2016). [Online]. Available: https://www.wired.com/2016/02/apples-fbi-battle-is-complicated-heres-whats-really-going-on/

[41] D. Sulivan, "How Google's New Right to Be Forgotten Form Works: An Explainer," May 30, 2014 (Last Accessed on 28 July 2016). [Online]. Available: http://searchengineland.com/google-right-to-be-forgotten-form-192837

[42] L. Clark, "Google's 'Right to Be Forgotten' Response Is 'disappointingly clever'," May 30, 2014 (Last Accessed on 28 July 2016). [Online]. Available: http://www.wired.co.uk/article/google-right-to-be-forgotten-form

[43] D. Sulivan, "Google to Remove Right-To-Be-Forgotten Links Worldwide, For Searchers in European Countries," February 10, 2016 (Last Accessed on 28 July 2016). [Online]. Available: http://searchengineland.com/google-to-remove-all-right-to-be-forgotten-links-from-european-index-242235

[44] "The Right to Be Forgotten – Between Expectations and Practice," November 20, 2012 (Last Accessed on 28 July 2016). [Online]. Available: https://www.enisa.europa.eu/publications/the-right-to-be-forgotten

[45] "Data Protection Laws of the World" (Last Accessed on 30 August 2016). [Online]. Available: https://www.dlapiperdataprotection.com #handbook/world-map-section

[46] "Global Heat Map" (Last Accessed on 30 August 2016). [Online]. Available: http://heatmap.forrestertools.com/

[47] H. Shey, E. Iannopollo, M. Barnes, S. Balaouras, A. Ma, and B. Nagel, "Privacy, Data Protection, and Cross-Border Data Transfer Trends in Asia Pacific," March 4, 2005 (Last Accessed on 30 August 2016). [Online]. Available: https://www.forrester.com/report/Privacy+Data+Protection+And+CrossBorder+Data+Transfer+Trends+In + Asia + Pacific/-/E-RES131051# figure2

[48] J. Rohlmeier, "International Data Protection Legislation Matrix" (Last Accessed on 30 August 2016). [Online]. Available: http://web.ita.doc.gov/ITI/ itiHome.nsf/51a29d31d11b7ebd85256cc600599b80/4947d6deb021a9648525 6d48006403af?OpenDocument

[49] Baker & McKenzie, "Global Privacy Handbook," 2016 (Last Accessed on 30 August 2016). [Online]. Available: http://globalprivacymatrix. bakermckenzie.com/

[50] Baker & McKenzie, "Firm Facts," 2016 (Last Accessed on 30 August 2016). [Online]. Available: http://www.bakermckenzie.com/-/media/files/about-us/firm-facts-final.pdf?la=en

[51] M. Cartwright, "Rosetta Stone," January 3, 2014 (Last Accessed on 16 December 2016). [Online]. Available: http://www.ancient.eu/Rosetta_Stone/

[52] "EU Countries Ranked for 'influence potential'," July 29, 2009 (Last Accessed on 28 April 2016). [Online]. Available: http://www.euractiv.com/ section/future-eu/news/eu-countries-ranked-for-influence-potential/

Chapter 12

Data provenance in cloud

Alan Yu Shyang Tan[1], Sivadon Chaisiri[1], Ryan Ko Kok Leong[1], Geoff Holmes[1], and Bill Rogers[1]

Abstract

One of the barriers of cloud adoption is the security of data stored in the cloud. In this chapter, we introduce data provenance and briefly show how it is applicable for data security in the cloud. Building on this, we discuss the underlying question of how data provenance, required for empowering data security in the cloud, can be acquired. The strengths and weaknesses of two methodologies for provenance acquisition, active collection and reconstruction, are discussed. The goal is to provide an understanding on the current state-of-the-art for generating provenance, such that better methodologies and solutions can be developed.

12.1 Data provenance and its application

12.1.1 What is data provenance?

Data provenance is defined as the information that depicts the derivation history of a piece of data [1]. Ideally, it shows how the data reaches its current state, since its creation [2]. Data provenance is often conceptualised as a graph that captures the entities involved in the derivation process and the relationships between those entities [3–5].

Because of its relational properties and the information it captures, data provenance is often used for tracking data transformations that happened in the past or tracing the source of the data. For example, quality and trustworthiness of a data is assessed by analysing its creation process, how the data is being published and accessed and the parties that signed the data using the data provenance [6]. In [7], the authors discussed several use cases in which provenance can be used to audit, reproduce and verify experimental workflows. Miles *et al.* discussed how provenance can be used to troubleshoot experimental workflows, such that the source of errors in data can be found and fixed [8].

[1]Cyber Security Lab, University of Waikato, New Zealand

From these examples, one can observe data provenance is useful for addressing issues questions the *why*, *how* and *where* [9] of data. Addressing these questions becomes more relevant when it comes to data in the cloud. Kaufman highlighted cloud users not knowing where their data is stored as a main concern in his discussion on data security in the cloud [10]. The abstraction offered in cloud services further complicate matters when it comes to enforcing legal requirements surrounding data management, such as the compliance checking and auditing. Because of these concerns, there is an incentive to apply data provenance to cloud. In addition, the use of data provenance is not limited to just data auditing and verification. It can also be used for data security.

12.1.2   Applying data provenance to data security

Instead of determining the security aspects (e.g. confidentiality, authenticity and integrity) of data by looking at opinions and viewpoints of its sources, Moitra *et al.* focused on how the data was communicated. Using subjective logic, each piece of data is assigned three information assurance values, *belief*, *disbelief* and *uncertainty*. Weaknesses and strengths of how the data has been managed are then uncovered by analysing the data provenance. The information assurance values of the data are then assigned according to the evidences discovered. For example, if a piece of data is found to have been signed using Message Digest 5 (MD5), the data will be given a low belief and high uncertainty rating. This is so as MD5 has been demonstrated to be vulnerable [11]. Through the information assurance values, a user of the data can decide whether the data is trustworthy. Park *et al.* discussed how the Open Provenance Model (OPM) [12] is used to model the sharing and modification of data in a group collaboration environment [13]. Using the modelled provenance, users can analyse and verify if the data has been modified or handled in an untrusted manner or by untrusted groups.

In [14,15], data provenance as a form of security control is discussed. Data provenance that captures the transformation and access of the data is attached to it. In doing so, different versions of the data (e.g. copying and pasting of data) can be audited and its integrity checked. These checks may be executed as part of a company's data security policies that govern the management and use of data.

Using data provenance collected from systems, References [16–18] discuss how it is used to detect and trace data leakages and how data leaked can be identified. The discussed approaches focused on identifying and analysing applications that have interacted with the data, so as to discover the source and point of the leakage. For example, Yu *et al.* [17] generates profiles of sensitive data leakage path through the analysis of the provenance graph. Generated profiles are then used to detect applications that are responsible for the leakage. Jiang *et al.* [16] used colour tainting techniques to taint system call traces of processes that interacted with critical data. Once detected, origins of the data leakage (e.g. infiltration point) and applications responsible are uncovered by back-tracing the diffusion of colour taints.

The literature discussed thus far is only a sample of the research looking at how data provenance can be used for the assurance and security of data. However, they offer a glimpse of what data provenance can offer to the cloud. Having said that, these research focus on the usage of data provenance. Few have discussed how the data

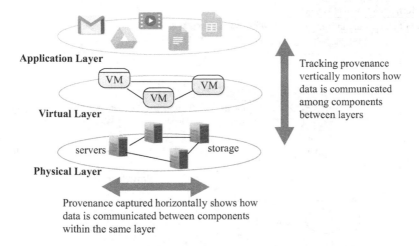

Figure 12.1   Tracking of data provenance in the cloud infrastructure

provenance, on which their proposed solution relies on, is obtained. In this rest of this chapter, we discuss how data provenance can be acquired in the cloud.

12.2   Data provenance in cloud

12.2.1   Scope of the discussion

Unlike traditional computer systems, the cloud infrastructure consists of multiple layers such as the application, physical and virtual layer [19,20]. Each layer may handle the same piece of data in a different manner and independent of other layers. For example, in the physical layer, a file may be stored as multiple blocks but in the virtual layer, the file may be stored as a virtual object. Data may also be passed between layers as users interact with the data. As a result, provenance needs to be tracked vertically as data is passed between layers. Likewise, provenance needs to be tracked horizontally as it is being managed by different components within the same layer. The two types of tracking required in cloud are illustrated in Figure 12.1. The challenges of tracking provenance across layers have been well discussed in literature such as [20–22] and as such, will not be discussed here. Instead, the discussion in this chapter focuses on techniques and solutions for acquiring data provenance within a layer.

12.2.2   Log files is not provenance

In the context of computer systems (e.g. cloud and servers), one of the common misconception of provenance is its equivalence to a log file. We use a mail delivery system, illustrated in Figure 12.2, as an example to explain the differences between the two.

Most mail delivery system used in modern world consists of a network of depots for collecting and sorting of mail items due for delivery. At each depot, items received are catalogued and sorted based on their destination addresses. The details of the items

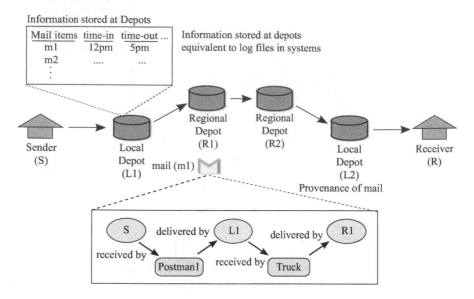

Figure 12.2   Illustration of the mail delivery system example

received, time it was received at the depot, time it was sent out of the depot and other information are tracked at the depot. However, each depot does not track where or which other depots the item had passed through prior to it reaching the depot. Similarly, log files are considered to be the result of logging mechanisms deployed at specific points within a computer system. Most of these mechanisms only capture events observed within their assigned scope and perspective. For example, a logger for an application only captures events happening in relation to the application and within the application's execution space (e.g. memory region or execution stack). Thus relationships between objects and processes outside the scope of the application (e.g. across other log files) are unknown.

On the other hand, provenance of a data describes how the data is managed and accessed by different applications and entities in a system. As such, it contains information that intersects with different log files. Referencing the mail example, provenance of the mail shows the origin of the mail, the depots that have processed the mail and other information that describes how the mail eventually reaches the current depot. This provenance can be retrieved from a centralised system, that stores information from all depots, using the bar code or ID assigned to each mail item.

Because of its relational properties, provenance is commonly visualised as a graph, as shown in the example illustrated in Figure 12.2. On the other hand, visualising events in a log file (e.g. an application log) will result in a graph that shows the states and objects the application interacted with directly connected to the node representing the application. The resulting graph is similar to a 'one-step' provenance graph, as illustrated in Figure 12.3.

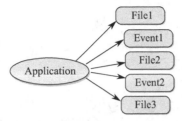

Figure 12.3 Example of a graph that visualises a log file

Hence, to capture information that allow the relational aspects and the entities of the provenance graph to be modelled, customised tools and techniques are required.

12.3 Acquiring data provenance from cloud

Approaches for acquiring data provenance from within a layer can be generalised into two categories – active collection and reconstruction.

12.3.1 Active provenance collection

Active provenance collection generally refers to pro-actively capture provenance during system runtime. In their discussion on the different types of provenance collectors,[1] Allen *et al.* [23] list the following methods of collection:

1. Operating system observation
2. Application reporting
3. Multiple system coordination points observation

12.3.1.1 Operating system observation

Provenance collectors that observe the operating system (OS) monitor key system components such as the kernel for events that can be used for inferring relationships between entities. For example, solutions such as PASS [24], SPADE [25], Komadu [26] and Progger [27], instrument the system kernel for capturing system calls pertaining to file and data communication executed by processes. Using a provenance model, such as OPM [12] or PROV [28,29], the captured events are modelled into provenance relations that describe the interactions between the processes, files and other observed entities.

The main advantage of capturing provenance through observing the OS is the breath of events that can be collected. System components such as the kernel and file system are jointly used by all applications running on the system. Hence, by

---

[1]We adopt the term provenance collectors for solutions that actively collects provenance from systems.

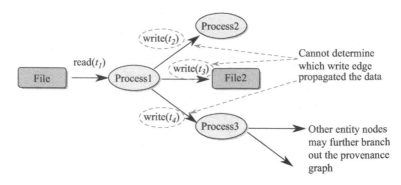

Figure 12.4   Inability to accurately determine causally dependent relations leads to an explosion of nodes and edges in the provenance graph

monitoring the system through these components, the proposed solutions are able to observe the activities of each application.

However, because these components operate at the fine-grained layer of the system. Events observed are detailed, high volume and semantically mismatched to user activities observed in the more coarse-grained layers of the system (e.g. user layer) [30]. For example, an event that shows an application reading data from a file can be translated to a series of *read* system calls in the kernel. Just by looking at the system calls, it is difficult to deduce whether the series of *read* calls are generated from a single or multiple *read* events in the application layer. Another major downside with capturing provenance through observing the OS is the dependency explosion problem [31].

Given two events, A and B, B is said to be causally dependent on A ($A \rightarrow B$), if, A happens before B and B is generally dependent on A [32]. An example of a pair of causally dependent system call is when an application *read* data from a file and *write* the data to other objects. If the *write* happens after the *read*, the *write* is considered to be causally dependent on the *read*. This is so as the application needs to first obtain the data before it can output the data.

Due to a lack of semantics, relating to the data or the activity, being captured, it is difficult to discern whether a pair of causally dependent input–output system call is related. A single *read* from an entity may be connected to a group of *writes* executed by the same entity after the *read*. In such situations, it is difficult to accurately determine which other entities did the data being read propagated to. As a result, all causally dependent edges and their sub-graphs will have to be included into the provenance. To complicate matters, the other entities may further branch out the graph, causing an explosion of nodes and edges in the provenance graph. This end result is an explosion of dependencies, as illustrated in Figure 12.4.

12.3.1.2   Application reporting

Another alternative to collecting provenance in systems is to modify applications managing the data to output provenance information whenever the relevant functions are executed. Although considered intrusive, it is less so compared to collectors that observes the OS as the modifications are confined to applications being monitored.

The advantages of solutions that instrument applications are its flexibility in how reporting can be done and the ability to capture a certain level of semantics. Because these solutions entail modifying the application source code, the programmer can decide how the reporting is to be done. Take for example a *while* loop function that reads all data from a file. The programmer instrumenting the application can choose to output a provenance relation to denote the application successfully reading the file by placing the reporting code outside of the loop at the end. Likewise, the programmer can also choose to output the number of reads executed by placing the reporting code within the loop. Similarly, because of access to the source code, the programmer can have knowledge of the behaviour of the application. Such knowledge can influence how and where the reporting codes are placed. As a result, analysts will be able to better relate the provenance generated to the activities of the applications or users.

The main limitation of instrumenting applications is that the generated provenance is constrained to the scope of the applications being modified. As explained in Section 12.2.2, data provenance can span across multiple applications. However, because the reporting codes are instrumented into the source code, only activities happening within the execution scope of the application can be reported. In the situation where the data is managed by applications not instrumented, gaps where no information is acquired will result in the generated provenance graph. Recognising this limitation proposed solutions, such as PASOA [8], Burrito [33] and E-notebook [34], target middlewares (e.g. workflow engines) used by a group of applications whose provenance is to be collected. This limitation also implies that users are constrained to the set of instrumented applications if provenance is to be generated.

12.3.1.3   Multiple system coordination points observation

The third method for actively collecting provenance off systems is by monitoring coordination points between different systems and applications. Examples of coordination points are external network interfaces, proxy servers and application messaging services. By monitoring requests made and the data passing through these coordination points, provenance collectors are able to capture and model activities happening between different entities (i.e. system and applications). The modification of the Enterprise Service Bus (ESB) [35] by Allen *et al.* [30,36] is an example of provenance collectors that monitor multiple system coordination points. Such a system is ideal for a cloud environment as it is fundamentally composed of a set of services coordinated by a set of key applications (e.g. cloud controller and hypervisor).

Because the modification is done at the coordination software (e.g. ESB, message queue services), the number of applications that needs modification is reduced. Users are also not constrained to a set of end user applications. Some coordination software even provides libraries and application programming interface (API) for logging and monitoring purposes. Due to these reasons, monitoring coordination points is considered less intrusive as compared to the other two methods discussed thus far. Having said that, because the monitoring is done outside the scope of applications

Table 12.1   Comparing methods used for active provenance collection

	Degree of intrusiveness	Scope of provenance	Granularity	Semantics of activity
OS observation	High	System wide	Fine-grained	✗
Application reporting	Moderate	Application specific	Coarse-grained	✓
Coordination point observation	Low	Point specific	Coarse-grained	✓

that managed the data, provenance that shows how the data is being transformed by those applications is unknown.

12.3.1.4   Overhead costs

Table 12.1 compares the discussed methods for actively collecting provenance from systems.

A point to note is that these methods are not mutually exclusive. Depending on the provenance required, one or more different types of provenance collectors can be used. However, the overhead cost that comes with actively monitoring the system should also be considered when deploying such solutions. Carata *et al.* [3] highlighted storage and computation as the two main overhead induced by active provenance collectors. Monitoring places extra load on the system as cycles are required to capture and output information. Depending on the volume and velocity of events, computational overhead may vary between 1% and 23% [24,37]. Similarly, storing the information on disk incurs disk storage overhead that increases with time. Another common disadvantage of actively collecting provenance is the requirement for modifications and the introduction of new monitoring software. Because most systems are by default non-provenance-aware, introducing new software or modifying existing applications are shunned due to concerns for security and stability of the system. Since cloud systems are fundamentally composed of a set of services working in tandem, it is important that the inter-operability, stability and security between services be tested when deploying active provenance collectors.

12.3.2   Reconstructing provenance

Due to its intrusive nature and potential overhead costs on the system, actively collecting provenance from the underlying system is not always practical. Recent research in provenance has turned to reconstruction as an alternative approach to acquiring provenance. The fundamental concept is to reconstruct data provenance using information found on the system. The following discussion focuses on research looking at reconstructing the entire provenance graph. While there are other related research looking at how an incomplete provenance can be reconstructed, they are not discussed here due to the assumption that some form of provenance is available. Such an assumption deviates from our discussion on how provenance can be acquired.

Assuming a scenario where the provenance for a set of critical files (e.g. medical records) or data is lost, an intuitive approach is to infer the relationship between files, thereby reconstructing the data provenance, by comparing the content between files. Magliacane *et al.* [38,39], Deolalikar and Laffitte [40] and Aierken *et al.* [41] proposed using similarity measures such as cosine similarity and longest common subsequence to compare and determine if two files are related. Files found to be related are then grouped and ordered based on timestamps, such as date of creation, found in their metadata. The ordered group of files then forms the coarse-grained provenance for the oldest file, showing the order of revisions for that file. The underlying assumption is that different revisions of a file would bear similarities in content between different revisions. However, there are two weaknesses in the proposed solutions. First, the reconstructed provenance only shows the possible order of transformation sequence, from the original file till the latest revision. The output does not capture details on how and what were the changes between revisions. Second, the approaches do not consider the case where the content of two revisions of the same file can be drastically different.

Nies *et al.* [42] recognised these two weaknesses and proposed a solution that compares two pieces of data (e.g. news articles, files) based on their semantic properties. Information such as *named entities* and descriptive metadata annotations that are embedded in the file are extracted as semantic properties of the data. The authors argued comparing two pieces of data at the semantic level allow the relationship between the data to be established even if the contents differed in length or words used. Details of changes made between two directly dependent revisions are then inferred by identifying the differences in content. These differences are then modelled into fine-grained provenance relations using concepts defined in the PROV-DM model [43].

Although these solutions show data provenance can potentially be reconstructed by comparing the similarity between two pieces of data, the approach is not scalable as the number of data pieces (e.g. virtual objects) or files increases. In public cloud storage services, such as Dropbox, it is common to find more than millions of file objects belonging to different users stored in the underlying infrastructure. As such, scalability of the approach is a factor that cannot be overlooked when considering alternative approaches for acquiring provenance from a cloud environment.

Groth *et al.* [44] explored the idea of formulating data provenance reconstruction as an Artificial Intelligence (AI) planning problem. The authors assumed the set of transformations that can take place between two pieces of data, the initial and final state of a piece of data are known. A prototype, based on A* search [45], that searches for all possible sequence of transformations that can explain how the data reaches its final state is built. However, the authors highlight the search space being unbounded and the possibility of the algorithm returning incomplete results as challenges that needs to be addressed before the approach is viable.

Deviating from the use of information surrounding the data, Huq *et al.* [46] analysed the source code of a given application.[2] Based on the grammar used in the

---

[2] In the cited paper, the authors analysed Python scripts. Hence, the term 'script' is used in place of source code.

analysed code, an abstract syntax tree is generated. The proposed graph building engine then parses through the syntax tree, generating a new object for every node in the tree. Users are prompted for details, such as whether the node is reading or writing data, for each object generated. The end result is a provenance graph that describes the workflow of the application and shows how data is being transformed within the application's execution space. Unfortunately, such a provenance graph does not show how data is being communicated or transformed outside of the application's execution space.

The type of reconstruction algorithm that can be applied to cloud heavily relies on the type of information obtainable from the environment (e.g. algorithm that works on the physical layer may not work for virtual layer). Current proposed approaches face issues such as unbounded search space for the possible sequence of transformation and ability to reconstruct fine-grained provenance. These issues will need to be resolved before provenance reconstruction can become a viable alternative for acquiring provenance in the cloud.

12.4   Conclusion and future challenges

On-going research on the applications of provenance have provided insights into its potential for enabling data security. However, little is mentioned on how the required provenance can be acquired in those work. In this chapter, we looked at two methodologies that can be used for acquiring data provenance in cloud systems – active provenance collection and reconstructing provenance.

Solutions that actively collect provenance monitor the underlying system or applications for events that are relevant to data provenance in real-time. Through the observed events, provenance relations that describe the interaction and relationship between data and other entities are modelled. Since the events are observed in real time, the resulting provenance relations are viewed with high confidence (e.g. users are assured that the relationship does exists and is valid). Having said that, the drawbacks of active provenance collection, such as the overhead cost and the need to modify the underlying system, are grounds for new and better methodologies for acquiring provenance. Acquiring provenance through reconstructing it from information found on the system is an on-going endeavour for alternative methodologies. Information that is leveraged on for the reconstruction can range from source code of applications running on the system to the data itself. Although reconstructing provenance does not have the associated overhead incurred from actively monitoring the system, provenance produced is by means of inference. This associates a certain level of uncertainty to the reconstructed provenance. In addition, there are still issues, such as the ability to reconstruct fine-grained provenance and the large search space for possible sequence of transformation, that needs to be resolved before reconstruction can be a viable solution for provenance acquisition.

The two discussed methodologies for acquiring provenance focused on how provenance can be collected from the underlying system. However, the following would need to be addressed before a complete and fool-proof solution can be arrived at.

- **Data provenance outside of cloud** – Regardless of whether it is actively collected or reconstructed, the discussed solutions focused on provenance that shows how data is transformed within the system. However, in practice, data is frequently communicated between different systems (e.g. the Internet). A 'blind spot' will result in the provenance if the data is moved off the system, modified and replaced with the modified version. New solutions will need to be developed for tracking provenance of data outside of the system. An example is the concept of encapsulating the data within a self-executing container before the data is allowed to leave the cloud, discussed by Tan *et al.* [47]. The container provides the platform on which changes made to the data can be logged and reported back to the main system. However, the issues such as integrity and security of the information collected still need to be addressed.
- **Correctness of provenance** – A piece of information is only as good as its source. An approach for verifying information collected using the monitoring mechanisms used for active provenance collection and information used for reconstruction is required. For example, Hasan *et al.* [48] discussed how encryption and chain-hashing can be used to provide provenance with tamper-evident capabilities. However, the correctness and integrity of the information produced by the source (e.g. monitoring mechanism) is not discussed. If an attacker tampers with the mechanism, such that incorrect information is generated, the errors induced will propagate to the resulting provenance. This applies for information sources used for provenance reconstruction. Hence, it is important that the source and the information can be verified.

References

[1]   Y. L. Simmhan, B. Plale, and D. Gannon, "A Survey of Data Provenance in e-Science," *ACM SIGMOD Record*, vol. 34, no. 3, pp. 31–36, 2005. [Online]. Available: http://doi.acm.org/10.1145/1084805.1084812

[2]   Y. S. Tan, R. K. L. Ko, and G. Holmes, "Security and Data Accountability in Distributed Systems: A Provenance Survey," in *Proceedings of the 15th IEEE International Conference on High Performance Computing and Communications (HPCC'13)*, 2013.

[3]   L. Carata, S. Akoush, N. Balakrishnan, *et al.*, "A Primer on Provenance," *Communications of the ACM*, vol. 57, no. 5, pp. 52–60, May 2014.

[4]   S. M. S. D. Cruz, M. L. M. Campos, and M. Mattoso, "Towards a Taxonomy of Provenance in Scientific Workflow Management Systems," in *IEEE Congress on Services*, 2009, pp. 259–266.

[5]   L. Moreau, "The Foundation for Provenance on the Web," *Foundations and Trends in Web Science, Journal*, vol. 2, pp. 99–241, 2010.

[6] O. Hartig, "Provenance Information in the Web of Data," in *Proceedings of the World Wide Web 2009 Workshop on Linked Data on the Web (LDOW'09)*, April 2009.

[7] S. Miles, P. Groth, M. Branco, and L. Moreau, "The Requirements of Using Provenance in e-Science Experiments," *Journal of Grid Computing*, vol. 5, pp. 1–25, 2007.

[8] S. Miles, E. Deelman, P. Groth, K. Vahi, G. Mehta, and L. Moreau, "Connecting Scientific Data to Scientific Experiments with Provenance," in *Proceedings of the Third IEEE International Conference on e-Science and Grid Computing (e-Science'07)*, 10–13 December 2007, pp. 179–186, Bangalore, India.

[9] J. Cheney, L. Chiticariu, and W.-C. Tan, "Provenance in Databases: Why, How and Where," *Foundations and Trends in Databases, Journal*, vol. 1, no. 4, pp. 379–474, 2007.

[10] L. M. Kaufman, "Data Security in the World of Cloud Computing," *IEEE Security and Privacy*, vol. 7, no. 4, pp. 61–64, Jul. 2009. [Online]. Available: http://dx.doi.org/10.1109/MSP.2009.87

[11] A. Sotirov, M. Stevens, J. Appelbaum, *et al.*, "MD5 Considered Harmful Today," http://www.win.tue.nl/hashclash/rogue-ca/ (Last accessed: 08/03/2017), Dec. 2008.

[12] L. Moreau, B. Clifford, J. Freire, *et al.*, "The Open Provenance Model Core Specification (v1.1)," *Future Generation Computer Systems*, vol. 27, no. 6, pp. 743–756, Jun. 2011. [Online]. Available: http://eprints.soton.ac.uk/271449/

[13] J. Park, D. Nguyen, and R. Sandhu, "On Data Provenance in Group-Centric Secure Collaboration," in *Collaborative Computing: Networking, Applications and Worksharing (CollaborateCom), 2011 Seventh International Conference on*. IEEE, 15–18 October 2011, pp. 221–230, Orlando, Florida, USA.

[14] B. Corcoran, N. Swamy, and M. Hicks, "Combining Provenance and Security Policies in a Web-based Document Management System," in *On-Line Proceedings of the Workshop on Principles of Provenance (PrOPr)*, Nov. 2007, http://homepages.inf.ed.ac.uk/jcheney/propr/

[15] A. Martin, J. Lyle, and C. Namilkuo, "Provenance as a Security Control," in *Proceedings of the Fourth USENIX Workshop on the Theory and Practice of Provenance*. Boston, MA: USENIX, 2012. [Online]. Available: https://www.usenix.org/conference/tapp12/workshop-program/presentation/Martin

[16] X. Jiang, A. Walters, F. Buchholz, D. Xu, Y.-M. Wang, and E. H. Spafford, "Provenance-Aware Tracing of Worm Break-in and Contaminations: A Process Coloring Approach," in *Proceedings of 26th IEEE International Conference on Distributed Computing Systems (ICDCS'06)*, 2006, pp. 890–902.

[17] J. Yu, S. Zhang, P. Liu, and Z. Li, "LeakProber: A Framework for Profiling Sensitive Data Leakage Paths," in *Proceedings of the First ACM Conference on Data and Application Security and Privacy (CODASPY'11)*, 2011, pp. 75–84.

[18] S. Jones, C. Strong, D. D. E. Long, and E. L. Miller, "Tracking Emigrant Data via Transient Provenance," in *Proceedings of the Third USENIX Workshop on the Theory and Practice of Provenance (TaPP'11)*, Jun. 2011.

[19] Y. Jadeja and K. Modi, "Cloud Computing – Concepts, Architecture and Challenges," in *Proceedings of the International Conference on Computing, Electronics and Electrical Technologies*. Piscataway, NJ: IEEE, Mar. 2012.

[20] I. M. Abbadi and J. Lyle, "Challenges for Provenance in Cloud Computing," in *Proceedings of the Third USENIX Workshop on the Theory and Practice of Provenance*, 2011, Heraklion, Crete, Greece. [Online]. Available: https://www.usenix.org/conference/tapp11/challenges-provenance-cloud-computing

[21] M. Imran and H. Hlavacs, "Provenance in the Cloud: Why and How?," in *Proceedings of the Third International Conference on Cloud Computing, Grids and Virtualization (CLOUD COMPUTING 2012)*, 2012.

[22] K.-K. Muniswamy-Reddy, P. Macko, and M. Seltzer, "Making a Cloud Provenance-Aware," in *Proceedings of the First Workshop on the Theory and Practice of Provenance (TaPP)*. USENIX, Feb. 2009. [Online]. Available: http://www.usenix.org/events/tapp09/tech/full_papers/muniswamy-reddy/muniswamy-reddy_html/

[23] M. D. Allen, L. Seligman, B. Blaustein, and A. Chapman, "Provenance Capture and Use: A Practical Guide," The MITRE Corporation, Tech. Rep., 15 June 2010. [Online]. Available: https://www.mitre.org/sites/default/files/publications/practical-provenance-guide-MP100128.pdf

[24] K.-K. Muniswamy-Reddy, D. A. Holland, U. Braun, and M. Seltzer, "Provenance-aware Storage Systems," in *Proceedings of the Conference on USENIX'06 Annual Technical Conference (ATEC'06)*, 2006, p. 4.

[25] A. Gehani and D. Tariq, "SPADE: Support for Provenance Auditing in Distributed Environments," in *Middleware 2012*, ser. Lecture Notes in Computer Science, P. Narasimhan and P. Triantafillou, Eds. Berlin: Springer, 2012, vol. 7662, pp. 101–120. [Online]. Available: http://dx.doi.org/10.1007/978-3-642-35170-9_6

[26] I. Suriarachchi, Q. G. Zhou, and B. Plale, "Komadu: A Capture and Visualization System for Scientific Data Provenance," *Open Research Software*, vol. 3, no. 1, pp. 1–7, 2015.

[27] M. A. W. Ryan and K.L. Ko, "Progger: A Efficient, Tamper-Evident Kernel-Space Logger for Cloud Data Provenance Tracking," in *Proceedings of the Seventh IEEE International Conference on Cloud Computing (CLOUD'14)*, Anchorage, Alaska, USA, June 2014.

[28] L. Moreau and P. Groth, *Provenance: An Introduction to PROV. Synthesis Lectures on the Semantic Web: Theory and Technology*. San Rafael, CA: Morgan & Claypool, 2013.

[29] L. Moreau, P. Missier, K. Belhajjame, *et al.*, "PROV-DM: The PROV Data Model," Retrieved: 04/09/2014 from W3C Recommendations, April 2013. [Online]. Available: http://www.w3.org/TR/prov-dm/

[30] G. B. Coe., R. C. Doty, M. D. Allen, and A. Chapman, "Provenance Capture Disparities Highlighted through Datasets," in *Sixth Workshop on the Theory and Practice of Provenance, TaPP'14*, 12–13 June 2014, Cologne, Germany.

[31]   K. H. Lee, X. Zhang, and D. Xu, "High Accuracy Attack Provenance via Binary-based Execution Partition," in *Proceedings of Annual Network and Distributed System Security Symposium*, April 2013, San Diego, CA.

[32]   L. Lamport, "Time, Clocks, and the Ordering of Events in a Distributed System," *Communication of the ACM*, vol. 21, no. 7, pp. 558–565, Jul. 1978. [Online]. Available: http://doi.acm.org/10.1145/359545.359563

[33]   P. J. Guo and M. Seltzer, "Burrito: Wrapping Your Lab Notebook in Computational Infrastructure," in *USENIX Workshop on the Theory and Practice of Provenance (TaPP)*, 2012.

[34]   P. Ruth, D. Xu, B. Bhargava, and F. Regnier, "E-notebook Middleware for Accountability and Reputation Based Trust in Distributed Data Sharing Communities," in *Proceedings of Second International Conference on Trust Management*, 2004, pp. 161–175.

[35]   Mulesoft.org, "Anypoint Platform," https://developer.mulesoft.com/ (Last accessed: 14/03/17), 2017.

[36]   M. D. Allen, A. Chapman, B. Blaustein, and L. Seligman, *Capturing Provenance in the Wild*. Berlin: Springer, 2010, pp. 98–101. [Online]. Available: http://dx.doi.org/10.1007/978-3-642-17819-1_12

[37]   K.-K. Muniswamy-Reddy, U. Braun, D. A. Holland, *et al.*, "Layering in Provenance Systems," in *Proceedings of the 2009 Conference on USENIX Annual Technical Conference*, ser. USENIX'09. Berkeley, CA, USA: USENIX Association, 2009, pp. 10–10. [Online]. Available: http://dl.acm.org/citation.cfm?id=1855807.1855817

[38]   S. Magliacane, "Reconstructing Provenance," *The Semantic Web – ISWC*, pp. 399–406, 2012.

[39]   S. Magliacane and P. Groth, "Towards Reconstructing the Provenance of Clinical Guidelines," in *Proceedings of Fifth International Workshop on Semantic Web Applications and Tools for Life Science (SWAT4LS)*, vol. 952, 2012. [Online]. Available: http://ceur-ws.org/Vol-952/paper_36.pdf

[40]   V. Deolalikar and H. Laffitte, "Provenance as Data Mining: Combining File System Metadata with Content Analysis," in *Proceeding of First Workshop on Theory and Practice of Provenance (TAPP'09)*, 2009.

[41]   A. Aierken, D. B. Davis, Q. Zhang, K. Gupta, A. Wong, and H. U. Asuncion, "A Multi-level Funneling Approach to Data Provenance Reconstruction," in *Proceedings of the 2014 IEEE 10th International Conference on e-Science – Volume 02*, ser. E-SCIENCE'14. Washington, DC, USA: IEEE Computer Society, 2014, pp. 71–74. [Online]. Available: http://dx.doi.org/10.1109/eScience.2014.54

[42]   T. D. Nies, S. Coppens, D. V. Deursen, E. Mannens, and R. V. de Walle, "Automatic Discovery of High-Level Provenance using Semantic Similarity," in *Proceedings of the Fourth International Conference on Provenance and Annotation of Data and Processes (IPAW)*, 2012, pp. 97–110.

[43]   L. Moreau and P. Missier, "PROV-DM – W3C Working Group Note," https://www.w3.org/TR/2013/REC-prov-dm-20130430/ (Last accessed: 13/06/2016), April 2013.

[44] P. Groth, Y. Gil, and S. Magliacane, "Automatic Metadata Annotation through Reconstructing Provenance," in *Third International Workshop on the role of Semantic Web in Provenance Management (ESWC)*, 2012.

[45] P. E. Hart, N. J. Nilsson, and B. Raphael, "A Formal Basis for the Heuristic Determination of Minimum Cost Paths," *IEEE Transactions on Systems Science and Cybernetics*, vol. 4, no. 2, pp. 100–107, Feb. 1968.

[46] M. R. Huq, P. M. G. Apers, and A. Wombacher, "ProvenanceCurious: A Tool to Infer Data Provenance from Scripts," in *Proceedings of the 16th International Conference on Extending Database Technology (EDBT)*, 2013, pp. 765–768.

[47] Y. S. Tan, R. K. L. Ko, P. Jagadpramana, *et al.*, "Tracking of Data Leaving the Cloud," in *Proceedings of IEEE 11th International Conference on Trust, Security and Privacy in Computing and Communications (TrustCom'12)*, 2012.

[48] R. Hasan, R. Sion, and M. Winslett, "The Case of the Fake Picasso: Preventing History Forgery with Secure Provenance," in *Proceedings of the Seventh Conference on Files and Storage Technologies (FAST'09)*, 2009, pp. 1–14.

Chapter 13

Security visualization for cloud computing: an overview

Jeffery Garae[1], Ryan K. L. Ko[1], and Mark Apperley[1]

Abstract

Cloud services continue to attract organizations with advantages that enable subsidiary costs. While there are advantages, security in the cloud is an ongoing challenging process for cloud providers and users. Cyber-threats are penetrating cloud technologies and exposing flaws in the cloud technologies. Data Provenance as a Security Visualization Service (DPaaSVS) and Security Visualization as a Cloud Service (SVaaCS) for cloud technologies are solutions to help track and monitor data in the cloud. Either data is *at-rest* or in *in-transit*, security visualization empowers cloud providers and users to track and monitor their data movements. Security visualization refers to the concept of using visualization to represent security events. In this chapter, we (1) provide our security visualization standardized model and (2) provide the security visualization intelligence framework model and finally discuss several security visualization use-cases.

13.1 Introduction

Providing security for data in cloud computing has been achieved in many ways and methods, mainly by past and existing research, technology solutions and innovations. Cloud providers and platforms are offering attractive services which spans across the wider spectrum of both business and home users. However, existing solutions are tailored towards the interests of cloud providers and largely for business organizations but less for the cloud end-users. Traditional computer security technologies such as firewalls, antivirus solutions and web proxies that scan and filter malicious packets were the foundation of computer security. These solutions faced challenges when cloud technologies emerged. The ability to protect data from exploitation, data breach and data leakage has been a challenge. And while cloud technologies provide efficient

---

[1]Cyber Security Lab, Department of Computer Science, University of Waikato, New Zealand

services to desirable users [1], current cloud technology providers are faced with data security challenges. For example, an attacker is able to:

1. Carry out a Denial of Service (DoS) attack on the server.
2. Intercept data sent from client to the server.
3. Intercept and/or spoof the reply from the server to the client [2].

This chapter emphasizes on enhancing existing cloud computing security solutions with security visualization and most importantly addressing the users' queries such as: *what has happened to my data?, is my data secure in the cloud?* and *how can I know what is happening to my data* or *who is touching my data in the cloud?* We will be addressing these queries from the data collection and data storage point-of-view with examples from law enforcement investigations and operations.

However, in order for security visualization to be an effective added feature into cloud computing technologies, datasets are needed on a real-time state [3]. Datasets are the key to understanding what has happened over internal networks and over cloud infrastructures. This means logging mechanisms are required. A vast amount of data collected from security-related events such as logging mechanisms and social media logs requires analytics and intelligence tools to explore, analyze and report on security events. These are seen in current cyber security trends in technologies demanded by security research organizations and industries. Technology trends are in the area of data analytics and threat intelligence. For example, for law enforcement investigations threat intelligence tools around malware and ransomware attacks are of interest. Understanding malware and ransomware patterns, behavior and attack landscapes are of prime importance [4]. However, with existing intelligence tools, lack of data processing power and effective reporting features affects the investigation process [5]. This creates a difficult and tedious task for the entire investigation process. A solution to improving the time spent on analyzing and investigating such complex and large dataset is with the use of security visualization. In this chapter, we introduce our "Security Visualization Framework for Cloud Computing." The framework proposes the following features for cloud platforms:

1. Data Provenance as a Security Visualization Service (DPaaSVS)
2. Security Visualization as a Service (SVaaS)
3. User-centric Visualization Intelligence (UVI).

13.1.1 Motivation and objectives for this chapter

The motivation for this chapter is to highlight the importance of data security in cloud computing, stating the importance of adding visualization methodologies to measure how effective security visualization to cloud service reporting features. In return, it is a solution to the common user question – *is my data secure in the cloud?*

This chapter aims to return control of data to users with the use of security visualization for interactions between users (cloud customers) and security technologies in the cloud. The overall goal of this chapter is to share security ideas and insights on how security visualization can enhance cloud technologies with user-centric visual approaches for customers when using cloud services and providing situation awareness to the cloud users [6].

While visualization has been used across multiple research domains, ranging from its origins in art to medical/pharmaceutical domain, researchers and businesses are tapping into using visualization mainly for two purposes: visualization for exploration and visualization for reporting. The reason is that visualization facilitates the missing gap between an anxious user and the given medium examined (visualization, reports, etc.). Visualization allows users to psychologically and intellectually build visual views of the examined medium which naturally being processed by human perception and cognition.

Although there are many visualizations used out in cloud technologies and visualization domains, the focus of this chapter is on effective security visualization with use-cases primarily for law enforcement – "Threat Intelligence and Data Analytics," the use of user-centric visualizations and generally in other security organizations such as financial and academia. Sub objectives are stated below to address effective intelligence reporting as follows:

1. Provide a way forward to establishing a standardized law enforcement security visualization standard and model for security events reporting.
2. Provide the Security Visualization framework for cloud platforms.
3. Develop a security visualization intelligence (SVInt) prototype that acts as a central visualization framework in providing reports to law enforcement personals when needed.
4. Discuss a Bitcoin block chain visualization use-case that shows Bitcoin transaction relationships between Bitcoin wallets and transaction IDs. The aim of this visualization is to identify possible suspicious Bitcoin tags that are involved in law enforcement investigations.
5. Discuss how security visualization can be used to show cyber-threats around the world.

13.1.2 Chapter outline

Section 13.2 begins with providing background information around cloud technologies, visualization and data security. Data security in cloud computing workflow challenges is discussed to identify the gaps and set the need to provide alternative solutions. Analyzing the research gaps, the challenges, and the need to find user-centric security solutions for cloud computing technologies emerges with reasons to establish security models is discussed in Section 13.3. Security Visualization standard (SCeeL-VisT) with guidelines of how security visualization should be developed and used are presented in Section 13.3.2. SCeeL-VisT going on to establish our security visualization framework that consists of two main services, DPaaSVS and SVaaS, is discussed in Section 13.4. Both DPaaSVS and SVaaS aim to provide cloud users with security and situation awareness. Security visualization application use-cases for data security in cloud platforms are discussed in Section 13.4.1. Section 13.5

presents new use-cases with the law enforcement approach of leveraging security visualization for Bitcoin investigations and malware threat visualizations. Finally, Section 13.6 provides the concluding remarks of this chapter.

13.2   Background: security visualization and data security

The term *Security Visualization* refers to the concept of using visualization for security measures [7]. For example, visualizing unauthorized access, information-leakage, and tracking malicious web traffic [8–10]. Other purposes include data visual analytics and threat intelligence, i.e., tracking and monitoring of security-related events [8,10,11,40]. For cloud technologies, adding the concept of security visualization to existing cloud services creates a "trust" relationship between the services used and the users. Although cloud technologies offer visualization features, it is for the purpose of analytics and reporting. The need for real-time security visualization framework to enable users to see and observe data movement and even being alerted by the service of a suspicious threat is crucial [12].

Whether its public or private cloud, high-performance parallel computing with the cloud environment and cloud technologies by vendors allows users to provision large quantities of instances efficiently [13]. Cloud technologies are expanding throughout the Internet realm, offering a wide range of services beginning from business management platforms, data analytics tools to facilitating efficient means for Internet of Things (IoT) [14,15]. However, security has become a major concern for every cloud provider and cloud user. For providers, implementing proper secure platforms is a priority whereas for users, the ever growing thoughts of how secure their data is on the cloud is their main concern [16]. Therefore, there are always great needs to implement security applications, tools and techniques specifically targeting cloud providers and users, for example, secure tracking and monitoring of data movement and processes in SaaS infrastructure [17].

13.2.1   Security visualization for data security

Cloud computing leverages and enhances day-to-day business operations. While it is successful and has been envisioned as the modern method for information technology enterprises, it brings about many new security challenges. This prompts cyber security researchers and experts to find ways to solve these challenges. These challenges revolve around data/information security namely confidentiality, integrity and availability of the data in cloud computing.

An increase in the number of users browsing the web daily has brought the world into a rapid change and ever increase advantages and also disadvantages. Business intelligence and global network are some of the advantages rising in parallel to the technological shift. However, cyber-attacks are increasing rapidly as reported by security firms around the world. This brings a lot of work for professionals concerned over cyber-attacks such as cyber security researchers, law enforcement, and security analysts. On that note, current cyber security workflow, techniques and methodologies lack the assessment factor. Security visualization in a quick-to-action form with presentable insights directed towards law enforcement is a catalyst to minimize the time spent on addressing/analyzing cyber security issues.

Data security in organizations and Internet is made aware of through security situational awareness. Adding visualization tools to provide data security such as NVisionIP [18], PortVis [19] and VisFlowConnect [20] allows security experts to increase their knowledge on the current state of their network. NVisionIP's primary focus is on detection by leveraging on visual representation of suspected segments of the network. PortVis's emphasis is on security event data discovery. It monitors data flow over Transmission Control Protocol (TCP) ports for security events. The VisFlowConnect tool enhances the ability of security administrators to detect and investigate anomalous data traffic between an internal local network and external networks. With all the various functionalities mentioned above, these tools are able to discover and observe varieties of interesting network traffic patterns and behaviors.

However, there are continuous data security challenges especially for cloud technologies. These challenges which are listed [21] include:

- data privacy issues [22],
- user data confidentialities,
- the ability to control and secure sensitive corporate data,
- trust relationships among cloud providers and cloud users [23],
- system monitoring services and logs [24].

The data security challenges mentioned also affect how security visualization is used when representing security events and scenarios. The introduction of security visualization into data security research has helped to identify and expose specific security needs that are targeted to data in the cloud.

13.2.2 The need for security visualization

There are existing methods of keeping track of events on the cloud and providing analytic reports for cloud services. For example, Google Analytics [25] is used for web traffic monitoring and effectiveness analytics [26]. Amazon Web Services, Google App Engine, and Microsoft Azure have transformed cloud technologies to whole new level and driving business management services. However, with these cloud technologies, security in the cloud is a challenge. There is a great need for user-centric security technologies to empower and alert users [1].

Alternatively, law enforcement is also facing greater challenge when more than half of the business environments are migrating into cloud service technologies. Investigations are becoming difficult due to existing security tools capabilities to help solve investigations. Tracking and monitoring data movement and threats over the Internet becomes a huge challenge. Investigation reports often fall short with evidence integrity and genuineness and are difficult to be admissible to courts. Issues of preserving evidence and sharing information across secure challenges are also a challenge.

Data or information loss is a concerning factor transporting information across cloud platforms. Investigation datasets grow at a fast rate and there is a need to store them securely. For example, a number of social media posts, images, physical evidence, dump files' application logs, system logs, and network logs have been significantly grown. In addition, analyzing complex datasets can be a tedious task. Security visualization is a potential solution for law enforcement reporting. It has the ability to simplify complex amount of data (evidences, work processes, etc.) into simple, clear, and efficient quick-to-action visual representation that has an effective impact on all targeted audiences (e.g., CEOs, researchers, technical specialists, and even the law enforcement officers in general). Overall, security visualization for law enforcement aims to provide useful insights that can aid investigations and reports on daily operations within the law enforcement sector.

With a clear understanding of how cloud technologies are contributing to the Internet and the challenges surrounding the technology services available, the next section provides a prominent approach to empowering cloud providers and cloud users.

13.3   A security visualization standardization model

Often security requires standards, policies, and guidelines to help safeguard a set of platforms when organizations handle sensitive data. In order for any security model to effectively function, certain requirements have to be met. The requirements include standards, guidelines, policies, and trainings around security visualizations with the aim of providing the users with the most useful insights on certain visualization purposes.

Security visualization standards are published materials that attempt to safeguard the security visualization environment. It is important and largely contributes to how visualizations provide security insights to users. Understanding what makes a visualization useful depends on how simple, clear, effective, and appropriate the type of security event is intended to be visually represented. Effective security visualization approaches heavily rely on user perceptions and cognitive abilities to connect the dots between users and visualizations.

13.3.1   *Effective security visualization approaches*

For a security visualization to stand out and capture its audience, it should take into consideration of certain prerequisites. In the field of security visualization for cloud computing, these prerequisites stem from two sources: users (targeted audience) and threat landscapes. Security visualization researchers and developers often ask themselves the following questions below in order to identify targeted audiences:

1. Who are the users?
2. What do the users want to see?
3. What security tasks can be performed using these visualizations?
4. When would these security visualization be used?

And from the threat landscape approach, researchers and developers often ask the following questions below:

1. What type of attack is visualized?
2. When did the attack take place?
3. What is the origin (source) and destination of the attack being visualized?
4. What is the reason of visualizing this attack?

The purpose of this section is to outline how effective and efficient the use of security visualization within law enforcement operations and investigations is. Regardless of existing security challenges faced by security firms [27] such as big data analytics, there is always the need to improve how security tools are performing. While there are other methods aiding law enforcement operations and investigations, the application of security visualization into the operations can minimize the time spent on investigations and other work processes. In order to achieve that, the law enforcement needs to create a set of visualization standards which act as indicators in various processes. For example, the current use of INTERPOL's "International Notice System [28]," the color Red in Red Notices indicates "Wanted Person," Yellow Notices indicates "Missing Person" and so on [29]. This helps law enforcement personals to quickly act upon such alerts when received at the National Central Bureaus (NCB) in different member countries and offices.

While the INTERPOL's Notice System uses colors to indicate different human investigation processes, there is a need to expand the idea and develop a visualization standard for law enforcement. This means, creating similar color and shape standards to visually represent various cyber-attacks. For example, over any network and system investigations, the color "Green" can be used to represent "normal web traffic." Suspicious traffic can be visually represented with the color "Yellow." Malware traffic can be visually represented with the color "Red." However, network traffic can be symbolized using "Circles" instead of "Rectangles," just to distinguish between the INTERPOL's Notice System and the network traffic.

Other cyber threats and attacks can be visualized differently, however keeping the standard consistent across different law enforcement visualization applications will gradually establish common grounds with visual reports and investigations. As a result, information processing will be fast and effective because humans naturally have the cognitive ability to process visual images and information faster than reading words.

13.3.2 Security Visualization Standard (SCeeL-VisT)

Security visualizations are often confusing when users do not have a fair idea of how a visualization platform works or what the intended purpose of confronting such visualizations. Therefore, establishing a security visualization standard helps to create scopes of how visualizations would impact business or organization. Standards also maintain and control the type of visual outputs required for the users to view. Organizations and users need security visualization to help make sense of complex data collected from cyber-attacks targeting cloud technologies. Establishing a security visualization standard as a component of the overall security framework for an organization would have a high impact on reducing intrusions and threats penetrating the cloud technologies. The visualization standards can provide guidance for developers during the design and implementation stage, and often the visual output provides situation awareness to the users of cloud technologies.

The SCeeL-VisT is a standard created to help standardize how security visualizations could be implemented and presented. The core targeted audience would be the visualization developers and users of the visualization. Having to bring the developers and users together into one realm, there is a higher probability of getting insights from the source to the users in an effective time frame.

SCeeL-VisT provides a brief content and overview of the work-progress security visualization standard visualizing security events out from complex datasets. It is important that the visualization developers and users understand what is needed to visualize. With a clear understanding, developing a visualization should gather all security features intended to visualize from the output. The two distinctive parts of the security visualization standard are as follows:

1. *Part 1: Understanding what is needed*: In this stage, the developers have to understand the purpose of the intended visualization, nature of the data collected, and most importantly the users who will be viewing the given visualization.
2. *Part 2: Security visualization process*: In this stage, a clear understanding of who the targeted audience are is very important. The right color choice and object selection are required for an effective visual output.

Security Visualization Standard (SCeeL-VisT)

Part 1: Understanding What Is Needed

1. **The Problem**: Identification of security events
   - Identify security events (e.g., malware attack, and SQL injection) and data type (raw data: log files, social media data, etc.)
   - Understand the nature of data (e.g., financial data and health data)
2. **The Purpose**: Know the visualization type and technique
   - Understand the intension of security visualization (e.g., show relationships)
   - Decision: exploratory or reporting visualization, security visualization technique (e.g., categorizing: time-base, provenance-base attack-base)
3. **Cyber-Attack Landscape**: Know the cyber-attack location (e.g., network, systems, and application layer)
   - Know the point of attack (e.g., network attack and identify source and destination of attack)
   - Attribution of cyber-attack

Part 2: Security Visualization Process

1. **Visual Presentation Methodologies**: How to present data visually
2. **Color and Shape Standard for Security**: Decision on choice of colors
   - Standardizing main color choices
     - Color: Red = High attack nature or violation (e.g., malware process)
     - Color: Yellow = Suspicious process (e.g., IP address)
     - Color: Green = Good or normal process (e.g., network traffic)
     - Color: Blue = Informational (intelligence) process (IP address)
     - Color: Black = Deleted, traces: non-existed (e.g., deleted file)
   - Standardizing main shapes choices
     - Shape: Circle = Nodes (e.g., network nodes)
     - Shape: Rectangle = Files (e.g., .docs and .jpeg)
     - Shape: Square = Data clusters (e.g., IP address – network traffic)
     - Shape: Diamond = Web/social media process (social media data)
   - Standardizing use of line types
     - Line: Single line (—) = Relationships, connections, links, provenance, time-base (e.g., between two network nodes)
     - Line: dotted line (- - -) = Possible relationships (e.g., .docs, .jpeg)
     - Line: Solid arrow (→) = Direction of relationship or interaction
     - Line: Dotted arrow (− − >) = Predicted relationship or interaction
3. **Security Visualization Techniques**: Provenance and attribution-base, user-centered, real-time base
4. **Security Visualization Type**: Animated, 3D, static, etc.

13.4 Security visualization intelligence framework

Past visualization technologies and threat intelligence frameworks have provided insights to users but often isolate most visualization separately for the purpose of just providing visualization for specific purpose. Our security visualization intelligence model aims to incorporate multiple security visualization landscapes to show relationships between several different attack landscapes.

Figure 13.1 provides an overview of the proposed security visualization model for cloud technologies, particularly for SaaS. A part of web applications in the cloud services, the "Added Security Visualization Framework," injects visualization options for users to use. This proposed security visualization framework aims to reduce the doubts in cloud users when using cloud technologies, by offering security visualizations to track, monitor and even alert them of any suspicious behavior.

13.4.1 Security Visualization as a Cloud Service

While cloud computing represents the most exciting computing paradigm shift in information technology, security over the data in the cloud is the concern for most

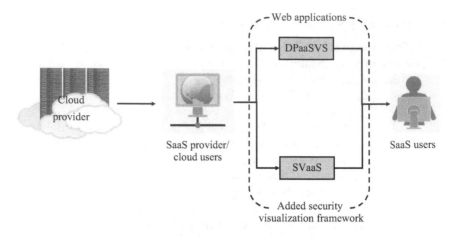

Figure 13.1   Security visualization framework – cloud computing[a]

users of the cloud today [30]. An added sub-component to working towards the concept of a Security-as-a-Service (SECaaS) model [31] is to observe user activities, web traffics and keeping track of what is happening in the cloud services [32]. Adding the security visualization as a service model into security in the cloud enables visibility in the cloud processes for both providers and customers. It installs confidence and a trust relationship between cloud customers and the service offered. Fujitsu's security visualization dashboard has helped to improve security governance in the cloud and enabled customers to visualize the efficiency and cost-effectiveness of information security measures [33].

The use of visual dashboards in business management software packages has provided businesses with the opportunity to include visual parts to the entire reporting framework. Amazon's QuickSight, a business intelligence for Big Data, provides visual analytics [34]. Google's cloud datalab tool offers data exploration, analysis, visualization and machine learning capabilities [35]. Microsoft Azure can produce Power Bi, a Big Data solution, with live dashboard and attractive visualization [36]. Microsoft Azure's Power Bi tool shown in Figure 13.2 displays how visualization dashboards are used to visually analyze data and present interesting insights. In Figure 13.2, Power Bi tool is used to show a persons' movement. Dashboard visualizations aim to consolidate most information onto a single screen view, showing users all the necessary information needed. However, adding the concept of Security Visualization as a Cloud Service (SVaaCS) into the cloud services to enhance dashboard visualizations helps to improve the way data security is presented with visualization.

13.4.2   Data Provenance as a Security Visualization Service

Data provenance is defined in the context of this chapter as a series of chronicles and the derivation history of data on metadata [37]. Incorporating the concept of data

---

[a]A colored figure of the "DPaaSVS and SVaaS: Cloud Computing Security Visualization Framework." [Online]: https://crow.org.nz/security-visualization/Figure-13.1_SaaSSecVis

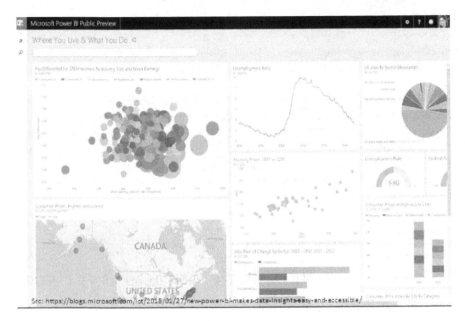

Src: https://blogs.microsoft.com/iot/2015/01/27/new-power-bi-makes-data-insights-easy-and-accessible/

Figure 13.2   Azure's Power Bi Analytic visualization[b]

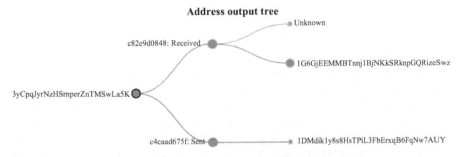

Figure 13.3   A Bitcoin transaction address visualization[c]

provenance into security visualization steps up visualization capabilities for customers using cloud services. The ability to track data actions on a piece of data stored on the cloud with the ability to observe past events and reconstruct any events when in doubt offers the data action to create the notion of Data Provenance as a Security Visualization Service (DPaaSVS). For example, tracking a Bitcoin payment of a service acquired by observing the Bitcoin transaction movement from the sender to the receiver is shown in Figure 13.3.

---

[b]A colored figure of the "Azure's Power Bi Analytic Visualization." [Online]: https://crow.org.nz/security-visualization/Figure-13.2_PowerBI_2
[c]A colored figure of the "A Bitcoin Transaction Address Visualization." [Online]: https://crow.org.nz/security-visualization/Figure-13.3_Bitcoin_Address_Output_Tree

13.5   Security visualization intelligence model

Security visualization intelligence (SVInt) model provides law enforcement person-nels with an enhanced investigation environment using visualization. The aim is to provide an effective visual method of analyzing complex datasets and outputting requested queries in a simple, clear, and efficient visual representation of the find-ings to aid the law enforcement of day-to-day investigation process. And due to an amount of workload and data complexity, SVInt is designed to incorporate various intelligence tools into one framework and add visualization as the main tool to be used for investigations, either for threat intelligences, observing criminal activities and normal day-to-day information sharing processes. The current SVInt framework provides:

1. A Bitcoin visualization platform for Bitcoin transaction relationship visualization.
2. Threat report visualization platform showing top malware threats using geo-locations.
3. A forensic taxonomy analytic tool.
4. A platform to support future intelligence visualization tools.

13.5.1   Bitcoin visualization

The SVInt enhances an in-house Blockchain Explorer tool that identifies and explores Bitcoin transactions relationships. The Blockchain Explorer allows law enforcement users to search for specific Bitcoin wallet IDs and analyze possible transaction connections with other wallet IDs and market places that are involved in criminal investigations. The current Blockchain Explorer acts as an identifier to suspicious address tags and with the introduction of the "Bitcoin Transaction Visual-ization," visual representations features of Bitcoin transactions are produced to show transaction relationships.

We later classify the transactions into different clusters to see possible transactions relationships and patterns. Our Bitcoin visualization is by default a suspicious-tag-centric visual approach where Bitcoin suspicious tags are the center of visual relationships. Based on suspicious-tag search on the Blockchain Explorer, the data collected are visualized in the Bitcoin visualization interface. An example of a visualization generated by the Blockchain Explorer is shown in Figure 13.4.

A classic Bitcoin live visualization intelligence map produced by BitNodes [38] shows the real-time Bitcoin transactions around the world as shown in Figure 13.5. Bitcoin transactions are indicated using IP address nodes used for the transactions. Comparing with the SVInt Bitcoin transaction visualization, BitNodes visualization provides users with a geo-location Bitcoin visualization while SVInt Bitcoin visual-ization provides visual transactions relationships amount from online Bitcoin explorer trading platform.

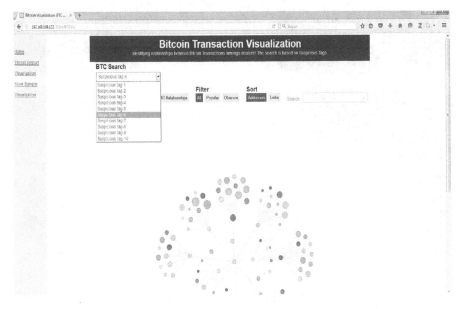

Figure 13.4   SVInt: Bitcoin transaction visualization[d]

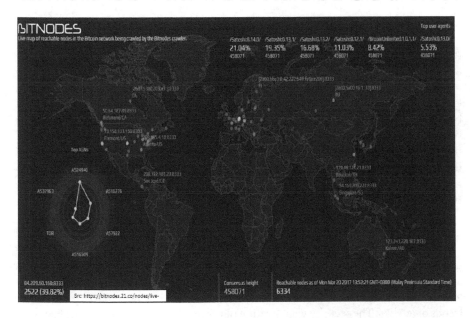

Figure 13.5   BitNodes – Bitcoin Live Map visualization[e]

[d]A colored figure of the "SVInt: Bitcoin Transaction Visualization." [Online]: https://crow.org.nz/security-visualization/Figure-13.4_Blockchain_Vis
[e]A colored figure of the "BitNodes - Bitcoin Live Map Visualization." [Online]: https://crow.org.nz/security-visualization/Figure-13.5_BitNodes

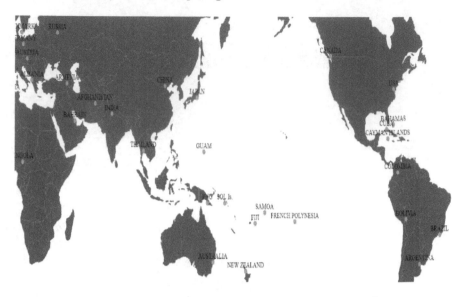

Figure 13.6   SVInt: threat visualization intelligence[f]

13.5.2   Threat intelligence visualization

Another example of live visualization that empowers security professional, especially aids law enforcement investigations is the ability to visualize malware threats affecting systems and networks around the world. The threat intelligence security visualization tool was developed specifically to analyze and monitor threats with the purpose of being able to attribute malware attacks back to the source and offenders. Based on weekly data collected from security logging tools around the world, the threat intelligence visualization highlights threats that were able to penetrate organization and individuals. With available datasets, the choice of using geo-location to visually represent the cyber-threats is to provide viewers of how cyber-attacks are affecting the Internet. Adding the concept of intelligence into the scenario, tracking and monitoring certain known cyber-attacks can be useful to track known cybercrime groups from known attack locations. Figure 13.6 represents malware attacks from around the world on a weekly time frame. This adds value to law enforcement investigations by using geo-location visualization and correlating it with other intelligence visualization such as Bitcoin transaction visualization. By providing multiple types of visualization visualized concurrently, investigators can help to connect both with patterns and possible trends of attacks. The security visualization platform allows users to view cyber-attack statistics with visual analysis capabilities based on preferred search of interest.

---

[f]A colored figure of the "SVInt: Threat Intelligence Visualization." [Online]: https://crow.org.nz/security-visualization/Figure-13.6_ThreatGeoMap

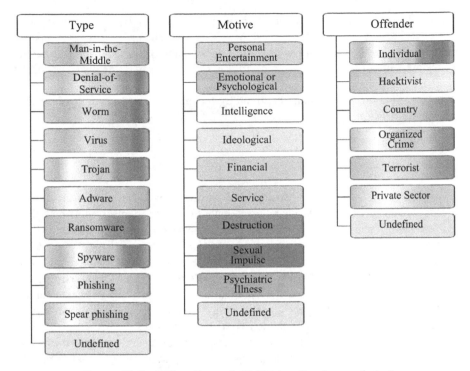

Figure 13.7   SVInt: ForensicTMO visualization analytics[g]

13.5.3   ForensicTMO – analytic tool

Although most security tools emphasize on preventing cyber-attacks, the post event of cyber-attacks requires security knowledge and situation awareness as well [18]. In order to understand how bad an attack is, forensic tools are required. As part of the SVInt, we have added external analytic tools, the ForensicTMO [39], a motive-centric Man-in-the-Middle-Attack (MITMA) investigation tool which aims to minimize the time spent on analyzing a motive behind a cyber-attack. The ForensicTMO application provides a preliminary forensic analysis of cyber-attacks that can be used by law enforcement officials as part of their investigations. It is a technical representation of the Forensic Taxonomy Extension shown in Figure 13.7, which is based on a classification framework developed for the classification of Man-in-the-Middle attacks. The forensic taxonomy extension illustrates the possible relationships between the taxonomy categories type, motive and offender. A visual representation used in Figure 13.7 do not have any implied meaning but allow a user to quickly identify relationships between motives and a particular type or offender, as well as the relationships within the type and offender category. The forensic taxonomy is designed to be motive centric,

---

[g]A colored figure of the "ForensicTMO Visualization Analytics." [Online]: https://crow.org.nz/security-visualization/Figure-13.7_Forensic_Extension_Attrib

as it is often the most apparent and easily identified characteristic of a cybercrime. Motives are tested throughout the course of an investigation resulting in revisions and changes to the motive until the motive can tie an offender to an attack type. During the course of an investigation it is common for the motive to lead to the discovery of the attack type and offender as a result of the investigation. As this is the natural behavior of an investigation, we continue this trend by making the taxonomy motive-centric, to streamline this process.

13.6   Concluding remarks

Cloud computing technologies change and shape the way Internet services were offered. When using cloud services, users have to remind themselves of how their data are being managed and stored. Security is always a challenge for both cloud providers and cloud users.

   In this chapter, SVaaS is used to bridge the gap between users and cloud platforms. With use-cases from the law enforcement domain, SVaaS – a sub-component of SECaaS – highlights how security visualizations are transforming cloud technologies. From an analytical perspective, DPaaSVS highlights security through tracking, monitoring, and enabling user interaction with visual features for cloud services. SVaaS and DPaaSVS connect the users perception of how users' data activities while their data are stored and processed in the cloud. Finally, security visualization creates the sense of trust and confidence to both cloud providers and customers.

References

[1]   Jin, H., S. Ibrahim, T. Bell, W. Gao, D. Huang, and S. Wu, "Cloud types and services," in *Handbook of Cloud Computing*, B. Furht and A. Escalante, Eds. Boston, MA: Springer, 2010, pp. 335–355.

[2]   Muttik, I. and C. Barton. "Cloud security technologies." Information Security Technical Report, 14(1) (2009): 1–6.

[3]   Hundhausen, C. D., S. A. Douglas, and J. T. Stasko. "A meta-study of algorithm visualization effectiveness." *Journal of Visual Languages & Computing* 13, no. 3 (2002): 259–290.

[4]   "Kaspersky Security Bulletin 2015. Overall statistics for 2015 – Securelist." [Online].   Available: https://securelist.com/analysis/kaspersky-security-bulletin/73038/kaspersky-security-bulletin-2015-overall-statistics-for-2015/. [Accessed: 12-Jan-2017].

[5]   Best, D. M., A. Endert, and D. Kidwell. "7 key challenges for visualization in cyber network defense." In *Proceedings of the Eleventh Workshop on Visualization for Cyber Security*, pp. 33–40. Paris, France: ACM, 2014.

[6]   I. Kotenko and E. Novikova, "Visualization of security metrics for cyber situation awareness," in *2014 Ninth International Conference on Availability, Reliability and Security*, 2014, pp. 506–513.

[7]   Goodall, J. R. "Introduction to visualization for computer security," in *VizSEC 2007*, pp. 1–17. Berlin: Springer, 2008.

[8]   L. SAS, "Linkurious – Understand the connections in your data," Linkurious. [Online]. Available: http://linkurio.us. [Accessed: 12-Jan-2017].

[9]   Wesley, R., M. Eldridge, and P. T. Terlecki. "An analytic data engine for visualization in tableau," in *Proceedings of the 2011 ACM SIGMOD International Conference on Management of Data*, pp. 1185–1194. Athens, Greece: ACM, 2011.

[10] Papadakakis, N., E. P. Markatos, and A. E. Papathanasiou. "Palantir: A visualization tool for the world wide web," in *INET 98 Proceedings*. 1998.

[11] Sarma, A., and A. Van Der Hoek. "Palantir: Coordinating distributed workspaces," in *Computer Software and Applications Conference, 2002. COMPSAC 2002. Proceedings. 26th Annual International*, Oxford, UK, pp. 1093–1097. IEEE, 2002.

[12] Lee, C. P., J. Trost, N. Gibbs, R. Beyah, and J. A. Copeland. "Visual firewall: Real-time network security monitor," in *IEEE Workshop on Visualization for Computer Security, 2005 (VizSEC'05)*, Minneapolis, MN, USA, pp. 129–136. IEEE, 2005.

[13] Ekanayake, J., and G. Fox. "High performance parallel computing with clouds and cloud technologies," in *International Conference on Cloud Computing*, pp. 20–38. Berlin: Springer, 2009.

[14] Weinhardt, C., A. Anandasivam, B. Blau, *et al.* "Cloud computing – A classification, business models, and research directions." *Business & Information Systems Engineering* 1, no. 5 (2009): 391–399.

[15] Tao, Fei, Ying Cheng, Li Da Xu, Lin Zhang, and Bo Hu Li. "CCIoT-CMfg: Cloud computing and internet of things-based cloud manufacturing service system." *IEEE Transactions on Industrial Informatics* 10, no. 2 (2014): 1435–1442.

[16] Carlin, S., and K. Curran. "Cloud computing technologies." *International Journal of Cloud Computing and Services Science* 1, no. 2 (2012): 59.

[17] Plaza, B. "Monitoring web traffic source effectiveness with Google Analytics: An experiment with time series." *Aslib Proceedings* 61, no. 5 (2009): 474–482.

[18] Lakkaraju, K., W. Yurcik, and A. J. Lee. "NVisionIP: Netflow visualizations of system state for security situational awareness," in *Proceedings of the 2004 ACM Workshop on Visualization and Data Mining for Computer Security*, pp. 65–72. Washington DC, USA: ACM, New York, NY, USA, 2004.

[19] McPherson, J., K.-L. Ma, P. Krystosk, T. Bartoletti, and M. Christensen. "Portvis: A tool for port-based detection of security events,' in *Proceedings of the 2004 ACM Workshop on Visualization and Data Mining for Computer Security*, pp. 73–81. Washington DC, USA: ACM New York, NY, USA, 2004.

[20] Yin, X., W. Yurcik, M. Treaster, Y. Li, and K. Lakkaraju. "VisFlowConnect: Netflow visualizations of link relationships for security situational awareness,"

in *Proceedings of the 2004 ACM Workshop on Visualization and Data Mining for Computer Security*, pp. 26–34. Washington DC, USA: ACM, 2004.

[21]   Morrow, B. "BYOD security challenges: Control and protect your most sensitive data." *Network Security* 2012, no. 12 (2012): 5–8.

[22]   Ren, K., C. Wang, and Q. Wang. "Security challenges for the public cloud." *IEEE Internet Computing* 16, no. 1 (2012): 69–73.

[23]   Popović, K., and Ž. Hocenski. "Cloud computing security issues and challenges," in *MIPRO, 2010 Proceedings of the 33rd International Convention*, pp. 344–349. Opatija, Croatia: IEEE, 2010.

[24]   Rong, C., S. T. Nguyen, and M. G. Jaatun. "Beyond lightning: A survey on security challenges in cloud computing." *Computers & Electrical Engineering* 39, no. 1 (2013): 47–54.

[25]   Armbrust, M., A. Fox, R. Griffith, *et al.* "A view of cloud computing." *Communications of the ACM* 53, no. 4 (2010): 50–58.

[26]   Plaza, B. "Google Analytics for measuring website performance." *Tourism Management* 32, no. 3 (2011): 477–481.

[27]   Agrawal, R., A. Kadadi, X. Dai, and F. Andres. "Challenges and opportunities with big data visualization," in *Proceedings of the Seventh International Conference on Management of Computational and Collective Intelligence in Digital EcoSystems*, pp. 169–173. Caraguatatuba, Brazil: ACM New York, NY, USA, 2015.

[28]   Notices/INTERPOL expertise/Internet/Home – INTERPOL [WWW Document], n.d. URL http://www.interpol.int/INTERPOL-expertise/Notices (accessed 3.30.16).

[29]   INTERPOL, 2015. International Notices System. INTERPOL, n.d. Notices/INTERPOL expertise/Internet/Home – INTERPOL [WWW Document]. INTERPOL Notices. URL http://www.interpol.int/INTERPOL-expertise/Notices (accessed 3.28.16).

[30]   Ren, K., W. Wang, and Q. Wang. "Security challenges for the public cloud." *IEEE Internet Computing* 16, no. 1 (2012): 69.

[31]   Hussain, M., and H. Abdulsalam. "SECaaS: Security as a service for cloud-based applications," in *Proceedings of the Second Kuwait Conference on e-Services and e-Systems*, p. 8. Kuwait City, Kuwait: ACM New York, NY, USA, 2011.

[32]   Delamore, B. and R. K. L. Ko, "Chapter 9 – Security as a service (SecaaS) – An overview," in *The Cloud Security Ecosystem*. Boston, MA: Syngress, 2015, pp. 187–203.

[33]   Okuhara, M., T. Shiozaki, and T. Suzuki. "Security architecture for cloud computing." *Fujitsu Scientific and Technical Journal* 46, no. 4 (2010): 397–402.

[34]   "Amazon QuickSight – Fast & Easy to Use Business Intelligence for Big Data at 1/10th the Cost of Traditional Solutions – AWS Blog." [Online]. Available: https://aws.amazon.com/blogs/aws/amazon-quicksight-fast-easy-to-use-business-intelligence-for-big-data-at-110th-the-cost-of-traditional-solutions/. [Accessed: 20-Mar-2017].

[35] "Cloud Datalab – Interactive Data Insights Tool," Google Cloud Platform. [Online]. Available: https://cloud.google.com/datalab/. [Accessed: 20-Mar-2017].

[36] "Azure brings big data, analytics, and visualization capabilities to U.S. Government." [Online]. Available: https://azure.microsoft.com/en-us/blog/azure-brings-big-data-analytics-and-visualization-capabilities-to-u-s-government/. [Accessed: 20-Mar-2017].

[37] Garae, J., R. K. L. Ko, and S. Chaisiri, "UVisP: User-centric visualization of data provenance with Gestalt principles," in *2016 IEEE Trustcom/BigDataSE/ISPA*, Tianjin, China, August 23–26, 2016, 2016, pp. 1923–1930.

[38] "Bitnodes live map." [Online]. Available: https://bitnodes.21.co/nodes/live-map/. [Accessed: 20-Mar-2017].

[39] Stricot-Tarboton, S., S. Chaisiri, and R. K. L. Ko, "Taxonomy of man-in-the-middle attacks on HTTPS," in 2016 *IEEE Trustcom/BigDataSE/ISPA*, Tianjin, China, August 23–26, 2016, 2016, pp. 527–534.

[40] Krasser, S., G. Conti, J. Grizzard, J. Gribschaw, and H. Owen. "Real-time and forensic network data analysis using animated and coordinated visualization," in *Proceedings from the Sixth Annual IEEE SMC Information Assurance Workshop*, pp. 42–49. IEEE, 2005.

Index

Printed in the USA
CPSIA information can be obtained
at www.ICGtesting.com
JSHW011509221024
72173JS00005B/1248